3D Management,

an Integral Theory for Organisations in the Vanguard of Evolution

3D Management,
an Integral Theory for Organisations in the Vanguard of Evolution

By

Marco A. Robledo

Cambridge Scholars Publishing

3D Management, an Integral Theory for Organisations in the Vanguard of Evolution

By Marco A. Robledo

This book first published 2020

Cambridge Scholars Publishing

Lady Stephenson Library, Newcastle upon Tyne, NE6 2PA, UK

British Library Cataloguing in Publication Data
A catalogue record for this book is available from the British Library

ISBN (10): 1-5275-5426-0
ISBN (13): 978-1-5275-5426-9

To my son, Alex and my daughter, Vera.

May you always find the space to be happy, reach your highest potential, and find meaning in your life.

This book is my humble contribution to make it easier for you.

Thanks for teaching me every day what truly matters.

"When the winds of change are blowing, some people are building shelters and others are building windmills."

Old Chinese saying.

TABLE OF CONTENTS

THE 3D MANAGEMENT MANIFESTO

Our world changes at breathtaking speed. Utopia is becoming a real place, unfolding into astounding chimerical forms: Hermes, the Olympian God of commerce, travels across cyberspace, the continent without borders; tweets from Dubai can create storms in Wall Street; we carry the office on a cell phone; computers diagnose medical conditions more reliably than human doctors; automobiles finally live up to their name and do not need a driver; 3D printers can't mend a broken heart, but they are able to make a new one. At the same time, dystopia extends its dark mantle over us: The 4 Horsemen run amok in a world where human rights are a privilege of the few, and the wealth of some comes at the expense of the suffering of many, where refugees of war die on our shores while we shamefully look away, where developing countries are the dumping grounds of our throwaway society, and where our fancy clothes come from factories right out of Dickens, and our phones are covered in the blood of conflict minerals and the sweat of slave labour.

Humanity stands at an evolutionary crossroads between a dream world and the worst of nightmares. It is our choice to reach for the light of hope or stumble on into the darkness of despair. Hence, this manifesto wants to be an invitation to dream.

I dream of purposeful enterprises that champion a conscious vision and aspire to something worthier than just making money. I dream of workplaces that are chrysalises of human flourishing, that empower people to reach the further limits of their potential and unleash the power of their ingenuity. I dream of organisations that treat people not as means, but as ends in themselves, and which are built on love rather than fear. I dream of governance models that reap the collective wisdom of all stakeholders and allow them to serve the organisational purpose rather than the whims of any powerful individual. I dream of corporations that are not passive instruments of the market but active agents of social transformation and planetary regeneration. I dream of a future where the minds of the smartest individuals are geared towards building a better world rather than skimping on taxes, or owning the latest smartphone.

I dream of a world of dreams fulfilled, a place where utopia has banished dystopia, and even as I dream, I do know that my dreams can come true in an integral and balanced world.

In this fateful moment, let's be the architects of our future. If we want to spend the rest of our lives in a better tomorrow, we need a positive vision to give direction to our present time, and a purpose to our lives. This is precisely what *3D Management* offers: an integral perspective to help individuals and organisations go beyond their current limitations and boost their evolutionary potential.

ACKNOWLEDGEMENTS

The book you are about to read has been written on the shoulders of giants. After more than 15 years of research and practice, and four years of writing, it is impossible to name all the works, theories, individuals, and organisations that have influenced or supported it; however, some stand out and cannot be omitted.

The first giant, whose canonical work has been the spark and the enduring influence for this modest attempt to develop an integral management theory, is the philosopher Ken Wilber. When I discovered his work in *A Theory of Everything* (2000b), my mind was blown open, and everything seemed to fall in place. For the first time, I had found a framework that integrated, with rigour, my scientific interests, my passion for arts, my ethical concerns, and my spiritual inclinations. It was a profoundly transformative experience, both at an intellectual and spiritual level. Upon reading that book, I became inspired to apply his integral approach to management, and thus my life changed in such an extreme way that I discovered my purpose: to help individuals and organisations in their transformation towards higher levels of consciousness. The best possible gift I could get is the amazing foreword he has written, and you are about to read. I have no words to express my gratitude for his generosity and support.

It was thanks to Ken Wilber that I also discovered the second most important influence of this book: *Spiral Dynamics* and its offspring *Spiral Dynamics Integral*. These evolutionary models, together with others presented by such authors as Clare Graves, Terri O'Fallon, Susanne Cook-Greuter, Lawrence Kohlberg, Michael Commons, and Robert Kegan, have been constant references for me.

Some management ideas that share the same principles and aspirations as 3D Management have also been deeply inspirational. Ricardo Semler's *Maverick* was probably the first book that made me realise that another kind of business is possible. Frederic Laloux's *Reinventing Organisations* is, in my opinion, the most relevant management book of the 21st century. All the seminal work of Richard Barrett has always been very present for me and has yet to be sufficiently acknowledged. John McKay and Raj Sisodia's

Conscious Capitalism is one of the leading theories of post-conventional management thinking. Brett Thomas' *Integral Leadership* is, in my mind, the most significant contribution to leadership theory in years. Gerard Endenburg's *Sociocracy,* Brian Robertson's *Holacracy,* and James Priest, Lili David, and Bernhard Bockelbrink's *Sociocracy 3.0* have achieved the incredible feat of making the workplace revolution accessible and replicable. Encode's *For-Purpose Enterprise*, is not only filling the gaps of *Holacracy* but taking it to the next level. There couldn't be better fertilisers for the growth of my ideas.

But thinkers go nowhere without doers. I want to recognise all the people that are walking the talk of organisational transformation. First, there are the pioneers. We wouldn't be here without companies like W.L. Gore, Johnsonville Sausages, Morning Star, Semco, Buurtzorg, HolacracyOne, Oticon, FAVI, or Irízar opening the way. I especially want to acknowledge those organisations and individuals that have worked with me or were so kind as to supply information for this book. The list is long but I would like to highlight the names of Tom Thomison, Christiane Seuchs-Seuler, and Dennis Wittrock from Encode.org, Koldo Saratxaga and Pablo Aretxabala from ner Group, Olivier Gesbert from Pressto Peru, Rainer Leoprechting from Pro Action Learning, David Tomás from Ciberclick, Pieter Spinder from Knowmads Business School, Ana Manzanedo, Albert Cañigueral, and Francesca Pick from Ouishare, Stellan Nordahl and Jens Rinnelt from Emprogage, Daniel Truran from B Corps, Lucía Zamora, Raquel Gutiérrez, and María Ruiz from DeLuz y Compañía, and Yan Eperon, the creator of Holycracy. To all the participants in the 3D Management Club of Conscious Organisations in Mallorca and especially to the president of Eticentre Miguel Ángel Benito who embraced the spirit of the idea from the very beginning. To Ricardo Martínez, the champion behind the Colombian chapter of the 3D Management Club of Conscious Organisations and an enthusiastic supporter and practitioner of 3D Management. To all the members of CineCiutat, for believing in this beautiful social innovation experiment against all the odds, and especially, to my fellow members of the board Javier Pachón, Pedro Barbadillo, Ignacio Bergillos, Rafael Goberna, Olga Titos, and Marta Pérez for their relentless belief in 3D Management.

I want to give a special mention to the few academics who are contributing with the introduction of *Integral Theory* in the university world as well as studying the cutting-edge of organisational evolution. We are not many, and we are swimming against the tide. In the top of my list is Julio Batle, who is like a brother to me. He is a penetrating thinker whose creative energy is in perpetual eruption and is always ready to challenge my views and take me one step further. Having him in the office next door is a privilege that has enriched my life over the years. He makes far too many bad jokes about Integral Theory, but we cannot expect those who have not reached an integral level of development to be perfect. Antonio Grandío and Ricardo Chivas from the Universitat Jaume I in Castellón are good friends, kindred spirits, and long-time supporters of my work. Mark Edwards, from Jönköping University, is one of my favourite experts in Integral Theory and is a distinguished contributor to its implementation in organisations. Tom Habib is developing, together with Bence Ganti, the International Consortium of Integral Scholars, a project that deserves all my praise and to which I have the honour of belonging. My recognition as well to Ana Moreno from Universidad Politécnica de Madrid, Aftab Omer from Meridian University, Lisa Norton from Parsons College, and Iñaki Heras from the Universidad del País Vasco.

I am most grateful to those creating spaces and communities to transform our society and our organisations for the benefit of all. I would like to draw special attention to the Enlivening Edge community and George Pór and Alia Bastet, the Journal of Integral Theory and Practice, edited by Sean Esbjörn-Hargens and managed by Lynwood Lord, the Integral Leadership Review and its editor Eric Reynolds, and Pim de Morree and Joost Minnaar's Corporate Rebels blog. My first contact with the integral community, apart from a small discussion group that Joan Umbert and I set up in Mallorca, was with the Spanish Integral Association, founded by Raquel Torrent and followed by Pablo Nebreda and Alberto Jiménez as presidents. It is no longer active, but I'm still in touch with many of the integral friends I met there. When it comes to conferences, three are very special to me. First, the Integral European Conference, created by Bence Ganti and Dennis Wittrock, and now headed by the former; then, the New Economy and Social Innovation Forum, organised by Diego Isabel de la Moneda; last but not least, Hispanoamérica Integral, led by my dear friends Santiago Jiménez, Gary Villar, José Ricardo Fuentes, Vidal Herly, Diana Murillo, Philip Watson, and Claudia Ramírez. Certainly, Facebook groups such as Integral Global, Teal for Startups, Teal for Teal International, Sociocracy 3.0, Reinventing Organisations, AQAL, or the Change-Maker's Collective are indispensable sources of information. All of them have been very receptive to my ideas and work, and I thank them.

Robert Perry will always be in my memory and my heart. He was the best teacher and one of the best communicators I have ever known. More importantly, his example made me deeply aware that a teacher is not only a knowledge transmitter but a soul transformer.

Special thanks go to Cambridge Scholars Publishing, and in particular, Adam Rummens for believing in this book from the very beginning, and helping nurture its creation with unwavering support. I also owe an enormous debt to Colleen Vollmer and Olga Zuyderhoff, who devoted extraordinary care and attention to the linguistic and editorial revision of this book. Their input has greatly enriched this book.

Finally, I am perhaps most deeply grateful to you, dear reader. It is only through your contribution that the evolution of organisations is going to be possible. It is a privilege to share my modest work with you in the hope it will inspire you.

FOREWORD

KEN WILBER[1]

"Integral Theory" (or "Metatheory") is a specific framework that is meant to be applicable to virtually any field or discipline that one wishes. As perhaps the major architect of this perspective in today's world, I originally created it as a way to make any specific discipline more inclusive, more comprehensive, and more "holistic" in the very best sense. I did an extensive search of dozens and dozens of world cultures—premodern, modern, and postmodern—and looked for any common elements that the "good theories" or "good ideas" of various times happened to share—whether that might involve a culture's idea of science, art, ethics, history, commerce, or religion. Odd as it might initially sound, I actually found several. What these shared patterns suggest is not a way that new facts are discovered and fitted (or not) to a particular theory, but rather what all good theories have in common. And the existence of these shared elements suggests that there are various aspects, dimensions, or areas of reality that human beings especially need to pay attention to, because they keep showing up again and again throughout our evolutionary history. To date, this Integral approach has been used to make over 60 different disciplines more comprehensive and inclusive.

To give only one quick example, take the notion of the Beautiful, the Good, and the True. This idea itself is several thousand years old, but it still has an enormous amount of importance for our postmodern culture. Why do I say this? One way to look at it is that these three dimensions are the actual basis of our 1st-person, 2nd-person, and 3rd-person pronouns (such as I, you, and it). There is the Beauty that is in the "eye" (or the "I") of the beholder (1st person); there is the Good, or how you and I are supposed to treat each other (2nd person); and there is the True, shorthand for "objective truth" (a 3rd-person approach). Every major language in the world has those three

[1] Ken Wilber is one of the most important philosophers in the world today. He is the creator of Integral Theory, the world's first truly comprehensive or integrative philosophy.

pronouns. It appears that they represent very real, very important dimensions of an actual reality; and thus, over the millennia, as human beings evolved, they were in touch with all three of those dimensions, and hence as their language began to emerge, it fully reflected all of them.

Another way to look at these dimensions (of the Beautiful, the Good, and the True) is as the specific disciplines of "art, morals, and science." It's very clear that those are indeed different areas or dimensions of reality. What's also not deniable is that all three of those dimensions exist. What's more, each of them has a very different methodology for disclosing its own specific types of truth. According to Max Weber, what specifically marked the emergence of the modern world was the "differentiation of the value spheres." That is, the differentiation of the Beautiful, the Good, and the True, which previously had been fused under the Church, which dictated exactly what each of them should be (so that the Church clergy did not have to look through Galileo's telescope because the Bible already told them what they would see). But with modernity, these three spheres were differentiated and allowed to go their own way with their own logic—and this produced a knowledge explosion in all of them that marked what we call "modernity."

So today, even Jürgen Habermas, whom some consider the world's greatest living philosopher, maintains that every time a human being speaks, they take up a relation to three different worlds—the subjective aesthetic, the intersubjective moral, and the objective scientific—that is, art, morals, and science (1st-, 2nd-, and 3rd-person realities). Further, each of those dimensions has very different validity claims or ways that you demonstrate what is true and what is false in each of those areas.

Here's the problem. Take something like "consciousness studies," which is the academic attempt to explain the origin and nature of consciousness or awareness. This discipline today is divided basically right down the middle between two very competitive schools: one that believes that consciousness can only be explained by actually looking within and introspecting (that is, by using a 1st-person approach); the other believes that consciousness is solely the product and function of neurophysiological brain processes (or a 3rd-person approach). Neither one of these has been able to decisively win the argument, and so they continue to go at each other's throats. What is rarely found is the approach that an Integral perspective takes, which is that both of those approaches are equally important and neither can be excluded—which is exactly why neither of them can win the argument. (Of course, a fully Integral view maintains that all of the Integral elements need to be included, but this is just a simple example involving what Integral calls the "quadrants," which also includes 2nd-person views—the point being to truly be comprehensive and inclusive.) No genuinely accurate and effective view of consciousness can be gained without including all three of those dimensions, yet how rarely it is done!

In the following pages, Marco Robledo approaches the world of business—its structure, function, leadership, investors, stakeholders in general—and he uses an Integral approach to do so. Thus, from the start, Marco includes the areas that he calls "art, ethics, and science"; in other words, these three major dimensions, with their different types of truth and validity claims. Now, in recent times, there have been movements that wish to include, in business, an ethical or moral dimension. But you always get the sense that these areas are just tacked on to their businesses, that somehow moral behavior is not a core of their enterprise. But how much different it looks if, from the start, you have a foundation that includes art and morals and science, as Marco does. The picture looks very different indeed, and you get the sense that this type of business has morals as part of its foundation—which, of course, it does.

And that's just the start. The Integral metaframework, as I suggested, has several elements that represent inherent qualities that all humans possess and that any human discipline that wishes to be truly inclusive and comprehensive needs to fully take into account. These elements include the quadrants that we just mentioned, as well as numerous stages of development, various lines of development, higher states of consciousness, various types, and shadow elements. These are all technical terms that you don't need to worry about now, except to notice that Marco uses all of those elements in his explanation of business and the revolutionary changes that we see happening to it right now.

But just as with consciousness studies, where we see the field fragmented into competing approaches, the world of business today, around the world, is largely still a badly fragmented affair. Even looking only at aesthetics, morals, and scientific technology, businesses today are having a hard time truly integrating all of those. And this applies just to the quadrants; you can imagine how poorly they are doing in all the other areas. So picture what you might think of as a truly comprehensive or holistic or integral business—and that is exactly what Marco lays out for you in the following pages.

Thus—along with approaches such as Alan Watkins's *Coherence*, surveys such as Frederic Laloux's *Reinventing Organizations*, and actual businesses like John Mackey's Whole Foods—Marco is one the pioneers in a truly Integral Business. As Laloux's survey indicates, this more Integral approach is already a feature of many of the most leading businesses in today's world. What Marco does is help show you, from the start, how to build a truly Integral Business, using virtually all of its central elements. Speaking again as the major architect of this framework, I can't say that I agree with every single little detail of how Marco lays this all out (who could?). But I can say that he does a brilliant job in using the framework in exactly the way I intended—which is to take a field that you love, and by filling in the gaps exposed by an Integral perspective, make it a field that you can love even more.

Most people, in most of the world, spend most of their time in a business venture of their choice. And the vast majority of them report that they are miserable. In large part, this is because the business where they work is still following a structure that is hundreds of years old. But evolution moves on, the stages of development move on; and most business owners, managers, and team members are completely unaware of these evolutionary stages (as well as most of the other elements of a truly Integral view). This is exactly what Marco's book can help you overcome. Whether you own a business, manage one, or simply use one, this book can help enlighten you, encourage you, and give you great hope for the future. One thing is certain: the more a truly Integral Business catches on, the more whole and fulfilled that humanity's future will be. And *3D Management* will have helped pave the way.

INTRODUCTION

"You never change things by fighting the existing reality. To change something, build a new model that makes the existing model obsolete."
Richard Buckminster Fuller

Many practitioners are allergic to theories. They are action-oriented people who think theorising is a form of mental masturbation with little to no practical application. When they say "give me action, not words," they are unconsciously implying there is no need to question our underlying assumptions. Let me quote Kurt Lewin to clearly express my utter disagreement: *"There is nothing more practical than a good theory,"* he asserted. Every action is theory loaded. In times of change, like the ones we live, it is critical to challenge the beliefs that shape our conduct.

Back in 2004, and with that purpose in mind, I wrote a book in Spanish (Robledo, 2004) that introduced a theory of my own making called *3D Management*. It was a pioneer application of Ken Wilber's *Integral Theory* to business and organisations, and a reaction and alternative to the mainstream model, due to my dissatisfaction with it. Yes, you read that correctly, a theory from a management scholar that is meant to be practical and disruptive. Rarer than hens' teeth.

Ever since, the theory has ostensibly grown and developed. I have presented it in many professional and academic forums, published several conference papers and peer-reviewed articles (e.g., Robledo 2011, 2013, 2014, 2016, 2018b), and applied its concepts and principles in the field. This new book introduces the evolution of 3D Management, as a result of the research I have carried out throughout these years, the hands-on applications of a community of practitioners that have worked with this or similar models, and my own practical experience in a wide range of contexts, such as the 3D Management Club of Conscious Organisations[1] which I founded and has chapters in Mallorca and Bogotá.

The original book received a limited but enthusiastic response. It was an unsurprising outcome for a work in the fringe of management theory that only appealed to the chosen few who shared my values and vision. I saw myself as a Spanish Quixote, hopelessly fighting against the invincible giant that was the established management paradigm.

But I was wrong. The tides are turning, and an ever-increasing number of organisations are experimenting with new models that are a better fit for the current conditions. My prediction now is that this revolutionary way of managing organisations will become the dominant management paradigm in the 21st century. Some leading-edge theories and models such as *Teal Organisations, Agile, Conscious Capitalism, Holacracy, Sociocracy 3.0,* and *Liberated Companies* are spreading as an alternative to the traditional model, laying out the foundations for a new paradigm[2]. Many prominent companies such as Zappos, Valve, W.L. Gore, Whole Foods, ner Group, Spotify, Netflix, Haier, Michelin, Patagonia, Buurtzorg, or Morning Star are already managed in this way, and they are just the visible side of an iceberg that could sink "business-as-usual". Different trends are pushing this revolution forward, I will highlight the four I consider most important:

Social dissatisfaction

The global economic crisis that originated in the US in December 2007, and spread like a virus to every part of the world, has contributed to an increasingly turbulent environment and deep questioning of some of the structures that define our model of living. The economic predicament is just one aspect of a much more profound and complex crisis that is also political, ecological, and axiological and is the result, first and foremost, of a fractured worldview. Crises are just the natural consequence of a world heading for disaster where the triad of capitalism, consumer society, and representative democracy is no longer working as it used to (Batle and Robledo, 2018). A capitalist model based on unlimited growth is a threat to our limited planet. Representative democracy, which not so long ago

[1] I define a conscious organisation as one that has a greater awareness of itself and the environment, understands the consequences of its actions better, and, thereby, acts more responsibly.

[2] See appendix 1 for a description of those and other related theories.

seemed unquestionable, is increasingly challenged for its shortcomings and problems, such as corruption, nepotism, focus on conflict, short-term thinking, and limited participation of the citizen. Finally, consumerism, based on a never-ending cycle of buying, throwing away, and buying again, is destroying the environment, reducing people to merchandise, and generating an aching spiritual vacuum.

The painful truth is that the system has failed the vast majority. Is it any wonder people feel cheated when companies make money and the economy keeps growing, but the system generates fewer and fewer jobs and favours only a small elite? A growing percentage of the population feels disenfranchised and has lost faith in a system based on Neoliberalism, consumerism, and a political structure controlled by corporations and elites. The social movements of the beginning of the century, like Syntagma Square in Greece, Indignados in Spain, or Occupy Wall Street in the US, campaigned against economic inequalities, financial instability, and precarious employment. More recent events like the election of Donald Trump, the rise of other populist candidates in other countries, or Brexit, can also be interpreted as people taking desperate means to show their utter frustration and disillusionment. They are also a reaction to the limitations and unreasonable premises of mainstream management and a sign of the erosion of trust in business and business leaders that has plummeted to unprecedented levels.

This trend is especially worrying when we consider the enormous influence business has over our lives. No government, no religion, no other social institution, past or present, has affected existence more than business does. It is the most powerful institution of all time. We could easily say that business rules the world. Not only do we spend most of our waking time working, but it also determines what we eat, what kind of information we receive, what we wear, etc.

Peter Parker learned from his Uncle Ben that *"with great power comes great responsibility,"* and he applied himself to live by that principle as Spiderman. Unfortunately, business is not the socially responsible institution we all would like it to be. On the contrary, if we take a critical look, we will see a picture of selfishness and a lack of moral compass. In fact, Joel Bakan's (2004) famous psychoanalysis of corporations concludes they act more like psychopaths in their pathological pursuit of power and profit, regardless of the harmful consequences they might cause to others[3]. The results are there. Business has a significant share of responsibility over the three major challenges we face today: excessive global inequalities, ecological unsustainability, and the alienation and neurotic anxieties of modern life.

Challenging environment

Heraclitus' maxims "*Everything changes, nothing is permanent*" and "*You can't swim twice in the same river*" are recurring clichés in business literature. But change is the only constant. It has been there since the beginning of time, what is different today is its pace. The analogy of a hurricane aptly describes its acceleration: the speed at the periphery is low, but it increases exponentially as you approach the centre. Hold on tight to your seat and take this whirlwind trip through human history, courtesy of Daniel Pinchbeck (2006: 102):

> *"The Stone Age lasted many thousands of years, the Bronze Age lasted a few thousand years, the Industrial Age took three hundred years, The Chemical Age or Plastic Age began a little more than a century ago, the Information Age began thirty years ago, the Biotechnology Age geared up in the last decade."*

Compare these facts: Homo Erectus used the same stone tools for 2 million years, it took 100 years to apply the steam machine to automobiles, but in just eight years the internet revolutionised our lives. Are you getting dizzy? As the Red Queen warned Alice, "*Nowadays we must run as fast as we can, just to stay in place, and if you wish to go anywhere, you must run twice as fast*".

Change not only happens faster than ever before. It also happens on a larger and more unpredictable scale, as current challenges have many factors and few solutions, and it is unclear the effects they may have. The acronym VUCA describes the volatility, uncertainty, complexity, and ambiguity of the current issues. Honestly, who could have predicted something like the coronavirus global pandemic? COVID-19 has shown us how unpredictable, complex, and deeply interconnected the world we live

[3] Bakan, in his book *The Corporation* (2004) and in the documentary of the same title he co-wrote in 2003 with Abbott and Achbar, examines the personality of corporations. He describes it as a self-centred, amoral type, with delusions of greatness and a lack of regard for the others. Based on those traits, he concludes it is a pathological, even psychopathic personality.

in is. For those of you who didn't fully understand how it was possible for a butterfly to flap its wings in Brazil and produce a tornado in Texas, let me give you a new metaphor for chaos theory: a person sneezes in Wuhan and causes a pandemic of planetary proportions. Indeed, it is such an extremely challenging environment that Tom Peters made the remark: *"if you're not confused, you're not paying attention."* He is not the only one. An IBM study of over 1,500 CEOs, cited by Petrie (2014), identified their number one concern was the growing complexity of their environments, with the majority of them saying that their organisations are not equipped to cope with such an amount of uncertainty, complexity, and ambiguity.

And it takes its toll: a wealth of research indicates that the average lifespan of organisations continues to shrink. More and more conventionally well-managed organisations fail to achieve sustainable long-term success. A recent study by McKinsey found that the average lifespan of companies listed in the Standard & Poor's 500 was 61 years in 1958. Today, it is less than 18 years. In the 1960s a company lived about as long as a human being of the time. Nowadays, they are dying once they reach adulthood. If the life expectancy of the human race had suffered such a massive downturn, it would have been considered a tragedy of biblical proportions. McKinsey forecasts that 75% of the companies currently quoted on the S&P 500 will have disappeared by 2027. They will be bought-out, merged, or will go bankrupt. None of the oldest and more resilient companies on the New York Stock Exchange (General Electric, Exxon Mobile, Procter & Gamble, and DuPont) are market favourites any longer. In Europe, the situation is similar. According to Eurostat, less than half of the enterprises born in 2011 were still active in 2016. It is not a matter of nostalgia, but of the enormous psychological, social, and economic repercussions such a mortality rate has.

The obsolescence of management

Our management models are too archaic and simple (taken individually) to effectively respond to the uncertainty and complexity of the current environment. The world has become so turbulent, new technologies are developing so rapidly, knowledge is multiplying so quickly, and we are confronting so many crises on multiple scales that we require explanations matched in complexity.

As authors such as Hamel (2009) and Carney and Getz (2016:45) point out, management was invented during the Industrial Revolution to solve two specific problems: The first was regulating the work habits of mostly untrained peasants and artisans, accustomed to working at their own pace, who were hired into factories to perform repetitive activities competently, diligently, and efficiently. The second was the need to obtain uniform, reliable output that enabled the large-scale production of goods and services. In a nutshell, the problems were efficiency, standardisation, and scale, the objective was doing the same thing over and over again, only changing with small increments, and the solution was bureaucracy, with its hierarchical system of command and control and its rules and procedures.

Our current management paradigm follows industrial age principles, now more than a century old. It worked well in the past when everything was stable and predictable, but it is useless in an unpredictable world of disruptive technology and highly autonomous and educated workforces.

Gary Hamel (2009) is one of the influential figures who have voiced their discontent with the current management paradigm:

> *"Why, for example, should it take the blunt instrument of a performance crisis to bring about change? Why should organizations be so much better at operating than they are at innovating? Why should so many people work in uninspiring companies? Why should the first impulse of managers be to avoid the responsibilities of citizenship rather than to embrace them? Surely we can do better."*

For him, it is time for change: *"Management, like the combustion engine, is a mature technology that must now be reinvented for a new age."* He elaborates:

> *"Managers today face a new set of problems, products of a volatile and unforgiving environment. Some of the most critical: How in an age of rapid change do you create organizations that are as adaptable and resilient as they are focused and efficient? How in a world where the winds of creative destruction blow at gale force can a company innovate quickly and boldly enough to stay relevant and profitable? How in a creative economy where entrepreneurial genius is the secret to success do you inspire employees to bring the gifts of initiative, imagination, and passion to work every day? How at a time when the once hidden costs of industrialization have become distressingly apparent do you encourage executives to fulfil their responsibilities to all stakeholders?*
>
> *To successfully address these problems, executives and experts must first admit that they've reached the limits of Management 1.0—the industrial age paradigm built atop the principles of standardization, specialization, hierarchy, control, and primacy of shareholder interests." (Ibid., 2009)*

Finally, he makes a call for action:

> *"All too often, scholars have been content to codify best practice instead of looking beyond it. Practitioners have been more inclined to ask "Has anybody else done this?" than "Isn't this worth trying?" What's needed are daring goals that will motivate a search for radical new ways of mobilizing and organizing human capabilities." (Ibid., 2009)*

Don't jump the gun, just yet. Mainstream management is neither something to be discarded or dismissed altogether. We can only reinvent management by understanding where it comes from and incorporating all the great achievements it has conquered. Otherwise, we risk throwing out the baby with the bathwater. Gary Hamel (2009) shares this point of view when he writes: "*The goal, though, is to overcome the limits of today's management practices without losing the benefits they confer. It would make no sense to find a cure for insularity and inertia, for example, if the side effects were imprudence and inefficiency.*" Organisations must become a lot more adaptable, agile, humane, and socially responsible without getting any less focused, disciplined, or performance-oriented. Giving it a little tweak won't be enough either. It is not a matter of rectifying, complementing, restoring or revitalising the current management paradigm. It is about fundamentally updating and reimagining it.

This book, using an integral approach, highlights the shortcomings of the current business model while guarding its virtues. It proposes a new theory that radically redefines management's ontology to make organisations a model of efficiency and prosperity, but also of integrity and commitment to people and society.

Employee disengagement

Most of us spend about a third of our waking hours working. Research shows that these hours are, on average, the least happy of our lives. For far too many people, work is a dispiriting, frustrating, and joyless experience they put up with only to make money:

> *"(...) you show up every morning, you punch a card, you go to your station, you're told what to do, you're not given the tools you need to do what you need to do, you get ten things right and nobody says a word, and you get one thing wrong and you get chewed out? You ask questions and it takes a week to get an answer back. It is no wonder many people feel pretty empty." (Chapman and Sisodia, 2015: 90)*

That is the management system we developed during the industrial revolution to turn farmers and artisans into automatons working in assembly lines to perform repetitive, predictable, and unintellectual tasks.

In his eye-opening *Throwing Rocks at the Google Bus,* Douglas Rushkoff (2016: 18) contends that industrialisation, under the disguise of the triumph of technology, was more about restoring the power of those at the top by disempowering workers, in particular merchants and artisans. Rather than having to learn how to make shoes, workers could be trained in minutes how to do one tiny part of the job. It was much more efficient and cheaper, especially if much of the cost was externalised or hidden (e.g., environmental and health costs).

Even though working conditions have improved since those early days, the daily reality for most people is still subject to a bureaucratic and hierarchical operating system that fosters predictability, mediocrity, and obedience. The result? Skyrocketing levels of disengagement and a colossal waste of human potential.

The leading and more often quoted study on employee engagement is *Gallup's State of the Global Workplace Report* (2017). It has been carried out since 2009 in more than 150 countries, and roughly 180 million employees have been interviewed. Its consistent results couldn't be more disheartening. Worldwide, the percentage of adults who work full time for an employer and are engaged at work (meaning they are psychologically committed to their jobs and enthusiastic about their work and the organisation they work for) is just 15%. The rest are looking forward to the end of the day, as soon as they arrive. Though engagement levels vary considerably by country and region (it ranges from 33% per cent in the US, to 10% in Western Europe or just 6% in East Asia), no country has more than four engaged employees out of ten. Out of the 85% of employees that are not engaged, we can separate between the merely disengaged workers that are not rowing as hard as they can and the actively disengaged ones that are rowing intentionally in a different direction or punching holes in the boat. The Gallup Research Institute estimates that active disengagement costs the US economy around 500 billion dollars per year and individual companies an average of 1/3 of the payroll.

When it comes to motivation, the results are equally distressing. Only two in 10 employees strongly agree that their performance is managed in a way that motivates them to do outstanding work. Moreno et al. (2018) gathered different studies that showed that 63% of employees are not motivated and are not willing to make an extra effort for the company, 24% consider themselves truly unhappy and unproductive in their work, and only 28% think that the company demonstrates a sincere interest in their welfare. Those staggering results represent an enormous cost for the organisation and show a grim picture of individuals wasting their lives doing something that does not make them happy. The founders of many of the vanguard organisations presented in this book (such as Buurtzorg's Jos de Block, Pressto Peru's Olivier Gesbert, Pieter Spinder from Knowmads Business School, and Corporate Rebels' Pim de Morree and Joost Minnaar, just to name a few) have in common being rejects of the traditional business world, and all suffered burnout or bore-out by their uninspiring jobs. Thankfully, they built their own paths to find meaning at work and have a real impact on society.

The journey

For untold ages, the kingdom existed in a serenity that seemed unchanging. Now winter is coming, and VUCA the dragon is at the gates of the kingdom. Its frozen breath will wipe out everything, and change the land forever. Brave individuals who dare to face the menace and tame the beast are needed. Only when that happens, will the gods allow the sun to shine once again[4].

The underlying assumptions of mainstream management are no longer relevant to our current situation. An unforgiving environment, social dissatisfaction, employee disengagement, and obsolescence of the industrial management model are mutually supporting trends that are making organisations increasingly dysfunctional. We can't cover our eyes with Virtual Reality goggles to hide in an alternate reality. The game is over, and a new game is coming up. A paradigm shift is going to happen very soon. The old model has become too incompetent and incomplete, so business as usual is no longer possible. Maintaining a system that doesn't work and is unacceptable for the vast majority is senseless. It might be even suicidal. Organisations have no choice about whether to accept a new world that differs fundamentally from the old. Ready or not, here it comes! That is the inevitable future.

---

[4] As I proofread the document, locked at home in the middle of the coronavirus pandemic curfew, this paragraph presents an entirely new meaning.

Does your organisation have what it takes to deal with the world ahead of us? Patching things up won't work. Working harder or smarter is no longer enough. We have to create everything anew and radically reimagine the way organisations are conceived and managed. Embracing change might allow us to shape it according to our needs. If we deny it, we will only suffer the consequences.

We are like trapeze artists hanging on to the bar. We must release our grip on this well-known bar and hurtle across space to the great beyond. Some of us have already leapt. We are in the bottomless chasm between the past and the future. It is scary, but also utterly exciting because this is part of our evolutionary growth.

This book features the cases of more than 60 vanguard organisations that made the leap into the unknown. These and many other organisations are paving the way in every sector and every country. They are legion.

Don't feel overwhelmed by what seems like a large gap between you and the best cases portrayed in this and other similar books. Every trip must start with a first step. If you don't want the future to leave you behind, join the (r)evolution. Take the path paved with yellow cobblestones, follow it, and we will meet somewhere over the rainbow.

CHAPTER 1

INTEGRAL THEORY

"The most exciting breakthroughs of the twenty-first century won't occur because of technology, but because of an expanding concept of what it means to be human." (John Naisbitt).

1.1. Jack of all trades and master of none

"It is necessary to be alert and to go out of one's job: to observe well the landscape of life that is always total. No science or trade will give you the supreme faculty to live, but the synopsis of all trades and all sciences." (José Ortega y Gasset)

Since I was a child, I have shown great interest in the most disparate things: art, philosophy, sports, science, everything attracted my innate curiosity and my craving for knowledge. My mother used to rely on a famous proverb to show her concern about my eclecticism: *"You will be a Jack of all trades and a master of none."* She wanted me to follow the right path of specialisation. I have to say that her well-intended advice went in one ear and out the other. I was well aware that it was hard to be Leonardo in the 21st century, but I still wanted to toy with a lot of different fields and see if I could join the dots between them. In hindsight, I think I was right.

Nonetheless, my mother had a point. Back then, the market wanted only specialists. Nowadays, specialised jobs are under the constant threat of automatisation and artificial intelligence, while more and more employers demand a broader set of skills that combine big-picture thinking, transferable skills, and flexibility. It is not that they are giving up specialist knowledge to hire pure generalists. They want it all. Survival in the new work environment requires a combination of depth and breadth. Deep specialists, they call it. Take Valve Corporation, an American video game company responsible for such popular series as *Half-Life, Portal, Counter-Strike*, and *Left 4 Dead*. They seek "T-shaped" people, that is, people who are both generalists (highly skilled at a broad set of valuable things—the top of the T) and also experts (among the best in their field within a narrow discipline—the vertical leg of the T). They want to avoid the problems of overspecialisation by adding breadth to our knowledge.

A broader perspective reveals that fragmentation and compartmentalisation of knowledge are the cause of many of our ills. We know a lot about too little and too little about most anything. We tend to concentrate on the parts of a general process and neglect the whole. We focus on our professional careers, and we don't look after our personal lives. We make a decision concentrating on its immediate or partial effects forgetting the old African adage that it never rains in a single house.

Blame it on the brain. Our inferior parietal lobe is dualistic and understands the world by dividing it into opposites. Everything is neatly sorted into black and white, with no tolerance for ambiguity or shades of grey. Differences of opinion are pitted against each other as opposing ideas rather than as pieces of the larger picture. Right-wrong, good-evil, man-woman, loss-profit, environment-economy, concentration-diversification, superior-subordinate, conforming-nonconforming... They are just mental chimaeras of this binary logic.

Our futile attempts to understand totality by classifying and separating it are the source of many of our problems: wars, racism, nationalism, etc. The focus is on the differences rather than on the similarities. The struggle of opposites, as Heraclitus called it, necessarily leads to the dualisation of ideologies. Those who don’t share my point of view are wrong (unfortunately, one of the hidden assumptions of our parliamentary democratic system). If you are not with me, you are against me. Economists against psychologists, lawyers against economists, marketing versus finance. In the war of all against all, there are no winners, only losers.

Science itself has proven that atomistic models are not the most adequate to explain reality. The current scientific paradigm rejects that the world is made of isolated independent parts. The new science that emerged in the twentieth century (including relativity theory, quantum physics, chaos theory, and complexity science) is holistic. It portrays a reality formed by intrinsically related systems.

The same holds for organisations. There was a time when a person was responsible for the totality of a task. In a medieval workshop, each shoemaker made an entire shoe. Industrialisation brought along the division of labour and responsibilities. Consequently, people carry out small narrow specialised jobs that don't let them see the whole picture. As the ideological father of capitalism, Adam Smith, advocated, the production of a pin factory will improve if some workers focus on the head and others on the body of the pin. Next, the principle of specialisation was carried to the vertical level, as somebody who sees the whole picture is needed, and authority and hierarchy appeared. In *The Republic*, Plato divided the city into three main streams of force: generating forces (artisans and peasants), emotional and vital forces (warriors), and intellectual-spiritual forces (kings-philosophers). Applying the same principle, organisations divided power and responsibility into three levels: bottom (generator or operational), middle (controlling), and top (intellectual and strategic).

Specialisation improved knowledge by breaking complex phenomena into their essential components. But just as everything else, it came with a dark side. For starters, when the individual submits to authority, he or she becomes an instrument, alienated from his or her actions ("this is company policy," "this is not my job," or "I don't make the rules"). Plus, departmentalisation often leads to blurry boundaries or grey areas. Business processes can't always be parcelled out in clear-cut categories. There is a myriad of problems straddled across disciplines. Something in no man's land is harder to classify or understand, and easier to dismiss. That partly explains why fundamental aspects such as spirit, emotions, or ethics remain in organisational limbo. Specialisation also hinders information exchange because people tend to look with suspicion at everything alien to their group or discipline, thus ignoring or disregarding the possible links between different sciences, schools, or theories. "Departmentitis" is one of the most common organisational pathologies characterised by barriers between departments and a kind of tunnel vision that prevents seeing the whole picture. Some typical symptoms are managers more concerned with protecting their own turfs than with cooperating across areas, or incriminatory or elusive behaviours that blame other departments ("This is not my job", "It's logistics' fault", "Don't call reception, they are good for nothing", "I'm sorry for the delay, administration always makes mistakes").

The tayloristic principle of specialisation, based on fragmentation and not letting the left hand know what the right is doing, may have been useful in the past, but today it is counterproductive. When things are so fragmented, what is needed is to put the pieces together again. The best glue I know of is Integral Theory.

1.2. The integral vision

> *"There has never been a time when integrative metatheorizing could be of greater importance."* (Edwards, 2010b:3)

The *Udana*, a canonical Hindu scripture, includes the following story: Once upon a time in the city of Sabathi there lived a Maharaja that had all the blind people gathered before an elephant so that they would tell, when they touched the elephant, what they perceived. After reaching the head, one said: *"An elephant looks like a pot."* Those who felt the ear answered: *"It looks like a basket of throwing";* those who touched the fang claimed: *"It is like a ploughshare";* finally, those who explored the body declared: *"It is a barn"*. And so, they began to quarrel among themselves. A partial perception brings more ignorance than knowledge. Only an integral vision brings us closer to the truth.

Since American philosopher Ken Wilber started talking about Integral Theory in 2000, it has become the most influential theory within the broader fields of integral studies[5] and metatheory[6] to the point that it has been considered "*the most integral of integral theories*" (Esbjörn-Hargens 2010a:11).

Wilber first began to use the word "integral" to refer to his approach in 1995. He explains its meaning in the following terms:

> *"The word integral means comprehensive, inclusive, non-marginalizing, embracing. Integral approaches to any field attempt to be exactly that: to include as many perspectives, styles, and methodologies as possible within a coherent view of the topic. In a certain sense, integral approaches are "meta-paradigms," or ways to draw together an already*

---

[5] As Esbjörn-Hargens clarifies (2010), integral studies encompass all visions and theories that offer a comprehensive view of reality and aim at the development of metatheories. Under its umbrella, we find thinkers like Wilber himself, Cowan, Aurobindo, Gebser, Laszlo, Sorokin, etc. Instead, Integral Theory is developed by Wilber and his followers, focusing on the AQAL model and its applications. However, it is not uncommon to find the term not only circumscribed to Wilber's work but broadly defined as a synonym of integral studies.

[6] A metatheory is a theory dedicated to the study of other theory or set of theories. In a general sense, it could be considered a "theory of theories." The metatheory field includes the work of George Ritzer, Roy Bhaskar, Gioia and Pitre, Lewis and Grimes, etc.

> *existing number of separate paradigms into an interrelated network of approaches that are mutually enriching." (Wilber, 2003: xii-xiii)*

The general field referred to as "integral" had its genesis in "cross-disciplinary studies," which tried to bring together the various areas of human inquiry in academic institutions. It initially resulted in a "heap" of knowledge rather than an integrated "system", but eventually, after many decades of research and synthesis, and some significant breakthroughs, what emerged was an "integrating" of these fields into one coherent whole knowledge system: Integral Theory, defined by Esbjörn-Hargens (2010b: 34) in this manner:

> *"Integral Theory is the comprehensive study of reality, which weaves together the significant insights from all the major human disciplines of knowledge acquisition, including the natural and social sciences as well as the arts and humanities. (...) Because integral theory systematically includes more of reality and interrelates it more thoroughly than any other current approach to assessment and solution building, it has the potential to be more successful in dealing with the complex problems we face in the 21st century".*

Ergo, Integral Theory aspires to a complete and holistic understanding of reality in all its facets. To do that, it tries to incorporate as many perspectives and methodologies as possible into a single coherent vision. An integral approach is, therefore, a metaparadigm approach, which joins previously separated paradigms in more complex metatheories.

According to Edwards (2010a: 387), "*metatheorizing is a form of conceptual research that recognizes the validity of each theoretical perspective, while also discovering their limitations through accommodating them within a larger conceptual context.*" Metatheories transcend and include partial and monistic views by identifying the orienting concepts that a particular theory applies, as well as those that it neglects or doesn't possess.

Putting it all together, *"Integral Metatheory is a form of scholarship that draws out and connects the insights of many different paradigms and theories to create a more integrated conceptual system"* (Edwards 2010b:3). It has the potential to bridge silos within and across disciplines, to overcome parochialism and to formulate theoretical frameworks capable of bending the limitations of each area of knowledge.

Integral Theory is becoming a school of thought of growing importance and influence, given its ability to synthesise human knowledge in all-encompassing maps and more complex theories. Since its first application in consciousness studies by Wilber himself (1997), it has been applied to disciplines and fields as varied as psychology, economics, ecology, art, political science, medicine, and spirituality. Indeed, there are very few fields of knowledge where it has not been applied.

Only an integrally-informed perspective can appropriately address the complexity of managing in the 21st century. Global issues and wicked problems, of the scale that we currently encounter, require an integral vision and some level of big-picture metatheoretical response. Ken Wilber, the central figure of the integral movement, maintains (2000: 12) that the only way we can heal the world and heal ourselves is by replacing the current fractured worldview with an integral worldview that honours the entire web of life.

Integral theory can become the cornerstone of a new paradigm of management that is in greater harmony with society and the essence of our beings. An integral vision can bring a broader, wiser, and non-marginalising conceptualisation of business and organisations and a deeper consciousness about why they exist and how they can create more value in all senses of the word.

1.3. The integral map

> *Watch your thoughts; they become words. Watch your words; they become actions. Watch your actions; they become habits. Watch your habits; they become character. Watch your character; it will become your destiny.* Lao-Tzu

Let's start with a little crash course on Integral Theory. I will try to relate it as much as possible to management and organisations, but you will have to wait for real applications until the next chapter. Stay with me until then. It will be worth it. If you are an advanced integralist, and you don't need a review of the basics, you can skip ahead to Chapter 2.

AQAL is Integral Theory's primary instrument. It has been defined as "*a map of maps, or a metatheory that incorporates the core truths from hundreds of other theories*" (Wilber et al., 2008). It is both instrument and metatheory, to the point that it has come to be assimilated with Integral Theory itself. AQAL is a robust, content-free metatheoretical framework suitable for virtually any context and scale and is regarded as "*one of the most versatile and dynamic approaches to integrating insights from multiple disciplines*" (Esbjörn-Hargens 2010b:35).

AQAL stands for “All-Quadrant, All-Level,” which itself is short for “all quadrants, all levels, all lines, all states, all types,” the five core organising principles of Wilber’s integral vision. They are the fewest possible factors that need to be taken into account in any truly comprehensive understanding of any given aspect of reality. Any integral approach should include an awareness of quadrants, lines, levels, states, and types as the fundamental reference points for decision making. These five elements are not merely theoretical; they are aspects of our own experience:

- We are aware we have a mind, a body, and relationships with other people, and that we live in a given environment (what the quadrants describe).
- We know there are different aspects of who we are, and different things that we are good at (lines).
- We acknowledge that we have grown and matured in several ways over time (levels).
- We experience different states of consciousness (such as waking, dreaming, deep sleep, altered, or meditative).
- We notice that we have our own way of being in the world, and expressing who we are (types).
- We see the world through different lenses (stages).

The integral map AQAL makes sure we don’t leave out any of those elements as we make a decision. It does not dictate what we should do; it merely helps us be aware of everything we should take into account. A good comparison is the operating system of a computer. Our Integral Operating System or IOS (Wilber et al. 2008) is fully compatible with all kinds of “software” we use in our life —such as business, work, spirituality, and relationships—. Let’s go briefly through its different elements.

1.3.1. States of Consciousness

Consciousness is the awareness or degree of knowledge (*"con-Scientia"*) we have of ourselves (including bodily sensations and thoughts) and the environment. The opposite of conscious is unconscious, senseless, or unaware. And yet, consciousness is more than just a dualistic "on" or "off" state, as it can be broken down into at least three different states: Ordinary waking consciousness, dreaming, and deep sleep[7]. Besides, we may also undergo "altered states" of various kinds that can be induced by different means (drugs, sleep deprivation, meditation, hypnosis, etc.). Finally, we can have a variety of "peak experiences," many of which can be triggered by intense events like making love, walking in nature, listening to exquisite music, or being deeply absorbed in an activity we love and have mastered. This last case, defined as the "flow state" (Csikszentmihalyi, 1990), is especially desirable at work. When in flow, we can focus our energy and attention to such an extent that full absorption can be achieved in the task before us, resulting in a performance of an almost miraculous deftness.

Being awake is the required state of consciousness in a traditional workplace. Every other option is either undesirable (nobody wants to get caught sleeping or daydreaming at work) or vastly unexplored. In my opinion, the study of non-ordinary states of consciousness -altered states, meditative states, visionary experiences, flow, and peak experiences – is one of the most exciting new frontiers of organisational development with benefits for the individual as well as for the organisation. Indeed, more and more organisations are turning to practices such as *mindfulness* to create a more positive and harmonious work environment and tap into the full spectrum of capabilities of the mind. It is conclusively proven that meditation sharpens focus, memory, creativity, and emotional intelligence (especially empathy and self-regulation) and can help to reduce stress and anxiety, thereby potentially boosting resilience and performance.

An alternative way to classify states is based on emotions (like joy, happiness, sadness, anger, anxiety, or fear). Emotions are mental states that arise spontaneously (rather than through conscious effort) and are often accompanied by physiological changes. Emotional intelligence (EI) is the ability to identify, assess, and control the states of mind of oneself and others. It is considered to be a critical measure of personal competence and work performance.

1.3.2. Structures, levels, or stages

Integral Theory holds an evolutionary view of humanity backed up by developmental psychology, a school of thought that explains how and why

---

[7] The whole spectrum of states is more precisely referred to as gross, subtle, causal, witness, and nondual.

human beings *grow up* through various structures of consciousness. Our development through those structures, levels, or stages (call them what you want) is a measure of our growth and maturity. As our consciousness grows, we become more awake, we better understand the consequences of our actions, we act more responsibly, our thinking grows in complexity, our circle of care widens, and we become more profound and spiritual.

Cross-cultural analysis reveals this transformation[8] follows an invariant and predictable hierarchy of developmental progression[9] ("holarchy" is the technical term we will use later on) where each higher developmental stage transcends and includes (or unfolds and enfolds) the stage that preceded it (just as organisms transcend and include cells, which transcend and include molecules, which transcend and include atoms). These nested structures of consciousness are like our internal operating system. They are, in the words of Wilber and DiPerna (2016), like "hidden maps" that determine the way we (individuals or groups) make sense of the world and how we process information. While all of us predictably conform to the particular stage of consciousness that we are at, most of us are not aware that we are following a pattern that largely determines our worldview[10].

---

[8] Following Wilber and DiPerna (2016), I will use the terms "development" and "transformation" interchangeably (with both of them intimately connected to evolution in general). The two concepts refer to our innate human capacity to both grow (and heal) through predictable, sequential patterns of mental, emotional, and spiritual unfolding.

[9] The philosophical underpinnings in Western thinking of this evolutionary view of reality were studied by Wilber in *Sex, Ecology, and Spirituality* (1995), not by chance subtitled *"The Spirit of Evolution."* They can be traced back to Plato and Plotinus, and were recovered and further developed by Hegel and Schelling:

"Each stage of development (or evolution) is thus Spirit knowledge of itself through the structures (and limitations) of that stage. Each stage is therefore a thesis (Fichte, Hegel) that eventually runs into its own limitations (Fichte: antithesis; Hegel: contradictions; Schelling: checking forces), which triggers a self-transcendence to a new synthesis (Fichte, Hegel; Schelling: organic unity), which both negates and preserves its predecessor (Schelling, Hegel). This dialectic, of course, is Eros, or Spirit-in-action, the drive of Spirit to unfold itself more fully and thus unify itself more fully." (Wilber, 1995: 513-514).

[10] *"A worldview is "the overall perspective from which one sees and interprets the world." This "overall perspective" is, in its essence, made up of values and universal beliefs. By values, I mean what a person considers "most important" (their priorities in life), and by universal beliefs I mean broad-based beliefs about self, people, and how the world (the system) works."* Thomas (2014:40)

The structures of individuals and groups of people (be it an organisation, an urban tribe, or a whole nation) are mutually interacting, as Volckmann (2104:250) explains:

> *"Individually, our consciousness is a product of our capacities and capabilities in relation to our life conditions, those elements that impact how we comprehend ourselves, others, and the contexts that shape our understanding. Collectively, we help to shape each individual consciousness and to bring that consciousness into a set of understandings, values, aspirations, and intentions that we call culture."*

The scientific study of stages of structure development starts with Jean Piaget (1896-1980), a Swiss psychologist who showed in a series of experiments that as children grow, the way they think advances through predictable stages. At each higher stage, their thinking becomes more complex and sophisticated, and they are able to deal with more challenging problems.

The traditional belief was that once you reach adulthood, these stages of development would stop. Today it is generally accepted that coming of age is not the final station of the developmental line and that development continues into adulthood. Human development is a never-ending process of spiralling and expanding transformation. There is not an omega point or state of psychological maturity. We may move through these hierarchically ordered levels of development infinitely, so long as life exists, or we may stabilise at one particular level. We may even regress to a lower position in some extraordinary circumstances. However, there are substantial differences between child and adult development. Whereas children move smoothly and rapidly through the stages, an adult's pace is not as predictable. While a child's development appears to happen automatically, for example, a toddler experiencing their terrible twos or an adolescent navigating their sweet sixteen, adults can't simply wait until they turn thirty to reach a new developmental altitude. They need to work to keep growing, or it will slow down dramatically, to the point of plateauing.

They determine, to a great extent, how we think and act:
"A person's worldview (values and beliefs) determine in large part: a) what facts they notice (and ignore) in the first place, b) how they interpret those facts (inevitably in a way that reinforces their pre-existing beliefs), c) what they value most and therefore deem important, d) what approaches and actions they think are warranted (or even acceptable), and e) what immediate action is called for now." (Id. 32)

Graves (2005: 29) provides an accurate description of the adult's development process:

> *"The psychology of the adult human being is an unfolding, ever-emergent process marked by subordination of older behaviour systems to newer, higher-order systems. The mature person tends to change his psychology continuously as the conditions of his existence change. Each successive stage or level of existence is a state through which people may pass on the way to other states of equilibrium. When a person is centralized in one of the states of equilibrium, he has a psychology which is particular to that state. His emotions, ethics and values, biochemistry, state of neurological activation, learning systems, preference for education, management and psychotherapy are all appropriate to that state."*

Following Piaget's pioneering work, those stages have been studied by developmental psychologists like Jean Piaget, Lawrence Kohlberg, Carol Gilligan, Abraham Maslow, Jean Gebser, and Clare Graves. Virtually all of the models they have created (including Maslow's hierarchy of needs, Kohlberg's stages of moral development (1973), Graves' emergent cyclic levels of existence (2002), Beck and Cowan's spiral dynamics (1996), Loevinger's stages of ego development (1998), Cook-Greuter's EDT and Leadership Maturity Framework (1999, 2004), Terri O'Fallon's STAGES (2011), or Barret's Seven Levels of Consciousness (2014), just to name a few) are variations on the same 6-to-8 universal and cross-cultural basic structures. Wilber offers a simplified version of just four basic stages: "egocentric" (self-focused), "ethnocentric" (group-focused), "worldcentric" (encompassing all of us, regardless of race, colour, sex, or creed), and "integral" (synthesising all previous stages). These stages necessarily happen in succession—that is, you have to go through the ethnocentric level of development before you can reach worldcentric.

The distinction between states and stages was brilliantly sketched by Ken Wilber (2017:84): *"States are something we can look at; structures are things we look through."* In addition to that, a state is temporary (now you are awake, but in a while, you might be sleeping, and I hope not because of this book) and a stage is relatively stable and permanent. Another fundamental difference is that stages are inclusive. Each new stage builds upon the last, and once you are there, it is an irreversible acquisition. For example, once a child grows to the linguistic stage, he or she has permanent access to language. In contrast, states of consciousness are exclusive, meaning you can't be awake and asleep, happy and sad or, drunk and sober at the same time, no matter how hard I have tried at times. Finally, while we can't skip stages of development (you must grow through the previous stage before you can crown the next one) states of consciousness can be experienced at just about any time. In Wilber's words, *"states are free, and structures are earned"* (Wilber 2017:216)

1.3.3. Types

Types are different styles of feeling, thinking, and acting in the world. The following are just some examples:

- Personality types: Our personality is made up of certain relatively enduring traits that make each of us unique. There are many personality typologies, some of them quite popular in organisational psychology. My favourites are the *Myers-Briggs Type Indicator* (that classifies people into 16 basic types based on Jung's archetypes of introversion/extraversion, thinking/feeling, sensation/intuition, and judgment/perception) and the *Enneagram* (that delineates nine basic personality types).
- Masculine and feminine: Certain behaviours are more feminine, while others are more masculine. I am not referring here to traditional genders (male and female), but rather to the energetic qualities of masculine and feminine. Feminine energy is intuitive, receptive, affectionate, creative, communicative, cooperative, and emotional. Masculine energy is action-oriented, to the point, competitive, rational, assertive, independent, problem-solving, risk-taking, etc. In Integral Theory terms, male values privilege agency (individuality) and female values privilege communion (relationships).
- Representational systems: Neuro-Linguistic Programming (NLP) classifies people according to the systems they use to experience and represent the world (visual, auditory, kinaesthetic, etc.)

The list of typologies could go on endlessly, including left-handers vs. right-handers (for example, lefties are thought of as being more creative), birth order (firstborn, middle, lastborn, or single child), etc.

If levels of development may be ranked in terms of "higher" and "lower," or less and more inclusive, types are horizontal categories that can be expressed at any level. Every type is entirely legitimate and is not necessarily "better" or "worse" than any other. Even so, they can be expressed wrongly or in unhealthy ways. For example, the feminine expression of nurturance can degenerate into over-protection, and masculine self-assertion can turn into aggressiveness. Equally, an introspective personality can lapse into negative self-criticism and isolation, and an extroverted style can neglect self-reflection. In those cases, our basic type needs to be untangled and distilled from its pathological expression to develop in more healthy ways.

Mainstream management prefers some types to others. Traditionally, recruiters looked for masculine values of rationality, power, and competitiveness in a manager. Hence, gender imbalance is not only a consequence of discrimination but also of typology preferences in management. Men tend to be better suited to the traditional management model because it builds on their strengths. Thus, many women who make it to top management positions are forced to lead with their masculine energy, projecting a hard, implacable, and autocratic image, and must behave as the prototypical alpha male, which is a disadvantage for them. But the cultural pendulum has swung back. If, in the past, women were considered defective men, (it was thought that they lacked logic, rationality, and sense of justice), today men are the defective ones (they are branded as insensitive, with poor relational skills, and unable to express their feelings). Many people, including the famous business guru Tom Peters, suggest that organisations need more feminine values and that women are better prepared for managing in the future:

> *"Women are better managers than men," men and women say. Definition of better? Better in relationships. (Not surprising, huh?). And better at planning, setting goals, and tracking. (...)*
>
> *"Men focus on separation ... getting away from authority/family/ whatever. Women focus on connection. Men focus on self. Women focus on others. As a spin-off of that, men worry about rights (and respect for others' rights). Women worry more about responsibilities. Men are more comfortable with hierarchies that clearly differentiate one from another. Women are more comfortable with network (web) organizations, where inclusiveness is the aim. And another manifestation: Men (surprise) go in for confrontation to solve problems. Women emphasize care and protection." (Peters 1997: 406).*

In my opinion, organisations don't have to choose between masculine and feminine. Both are the interdependent extremes of a continuum that needs to be balanced. As Wilber (2000:53) explains, privileging male values can result in hyperagency, or fear of relationship, *"where too much agency, too much individuality, leads to a severing (repression and alienation) of the rich networks of communion that sustain individuality in the first place."* Privileging female energies is equally problematic as "*too much communion [i.e., hypercommunion or fear of autonomy] leads to a loss of individual integrity, leads to fusion with others, to indissociation, to a blurring of boundaries and a meltdown and loss of autonomy (...) the one leading to domination, the other to fusion (...)"*

We are not doomed to be stereotypes of masculine or feminine behaviour. Within all of us, there are masculine and feminine energies that can combine in multiple ways. Virtue is in the middle point, and organisations should aspire for androgyny. In alchemy, androgynous entities achieve the conjunction of opposites and the cessation of the torment of separation. A genuinely integral approach avoids confrontation between opposites and integrates masculine and feminine values into a single reality with a broader perspective. Organisations need as much the masculine capacity for abstraction and sense of justice, as the emotionality, practicality, and relational ability of the feminine.

1.3.4. Lines

Our capacity to move sequentially through different stages can be expressed in a complex array of "lines" of development. The theory of multiple intelligences suggests that we all have up to a dozen different lines of intelligence, including cognitive intelligence, emotional intelligence, moral intelligence, interpersonal intelligence, linguistic intelligence, mathematical intelligence, kinaesthetic intelligence, aesthetic intelligence, and spiritual intelligence, as well as others. There is a growing body of developmental studies on specific lines, such as moral development (Kohlberg, 1973; Gilligan, 1993); values (Graves, 2002); general and ego development (Cook-Greuter, 2004; Kegan, 1994; Loevinger, 1998); worldview (Gebser, 1985); or cognitive development and systems (Commons, 2008), each categorising developmental stages in their own particular way. Even though many of these researchers worked independently from each other, their models show strikingly similar stages (Wilber, 2000).

The degree of development of each line varies according to capabilities and effort. Roger Federer was born to play tennis and Dave Mckean to draw and paint, but they have both excelled in their disciplines thanks to a combination of talent and training.

The literature also indicates that different developmental lines unfold in a relatively independent manner. The Integral Psychograph illustrates the relationship between stages and lines of development (Wilber et al., 2008:

81-82). Vertically it maps altitudes or levels, and horizontally, lines, as figure 1 shows. It usually reveals that development is not homogeneous. One person may have a very high level of IQ (high cognitive development) and excel in that area while remaining at low levels of EQ (emotional development), and SQ (spiritual intelligence) and thus behave with the emotional and spiritual maturity of a child.

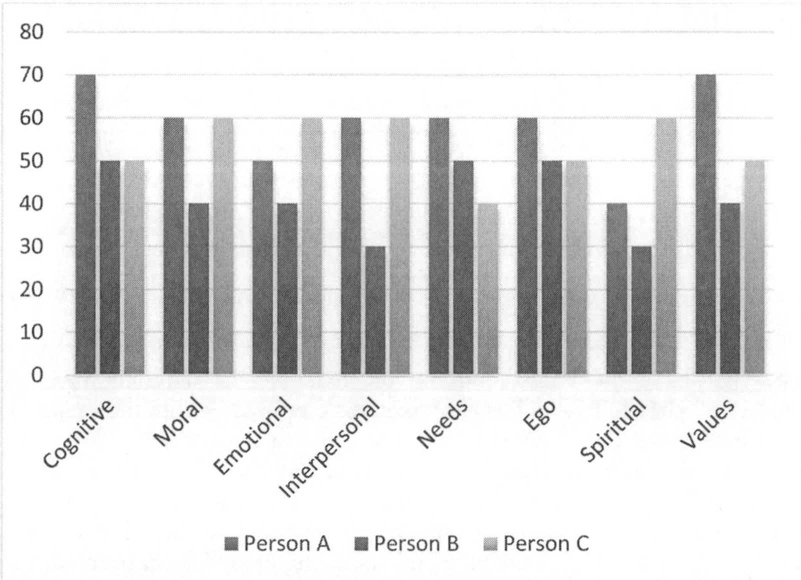

Figure 1: A comparative integral psychograph.

1.3.5. Quadrants

The foundation of the AQAL model is the matrix of the quadrants of development. It suggests that all dimensions and perspectives of human knowledge and experience can be summarised in a four-quadrant grid that includes the subjective experience, the physical or objective world, and the subjective relations with others[11]. All of them find their place in the

[11] On a technical note, I am using AQAL in this chapter as a Theory of Everything (TOE) to represent the ultimate big picture, i.e., the dimensions of the All as a whole. Alternatively, it can be used as an interpretive lens of the structure and

matrix, with each quadrant being a dimension defined respectively as inside and outside, and singular and plural, (see table 1). This versatile model brings simplicity on the other side of complexity and has been applied in many disciplines and contexts since Wilber first used it to analyse the paradigms that influence psychology.

	INTERIOR	EXTERIOR
INDIVIDUAL	**Subjective dimension** Thoughts, feelings, emotions, motivations, intentions.	**Objective dimension** Body, behaviour, organism.
COLLECTIVE	**Intersubjective dimension** Relationships, shared meanings, culture, ethics.	**Interobjective dimension** Social systems, environment, laws, technology.

Table 1: Quadrants of development and dimensions of human existence (Wilber 1996, 2000b).

The right-hand quadrants focus on the exterior, the tangible world of objective behaviour, which can be assessed empirically with the senses or their extensions. They are the "scientific ones" par excellence, given the preference of Western science to the external and objective. Its language is in the third person. Research dominated by the external perspective is objective and impersonal, excluding any consideration to the idiosyncrasies, values, and personalities of the members of the organisation because that interior space is not accessible in an empirical way. They derive, according to Zohar (1997: 100-107), from the division that liberal democracies, following Locke, made between the public and the private sphere of person and society. Indeed, in our Western civilisation, we have established clear boundaries between what can be shared and what should be protected from intrusion. Hence, the division between body and mind, and body and soul. The body and its actions belong to the sphere of the public. In contrast, the soul and the mind are private, and I must keep them for myself (for example, by not showing my feelings).

The left quadrants focus on the interior, intangible world of subjective experience. If the right quadrants were perceptible, and therefore likely to

---

dynamics of anything. In that case, AQAL acts as a Theory of Anything (Edwards, 2002b). I will take that perspective to analyse organisations in chapter 4.

be objects of observation, those on the left can only be interpreted through communication and hermeneutics. They are "*subjects of communication,*" and their meaning is context-dependent.

The famous psychologist Jordan Peterson (1999: xxi) describes the world as a forum for action, as well as a place of things. Inadvertently, Peterson's model describes the difference between the right and the left quadrants. We describe the world as a place of things, using the formal methods of science, those of the right quadrants. In contrast, the world as a forum for action is a world of perception and experience, only transmittable to others through techniques of communication and mapped in the left quadrants. The two forms of representation have been unnecessarily set at odds because, without an appropriate framework such as AQAL, we could not accurately differentiate their respective domains. The territory of the former is the "objective world" (i.e., what is, from the perspective of science). The realm of the latter is "the world of value" (i.e., what is and what should be, from the standpoint of emotion, culture, and action).

Now, let's proceed to examine each of the quadrants:

- The first of the external quadrants is the upper-right quadrant (UR) or behavioural. It refers to the exterior of individuals in an objective, empirical, and scientific way. It reduces people to *"organic bodily states, biochemical, neurobiological factors, neurotransmitters, organic brain structures, (...) and so on"* (Wilber, 2000: 49) and its observable behaviour. As applied to organisations, this quadrant would focus primarily on the behaviour of any individual who is an organisational member (employee, manager, owner) or stakeholder (customer, supplier, etc.).
- The upper-left quadrant (UL) investigates the psychology or inner consciousness of individuals. It considers their wants, needs, feelings, emotions, and motivations. Its study is undertaken primarily by some branches of psychology.
- The lower-right quadrant (LR) focuses on the outside of the collective. It is characteristic of the social sciences, and it concentrates on the "systems," i.e., all external, material, and institutional forms of a community. It is essentially the perspective adopted by management as a social science. It conceives organisations as objective realities from a techno-economic and social perspective. It highlights the exterior aspects

of organisational life –structures, processes, systems, and routines- that determine how to get things done and how to organise work.

- The lower left quadrant (LL) is about the interior of the collective, in other words, culture, that *"includes all patterns of consciousness shared by those who are part of a particular culture or subculture"* (Wilber 2000a: 50), including shared values, perceptions, beliefs, ethics, and cultural contexts as studied by organisational culture.

Psychology, behaviour, systems, and culture, each quadrant represents a different dimension, but they are interrelated and correlated with each other. For example, the emotion of fear -UL- pairs up with the limbic system –UR-, and an authoritarian kind of culture –LL- that will generate a hierarchical organisational structure –LR-. Table 2 shows an example of a developmental sequence in each of the quadrants.

Following the AQAL structure, an integral kind of management should take into account the individual and the collective, together with the objective and the subjective. It should address and support the development of the feelings, emotions, needs, desires, and motivations of the people –psychology-, their physical wellbeing and conduct –behaviour-, the beliefs, values , and symbols of the organisation -culture- and all the technical, social and economic aspects –systems or social dimension.

The four-quadrant matrix is an antidote against our deep-seated tendency to look at a phenomenon in a simplistic and biased way, without recognising all possible perspectives. When you blame it all on a single cause like the crisis, the system, patriarchy, the government, the boss, or your parents, you are not making a rigorous analysis. You are simply scapegoating. AQAL takes into consideration even the most complex issues in a balanced and comprehensive manner and develops full-spectrum solutions to today's increasingly complex business challenges.

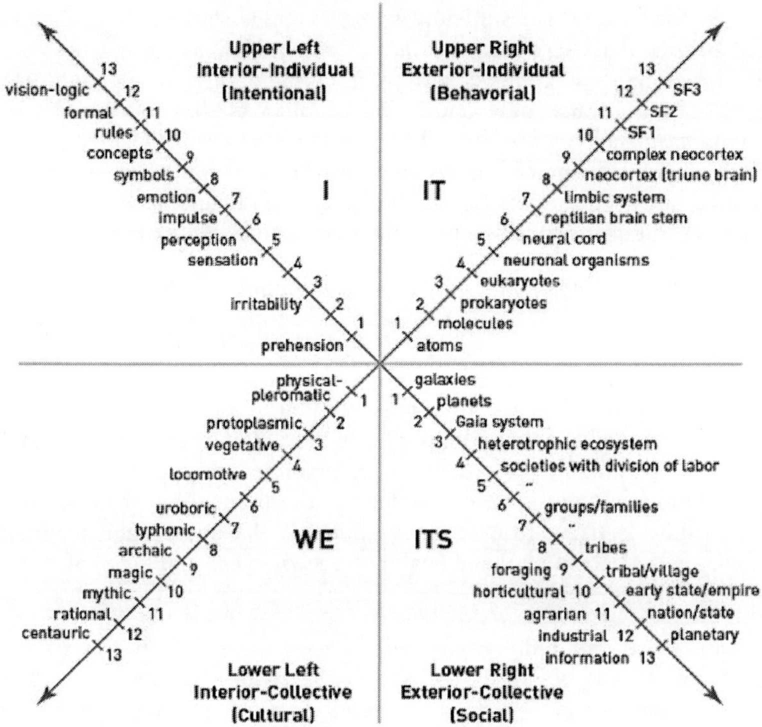

Table 2: The quadrants of development (Wilber 2000a).

As an illustration, let's apply AQAL to a downsizing scenario. Firing someone is a serious thing to do. In my opinion, it should be the last resort, but much too often, it is one of the first measures to be adopted. Can't make your numbers? Cut payroll. Companies pay crazy amounts to new CEOs whose first action is to start carving branches without a second thought[12]. Stock markets usually applaud the slaughter. Certainly, some companies are oversized and need to readjust, but numerous studies show

[12] The world record is that of Carly Fiorentina, who after dismissing 25,700 Hewlett Packard's employees in 2001 saw her pay increased 231% from $1.2 million to $4.1. Though she is not there anymore, the culture of layoffs is still very present in the company. Between 2002 and 2015, the current CEO Meg Whitman fired more than 120,000 people and in 2017 a further 5,000. Only 45,000 people have survived so far.

that after downsizing, the situation worsens. Ridderstrale and Nordstrom (2000) believe that these measures are often as crazy as cutting off your leg to slim down. You certainly lose weight, yet not only the root problem remains, but it creates new ones. The problem is that these kinds of decisions are usually made only from the perspective of the lower right quadrant. It is a "technical" analysis based on finance and productivity. Employees are reduced to mere numbers, and the process is objective and impersonal, disregarding personal feelings or particular situations.

A full-spectrum analysis should take into account all of the quadrants. Firstly, the collective effects should consider the left-hand quadrant: What are the consequences on the morale of the workers left in the company? How does it affect the company's culture and collective identity? What happens to customer loyalty? In addition to that, the individual should be included in the analysis. In the upper-left quadrant, the issue of emotional distress is of paramount importance. The person laid off is the victim, but the remaining employees are also affected (the motivation of those who work fearfully is likely to deteriorate). Finally, the upper-right quadrant would study the behavioural and health effects of every individual affected (stress, depression, etc.).

There are more and more organisations recognising the power of the AQAL matrix as a practical tool to make full-spectrum decisions. For instance, Decurion, an American corporation with a portfolio centred in movie theatres and real estate, makes use of the quadrants to develop more effective leaders and managers and to seek robust solutions to common problems. Here is an example extracted from the corporation's interesting blog (Forman 2014): Many theatres found that popcorn poppers were breaking down frequently; to address this issue, managers and talent members (i.e., employees in Decurion's jargon) met to find a solution. First, they asked whether some individual skills or competencies could be enhanced (UR). Then they evaluated whether there were systems, technologies, or processes that could be implemented to forestall the breakdowns, such as periodic cleaning or checking (LR). Next, they examined whether there were cultural barriers to keeping the poppers operating or collective assumptions about who was responsible or about how to handle stressful situations (LL). Finally, they considered whether they, as individuals, needed to improve their ability to remain calm in the face of anxiety (UL).

1.4. Spiral Dynamics or why I see people in colours

Someone is hearing me without knowing it,
But those I sing of, those who know, go on being born and will overflow the world.
Pablo Neruda. *The People.*

The kind of world I would like to live in requires major changes. As Einstein notoriously said, *"We can't solve our problems with the same thinking that created them"*. As the objective world (in the right quadrants) is becoming more and more complex, we need a corresponding increase in individual and collective consciousness (in the left quadrants) for a balanced evolution[13]. In other words, we need a significant number of people acting out of a higher level of consciousness, as opposed to those that have brought us to the state we are in now if we want to have a good chance of getting out of the mess we have created.

At the end of the opening scene of Stanley Kubrick's masterpiece *2001: A Space Odyssey*, an Australopithecus throws a bone into the air, after using it as a weapon. The shot of the flying bone crossfades into a spaceship. This transition is the longest ellipsis in film history and pays tribute to 4 million years of human evolution. Both the bone turned into a weapon and the futuristic spacecraft, are expressions of our human ingenuity at different stages of our journey as a species.

Despite all our mistakes and the fact that we are not taking our stewardship responsibilities seriously enough, our history shows a progression towards higher levels of consciousness. Consider the many practices that we found acceptable in the past which are unthinkable today: human sacrifice, slavery, racial segregation, and bell bottoms are just a few examples that come to my mind. As Wilber argues, nowadays with a nuclear bomb, we can cause much more harm than when bows and arrows were cutting-edge technology, and if Genghis Khan had had nukes, cockroaches would have replaced us as the dominant species of the planet.

As we saw in the last chapter, several models analyse the structures of human development as applied to individuals and entire societies[14]. *Spiral Dynamics* (SD) is among the most popular ones, especially in the integral

---

[13] This is Teilhard de Chardin's law of complexity and consciousness.
[14] In *Integral Psychology* (2000b), Wilber charted over 100 developmental models, East and West, ancient, modern and postmodern.

community. It is simple and easy to learn, and, at the same time, quite precise and descriptive. It was originally developed by Don Beck and Chris Cowan (1996) based on the *Emergent-Cyclical Theory* of Dr Clare Graves, who in turn, was also inspired by the *Hierarchy of Needs* of his contemporary Abraham Maslow.

Spiral Dynamics organises the complexity of all human evolution into a series of stages encoded in an ascending spiral, representing levels of biopsychosocial complexity, with each new one being a developmental feat. This process, labelled by Clare Graves as *"the human existential helix"* (Graves 2005:2), is the result of an adaptive response to life circumstances and challenges, what Spiral Dynamics calls *"life conditions"*. In other words, individuals and human societies pass through recognisable paradigm shifts, or stages of growth in consciousness, as the way to keep up with an increasingly complex world. The different stages categorise broad spectrums of people, according to generalised stereotypes, by how they see the world and what they value. Ultimately, they come to govern how we think and feel, as Wahl has emphasised (2016:131):

> *"How we see the world influences the real or perceived needs that inform our intentions. If I see a place dominated by fierce competition for limited resources, I will fight others to get my own needs met. I will live a different life, interpret experiences in a different way and design different products, services, and systems than if I see the world as a place of abundance to be shared in solidarity and collaboration within the human family and with deep care for the ecosystems functions that are the basis for this abundance."*

In Spiral Dynamics, the levels or stages are also called "memes," a concept first defined by biologist Richard Dawkins. Memes (or, more precisely, *vmemes*[15]) represent differing value systems which are articulated at various developmental stages of individual and human histories. Each

[15] Dawkins' memes are self-replicating ideas that are like our cultural DNA. Much like a gene is a unit of biological selection, a meme is a unit of cultural selection. Ideas originate, mutate, and are passed on through culture, much as genes do through genetic inheritance. According to this notion, skinny jeans, emojis, and prog rock are examples of memes. However, for Spiral Dynamics, they are little memes. Beneath these surface values, there are big memes or, as Beck and Cowan named them, "value-memes" or "vmemes" which form the levels of the spiral and are conceptual frameworks, paradigms, worldviews, deep-level decision systems, or mindsets from which the little memes emerge.

one generates a different cognitive style, morality, self-identity, and motivation for the individual, with distinctive rules and laws, institutions, productive forces, religions, economic systems, and technology for society.

There are two versions of Spiral Dynamics, the original one (SD) developed by Beck and Cowan (1996), and *Spiral Dynamics Integral* (SDi), which resulted from the collaboration and subsequent split between Beck and Wilber.

It is important to distinguish between them because their differences are deeper than they seem[16]. On the surface, they only differ in the colour

[16] Ken explained to me that the reason for the discrepancy was that he contended that SD only covers one line of development -a line that Graves called "value systems" (and "value" is what the "v" in *vmeme* stands for), while Don Beck believes that it covers everything. Ken (2006) decided to change the colour system in order to emphasize that Integral was presenting overall altitude or level of development (which had many different lines of development, one of which was SD). I agree with Ken. For my academic research, I wouldn't use a supposedly good-for-all-lines model, because I need to get the highest possible statistic validity. An SD test will obtain a high predictive validity in the value line, but it will not get such a high score when it comes to predicting moral development. In that particular area, Kohlberg's model will get a much better concurrent validity.

The classic SD model draws from basic colour psychology: beige is the tone of the savannah grasslands where early hominids lived; purple the colour of royalty; red is associated with passion and bloody excitement; blue comes from heaven, blue-bloods, and "true blue" loyalty; orange is inspired by industrial-age furnaces at work; green because of nature; yellow relates to solar energy and post-industrial new technologies; and turquoise is the colour of Earth from outer space. The alternation of warm and cold colours form a spiralling sequence. Warm colours (beige, red, orange, yellow) represent the self-expressive systems or I-stages (the odd numbers in the series), while the self-sacrificing, collective-oriented systems or We-stages form a family of cool hues (purple, blue, green, turquoise).

Instead, Wilber retained only half of the original colours (i.e., red, orange, green and turquoise) and changed the other half. Beige was replaced by infrared, purple by magenta, blue by amber, and yellow by teal. This new spectrum of colours (running from infrared to magenta to red to amber to orange to green to teal to turquoise) is meant to match a real rainbow, to reflect the unified nature of the Kosmos, where the light of the One diffracts in the many. Additionally, following the yogic and tantric chakra traditions, each colour corresponds to a subtle energy or frequency of the body. The sequence goes from the warm, reddish hues (which are low frequencies of "violent" colours associated with anger or code they use to describe the different stages and the number of levels in which they are grouped[17]. Here I will use Wilber's model.

1.4.1. First-tier levels

The first tier encompasses 200,000 years of human history and includes six different levels of evolution. Graves used to call them the subsistence levels because they are all concerned with ending feelings of shortcoming.

Infrared: Archaic[18]

This category includes all the structures of consciousness that emerged as humans began to evolve from the great apes. Today they are limited to some hunter-gatherer tribes like the bushmen of the Kalahari Desert, and they represent roughly 0.005% of the world population (about a quarter-million people). In individuals, we can find it in infants until 18 months old, mentally disabled, severe senile elderly, and *enfants sauvages*.

It is an automatic, autistic, instinctual, existential state centred on survival. It operates at the base of Maslow's pyramid, having as a priority the satisfaction of physiological needs, namely food, shelter, water, sex, and

---

hatred) to the cooler, bluish tones, representing more advanced/evolved levels, and culminating into ultraviolet and white at the highest end of the transpersonal levels.

Unfortunately, we ended up with two different colour-dialects, which is confusing, to say the least. The reasons I have chosen Wilber's SDI as a frame of reference have been explained above. His model (as could not be otherwise) is integral, it honours all the different developmental lines, and lets you resort to the best models of each line (including SD in the values line), as you will see I do, for example, relying on Kohlberg's when talking about moral development (cf. 6.3).

[17] Contrary to the original SD-model, Wilber's SDi recognizes Third-Tier or "super-integral" stages (as well as other authors such as Aurobindo, Cook-Greuter or O'Fallon). They demarcate the transition from personal to transpersonal, where one's identity shifts to higher, supraindividual, transpersonal, or spiritual levels. Third-Tier colours are indigo, violet, ultraviolet, and white. Research suggests that only about 5 per cent of individuals are at 2nd-tier at this time, while those at the upper level of the 2nd-tier –turquoise- are not much more than 0.5 per cent (i.e., one in every two hundred people), and those at 3rd-tier are estimated to be just a tenth of 1 per cent. This book will stop at the Second Tier, but if you want to know more about the Third Tier, you can always check on Wilber (2017).

[18] I prefer to accompany each colour with an adjective, to describe the essence of the level. Those terms are either taken from the developmental models of other authors, such as Gebser, or my own.

warmth. Individuals operating from this altitude are characterised by primary narcissism. As the ego is not fully formed, they have little awareness of self as a distinct being, as Laloux notes (2014: 16):

> *"(...) people don't perceive themselves as entirely distinct from others or from the environment (which causes some to romanticise about this period, seeing it as pre-dualism bliss, ignoring the extremely high rate of violence and murder at this stage)."*

Like other animals, they live "off the land", foraging, and organised in survival clans of a few dozen people:

> *"This model requires no division of labor to speak of (other than women taking responsibility for the bearing and rearing of children), and so there is nothing like an organisational model at that stage yet. In fact, there is no hierarchy within the band—there is no elder, no chief that provides leadership."* (Laloux, 2014: 16)

Beck and Cowan (1996: 199) remind us that someone operating from this level is not necessarily a deficient human being; only one going through extremely harsh living conditions. We begin our development at Infrared; some of us will go back to it at the end of our existence or in extreme situations, to take advantage of our survival instincts.

Magenta: Tribal

As soon as the problem of physiological existence is solved, we move to the second milestone of human development. In individuals, it is characteristic of children between 1 and 3 years old. As a culture, it appeared around 40,000 years ago, when there was a shift from small family bands that huddled together in caves for safety and warmth to tribes of up to a few hundred people. We can still find it today, in ethnic tribes in Africa, America, and Australia.

As body and mind are still relatively undifferentiated, and the self sees itself as the centre of the universe, people at this level believe that mental intentions can magically alter the physical world, and they use magical thinking to explain things: clouds move to follow me; bad weather is the punishment for my evil deeds; the Tooth Fairy left a coin under my pillow.

The basic drive of this value meme is safety and security. The world is seen as a dangerous place, imbued with mysterious powers and inhabited by spirits, which must be appeased. As they are full of superstitions, they try to manage life by incantations and rituals to invoke a continuance of what is desirable or to control the unexpected.

The interest of the group always comes first. For that reason, they show strong allegiance to tradition, custom, and tribal leaders. People live mostly in the present, with some blending in of the past, but little projection toward the future.

Red: Egocentric

> *"Hey, you wanna hear my philosophy of life? Do it to him before he does it to you.* Terry Malloy in "*On the Waterfront*" (Elia Kazan, 1954).

> *"Punishment. Can't do anything without that. Punishment is how we built everything we have."* Negan in "*The Walking Dead*" S07E16.

About 10,000 years ago, during the Neolithic, humankind leapt from a tribal world subsisting on horticulture to the agricultural revolution. As Habermas explains, there was a transition from tribes to societies organised through the State, which required an evolution of membership from common descent to territorial belonging, and the legitimation of the figure of a ruler not genetically related. Empires like Egypt, Greece, Rome, Persia, the Mongols, the Aztecs, and the Incas emerged in this stage of human history as forerunners of our globalised world. Wilber (1995: 234) points out that this was accomplished, in part, by the development of religious narratives that unified different tribes, not by blood or kinship (for that was impossible since each tribe had a distinct lineage), but rather by a common mythological origin (the twelve Tribes of Israel, united under a common God, are a perfect example).

The world through a Red lens is a jungle filled with predators where only the strongest and most cunning survive and thrive. Therefore, people operating from this mental mode aspire to be strong, courageous risk-takers, who are capable of defending themselves and getting what they want, when they want it. Red consciousness is egocentric, impulsive, amoral, uninhibited, our inner 3-year old, driven towards instant gratification without guilt or remorse but with a strong element of shame. Selfishness and hostility are self-preservation mechanisms to get ahead in a world they perceive as violent and unfair.

People with such a mindset make their own rules or die trying. They are driven by power, respect, and dominance as the way to conquer freedom and gratify their desires. People are divided into two types: the strong and the weak. The big fish eats the small fish. Those who have power, get what they want, and those who don't, have to submit.

A Red centre of gravity is frequent in tough environments (e.g., slums, reform schools, or prisons), but it can be found anywhere. People coming from as comfortable backgrounds as Donald Trump or Jordan Belfort (the famous *Wolf of Wall Street* as depicted by Martin Scorsese in his brilliant adaptation of Belfort's autobiographical novel) show evident Red traits in some of their lines of behaviour.

Don't make the mistake of labelling Red as negative. When it emerged, it was the best response humankind could offer to the existing conditions, and it still is vital for harsh environments. Plus, Red consciousness shows highly desirable features such as independence, spontaneity, creativity, struggle, will, and nonconformity. It is from here that the impulse to question everything, especially one's place in the world, is born. It is from here that personal power and self-assertion arise. The Promethean underlying aspect of heroism in Red makes people at this level do whatever is needed to survive.

Amber: Traditional

> *"Tradition: one of those words conservative people use as a shortcut to thinking."* Warren Ellis. *Transmetropolitan.*

The Red mindset is problematic. The "might makes right" thesis generates widespread opposition. The math is easy: in a Red world, there are a few with power and many powerless. Sooner or later, the individual will have to control his or her egocentric behaviour or have it regulated by others, and society will have to create rules to get unbridled lusts and impulsive desires under control. Though today we consider amber as a traditional or premodern worldview, it was born as a radical critique of the negative aspects of Red consciousness: the arbitrary use and abuse of power.

Amber societies emerged across the Eurasian continent, around 10,000 BCE and flowered between 2,000 BCE to 1,500 BCE, in a period known as "the Axial Age," right when many of the classical religions, wisdom traditions, and philosophical schools were founded. Religion enforced codes of conduct based on eternal, absolute principles that, if followed, produced stability and gave rewards in this world or the next. Institutions control the rules, and nobody can have any ultimate authority beyond serving the universal truth.

The big psychological shift from Red to Amber takes place at approximately seven years old. At that point, we learn how to bind our impulses within, discover there are rules, and develop a desire to conform to conventional norms and behaviours. We also understand that deferred gratification may benefit us and that saving up is a good idea, so we can wait longer or work harder for better outcomes. It is the taming of the egocentric rebel.

From the Amber rung, the world is seen as orderly, predictable, stable, and unchanging. People at this level accept their assigned role and identity in the world. It is one's duty to submit to the order of things, follow the one true way of being, and strive for perfection. Needless to say, this traditional worldview brings about a very rigid society:

> *"Amber societies tend to be highly stratified, with social classes or caste systems, and rigid gender differences as defining features. A lottery at birth defines what caste you are born into."* (Laloux, 2014: 20)

People who gravitate towards Amber identify with being responsible, purposeful, and self-sacrificing. They seek a reassuring sense of stability, security, and belonging by conforming to the long-standing traditions of the culture in which they were socialised. As the belonging needs come to the foreground, an ethnocentric type of ethics emerges. It is a significant expansion of our circle of solidarity, as Freinacht (2019: 64) notes: Suddenly, people not only care about their acquaintances but about people they don't even know yet who share the same nationality or religion. "Love to your kind" is their motto; however, if you are not one of them, you are in trouble. The opposite of love is fear, not hate. Fear of those who are different from you.

In Amber, thinking is categorical, absolutistic, rigid, and dogmatic. It is universal by imposition. There is one truth, and only one right way to think and behave. All others are wrong. They see themselves as the paragon of virtue. They know the rules of proper living, follow them, and require all others to do so. If they don't, they deserve to be punished. Amber loves those who follow the rules but is hostile and belligerent to those who don't.

Orange: Competitive

> *"Work until your bank account looks like a phone number."* (*The Wolf of Wall Street*. Martin Scorsese. 2013)

The "Modern Worldview" first appeared in the Age of Enlightenment (late

18th century), only to bloom fully during the Industrial Revolution. Modern values eventually replaced traditional Amber cultures, and today, Orange is still the average effective value meme of the Western world.

People at Amber are slaves to the authoritative claims of others. From Amber to Orange, the individual experiences a transformation from an external locus of control to an internal locus of control. The Orange mindset is capable of questioning authority, group norms, and the status quo. Science was the mechanism that Orange cognition invented to make that possible. It was the end of a long history of darkness, ignorance, and prejudice. You couldn't possibly have any real science with a traditional absolutistic mode of thinking. Science uncovered the unchangeable, mechanical rules of the Universe, and became the true universal, creating a new moral order where right is not what satisfies one's needs (as in Red) or what the authority says is right (as in the Amber stage), but what the evidence shows is correct. It is a kind of truth not imposed by religious dogma or political ideology. Reason rose above the narrow interests of an egocentric or ethnocentric stance, discovering and affirming what was good and fair for all beings, and not merely for me, my tribe, or my nation. If Red was egocentric and Amber ethnocentric, Orange became worldcentric, a quantum leap for humanity that brought about democracy, human rights, and equality.

Orange is highly rational, competitive, ambitious, autonomous, and elitist. People with this mindset are driven by success, achievement, and status. The world, through this lens, is a playing field full of possibilities to explore and opportunities to achieve. The way to get ahead is to compete, so people are hungry for tools and techniques that will make them more competitive. If you learn and master the rules, you can win the game[19]: go to the best school, get the best marks, choose the right job, and make it to the top. In the words of Laloux (2014: 24):

> *"Effectiveness replaces morals as a yardstick for decision-making: the better I understand the way the world operates, the more I can achieve;*

---

[19] Although both Red and Orange mindsets are driven to win and value the will to power, the power they value is different. In the Red system of thinking, it is the power of self that is important whereas in Orange, one's importance lies in the power of ideas. Where one wields muscle, the other wields intellect. The Orange drive is fuelled by excellence, competitiveness, and status, while Red is motivated by power, respect, and glory. You can't conquer the Orange world through raw, naked force, but by learning its secrets.

the best decision is the one that begets the highest outcome. The goal in life is to get ahead, to succeed in socially acceptable ways, to best play out the cards we are dealt."

The Orange system holds a very materialistic view, where only what can be seen and touched is real, and more is generally better. It is a flat and simplistic epistemology, more concerned with the "how" than the "why." "What does it mean?" is replaced with "what does it do?" Value is reduced to money in a process where quantitative distinctions substitute qualitative ones. Because of the difficulty in believing something that can't empirically be proven or observed, AQAL's 4-quadrants are reduced only to exteriors, and the left-hand path (where emotions, values, ethics, and spirituality, among others, find their place) is marginalised as a result of this monological gaze.

Individual results and success are measured by material acquisition and "upward mobility." Orange individuals value excellence, advancement, prosperity, achievement, and status. They are driven to achieving and getting, having and possessing, to prove they are better than you. When Donald Trump valued his fortune at $9bn as he officially entered the race for the White House, he was not doing that to brag. He was proving a point: *"I'm the most successful person ever to run for the presidency, by far,"* he said.

As Laloux notices (2014: 25), the emphasis on achieving and getting tends to project people with an Orange mindset consistently into the future:

"We live our lives on the assumption that achieving the next goal (getting the next promotion, finding a life partner, moving to a new house, or buying a new car) will make us happy. In Orange, we effectively live in the future, consumed by mental chatter about the things we need to do so as to reach the goals we have set for ourselves. We hardly ever make it back to the present moment, where we can appreciate the gifts and freedom the shift to Orange has brought us."

Autonomy, equal opportunity, and meritocracy are other fundamental values of this mindset. One must evidence independence and the ability to think and act autonomously. Those who make it have brought themselves to this position by their own efforts, so they deserve it by proven superiority. The emphasis is on action and results: It is better to act and fail than not having tried.

As I said, the Orange value meme brought about a worldcentric stance interested in what would be fair for all peoples and not merely one's own. That capacity has solved, in just two centuries, the material needs for more people than any other previous way of life and has provided the highest increase in welfare in the history of humanity. But these dazzling lights cast an ominous shadow: the Anthropocene dawned Orange. Orange modernity conceives the planet as a set of resources waiting to be converted into capital. It is a worldview that has led to reckless exploitation of the world's ecosystems, impacting the planet in a much deeper way than the previous stages, to such an extreme that we are flirting with extinction. Socially speaking, the promises of equality for everyone regardless of race, creed, nationality, or gender, only worked for a chosen few, while the rest always end up getting the short end of the stick. Humanity has globalised the economy, but it has failed to humanise globalisation.

The Orange shadow also hovers over the individual, as Laloux points out (2014:29):

> *"Another shadow appears when success is measured solely in terms of money and recognition. When growth and the bottom line are all that count, when the only successful life is the one that reaches the top, we are bound to experience a sense of emptiness in our lives (...)*
>
> *The midlife crisis is an emblematic disease of life in Orange Organizations: for 20 years, we played the game of success and ran the rat race. And now we realize we won't make it to the top, or that the top isn't all it is made up to be. In principle, work in Orange Organizations can be a vehicle for self-expression and fulfilment. But when year after year things boil down to targets and numbers, milestones and deadlines, and yet another change program and cross-functional initiative, some people can't help but wonder about the meaning of it all and yearn for something more."*

Green: Pluralistic-relativistic

> *"Success without fulfillment is the ultimate failure."* Tony Robbins

The next leap comes when the person stops thinking in terms of his material gratification and starts thinking in terms of others. Satisfying self alone, in a materialistic way, does not bring the level of happiness expected beforehand because it neglects the interior dimensions.

The Green meme is only about one century old. It first appeared in the late 19th century in industrialised countries as movements such as Romanticism reacted against Modernity. It only became mainstream after 1968, with the advent of the postmodern movement. The purpose of Postmodernism and the Green worldview was to deconstruct the rigid hierarchies, formalisms, and oppressive schemes created by Amber and Orange (Wilber 2000a: xi). Scholars refer to this stage as postconventional and postconformist, for its rejection of the status quo.

The postmodern movement[20] differs from modernity in its attempt to not marginalise the voices and points of view that modernity obviates and to

[20] Ken Wilber (2000a: 163) summarizes the three central tenets of postmodernism:

- Constructivism: Constructivism is a rebellion against the myth of the given. It was Kant who first stated that if we want to understand reality, we don't have to look outside, but within ourselves, as we never perceive "things in themselves" but "things as we perceive them." Reality is not a given, but a construction and interpretation of our brain. It is inescapably virtual. Therefore, for postmodernists, science is nothing more than another form of "conversation" about our beliefs, and the supposedly "hard facts" are only prior agreements of a particular community.
- Contextualism: A term used in quantum physics to refer to the ambiguous and relational nature of quantum entities. Quantum physics argues against a world formed by solid and separate entities. At the most fundamental level of reality, physical systems consist of interactive patterns of dynamic energy. A quantum object must be seen in the context of its relationships to be understood, measured, or used. Each one (e.g., a photon) functions as a particle or wave depending on the possibilities and identities of the other elements it interferes with. Heisenberg's *Principle of Uncertainty* postulates that quantum reality has infinite possibilities, and we can only see some of its aspects. Therefore, reality is not immutable. It shows a different face according to how we look at it. If we believe that the photons behave like particles, we will find particles, if we think that they do as waves, that's what we will see. Nothing can be abstracted or contemplated in itself. Reality is contextual, and contexts have no limits.
- Perspectivism: Postmodernists claim there are no absolute truths. Therefore, no perspective can be privileged. The previous levels of development argued that their way of seeing things was the only right one. That makes many people believe they have the absolute truth. A boss says something is wrong, not that he does not like this way of doing things, a customer complains a product is too expensive, instead of saying that he is not willing to pay that price, the CEO announces downsizing as the only option, instead of saying that he doesn't know how to turn the company around without reducing labour costs. Postmodernism denies the Taylorist principle of "one best way." At best, one can speak of "subjective truth" because different agents hold different values and beliefs.

be inclusive, pluralistic, and multicultural (Wilber 2000a: 159). Movements like feminism, environmentalism, animal rights, slow food, or LGBTQ+, are the offsprings of a Green mentality.

People with this mindset are driven by human connection and changing things for the better. They value tolerance, cultural sensitivity, diversity, sustainability, and interdependence. They strive for fulfilment as defined by personal growth, increased awareness, harmonious relationships, and making a difference.

The pluralistic-relativistic view has profound social concerns, powerful drives of social justice, and is nonjudgmental, egalitarian, antihierarchical, postmaterialistic, antipatriarchal, profeminist, and is socially and environmentally engaged.

This perspective abhors the competitive Orange mindset. 'Getting along with' is preferred to 'getting ahead of'. Relationships are valued above outcomes, and communal values like caring, sharing, and fairness come top on the Green agenda (Laloux 2014:31).

The Green mindset builds communities that value tolerance, interdependence, creativity, diversity, activism, and progressivity. They prefer non-traditional, "humanised" workplaces with a non-hierarchical, egalitarian approach, where ongoing growth and development along with "work-life balance" are encouraged, and contribution to social, political, and environmental causes is central.

Relativism is one of the characteristics of postmodernism most openly criticised by Wilber and other thinkers. From a correct observation ("no perspective has the whole truth"), they jump to a completely false conclusion ("anything goes"). Another apparent contradiction of Green relativism is when others abuse their tolerance and present bigoted ideas. It is a performative contradiction since the statement "there is no absolute truth" is an absolutist statement in itself.

1.4.2. Second-tier: The integral levels

Evolution is accelerating at breakneck speed. There has never been a time in human history where so many people operated from so many different levels of consciousness at the same time.

If I may borrow Ernst Bloch's concept of "simultaneous non-simultaneity", the coexistence of so many different stages in time and space gives way to a broad, flexible, and thoroughly dynamic "multiverse" (yet another term from Bloch) in which the voices of history join in a perpetual, and often intricate, counterpoint that results in an ongoing cultural war between the three most common worldviews today: Traditional Amber, Modern Orange, and Postmodern Green. Paradoxically, the origin of this confrontation is something they have in common: they only value their own perspectives. Their worldview is the right one, and all the other levels are wrong. Consequently, they are at war against the rest of the value memes, especially the previous and the next. Amber despises Red's impulsiveness and Orange's egoism. Orange hates Amber's blind respect for tradition and thinks of Green as naïve and weak. Green rejects Orange's materialism, Amber's authoritarianism, and reacts strongly to anything post-Green.

First-tier consciousness has led to confrontation, hatred, distrust, and injustice in the world. Me against you, my department against the others, my company against its competitors, my country against the world. "*With any of those levels in place –which at this particular time in history covers 95%*[21] *of the population- humanity is destined to disagreement, conflict, terrorism, and warfare.*" (Wilber, 2017:37).

Clare Graves defined the emergence of the second tier as a *"momentous leap,"* where *"a chasm of unbelievable depth of meaning is crossed."* In essence, with second-tier consciousness, one can think both vertically and horizontally. Second-tier awareness includes the overall spiral of existence in its thinking, and not merely one level. The second tier includes, for the first time, all previous stages appreciating the role that all of the other memes play and finding some value and partial truth at each of them.

Up to 5% of the worldwide population has reached second-tier levels, and some experts see this increasing to 10% within the decade. The 10% is a significant tipping point[22] for Wilber (id: 38-39) that will result in the emergence of the Integral Age, an evolutionary revolution greater than any

[21] We find about 10% of the population at Red, 40% at Amber, 45% at Orange and 20% at Green (Wilber 2017: 46)

[22] Evidently, people copy each other and so, the more members of a social group exhibit some behaviour, the more the remaining members will feel pressured into adopting it, and before you know it, the whole group is doing the same. Elites (of the worlds of theory and practice) play, in particular, an important catalytic role.

previous one:

> *"What researchers have found is that during human history whenever the leading edge of evolution and development becomes around 10% of the population, major profound and extensive changes occur throughout the overall population (...)*
>
> *In other words, the human race, for the first time ever in its history, is heading toward at least the possibility of a world beyond major and deep-seated conflict, and toward one marked more and more by mutual tolerance, embrace, peace, inclusion, and compassion."*

He concludes:

> *"This is not just a stage transformation, as in the transformation from archaic foraging to magic horticulture to mythic traditional agrarian to rational modern industrial to pluralistic postmodern informational, but also a major tier transformation: from the first-tier of stages built by deficiency needs, scarcity motivations, absolutistic thinking, non-inclusive and exclusionary practices, and hence human conflict and suffering, to a second tier of stages built by inclusiveness, embrace, abundance motivation, being values and caring kindness in its actions, tender mercies in its thoughts, exquisite patterns that connect in its ideas, and wholes upon wholes upon wholes in its awareness." (Id: 651)*

Teal: Holistic

The Teal level represents the cutting edge of evolution. The levels above are not significant enough in terms of numbers and degree of influence. So, watch out, these people are going to take over the world[23].

[23] Teal consciousness is more easily found within what Freinacht (2017b) calls the triple-H population: hipsters, hackers, and hippies. By hackers, he means people at the avant-garde of the digital and technological revolution. By hipsters, people in the leading edge of culture, including artists, designers, thinkers, social entrepreneurs, writers, and bloggers that are responsible for transmitting new values and ideas by creating music, fashion, movies, books, and games. By hippies, those who produce new lifestyles, habits, and practices that make life in post-industrial society happier, healthier and, perhaps, more enchanted. He concludes: *"The triple-H folks are usually more artsy, creative, well connected, socially intelligent, emotionally developed, idealistic, digitalized, diversified and educated – and thus more likely to become rising stars of the new society."*

If the Amber meme shaped traditional societies, the Orange meme the modern society, and the Green one is behind the postmodern, Teal consciousness is bringing about the metamodern society (Freinacht 2017a). And that is happening right now. Our globalised and digitised society has metamodern DNA in its blood. Van der Akker and Vermeulen (2017: 11) situate the emergence of metamodernism[24] in the 2000s. As a cultural stage, Teal is less than twenty years old.

The Teal altitude signals the beginning of an integral worldview that sees wholes everywhere and strives to bring the world together. Pluralistic relativism is transcended and included in universal integralism. As Wilber puts it (2000: xi), where the Green meme freed many different voices previously marginalised, the Teal one begins to bring them together into a harmonised chorus. Not only it is capable of seeing all points of view (as Green does) and honouring them, but it can also evaluate them critically, noticing universal common patterns, to provide unifying solutions. If the Green level tries to equalise everything and everyone, Teal tries to "aqualise" it all.

The Teal value meme is deeply aware there is an evolution in consciousness. It is the first one that can include all perspectives, giving each one its due credit, as a relevant part of reality. Teal begins to see the process of development itself, acknowledging that each one of the previous stages reveals a partial truth and has a relevant role to play. Thus, it pulls them together to construct a synthesis or *summum bonum* of all the earlier stages (transcending and including them).

Teal embraces the paradoxical and complex nature of reality. The ability of people that own Teal to intellectually see, and intuitively sense, the intimate interconnectedness of all things allows them to grasp big pictures and handle paradoxes. For this reason, they are better equipped to solve complex problems without necessarily being more intelligent. Their integral mindset makes them strive for wholeness in their lives:

---

[24] Metamodernism is a twin concept to Teal, proposed by Hanzi Freinacht (2017c) as an elaboration and extension of the original one coined by cultural theorists Vermeulen and van den Akker (2010). As a philosophy and worldview, it oscillates somewhere in the middle between the pre-postmodern (and often the modern) and the postmodern, but in a higher ground. Not in vain, the prefix "meta," as used by Vermeulen and van den Akker (2010), refers to the metaxy of Plato, i.e., the "in-between" or "middle ground," where virtue is.

> *"With this stage comes a deep yearning for wholeness — bringing together the ego and the deeper parts of the self; integrating mind, body, and soul; cultivating both the feminine and masculine parts within; being whole in relation to others; and repairing our broken relationship with life and nature. Often the shift to Teal comes with an opening to a transcendent spiritual realm and a profound sense that at some level, we are all connected and part of one big whole. After many successive steps of disidentification, as we learn to be fully independent and true to ourselves, it dawns on us that, paradoxically, we are profoundly part of everything." (Laloux 2014: 44)*

People gravitating towards Teal hate polarities, and rather than looking for differences, they try to find the similarities between contesting opinions. They are self-critical and see the flaws in every position, even the one they defend. Bearing this in mind, it is difficult to see them band with any given one. More characteristics: They are driven by transcendence, contribution, and service, have a "kosmocentric"[25] consciousness, and hold progressive and post-materialistic values.

If ego is extremely present at Red and Orange, the essential quality of an individual at the Teal stage of development is, in Pór's words (2015), *"sensing, thinking, speaking, and acting beyond "small self", with increasing consistency."* That is incredibly liberating:

> *"By looking at our ego from a distance, we can suddenly see how its fears, ambitions, and desires often run our life. We can learn to minimize our need to control, to look good, to fit in. We are no longer fused with our ego, and we don't let its fears reflexively control our lives. In the process, we make room to listen to the wisdom of other, deeper parts of ourselves.*
>
> *What replaces fear? A capacity to trust the abundance of life. All wisdom traditions posit the profound truth that there are two fundamental ways to live life: from fear and scarcity or from trust and abundance. In Evolutionary-Teal, we cross the chasm and learn to decrease our need to control people and events. We come to believe that even if something unexpected happens or if we make mistakes, things will turn out all right,*

---

[25] "Kosmos" is an old Pythagorean term that Wilber uses to describe the entire universe in all its dimensions: physical, emotional, mental, and spiritual. It is more than the Cosmos or physiosphere, that encompasses just the physical universe, to include also the biosphere, or life dimension, and the noosphere, or the dimension of the mind. To be kosmocentric is to identify with the entirety of reality itself – not just physical reality but also the reality of mind and consciousness.

> *and when they don't, life will have given us an opportunity to learn and grow."* (Laloux 2014: 43).

This disidentification with the ego makes Teal the first genuinely autonomous level:

> *"When we are fused with our ego, we are driven to make decisions informed by external factors — what others will think or what outcomes can be achieved. In the Impulsive-Red perspective, a good decision is the one that gets me what I want. In Conformist-Amber, we hold decisions up to the light of conformity to social norms. Decisions beyond what one's family, religion, or social class considers legitimate cause guilt and shame. In Achievement-Orange, effectiveness and success are the yardsticks by which decisions are made. In Pluralistic-Green, matters are judged by the criteria of belonging and harmony. The Teal mindset works by another social and economic logic than any of the old groups in industrial society. People switch to intrinsic motivation and self-realization, rather than extrinsic motivation, such as monetary rewards, consumption, and security. Doing what feels right in relation to inner values and assumptions.*
>
> *We are now concerned with the question of inner rightness: Does this decision seem right? Am I being true to myself? Is this in line with who I sense I'm called to become? Am I being of service to the world?*
>
> *(...) In contrast with previous stages, the order is reversed: we don't pursue recognition, success, wealth, and belonging to live a good life. We pursue a life well-lived, and the consequence might just be recognition, success, wealth, and love." (Id. 2014: 43)*

Turquoise: Wholistic

Note I deliberately wrote "wholistic" rather than "holistic." The distinction between holistic and wholistic is at the roots of the difference between Teal and Turquoise. I borrow it from Yan Eperon, creator of holycracy, the only management theory I know with a Turquoise perspective. As you all know, a holistic approach takes into account the whole of something or someone and not just a part. It emphasises the importance of the whole and the interdependence of its parts. On the other hand, Yan defines "wholistic" as "*A state of consciousness where we realize that we are the whole manifested as inter-dependent individuations to enjoy and serve ourselves as the whole.*"

People centred at Turquoise are fully present, self-reliant, autonomous individuals, deeply connected to their higher selves, as well as to others and the whole web of life. They follow a transcendental purpose, and always go for nothing less than what reflects their most authentic desires, honouring their deepest calling at any moment.

At this level, everything is seen in its right place. Turquoise trusts the living process and its self-organising power. Life is meant to work out; it does not need to be improved. It needs to be tuned in to and never fought. Systems are consciously woven together to make a better whole. Different tiers of interaction are detected at once, with the Turquoise view being a flow-state that would be seen as mystical from further down the spiral.

Turquoise is the first level to begin to grasp Spirit as a living force in the world (manifested through any or all of the Three Faces of God identified by Wilber (2006): "I"—the "No self" or "witness" of Buddhism; "we/thou"—the "Great Other" of Christianity, Judaism, Hinduism, Islam, etc.; or "it"—the "Web of Life" seen in Taoism, Pantheism, etc.).

Freinacht (2017c: 32) points out that Turquoise has not appeared yet at a societal level. The amount of people at this stage (one in a hundred thousand, according to his estimates) is still too small to organise themselves socially. The fact that there is still no Turquoise critique of Teal supports his statement.

1.5. Understanding Spiral Dynamics

"Psychosocial man, his institutions, and his life are processes in transit from the earliest order of adult behavioural organization, through a series of way stations, to no knowable destination" (Graves 2005: 416)

1.5.1. Colouring by numbers

"Change is inevitable. Evolution, however, is optional." Tony Robbins.

SDI and any other model of human development are simplifications of reality, just like a geographical map is a simplified representation of a territory. When one first learns SDI, the immediate reaction is to tag oneself and everybody else with a colour. It would be extremely reductionistic to label your friend Peter as Orange. Peter is not Orange; he is just exhibiting the characteristics of that value meme. He is too complex to be reduced to a colour tag.

Stages are not types of people. They are systems operating in people (or even whole societies) in a complex mix. Each of them includes, and transcends, all the previous ones that are still part of us and available to us. We are like Russian dolls, with many layers of psychological and cultural evolution available within us. New life circumstances can make us resort to them. For example, if someone becomes a father, he might start giving more importance to Amber values such as security. By no means can this be considered as a regression to Amber; he is just adapting to his new life circumstances and taking advantage of what he needs from that level. Even the opposite is possible to some extent: if Peter finds himself in an environment where people dominantly operate from Green, he will try to blend in by displaying Green behaviours, even though he has not owned the stage yet. Also, don't forget there are many lines of development—cognitive, moral, intrapersonal, interpersonal, spiritual, and so forth— and we don't grow at the same rate in all of them. For example, Peter has internalised Orange cognition, as he has a PhD degree, but on the spiritual line, he still shows Amber mythical beliefs. At best, we could generalise that, at this particular time, Orange is the stage he is operating from more often. In other words, Orange is his centre of gravity.

The same happens to organisations. An organisation's centre of gravity reflects the average mode of consciousness of its members and around which the organisation orbits as a whole. For example, if the predominant worldview of most of the members is Amber, then the organisation's gravitational pull is likely to be Amber.

Finally, it would be very simplistic to believe that two people operating from the same stage are mostly alike. Despite the apparent similarities, they can see the world very differently from each other. For example, Sheldon and Penny, two of the characters of *The Big Band Theory*, view the world through an Orange lens, but they are almost opposite poles. A white neo-Nazi and an African-American gang member might share the same Red worldview, yet violently disagree (literally) on nearly every issue. The same would happen with two Amber fundamentalists, one Christian, and the other Muslim. As for Green, compare a New-Age eco hippy with a gloomy postmodern intellectual.

1.5.2. King of the hill

- Mr Kralik, it is true we're in the same room, but we're not on the same planet.
- Miss Novak, although I'm the victim of your remark, I can't help but admire the exquisite way you have of expressing yourself. You certainly know how to put a man on his planet.
(The Shop Around the Corner, Ernst Lubitsch)

SDI is a hierarchical model. People who like hierarchies (like those operating from Competitive-Orange) tend to overrate themselves[26] while those with an anti-hierarchical Green outlook usually despise the model for being socially elitist and even fascist. Both share the misconception that later stages are "better" than earlier stages. They both fail to understand that higher is not necessarily better. I prefer a sensible and righteous expression of Amber to a bigoted and dogmatic version of Green. As it turns out, inclusion is much more critical than transcendence. Otherwise stated, it is preferable a healthy development of the value memes acquired than to rush into higher ones. Petrie (2014: 12) refutes the idea of "the higher, the better" with this elegant argument:

"There is nothing inherently "better" about being at a higher level of development, just as an adolescent is not "better" than a toddler. My five-year-old can think in more advanced ways than my three-year-old. That doesn't make him a more valuable human being, just a fraction more developed. However, the fact remains that an adolescent is able to do more because he or she can think in more sophisticated ways than a toddler. Any level of development is okay; the question is whether that level of development is a good fit for the task at hand. In terms of leadership, if you believe that the future will present leaders with an environment that is more complex, volatile, and unpredictable, you might also believe that those organizations that have more leaders at higher levels of development will have an important advantage over those that don't."

It is more accurate to say that a higher level of consciousness owns a greater repertoire of options and more sophisticated ways of dealing with the world than a lower one. Each new stage shows an increasing degree of emotional, intellectual, relational, and moral development. In practice, it

---

[26] After a lecture I gave on SDI, a guy came to tell me he was Turquoise. How little he knew that was the infallible proof he didn't own that stage. Somebody operating from Turquoise would never ever boast about being Turquoise.

means that each higher stage is able to handle more complexity, is more caring, and can take more perspectives. For instance, a person operating from Green can integrate people's conflicting views in a way that a person functioning from Red simply can't.

In general, the more complex the conditions, the higher the developmental altitude we need to face them. Research proves that in complex situations, people at more upper stages outperform those at lower levels. The more refined our worldview and cognition, the more effectively we can deal with our predicaments. The world is even more complex for those whose level of mental complexity is not high enough.

Kegan and Lahey (2009: 23) quote a study by Keith Eigel that looked at 21 CEOs and 21 middle managers from various companies, each with annual revenues of over $5 billion. The study revealed that across a range of leadership measures, there was a clear correlation between higher levels of vertical development and more effectiveness. The reason that managers at higher levels of development perform more effectively is that they think in more complex ways. This finding has since been replicated in several studies.

Clare Graves came to a similar conclusion in another experiment: people operating from Teal found many more solutions than all the others put together (Red plus Amber, plus Orange, plus Green). More importantly, the quality of their proposals was superior, and they reached the completion of them much more quickly than all the other groups.

Failure to meet life's challenges is, more often than not, a function of an inadequate level of development. Humans may adapt to new conditions by creating greater complexities of thinking that can handle new problems. Consciousness has a holarchic[27] structure, and transformation is an evolutionary process, whereby one achieves a more precise and more expanded vision of the world. When it leaps to a new holon, a whole new

[27] A holarchy is a natural hierarchy of holons. The holon is a fundamental concept of Integral Theory borrowed from Koestler (1967:48) to describe a fundamental unit that is simultaneously a whole and a part of a holarchy in which each higher level is more whole than the previous levels (Wilber 1995: 26). E.g., an atom is part of a molecule, which is part of a cell, which is part of an organism; or a letter is part of this word which is part of this sentence, which is part of this paragraph, which is part of this chapter, which is part of this book. In chapter 4, I will come back to the theory of holons and holarchies as applied to organisations.

world of possibilities opens up. The fresh holon (i.e., the newly achieved structure) can respond to deeper or higher worlds because its translation processes transcend and include those of its subholons. Paraphrasing Hegel, Wilber likes to say that each stage is true and adequate, and each higher stage is more true and adequate (for the new conditions and new emergent phenomena). For instance, when evolution developed rationality, it didn't wipe out the emotional mind but was integrated into a higher structure. Likewise, the Orange meme is a senior holon that transcends and includes the Amber meme. To the previous holon, these new realities are all "otherworldly". In SDI terms, we could say that an individual operating within the Red meme can only relate fully with exchanges up to the Red level. In the same way that humans are not able to listen to ultra-sound frequencies, they won't be able to get concepts coming from Orange because they are, to use Kegan's expression, "in over their heads".

A further advantage of the higher levels benefiting the lower levels. The higher our position in the spiral, the higher the tolerance towards the lower structures. For example, Galileo Galilei was judged by the Inquisition because his heliocentric theories didn't conform to the prevalent Amber worldview of the Church. They violated the supposed infallibility of the Sacred Texts, written according to the Ptolemaic ethnocentric paradigm. He saved his life only after publicly declaring he was wrong. He was lucky because if the centre of gravity of the members of the jury had been Red, he would have been condemned to the stake right away. In our contemporary Orange or Green cultures, someone in a similar situation would simply be ostracised.

As Laloux (2014: 38) pinpoints, a way to avoid attaching judgment to stages is to recognise that each stage is the best available solution for a particular life condition:

> *"If we were caught in a war, Impulsive-Red would be the most appropriate paradigm to think and act from to defend ourselves. On the other hand, in peaceful times in post-industrial societies, Red is not as functional as some of the later stages."*

The standard process of development transcends an old stage by acquiring a new one while integrating the preceding ones. Beck and Cowan (2006) explain that a healthy expression of each value system is essential to the health of the entire spiral. The lower levels are just as necessary as the higher levels.

One more caveat for your inflated egos: No matter how high you are in the spiral, you are just able to operate from there at particular times, and in certain lines (cf. 1.3.3). I found out reading Freinacht (2019: 477) that people tend to descend by two stages in Common's *Model of Hierarchical Complexity* (2008) when they are very upset about something, they are very invested in a belief, or something is a very touchy spot. Sorry to disappoint you, but you operate from Teal only on a good day. Sometimes you may be Dr Jekyll, and other times Mr Hyde.

1.5.3. Holding out for a Hero

> *I, I will be King*
> *And you, you will be Queen*
> *Though nothing will drive them away*
> *We can be heroes just for one day*
> *We can be us just for one day*
> (*Heroes*, David Bowie)

Once upon a time, a formerly prosperous land was floundering. The king was corrupt and only cared about the perpetuation of his power. One hero took on a journey, full of obstacles and perils, to return the lost prosperity to his land. He found wisdom and enlightenment, and he came back home profoundly transformed. He became the new king, sharing his new-found treasures with all his people.

This outline is very similar to the narrative pattern of many classic tales and myths that Joseph Campbell (1949) identified and called the hero's journey. They all describe the same "monomyth": the adventure of the archetype known as The Hero, who goes out and achieves great deeds on behalf of the group, tribe, or civilisation. It is a beautiful metaphor to describe the transformational experience that everyone goes through towards becoming whole and contributing members of society. Life is a journey, and every stage is a different station. The hero's journey is the adventure of living, and we are all heroes destined to leave our comfort zone, travel to our inner depths, face dangers, defeat dragons, and find the treasure of our True Self through a continuous developmental process (Robledo and Batle, 2014). When transformation occurs, the individual adopts a new self-definition and a greater sense of power and freedom that Wilber summarises as "self-realisation through self-transcendence."

According to Integral Theory and Spiral Dynamics, the universe is continuously pushing us to grow as an adaptation mechanism to cope with entropy and chaos.

> *"At each stage of human existence, the adult man is off on his quest of his holy grail, the way of life by which he believes men should live. (...) Yet, always to his surprise and ever to his dismay he finds, at every stage, that the solution to existence is not the solution he thinks he has found. Every stage he reaches leaves him discontented and perplexed. It is simply that as he solves one set of human problems, he finds a new set in their place. The quest he finds is never-ending." (Graves 2005: 476)*

We tend to stay stable at every stage of development for a while. When the time is ripe for change, a new level is activated, and we change our worldview, value system, belief structure, and rules for living. It is a leap both liberating and frightening. We might experience the death of our old self as a tragedy, but it is an adaptive transformation toward a more viable existence, same as when a caterpillar changes into a butterfly. In time, we will become as familiar with the higher stage as we were with the lower.

Robert Kegan estimates that, on average, it takes approximately five years to change stages. However, it all depends on the person. What makes a person open up to a later stage of consciousness? It will depend on age (the younger, the faster you evolve), environment, and life circumstances (both of them make us aware of the degree of suitability of our current patterns of behaviour, and their limitations). More often than not, movement from one stage to the next is driven by constraints in the current stage. We could say that need is the mother of development. Need satisfaction fixates it, need deficiency fosters it. As Graves explained (2005:30), by the time people are centralised at a particular level, they have only the "degrees of behavioural freedom" afforded at that level. When they confront situations, dilemmas, or challenges of a complexity that can't be reconciled by the degrees of freedom that determine what they know and can do at their current level, they consistently feel frustrated in their lives. When many small challenges or a major one can't be resolved from the current worldview, they are pushed to take the next step. At that point, they can choose one of two approaches: ignore the problem and cling to their existing meaning-making framework (or even shift back to the reassuring simplicity of an earlier worldview), or grow into the new and more complex level.

In that last scenario, development accelerates when people can identify the deeply embedded assumptions that are holding them at their current level and test their validity. When we are fixated on a particular stage, we are subject to its specific beliefs, motivations, and behaviours. We may be so identified with them that we are not even aware of their existence. Each shift in consciousness occurs when we reach a higher vantage point from which we see the world from a broader perspective. Like a fish that can see water for the first time when it jumps above the surface, gaining a new angle requires that we disidentify from something we were previously engulfed by. Not an easy thing to do, Laloux admits (2014: 40):

> *"Cognitively, psychologically, and morally, moving on to a new stage is a massive feat. It requires courage to let go of old certainties and experiment with a new worldview. For a while, everything can seem uncertain and confused. It might be lonely, too, as sometimes in the process we can lose close relationships with friends and family who can no longer relate to us."*

Transitioning to higher stages requires what Harvard Professor Kegan defines as a "s*ubject-object shift"*. Suddenly, people become objectively aware of those aspects of themselves to which they were formerly subject. As Kegan puts it, "*The subject of one level becomes the object of the subject of the next level."* When you are subject to a part of yourself, you are more attached to it. You can't disidentify from it, reflect on it, or take an objective look at it. You *are* a Catholic, or a manager, or a socialist. When you finally get to see these aspects as objects, you are able to be free from its control; in other words, the more we understand these as objects, the freer we are, and the more clearly we see the world, ourselves, and others. The shift to Amber, for instance, happens when Red disidentifies from its needs and impulses and is able to internalise rules that allow it to control them; next, the shift to Orange happens when Amber starts to question its identity and when its beliefs are no longer embodied (the change occurs when one moves from "I am a Catholic" to "I have Catholic beliefs") whereby one can step back and question the validity of the rules previously blindly adhered to.

The pattern of evolution follows a sequence that goes from subordinating self-interest in favour of the group in one stage to affirming self-interest in a new and higher form. As Beck and Cowan (1996: 57) emphasise: *"If too much 'me'-ism is the problem, then a form of 'we'-ness will then be required to restore balance. If the 'we' is excessive, then liberation of some 'me' becomes attractive if harmony is desired."* Thus, the overall spiral zig-zag between individualistic systems oriented to change and control the external world (Infrared, Red, Orange, Teal), and collective and conservative systems (Magenta, Amber, Green, Turquoise). Every other system is like its alternating partner, but more evolved, progressively reducing narcissism and increasing the complexity of thinking, inclusiveness, and care. With each successive level, the degrees of behavioural freedom increase, but is higher in odd-numbered (I) than in even-numbered (we) systems.

Personal transformation is a change in the way we feel about ourselves and the world. It entails an expansion of consciousness through a change in the underlying worldview and specific capacities of the self. It goes through a non-linear process, involving self-reflection and the development of consciousness, moving through the transformation of the basic worldview and the adoption of new, broader self-definition and capacities of the self. Ross' definition of personal transformation incorporates a three-stage process:

> *"...a dynamic socio-cultural and uniquely individual process that (a) begins with a disorienting dilemma and involves choice, healing, and experience(s) of expanding consciousness towards the divine; (b) initiates a permanent change in identity structures through cognitive, psychological, physiological, affective, or spiritual experiences; and (c) renders a sustained shift in the form of one's thinking, doing, believing, or sensing due to the novelty of the intersection between the experiencer, the experience, and the experiencer's location in time." (Ross 2010: 54)*

Those three stages are ubiquitous in the literature[28] and are analogous to the hero's journey model consisting of a departure from the known world, initiation to some source of power, and a return to live life more meaningfully:

> *"The standard path of the mythological adventure of the hero is a magnification of the formula represented in the rites of passage: separation—initiation—return: which might be named the nuclear unit of the monomyth. A hero ventures forth from the world of common day into a region of supernatural wonder: fabulous forces are there encountered, and a decisive victory is won: the hero comes back from this mysterious adventure with the power to bestow boons on his fellow man." (Campbell, 1949: 30)*

The hero's journey can thus be conceived as a rite of passage from one level of consciousness to the next, structured in a three-fold sequential

---

[28] Graves (2005: 483) mentions three periods involved in the transition to a higher stage: preparation, relative equilibrium, and disintegration. Likewise, McGuire and Rhodes (2009) describe vertical development as a three-stage process: (1) Awaken to a new way of making sense of the world, (2) Unlearn the old assumption and discern the new possibilities, (3) Advance to a new way of being.

structure:

1. Departure: The story begins in the familiar everyday world, which psychologists describe as "the comfort zone." Often when the hero hears the call (suppose a job offer for which the person has little experience), he first refuses to heed it. There is a whole range of reasons that try to hold us in our current circumstances (a sense of duty or obligation, fear, insecurity, a sense of inadequacy, etc.). An unusual personal situation, such as a life crisis or major life transition, is a common catalyst for change that initiates the stage of departure. It triggers a process of self-examination and critical assessment that ends up in discontent and recognition that others have travelled the same path:

   "The usual hero adventure begins with someone from whom something has been taken, or who feels there is something lacking in the normal experience available or permitted to the members of society. The person then takes off on a series of adventures beyond the ordinary, either to recover what has been lost or to discover some life-giving elixir." (Campbell 1949: 152)

   Finally, the hero takes a step forward, expressing his or her commitment to undergo the metamorphosis (what Campbell calls "The Crossing of the First Threshold"). The decision involves a metaphorical "death," as the initiate is forced to transform and prioritise values from a new perspective, and to break with previous roles, practices, and routines. It might even require the hero to go through a separation from his or her old environment.

2. Journey: The person leaves the known limits of her world and ventures into a new place of unknown rules. It usually requires confronting a series of tests and trials that start the transformation process. Dragons must be conquered[29], and difficult barriers overcome. The encounter with the unknown can provoke, using Mezirow's terminology (1995), a "disorienting dilemma" through

[29] The dragon symbolises the unconscious and our instincts. In the West, it is often associated with the obstacles to overcome to realize one's true self. I have noted an interesting evolution of the archetype. Traditionally, the hero (St. George, for example) had to slay the dragon, as part of his journey of self-completion. More recently, it is increasingly common than the hero or heroine tames the dragon (see, for instance, *A Game of Thrones*, or the series of movies *How to Train Your Dragon*). The dragon is no longer a threat to get rid of, but an ally of our evolution.

which a person's "orienting frames" and "habits of mind" are questioned, driving the transformational process. When one adopts a different perspective, a feeling of crisis is often experienced. The new way of seeing might come with the realisation that our old life does not make sense anymore; that all our previously held values have changed their meaning; and that people who used to share our perspective don't understand us anymore so that we can't relate to them the way we used to. Some progressive organisations use an anti-structural activity such as tourism, marked by the separation and the absence of the known structures of the home/the known, to make more feasible the possibility of experiencing new and different ways of being. A case in point is &samhoud, a Netherlands-based consultancy firm that uses transformational tourism (Robledo and Batle, 2017) as a strategy to foster personal development. New hires are sent out with their peers to places like Delphi, in Greece, to know themselves, or to the medieval route of Santiago de Compostela, in Spain, to reinforce interpersonal connection and one's own journey.

3. Return: When the young Goethe came back from Italy, his father asked him if he had seen anything new. He replied, *"No, father, but I have learned a new way of seeing."* The full round of the monomyth requires that the hero does not abandon social order and responsibilities altogether. When the quest has been accomplished, the hero must return with his life-transmuting trophy. He has to bring the runes of wisdom back to the kingdom. His goal is to retain the wisdom gained, integrate it into his life, and figure out how to share it with others.

Can you hear the calling once again? Are you going to keep ignoring it? Last time it was the mortgage. What excuse will you use this time to silence your yearning? Will you dare to be a hero?

1.5.4. Shades of colour

> *"Every challenge you encounter in life is a fork in the road. You have the choice to choose which way to go -backward, forward, breakdown, or breakthrough."* Ifeanyi Enoch Onuoha

Every level has lights and shadows, healthy and unhealthy expressions. Red can be heroic as well as tyrannical, Amber organised or inflexible, and so on. Evolution is not a path of roses, and every higher stage brings new and sublime potentials, combined with new and potentially disastrous pathologies.

A further area of concern, as Wilber (1995: 109) conveniently reminds us, is the possible dissociation, or even repression, of previous stages as well as the domination of the lower stages to the higher:

> *"(...) the fact that evolution always produces greater transcendence and greater differentiation means that a factor of possible pathology is built into every evolutionary step, because transcendence can go too far and become repression—the higher does not negate and preserve the lower, it tries only to negate (or repress or deny) the lower, which works about as well as denying our feet.*
>
> *Likewise, differentiation can go too far and become dissociation—a failure to adequately integrate the newly emergent differences into a coherent whole that is both internally cohesive and externally in harmony with other correlative holons and with all junior components. Whenever a new differentiation is not matched by a new and equal integration, whenever there is negation without preservation, the result is pathology of one sort or another, a pathology that, if severe enough, evolution sets about to erase in earnest."*

If during our transformative path, rather than transcending and including a lower level, it is transcended and repressed, then a shadow emerges, because the lower level is split off and marginalised. On the other hand, the pathology associated with dissociation is a regression to a lower level.

Richard Barrett makes a pivotal contribution to the understanding of human development with his distinction between primary and secondary motivations[30]. According to him (2014: 31), *"you must build a solid platform at each stage of development before you can establish yourself at the next higher stage of development."* If you fail to master a stage fully, it becomes a potential weakness that can undermine your progress.

Typically, the level of consciousness you are operating from will be the same as the stage of psychological development that constitutes your centre of gravity. This level will determine your primary motivation; however, in certain situations, this could threaten your internal stability or external equilibrium. You may temporarily revert to a lower level of consciousness. If that's what the event requires, then everything is fine

---

[30] For a full account of people's primary and secondary motivations, please refer to Richard Barrett's book *Evolutionary Coaching* (2014).

(e.g., in a life-or-death situation, you will have to shift temporarily into an Infrared consciousness to ensure your survival). The problem arises when a particular level recurrently hijacks you because of unmet needs at an earlier stage. When situations arise that consciously or subconsciously remind you of those needs -when you are holding onto fears about being able to meet your deficiency needs- your secondary motivations will take precedence over your primary one. In Integral Theory's terms, you have developed a maladaptive schema or a fixation. For example, if you had difficulties getting your survival needs met when you were a child (e.g., you were abandoned, your parents ignored you when you cried or, just the opposite, they were excessively concerned and anxious about your survival), whenever you have anything that feels like a survival challenge, your fear-based limiting beliefs from childhood will be triggered, and they will make you operate unnecessarily from the Infrared level of consciousness. You will see the world as a dangerous place, and you will trust no one. You will always be on guard, trying to control everything and everyone around you, or you will be overly conscientious and risk-averse.

Barrett (2014: 45) summarises it in the following terms:

> *"Your primary motivation will always be the need of the stage of the psychological development you have reached, and your secondary motivations will always be the needs of the stages of psychological development you have passed through which you have not yet mastered"*

Secondary motivation is intimately intertwined with shadow. At a particular moment of our developmental journey, the motivation was repressed, banishing from our personality the feelings and abilities necessary to get them. Actually, all of the first-tier levels of development have strong tendencies to turn into the shadow of the previous levels, especially the one most recently left behind. That is why, for example, so many people operating from Orange repress their spiritual sides or those at the Green level have disproportionate opinions against money.

In Barrett's opinion (2014: xxii), every goal a person is trying to achieve, every challenge they are facing, and every choice they are trying to make, is not only reflective of the needs associated with the stage of development they have reached, but also of the one they have passed through but have not yet mastered. Barrett (2014: 16) claims that those secondary motivations distract us from focusing on our primary motivation and inhibit our evolutionary progress. It is necessary to uncover them and reprogram the limiting beliefs.

CHAPTER 2

APPLICATIONS OF INTEGRAL THEORY TO ORGANISATIONS

2.1. Applying the AQAL model to Management Theory: Putting together the great puzzle

> *"In every intellectual debate, both parties are often right in what they claim, and wrong in what they deny."* (Stuart Mill)

Accountants, auditors, and ISO 9000 fans should have Aristotle as a patron (or if they prefer a proper saint, his acolyte Thomas Aquinas would be the man). Aristotle was the Great Categoriser. Influenced by Democritus and the atomists, he conceived the world as a composite of different independent parts. Armed with a scalpel, patience, and countless filing cabinets, the Greek philosopher was the first one to take the enormous task of ordering and classifying existence. Among other achievements, he managed to place every object of human apprehension under one of ten categories, and he devised two classification systems of living organisms. His work has been of paramount importance for the development of science and philosophy.

I know it is ugly to point the finger of blame, but if today we consider organisations as a multidisciplinary reality it is because of him. Management, economics, psychology, sociology, law, accounting, anthropology, engineering and informatics, are just some of the disciplines from which one can face the study of a reality as complex as an organisation. However, disciplines can be mentally suffocating. Delimiting is limiting and separating entails marginalising. If we divide too much, we might not be able to recompose the original puzzle, and we won't see the forest for the trees.

Each organisational discipline is subdivided into areas and these areas into schools, which regularly present their theories to the coveted leading-theory prize. Every school of thought, sometimes even every management theory, creates a particular paradigm that conceives organisations in a specific way. Their differences don't come from errors in their methods or conceptions but from different ways of seeing the organisational world. Every one of them offers only a partial vision of reality; none can give a useful solution for every single problem; none is complete enough to structure everything an organisation does.

Indeed, no theory is absolutely right (including Integral Theory), because it is only an imperfect approximation of reality. Theories are like maps that guide us through a complex reality. We tend to forget how incomplete the map is, and we mistake it for the territory. Hence, instead of paying attention to the territory, we end up noticing only the internal map we carry. Think about the platypus, that strange animal that lays eggs like the reptiles and suckles its babies like the mammals. When the zoologists of the eighteenth century found it, they considered it a paradox of nature, an enigma, and an impossible animal. Being older than man, the platypus must have found it very amusing. Obviously, the problem was not the platypus, but the imperfect categories made by the zoologists.

As I was saying, every partial view is wrong if it is exclusive, but it may have a component of truth we can't let go of. If we have a partial, truncated, and fragmented map, we will end up having a partial, truncated, and fragmented business approach. It is in the interplay between different theories that we can gain a better understanding of management phenomenology. That's why we need integral and pluralistic visions that include and transcend partial and monistic visions and also take into account all of the possible perspectives. Only an integral theory, based on epistemological pluralism, can capture the relations between theories, overcome the provincialism of the specialities, and formulate a theoretical framework that overcomes the limitations of each sphere of knowledge[31].

---

[31] Ken Wilber (2002) defines the three principles of an integral kind of thinking:
1. Nonexclusion - "Everyone is right"-. We can accept different validity claims (i.e., the truth claims that pass the validity tests for their own paradigms, in their own fields) insofar as they make statements about the existence of their own enacted and disclosed phenomena, but not when they make it about the existence of phenomena enacted by other paradigms. That is, one paradigm can competently pass judgments within its own worldspace, but not on those spaces enacted (and only seen) by other paradigms.
2. Enfoldment - "Some are more right than others." Everybody can be right, but some views are more right than others because they are more inclusive, more encompassing, more holistic, more integrative, more depthed, more transcending-

The AQAL model is an excellent epistemological framework for classifying the main theories of management and organisation and furthering the understanding of the underlying structures of thought that generate them. Table 3 represents a non-comprehensive attempt of classification[32].

	INTERIOR	*EXTERIOR*
INDIVIDUAL	*INTENTIONAL* Motivation Theories Psychoanalytical Organisation Theory Managerial theories Strategic Negotiation Spirituality at Work DDO Teal Organisations 3D Management	*BEHAVIOURAL* Behaviourist School Organisational Development Theory of Economic Behaviour Radical Theory Spirituality at work Teal Organisations 3D Management
COLLECTIVE	*CULTURAL* Cultural Theory Anthropological Theory Quality Management Postmodernism Power Theory Business Ethics Corporate Social Responsibility Knowledge Management Excellence Theories Conscious Capitalism Spirituality at Work DDO Teal Organisations	*SOCIAL* Industrial Economics Theory of Economic Behaviour Theory of the Firm Managerial theories Organisational Economics Agency Theory Transaction Cost Theory Evolutive Economics Theory Resources and Capabilities Structural Theories School of Administrative Process: Fayolism. Bureaucratic School Classical Theory of Public

and-including.
3. Enactment - "If you want to know this, do that." Most "paradigm clashes" are usually deemed "incommensurable"—meaning there is no way for the two paradigms to fit together— but this is so only because people focus on the phenomena, not on the practices. If we realize that phenomena are enacted, brought forth, and disclosed by practices, then we understand that what appeared to be "conflicting phenomena" or experiences are simply different (and fully compatible) experiences brought forth by different practices. Adopt them, and you will see the same phenomena that the adherents of the supposedly "incommensurable" paradigms are seeing. Hence, "incommensurability" is not an insurmountable or even a significant barrier to any integral embrace.

[32] I have tried my best that all the theories included are at the same level of specificity; however, it is a challenge to do so. I apologise for any inconsistencies.

	3D Management	Administration Neoclassical Theory Quantitative Theory Behaviourist School Social Systems School Organisational Development Systems Theory Sociotechnical Theories Contingency Theories Excellence Theories Population Ecology Chaos Theory Resource Dependency Theory Interorganisational Analysis School of Human Relations Organisational Learning Institutional Theories Organisational Ambiguity Quality Management Strategy Schools Organisational Configuration Organisational Change Theory Network Analysis and the Theory of Cooperation Knowledge Management Conscious Capitalism Sociocracy Holacracy Spirituality at Work Teal Organisations 3D Management

Table 3: Main organisational theories for each of the quadrants of the AQAL model

Now let's undertake a more thorough analysis by going through every quadrant:

1. RIGHT QUADRANTS

The Lower Right quadrant (LR), focused on the exterior of the collective, is, by far, the most populated one. The immense amount of theories in this box study organisations as a social enterprise and try to objectify everything happening in them. This quadrant reduces the complex organisational nature to an objective reality from a techno-economic or a sociological perspective. It focuses on the external aspects of the organisation, i.e., those items that can be seen with the senses or their extensions (Wilber 1996:80). From this "scientific" perspective, only the phenomenic deserves attention, i.e., the material aspects that are precise and measurable. As such, the only variables allowed in the discussion are purely objective and exterior realities. Everything immaterial is subsequently dismissed. Management dominated by this perspective is designed to be objective and impersonal, excluding any consideration of idiosyncrasies, motivations, values, or personalities, as that internal space is not empirically and objectively accessible. This penchant towards the objective, the material, and the measurable, results in an obsession with the quantifiable. The underlying principle is "to measure is to know." Ideally, everything should be reduced to an equation or a number through econometric measures, balance sheets, market reports, or business ratios. The resulting management practice is based primarily on economic measures of profitability and its by-products of productivity and quality, also expressed in quantifiable terms. Mintzberg (1994) refers to the "myth of quantification" to denounce the excessive importance that organisations give to data.

Less populated is the Upper-Right quadrant (UR), the exterior of the individual or behavioural, which represents *"the individual viewed in an objective, empirical, "scientific" fashion"* (Wilber 2000a:49). The theories that appear in the UR quadrant take the individual as an objective object of research, whether they are members of the organisation (employees, managers, owners) or other stakeholders (customers, suppliers), and focus basically on the analysis of their behaviour.

2- LEFT QUADRANTS

The Left-Hand quadrants focus on the interior, the subjective aspects of human experience. Their area of study is what is commonly called, the "soft" organisational factors, as opposed to the right-hand "hard" factors. Classically, Left-Hand quadrants were practically absent from the study of organisations, but in recent times they are becoming increasingly popular, especially with the growing importance of customer orientation and the rise of the human side of organisations.

The Upper Left (UL) investigates individual inner consciousness. From this standpoint, subjective experience is the only relevant one. Therefore, the theories and schools that belong to this quadrant analyse desires, needs, feelings, emotions, and motivations of individuals.

The Lower Left (LL) investigates the interior of the collective, "*all those patterns in consciousness that are shared by those who are <in> a* *particular culture or subculture"* (Wilber 2000a:50). The theories in this quadrant study organisations as a cultural phenomenon. These shared values, perceptions, beliefs, meanings, worldviews, and ethics, referred to as organisational culture, are the intersubjective organizational patterns.

What is the relevance of this exercise? Well, if theories are the basic epistemological structures of management science, identifying their paradigmatic underpinnings becomes critical. Every quadrant takes a different perspective of reality, and is, in its own right, a paradigm. Each one, while valid and useful, is partial.

However, if we believe scholars, management is characterised by the absence of a dominant paradigm. So far, none of these competing theories has been able to impose its perspective over the others. As a result, research in this field seems to evolve not towards normal science (i.e., a convergence of knowledge), as Kuhn predicted (1962), but towards a growing diversity of research perspectives, theories, and schools of thought[33], as defended by Feyerabend (1970).

Indeed, the application of the AQAL model shows that there is not a dominant paradigm at the theoretical level, as there are just too many theories in every box of the matrix. However, more careful analysis challenges conventional wisdom. Taking a bird's-eye view at Table 3, something is immediately noticeable: since organisations are a collective enterprise, the lower quadrants are the most important ones, but if we compare left and right, the right-side is more populated, and the lion's share is in the lower-right. This quadrant is like the tail wagging the dog, in a notorious case of quadrant imperialism. The implication is that there is an underlying paradigm at the metatheoretical level that dominates management and organisation theory: "scientific materialism," not by chance, the most common Western worldview, and a manifestation of the Orange value meme. Under the influence of scientific materialism, the typical management researcher or practitioner will tend to consider fundamentally real only that which is revealed by the methods of science. This is a limiting view that excludes all consideration to the idiosyncrasies

[33] Like everything else, it has its pros and cons. On the one hand, this is an indication that the complex nature of organisations is being understood and that researchers have a more refined outlook. On the other hand, it leads to excessive theoretical compartmentalisation, difficulty in the integration of the facts and data supplied by the different schools with their incompatible methods, not to mention the problem of incommensurability between theories and schools.

and personalities of the individuals, and the cultures of the groups involved. Everything is reduced to quantitative data, to numbers you can measure, such as revenue, expenses, profit, and taxes. It all boils down to maximising the bottom line.

In his foreword to Arnsperger's book on Integral Economics, Wilber reflects upon the danger of having a specific and often implicit worldview such as scientific materialism: *"What if the worldview of scientific materialism is in itself corrupted, deficient or inadequate in several fundamental ways (inadequate in methodological, ontological, and/or epistemological ways?)* (Arnsperger 2010, xvii). He answers that the discipline itself would be deficient and inadequate since it would not cover all of the areas or dimensions "*that need to be included in order to produce a full, balanced, comprehensive, and integral approach.*"

Since the birth of management (with early pioneers such as Taylor and Fayol, and the pervading influence of Adam Smith) at the beginning of the 20th century, business activity is evaluated based on profit and material growth. Up until the 70s, there was an almost undisputed monologue of the LR quadrant and a profoundly limited and fragmented view of the organisational world. Later on, with the recognition of the, until then, repressed voices of customers and employees, some pluralism was accepted. The individual began to be recognised and studied (i.e., the upper quadrants), trying to understand concepts such as motivation (to work and shop) and leadership, and their effects on the organisation. Also, as the interior of the collective was being seriously taken into account, the study of organisational cultures and ethics resulted.

All in all, the scientific-rational paradigm massively dominates management. When other perspectives are included, they end up subordinated to the positivist approach, both in academic research (that clearly favours statically measurable and tractable research, often at the expense of depth and interest), and management practice (where the only interiors valued are the ones that affect the bottom line, often leading to category errors[34] as a result of trying to measure the immeasurable).

Such a particular view of the world has dire consequences. Creating economic value as the only business goal (quite often with a short-term

---

[34] A category error is a semantic or ontological error in which *"things of one kind are presented as if they belonged to another"* (Blackburn, 1994, p.58). More about that in chapter 3.

lens) involves significant trade-offs: diminishing public trust in organisations, shortening life spans of organisations, plummeting levels of employee engagement, and damaging the environment around us.

A truly integral theory should take into account, and balance, all of the quadrants. Table 3 shows very few schools or theories in more than one quadrant, and only three in all of them, namely the new field of inquiry of Spirituality and Religion at Work (SRW), and obviously, the distinctly integral theories of Teal Organisations and 3D Management. That is an indicator of how reductionist management science is[35].

The moment has come to focus not on the confrontation of reductionisms, but in the integration towards increasingly holistic and complex theories. If no theory is complete enough to describe, with sufficient precision, the complexity of organisations, why don't we try to combine as many as possible in a rich tapestry, a multi-coloured but unique rainbow? The more theories we combine and place in a proper fit, the more accurate our map and our vision of management. If we can do that, we will be able to find the pot of gold at the end of the rainbow.

What we are looking for is an all-quadrant, all-level approach that provides a more comprehensive view of organisational phenomena to reflect the multifaceted and evolving nature of these institutions. That is precisely what 3D Management brings to the table: an alternative approach of theory building based on multiparadigm research that integrates all previous organisational knowledge in a comprehensive, balanced, and non-marginalising framework. Its metatheory-building process takes into account all possible perspectives from which organisations can be studied for truly integral management. This is something we will examine further in the next chapter.

2.2. The evolution of organisations through the Spiral Dynamics lens

Some people imagine that to know the future a crystal ball is needed, but who needs one when we have developmental models such as spiral dynamics that map the future of human development? As Sci-Fi writer William Gibson once said: *"The future has already happened."* What he meant is that most of what will be common in the future, at least in short

[35] For a more detailed explanation, see Robledo (2014).

to midterm, is simply the spread of the value memes that are ahead of their time, but that will eventually become hegemonic in a particular culture.

Systems grow out of the prevalent value memes of the time in which they emerge. Magenta is linked to tribal societies. Red is associated with feudalism and imperialism. Amber was responsible for the birth of the Nation-State, together with law, politics, and religion. Orange engendered the Enlightenment and the Industrial Revolution and brought about democracy, capitalism, and consumerism. Finally, Green set off movements such as feminism, environmentalism, and political correctness.

Organisations evolve in the same recognisable packages. Frederic Laloux, in his famous book *Reinventing Organizations* (2014), applied the SDI model to the evolution of organisations and identified Teal as the next stage of organisational evolution. His groundbreaking work will, obviously, be the primary reference for my description.

Without further ado, let's start our voyage through the spiral of organisational development. We will set sail to go to Red, which represents the marginal pre-conventional level of authoritarian organisations. Our next port will be Amber, the colour of the still very present, traditional bureaucratic management. We will stop in Orange, the prototype of mainstream modern management. Together with Amber, these constitute the conventional stages. As a grand finale, we will behold the wonders of the post-conventional organisations, the vanguard of management evolution, made up of Green, Teal, and Turquoise.

Impulsive-red organisations: The wolf pack.

> *"Was all this legal? Absolutely fucking not, but we were making more money than we knew what to do with."* (*The Wolf of Wall Street,* Martin Scorsese, 2013)

Consisting of small bands of up to 10 people, the Infrared and Magenta levels of development present extremely rudimentary forms of organisation. For Laloux, the first forms of organisational life worth studying are shaped by a Red worldview: "*Organisations molded in Impulsive-Red consciousness first appeared in the form of small conquering armies when the more powerful chiefdoms grew into proto-empires*." (Laloux 2014: 17)

The defining element of a Red organisation is the continuous exercise of power in interpersonal relationships. According to Laloux, Impulsive-Red

Organisations can only be found in developed societies at the fringes of legal activity. The examples he provides are street gangs and mafias. In my opinion, we can find other less extreme cases of organisations with a Red culture. I would include in this category any organisation with a strong and authoritarian leader who is operating from the Red level of development. This leader, usually the owner, monopolises all the power and trusts no one, even if they are close relatives. Indeed, a textbook example of Theory X[36]. As his or her word is law, his or her worldview will determine the structures and practices of the organisation, resulting in a highly autocratic management style, with control mechanisms mostly based on mistrust and punishment, and an extremely egocentric moral stance. Organisations like this are dwindling to marginal numbers, with only about 2% of organisations centred at this level, usually small family businesses.

Laloux (2014: 17) resorts to the metaphor of the wolf pack to describe them[37]:

---

[36] Douglas McGregor, a professor at the MIT, identified in its classic book, *The Human Side of Enterprise (1960)* two opposing management styles based on a different set of assumptions about human nature that, despite their unoriginal names, have come to define the ways to manage and motivate people: *"Theory X"* and *"Theory Y"*. Theory X is based on a pessimistic view of human beings. Its underlying assumptions are: workers are naturally lazy, they don't like to work, and they do it only for the money. Theory X argues that the typical workforce operates more efficiently under an authoritarian style because workers can't be trusted, and they have to be controlled. Theory Y is a radically different style that acts on the belief that people are trustworthy and active, they can enjoy work, and they can be intrinsically motivated. Consequently, a participatory management style that involves them in the decision making and gives them freedom, is more desirable.

[37] Laloux offers a guiding metaphor for every level of organisational development. His premise is that our theories and explanations of organisational life are based on metaphors that lead us to see and understand organisations in distinctive ways. He has been, probably, inspired by Morgan *"for the use of metaphor implies a way of thinking and a way of seeing that pervade how we understand our world generally"* (Morgan, 1986:17). Morgan developed one of the most influential models of classification and analysis of organisational theories based on the following metaphors: organisations as machines, organisations as organisms, organisations as brains, organisations as change, organisations as culture, organisations as political systems, organisations as instruments of domination, and organisations as psychic prisons.

> *"Rather like the "alpha wolf" uses power when needed to maintain his status within the pack, the chief of a Red Organisation must demonstrate overwhelming power and bend others to his will to stay in position. The minute his power is in doubt, someone else will attempt to topple him."*

Organisations that sprout in the shadow of this metaphor, frequently exhibit a very informal and adhocratic structure, with no clearly defined roles. On the upside, this makes Red Organisations highly reactive to new threats and opportunities. Their excessive reliance on one single person, management by fear, and weak planning capacities, significantly hamper their functioning.

This kind of organisations, with a Red-centred feudal lord calling all the shots, shows an egocentric level of moral development. They will try to maximise profit and power no matter who gets hurts in the process. Ethics is not on the agenda, nor even respect for the law. They will do whatever it takes to achieve their objectives. Tax evasion, corruption, environmental damage, health and safety violations, illegal employment, fraud, counterfeiting, or piracy, are not a problem for them as long as they don't get caught.

Conformist-Amber organisations: The disciplined army.

"*Listen, this old system of yours could be on fire, and I couldn't even turn on the kitchen tap without filling out a 27b/6... Bloody paperwork.*" (*Brazil*, Terri Gilliam, 1998)

The second stage in the history of organisational development is the Amber stage:

> *"Historically, Amber Organisations are the ones that have built irrigation systems, pyramids, and the Great Wall of China. Conformist-Amber Organisations ran the ships, the trading posts, and the plantations of the Colonial world. The Catholic Church is built on this paradigm—arguably it has been the defining Amber Organisation for the Western world. The first large corporations of the Industrial Revolution were run on this template. Amber Organisations are still very present today: most government agencies, public schools, religious institutions, and the military are run based on Conformist-Amber. Authority to define what is right and wrong is now linked to a role, rather than to a powerful personality (as was the case in Red); it is the priest's robe, whoever wears it, that counts." (Laloux 2014:20)*

The metaphor that guides Amber organisations is the army, a steep and rigid hierarchical system with a well-defined chain of command, strict control from the top, and a focus on order and certainty achieved through documented processes and precise rules that stipulate who can do what.

Denning (2010:29) provides an accurate description of the organisational model of an army:

> *"The practices were founded on distrust: unless people were tightly controlled, they might do the wrong thing. The goal was to reach optimal decisions, even if they were not the most rapid. The linchpin of the approach was the brilliant general at the top who would study the situation, make the right decisions, give orders, and win the battle. This had proved to be a successful model of military organisation down the centuries. The more disciplined the army, the more successful it was. The communications were top-down, explicit, and linear. It was a hierarchy in which the management style was directive and transactional. The assumption was that the world was knowable and people at the top were best placed to know what was going on and to run the organisation."*

The organisational structure is pyramidal, with a very rigidly ordered superior-subordinate relationship defined in job descriptions: *"Foot soldiers at the bottom of the pyramid are expected to follow orders scrupulously, no questions asked, to ensure the battalion marches in good order."* (Laloux, 2014:20)

Amber organisations are hierarchical, and they apply individualistic or bureaucratic command-and-control management styles with rigid lines of responsibility, authority, and accountability. They are traditional and highly formal, with rigorous codes of behaviour and dress. If you have to wear a tie, you are likely working in an organisation deeply influenced by the Amber worldview. Their fundamental values are efficiency, certainty, and the belief in the existence of a correct solution to every problem. As it was the case with Red Organisations, "management by instructions" is the rule, led by the "top-down" principle, with a rigid subordination and control over the execution of every activity. Challenging authority is not permitted. Employees are paid to do as they are told.

According to Laloux (2014: 21), the Amber worldview brought about two major organisational breakthroughs:

- Process systematisation and long-term perspective: The introduction of standardised work processes replicated past experience into the future. Amber Organisations are able to survive for centuries because critical knowledge is no longer dependent on a particular person; it is embedded in the organisation and can be transmitted across generations. Hence, any person, including the chief, is replaceable.

- Stable structures: Amber organisations bring stability to power, with formal hierarchies represented in organisation charts, job titles, and job descriptions. People, depersonalised and anonymous, are rectangles in the organisational chart. Work is divided to control them more easily and maximise performance. Thus, each person has a perfectly defined position, where tasks are assigned and included in his or her job description. Laloux's (Ibid.) depiction is very graphic:

> *"The overall structure settles into a rigid pyramid (...) The plant manager is in charge of the department heads, who in turn oversee unit managers, line managers, foremen, and machine operators. (...) Planning and execution are strictly separated: the thinking happens at the top, the doing at the bottom. (...) Jobs are organized by rigid job descriptions. Control is maintained through compliance with a catalog of rules and procedures. (..) The underlying worldview is that workers are mostly lazy, dishonest, and in need of direction. They must be supervised and told what is expected of them."*

The Golden Years of the Amber organisations spanned from the Industrial Revolution until the 1950s due to both scarcity and high demand for mass-produced goods and services. These were times of stable environments, with little competition, and excess of demand. The key to market success was to produce high-quality products that were durable and worked well. The other element of the profit equation was minimised, taking advantage of economies of scale to reach maximum operational efficiency at the lowest cost.

Taylor's Scientific Management, Fordism, and Weber's bureaucracy are the more influential Amber theories and models. They may seem a thing of yesteryear, but many contemporary management theories are influenced by them. Many current business models and practices, including management by objectives, systems planning, programming and budgeting, and quality assurance systems like ISO 9000, follow their principles. In fact, we can still find many traditional companies centred in Amber (my estimate is around 25%). The order they create makes them exceptionally well suited for stable markets and sectors with little need for adaptation to market changes, as is commonly seen in the public sector.

On the downside, this kind of organisations has little to no creativity and almost no sense of urgency. They work under the assumption that there is one right way to do things, which makes them adverse to change and innovation. Furthermore, the bureaucratic approach demotivates people and disengages them from organisational concerns. Workers tend to do the minimum to get by, showing almost no initiative or passion.

Achievement-Orange Organisations: The perfect machine.

After the Second World War, products were not selling as well as they used to due to the progressive saturation of markets. The Amber business model gradually became outdated as the marketplace became increasingly crowded, competitive, and global, thereby forcing companies to develop products based on customers' desires. Orange organisations emerged from these new market conditions, staging a professional model, that was optimised for highly competitive environments. Modern global corporations are the paragon of the Orange mindset, a mindset that constitutes the culture of approximately 50% of organisations.

Laloux (2014: 26-28) identifies three breakthroughs induced by Orange organisations: innovation, accountability, and meritocracy

1. Innovation: Businesses operating in highly competitive environments need to be very innovative to differentiate themselves from the fierce competition. The traditional, inflexible, conservative, hierarchical, and normative approach of the Amber stage is not appropriate for innovation. The Orange organisation had to deconstruct the outdated Amber model, reducing the bureaucratic structure to be more flexible and adaptable. The film industry is a good example: Film companies reinvented themselves after the collapse of the traditional studio system, characterised by vast, vertically integrated empires, and long-term contracts with the stars, screenwriters, and directors. With the new model, each film is a new project with a different team each time.

2. Accountability: According to Laloux (2014: 26-27): *"Amber command and control becomes Orange predict and control. To innovate more and faster than others, it becomes a competitive advantage to tap into the intelligence of many brains in the organisation. Larger parts of the organisation must be given room to manoeuvre and must be empowered and trusted to think and execute."*

3. Management by Objectives replaces Red and Amber "management by instructions". Organisational goals decided on top are cascaded down and translated to employee level into individual objectives. Employees are no longer told what to do, only what objectives to achieve, and they are assessed and monitored accordingly. With such a system, motivation becomes increasingly important and requires different tools than the ones used by Red and Amber organisations:

   "Orange Organisations have invented a host of incentive processes to motivate employees to reach the targets that have been set, including performance appraisals, bonus schemes, quality awards, and stock options. To put it simply, where Amber relied on sticks, Orange came up with carrots. The breakthrough in terms of freedom is real. Managers and employees are given room to exercise their creativity and talent and the latitude to figure out how they want to reach their objectives, which can make work considerably more interesting." Laloux (id.)

4. Meritocracy: Equal opportunity is the fundamental principle of a meritocracy. Prosperity, success, and upward mobility is based on talent, competency, and hard work regardless of age, creed, sex, nationality, religion, or social class. The American Dream comes true, and the errand boy can become the next CEO. Thanks to meritocracy, *"identity is no longer fused with rank and title; instead, it is synonymous with our need to be seen as competent, successful, and ready for the next promotion."* As Orange organisations usually measure success on an individual basis, there is fierce competition to work harder and appear smarter and better than others. The belief that some people got where they are because they worked for it has the cruel and unfair flipside that those who aren't successful didn't try hard enough.

The success of the Orange worldview, as a blueprint for the business world, was due initially to the accidental coincidence between pioneering leaders at the Orange level of development and a workforce predominantly operating from Amber. It was a marriage made in Heaven. On the one hand, you had leaders with a tremendous need to accomplish something and, on the other hand, a vast number of subordinates ready and willing to follow someone else.

In the final analysis, the Orange organisation is an upgrade of the Amber organisational model to adapt to increasingly complex environments and technology. Basically, it relies on the same Amber principles of hierarchical systems based on command and control.

Indeed, the metaphor Laloux chooses for Orange, the organisation as a machine, could easily be applied to Amber but is in Orange organisations where it achieves its maximum expression. The comparison between a modern organisation and a machine is a recurring theme (from Morgan to Chaplin and Fritz Lang) that is a consequence of the mechanistic view of reality imposed by Cartesian rationalism and Newtonian mechanics: these are simple to understand systems based on action-reaction, predictable, and easy to control. Thus, organisations are built in the image of machines formed by independent parts working with mechanical precision, like clockwork. Its foundational exponents were Taylorism and Weber's bureaucratic model, both unambiguously Amber theories. Still today, most companies are seen as a machine designed for a single purpose: to create profit.

The main problem of this metaphor is that it tends to suppress the human side of the organisation, reducing people into pieces of corporate machinery. Individuals are like cogs in the wheel, passive production units, thoughtless automatons. When people are treated as replaceable parts, it is only natural they lose connection to themselves and each other. As the wise Chuang-Tzu said, *"He who works as a machine develops a mechanical heart."* All those dehumanising and alienating effects have been perfectly portrayed in movies like *Metropolis, Brazil, The Hudsucker Proxy, or Modern Times* (that shows the famous scene where the machine eats the Tramp).

Yes, people have components that seem mechanical. Muscles operate like machines, and the brain works like a computer; however, they are some of the less essential aspects of human beings. A crane can lift more weight than a person, and a computer is faster and more reliable than any brain. One of the consequences of the Industrial Revolution was to substitute people with machines that did physical work more efficiently. The same happened during the Information Revolution when computers replaced many people because they were able to do some clerical tasks faster, more accurately, for less money, and without any health insurance costs. And it is happening again and on a bigger scale: most of the technologies currently being developed replace or obsolesce human jobs, and not just the unqualified ones but even mid-level executive positions. The supermarket cashier is replaced by a touchscreen, the factory worker by a robot, and the stock researcher and the market analyst by a computer algorithm. Experts estimate than by 2025 advances in artificial intelligence and robotics are going to replace at least 50 per cent of the workforce.

Don't fight it; it is a lost battle. Humans are inferior to machines in everything mechanical and algorithmic. The only alternative for us is to move up the food chain, so to speak, to become more human and less like machines. Human beings are infinitely superior in non-programmable facets. It will take a long time before a computer gets even close to humans in anything requiring autonomy, complex thinking, decision-making, creativity, or empathy. AI can be better at diagnosing but cannot replicate or measure up to the high-touch connection and care that a good nurse provides. So, if humans make use of their best talents, machines could allow us to focus our collective energy in activities like education, care, and development.

What makes us superior as humans is precisely what mechanistic organisations waste in their stubborn attempt to turn us into mechanical components made of flesh and bones. No matter how hard they repress the human element, it ultimately manifests itself, often to their disadvantage, as politicking, stress, depression, etc.

A further disadvantage is that, despite the fact that mechanistic organisations are efficient and reliable in stable conditions when change happens and the rules don't accommodate the exceptions, they tend to be inflexible. It takes time to reprogram the machine to suit the new circumstances, sometimes too much time. Resistance to change is much more significant in Amber organisations but is not unknown in Orange ones.

Being the dominant kind of organisation of our times, Laloux (2014: 29) devotes a significant amount of space to examining the shadows of the Orange management model:

> *"One of Orange's shadows is "innovation gone mad." With most of our basic needs taken care of, businesses increasingly try to create needs, feeding the illusion that more stuff we don't really need— more possessions, the latest fashion, a more youthful body— will make us happy and whole."*

Unethical behaviour is the most prominent shadow of the modern organisation. Orange organisations have profit as their only goal, and much too often, they shamelessly prioritise that to an ethical obligation. Fraud, mobbing, violations of consumer rights and safety, destruction of the environment, or discrimination, are examples of regular business practices almost as normal as taking inventory.

Pluralistic-Green Organisations.

Are you full of tattoos and piercings, and that was not a problem when you were being hired? More likely, you work in the 20% of organisations that are centred at the Green level. If nowadays most of us can dress casually at work, it is thanks to the influence of Green values.

Green or postmodern organisations have alternative values compared to modern (Orange) organisations. The main difference is that they give their right status to the left quadrants. If Amber and Orange organisations recognise only the existence of the hard factors in the lower-right quadrant, Green questions the economic (or hard) vision and affirms in its epistemology non-economic (soft) values coming from the left quadrants (culture, values, employee satisfaction, coaching, mentoring, etc.)

Heydebrand (1989: 327) describes a Postmodern-Green organisation as informal and flexible, with a decentralised, eclectic, participatory management structure, and a post-bureaucratic control structure. Concurrently, it can use pre-bureaucratic elements such as clannish personalism, informalism, and corporate culture, to integrate a generally scantly integrated system. Where modernism opted for rationality, centralisation of power, hierarchy, structure, standardisation, and control, postmodernism advocates a more organic type of enterprise committed to decentralisation, empowerment, flexibility, trust, and confidence.

Now let's see their traits and contributions. Laloux (2014: 32-33) identifies three breakthroughs of Green organisations:

1. Empowerment: Employee satisfaction and involvement are very important for Green Organisations. The creation of a good working atmosphere where every voice is heard is of paramount importance. Not in vain, the metaphor Laloux recurs to describe Green organisations is "the family":

> *"Green Organizations retain the meritocratic hierarchical structure of Orange, but push a majority of decisions down to frontline workers who can make far-reaching decisions without management approval."*

> *"For instance, where Achievement-Orange seeks to make decisions top-down, based on objective facts, expert input, and simulations,*

Pluralistic-Green strives for bottom-up processes, gathering input from all and trying to bring opposing points of view to eventual consensus."

Accordingly, managers listen to subordinates, empower them, motivate them, develop them, and evaluate them based on 360-degree feedback, to make them accountable. In some companies, employees choose their bosses, and they practice servant leadership.

2. Values-driven culture and inspirational purpose:

   "A strong, shared culture is the glue that keeps empowered organizations from falling apart. Frontline employees are trusted to make the right decisions, guided by a number of shared values rather than by a thick book of policies (...)

   In many cases, Green Organizations put inspirational purpose at the heart of what they do. Southwest doesn't consider itself merely in the transportation business; it insists that in reality, it is in the business of "freedom", helping customers to go to places they couldn't without Southwest's low fares. Ben & Jerry's is not just about ice cream, it is about the Earth and the environment too." (Laloux 2014:33)

3. Multiple-stakeholder perspective: Green Organisations hold the belief that *"businesses have a responsibility not only to investors, but also to management, employees, customers, suppliers, local communities, society at large, and the environment. The role of leadership is to make the right trade-offs so that all stakeholders can thrive."* They also recognise the benefits of a diverse workforce and strive to create inclusive environments. For this reason, it is not uncommon to find features like prayer rooms for different faiths, different meal options, work opportunities for the disadvantaged, or accessible facilities for the disabled.

There are other kinds of more radically Green organisations. They result from experiments of the Green counterculture in the non-profit sector, the cooperative movement (with long-standing examples such as Mondragón Corporation, that began in 1956 in the Spanish province of Gipuzkoa, or 21st-century-digital representatives such as EthicalBay or Fairmondo), the communes that started in the 1960s with the hippy and beatnik movements (some of them are still functioning, such as Twin Oaks in the US, or Christiania in Denmark that has achieved micro-nation status), or many intentional communities, including ecovillages (e.g., Findhorn, Scotland), transition towns (e.g., Totnes, Britain), or spiritual communities (e.g., Auroville, India). They are mostly egalitarian organisations that have developed very interesting techniques on community building, group dynamics, collaborative processes, emotional management, conflict resolution, and active listening, and tools as valuable as Sociocracy, Open Space, Dragon Dreaming, Forum, Appreciative Enquiry, etc., that are starting to make some inroads in business environments.

One of the main problems with people operating from Green is that they repress the Orange in them and tend to despise everything that sounds Orange, such as the business world, profits, marketing, or hierarchies. Consequently, many Green organisations have survival problems, as the commercial and the operational aspects are likely to be marginalised.

Evolutionary-Teal Organisations.

Teal is the new management buzzword since Frederic Laloux's book "*Reinventing Organisations*" (2014) was published. Today, around 2% of organisations have joined the ranks of this stage of development.

Laloux identifies three breakthroughs of Evolutionary-Teal organisations (2014:56)[38]:

- Self-Management: Teal organisations manage to transcend the classic problem of power inequality through a system where no one holds power over anyone else. This is based on a distributed authority and peer relationships without the need for either dominance hierarchies or consensus.
- Wholeness: Teal Organisations allow us to bring the whole of ourselves to work. They no longer demand you show up with a narrow, professional, masculine, rational self, and to leave your emotional, creative, and spiritual parts at the door.
- Evolutionary Purpose: Teal Organisations have a life and a sense of direction of their own. Instead of trying to predict and control the future and create strategies for it, members of the organisation are invited to listen in and understand what the organisation wants to become and what purpose it wants to serve.

---

[38] My friend Tom Thomison, of Encode.org, talks about five alternative markers of a Teal organisation: purposeful, holarchic, dynamic, autonomous, and transparent.

He labels the Teal culture as evolutionary, resorting to the metaphor of a living system[39]:

> *"Life, in all its evolutionary wisdom, generates eco-systems of unfathomable beauty, ever-evolving toward more wholeness, complexity, and consciousness.*
>
> *In these organisms, change happens everywhere, all the time in a self-organizing urge that comes from every cell, with no need for central command and control to give orders and pull the levers."* (Laloux 2014: 56).

Competition is no longer relevant at this level. Teal organisations compete with what is possible, not with other companies. The first time Logan et al. (2011) walked into Amgen, they asked about their competitors. Rather

---

[39] It is not uncommon to compare organisations with organisms. For example, we say that some company is aggressive as a lion, or flexible as a reed. The most usual comparison is with people, to the extreme that from a legal point of view, corporations are regarded as legal persons, subject to rights and obligations as any human being. Thus, the metaphor explores the parallels between organisations and organisms in terms of performance and relationships with the environment and other species. Usually, it establishes certain analogies between the life cycle of living things and organisations, which are credited with goals, and survival and development needs. Therefore, many theories are about life cycles, such as the *Product Life Cycle (PLC)* in engineering and marketing, the *Enterprise Life Cycle (ELC)* in enterprise architecture, the *Project Life Cycle* in project management, and the *Destination Life Cycle* in tourism. They describe the stages of life from conception or birth, to decline, and define suitable policies for each of them.

Theories that use this metaphor tend to emphasize survival as the primary goal of any organisation. Businesses must adapt to changing environmental conditions and compete with other companies to survive. There has been an evolution from the cruellest Darwinist principles of competition based on the survival of the fittest. In recent times, some theories are beginning to replace the simplistic vision of the business environment as a hostile jungle, adding new variables such as cooperation (resulting in theories and practices such as benchmarking and coopetition -a neologism coined to describe cooperative competition-).

It is also quite common to compare organisations and living organisms in their evolution. The theories in this group study organisations not statically, but dynamically (e.g., evolutionary economics theory, population ecology theory, or organisation change theory). Thus, in stable environments, ordered and methodical firms will have more chances to succeed. In contrast, in turbulent conditions, companies should encourage mutations, introducing new products to compete even with their own.

than Pfizer or Genentech, the answer they got was cancer, arthritis, obesity, Parkinson's, and human disease in general.

Turquoise Organisations: Holycracy

Laloux's journey ends at Teal, but the spiral carries on, and after Teal comes Turquoise. Yan Eperon has created *Holycracy*, the only Turquoise management philosophy I know[40]. It is a profoundly visionary and speculative theory, and I don't know of any organisation even close to that level of consciousness, but it is a fascinating yardstick for future development.

Eperon describes Holycracy as a highly disruptive management and organisational proposal:

> *"It provides a framework for self-organization of people who are connected intuitively and soulfully to wholeness. Beyond this, it is intended to support a planetary shift towards an enlightened society which thrives and blossoms in deep harmony with Self and nature. Holycracy is synthesizing cutting-edge spiritual understanding with the most daring forms of self-management, the former being the key to the potency and workability of the latter."*

He adds:

> *"Holycracy is a frame that supports our highest potential in the form of inspired synergistic - and at its best ecstatic - co-creations. It shows a higher platform of human expression, coming from a shared state of consciousness where we see all as individual expressions of a unique Reality – that we all ARE -, manifesting and exploring through infinite diversity its most exquisite and fulfilling potentials."*

Etymologically, holycracy means "sovereignty of the sacred." From a Turquoise perspective, Eperon considers sacred our innate and absolute connection to "all that is" and to our most authentic heart-centred desires.

Eperon summarises the essential elements of holycracy:

- Individual freedom in universal oneness is the cherished ideal.

---

[40] Holycracy, as an expression of the Gift Economy, offers a free, open-source organisational toolkit. You can download all the materials available in English at https://docs.google.com/document/d/1Vv5C6Rcz2wH0jg4RSg6KciGRfixul1WsYh6DyaSD5Ls/edit#

- Support each other's deepest and sincerest inner calling.
- What supports your highest fulfilment is my highest blessing and vice-versa.
- Open up to the infinite potential of co-creation and see what naturally wants to unfold. Surf on synchronicities.
- Embodying our wholocentric self: Realise ourselves being the whole expressed as parts serving ourselves as the whole. That translates into purely transpersonal drivers.
- Move from evolutionary purpose to attunement, to the purpose of evolution itself.

For Eperon, holycracy constitutes the peak and deeper embodiment of the second-tier organisational revolution:

> *"It goes further and more radically into personal empowerment, individual freedom, organizational agility, organic governance, wholeness, and evolutionary purpose by relying much more fully upon supra-conscious capabilities, spiritual intelligence, transpersonal drivers and the self-organizing nature of a wholistic reality."*

This brief introduction to holycracy may sound outlandish and vague, but don't be mistaken: Eperon provides a complete toolkit of guidelines and practices that includes governance structure, meeting protocols, decision-making procedures, financial organisation, etc.

2.3. The new paradigm

> *"Crisis takes place when the old does not just die, and the new is not yet born."* Bertolt Brecht

That is the evolutionary journey of organisations, from Red to Turquoise. Each level determines a different management paradigm and worldview, and a corresponding set of values and rules of conduct as a response to the changing conditions of the environment. Any organisation can be classified somewhere in this spectrum of development. I have devised a questionnaire to diagnose organisational culture based on the influential "Competing Values Framework" (Quinn and Rohrbaugh, 1983; Cameron and Quinn 2011). The assessment instrument classifies organisations in Amber, Orange, Green, or Teal, based on compliance with two major dimensions. The first one differentiates organisations that emphasise flexibility and autonomy from those that value stability and control. The second dimension differentiates organisations that prefer internal orientation from those that have a more external focus. Table 4 displays the four different cultures in a matrix:

Flexibility and autonomy

GREEN (Collaborate)	TEAL (Co-create)
AMBER (Control)	ORANGE (Compete)

Stability and Control

Table 4: Organisational culture matrix

Pre-conventional organisations at the Red altitude are remnants from the past; the present is dominated by conventional organisations at Amber and especially Orange levels, while post-conventional ones at Green and Teal are the future. What lies ahead of us is the fact that the number of pre-conventional and conventional organisations will progressively dwindle, to be substituted by Green and Teal ones.

Getting to Green or Teal is a significant paradigm shift. A real one, I should add, because paradigm is one of the more overused and degraded words in management. Everything is labelled as "paradigm-shifting" from Customer Relationship Management to *Post-It Notes*[41]. Technology is often coupled to paradigm shifts, and with a reason. But new technologies, however disruptive, more often than not, are only so on the surface, and primarily reinforce the existing paradigm churning beneath it all. In fact, Rushkoff (2016) condemns that premise and maintains that with digital technologies, everything changes except the underlying Orange paradigm. New machines upholding the same old purposes:

> *We still tend to see digital technology as a new tool through which to scale up industrialism. So instead of mechanical looms replacing humans, it is robots and algorithms. Instead of creating distributed mechanisms to enhance the emergent peer-to-peer marketplace, we create platforms to extract value from its participants and deliver it upward."*

With all the misuse and abuse of the term, maybe we should start by clarifying what a paradigm is. The notion was coined by Kuhn (1962) as the central concept of his philosophy of science. He defined it as a set of overarching and interconnected assumptions shared by a particular community that, for a time, allows its members to work within a common conceptual framework providing model problems and solutions. Peterson (1999: 236) compares a paradigm to a game: play is optional, but once undertaken its rules cannot be questioned while the game is on (and if they are it becomes a different game). Paradigms determine our expectations, our focus, and even our perception of reality. For example, during the Middle Ages, they would have laughed at anyone saying that the horizon is not straight but curved. Trying to convince them that the Earth is round would have been as tricky as explaining brown to a dog.

The progress of scientific knowledge, according to Kuhn, begins with the competition between theories until one of them succeeds in attracting a majority of followers and becomes the dominant paradigm. Let's see the process as applied to management science. In the 19th century, management was in a pre-paradigm phase. Then in the early 20th century, scientific management came in, and scientific materialism became the dominant paradigm, as I already explained. It was the onset of a period that Kuhn calls "normal science", oriented by the rules of this paradigm.

[41] 3D Management is beyond that game. It does not claim to be a new paradigm. It is a metaparadigm. Top that if you can ;-)

The essential feature of normal science is its cumulative and incremental character as a result of the continuous extension of the scope of the knowledge that emerged under the shelter of the hegemonic paradigm. During that period, there is no predisposition to the discovery of new theories, to the point of intolerance of novelty, as the whole community tries to protect the paradigm. In the case of management, it has been extremely well protected, since it has reigned supreme for two centuries.

Nothing lasts forever. Sooner or later, the current paradigm is going to be undermined by the accumulation of so many abnormalities that they become the general case. I hope you agree by now that our current management model, built on Traditional-Amber and Modern-Orange industrial structures and based on a linear and Newtonian worldview, is clearly dysfunctional and unable to cope with the many anomalies that have emerged because of a much more turbulent environment, an exponential rate of change, and the increasingly adverse impacts that the traditional model has over society, workers and the planet.

The recognition of anomalies marks the beginning of a crisis. One after the other, the advocates of the dominant paradigm lose confidence, and a scientific revolution occurs. Competing theories proliferate, fuelled by the need to find a better paradigm. I think that is the point we have now reached. Many theories including Agile, Management 3.0, Radical Management, Teal Organisations, Conscious Capitalism, Holacracy, Sociocracy, Holycracy, and 3D Management, are trying to raise the bar to help companies grow to post-conventional levels and are laying the foundation for a new management paradigm inspired by more evolved worldviews[42]. Most of them come from Green, but some theories come from the second-tier, in particular from Teal, or even from Turquoise, as we have seen.

Consequently, a change of paradigm is fast approaching. More and more organisations are "going Teal," "getting conscious," or "liberated", and they are impacting both for-profits, and non-for-profits, where their involvement is even more significant.

This process may not be as rational as would be desired. Organisations plagued by uncertainty, lack of time, and information overload, succumb

---

[42] See appendix 1 for a detailed analysis of some influential post-conventional theories.

to the temptation to simply follow the crowd. If the competition implements agile, they will too, not by conviction but by peer pressure. To top that off, scientific development is characterised by the incommensurability of paradigms. Competition between paradigms cannot be solved using logical criteria of evaluation (verification-falsification), as they employ different concepts and methods to address the same problems. As a result, the proponents of each competing paradigm see different things even when looking in the same direction:

> *"If there were only a set of scientific problems, a world in which to be able to deal with them and a set of rules for their resolution, competition among paradigms could be solved by some particular process, such as counting the number of problems solved by each of them. But, in reality, those conditions are never fully satisfied. Those who propose competing paradigms are always, at least slightly, in an involuntary struggle. None of the parties will take for granted all the non-empirical assumptions that the other needs in order to develop his argument ... Competition between paradigms is not a type of battle that can be solved by evidence."* (Kuhn 1962: 229)

Let me give you an illustrative example: Douglas McGregor's two opposite management styles, *"Theory X"* and *"Theory Y"* are based on different assumptions about the human nature. The assumptions that managers have about their employees often turn out to be self-fulfilling prophesies as a result of the so-called *Pygmalion Effect*. This psychological effect says everyone tends to fulfil the expectations of others. If I believe that my workers are trustworthy (Theory Y), they will prove me right. Netflix, the world's leading internet TV network, is a good example, as its core precept is "*Use your best judgment.*" Trust employees' good judgment is the antecedent, and excellence is the consequence. On the contrary, if I believe that my employees are a bunch of lazy and unreliable people, as Theory X maintains, they will also prove me right, and then I am in big trouble because no matter how sophisticated my control systems are, they will be foiled. People will spend all their time and ingenuity cheating the system. Perhaps the best example I have found is the following real story I once was told: a mechanic was enjoying his well-deserved Sunday rest with his family when his boss phoned him. His boat had just broken down, and he asked him if he could go and fix it. Our protagonist drove 80 kilometres to repair it. Days later, the boss called him complaining that he had included two undue overtime hours. The worker replied that it was because of commuting time and that he had not even invoiced the cost of gas. The boss paid grudgingly, but the damage was done. The mechanic told me: *"That's fine if he doesn't trust me, from now on, I will give him a reason. I won't ever do him any favours again. I will cheat on him whenever I can."*

Kuhn's theory adequately captures how new organisational theories triumph. Gill and Whittle (1993) have identified an "organisational life cycle" for ideas whose evolutionary graph is a bell-shaped curve that begins with the "birth" stage, when a new theory is introduced in a seminal book or article; then goes to "adolescence," in which consultants and companies begin to apply the theory; later it reaches "maturity," as the approach spreads and is used by the entire community; and then finally enters "decline", when it starts losing acceptance and is gradually replaced by new ones.

2.4. The Atlas of Organisational Evolution

Figure 2 shows an AQAL map that puts together, in one comprehensive framework, quadrants and levels of development (from Amber to Teal, shown in concentric circles). It is called the Reinventing Organisations Map, a fantastic piece of work developed by Szabolcs Emich. It is a map of what the four quadrants of an organisation, when integrated, might look like and how they would evolve, with each quadrant given its own respected and honoured place and divided into different subcomponents. Emich and his team use the map as an assessment tool to help organisations make conscious decisions about the steps to take in their spiralling climb to the next stage, by providing a detailed view of the organisational consciousness levels and its correlations. They have even created a platform called Atlas, where you can take a self-assessment.

The dynamic combination of quadrants and levels prevents us from reducing the quadrants to separate boxes, as if they were autonomous entities, and help us see the possibilities of organisational evolution in all its splendour. As we have seen in this chapter, the cultural transformation (LL) of an organisation, as it moves from Impulsive-Red, to Traditional-Amber, to Competitive-Orange, to Pluralistic-Green, to Integral-Teal, goes hand-in-hand with a correlative moral evolution from egocentric, to ethnocentric, to worldcentric, to kosmocentric. It is also affected by the other quadrants, the individual (UL and UR), the evolution of the social systems (LR), from autocracy, to bureaucracy, to meritocracy, to

Sociocracy, to Sociocracy 3.0 or Holacracy[43], coupled with a social organisation (LL) that goes from hierarchies to heterarchies, to holarchies. The four quadrants have been differentiated, and although they are not yet wholly integrated (something the 3D-Management model aims to achieve), they are not dissociated either. At this point, each is pursuing its own truth unhampered by domination from the others.

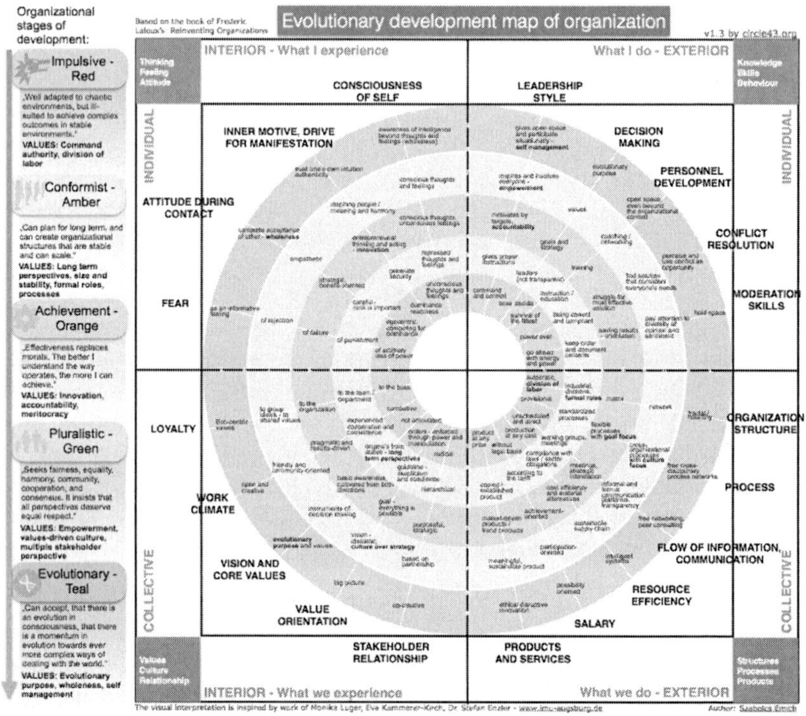

Figure 2. The Reinventing Organisations Map
(reproduced with permission from the author).

[43] Sociocracy, Sociocracy 3.0, and Holacracy are self-organised governance models we will explain in Chapter 4.

2.5. Join the Silent Revolution

"We are on the verge of taking down this virtual reality."- Mr Robot

Most probably, some of you are hesitant about the feasibility of some of the principles that define the next stages of organisational evolution. There are many pages left to dissipate your doubts, but let's stop here for a minute because I might have some answers for some of your concerns.

I have given countless talks, courses, and conferences on the new management paradigm proposed by 3D Management and other analogous theories like Teal organisations, Holacracy, Sociocracy 3.0, and Conscious Capitalism. The most common sceptical reactions go something like this: "This is wonderful, but it won't work here because..." followed by a panoply of excuses such as "it can't be generalised", "this is for tech companies", "that wouldn't work in our sector", "it is not possible in big companies", "this is not the US or Northern Europe", "there is a union here", "this would only work with a highly-educated workforce", or similar misgivings.

My research and experience tell me that this new paradigm can work in *any* organisation, regardless of country, sector, or size. I have intentionally picked the organisations portrayed in this book to show a vast array of examples. If you gaze upwards and behold the star system of post-bureaucratic organisations I have compiled for your amazement, you will see not only the bright stars everyone is talking about (Zappos, Buurtzorg, Morning Star, W.L. Gore, etc.), but a good sample of rising stars that fill up the heavenly vault of light, colour, and variety. Now, let us take some time to address some of the most common objections I have encountered, with concrete examples from my particular sky map:

- **"It is only for companies with a highly-educated workforce":** False. People don't need to have a PhD or an Ivy-League MBA to work in these kinds of organisation. The Californian company, Morning Star, implemented its self-management philosophy in 1990 with the construction of its first factory. Today it is the world's largest tomato processor, supplying approximately 40% of the US industrial paste and diced tomato markets. It has 400 full-time employees. They produce over $700 million a year in revenues. It also comprises a trucking company that moves over two million tons of tomatoes annually and a business that handles the harvesting. Other companies included in this book like Deluz,

FAVI, Irizar, Pressto Peru, Semco, FIFCO, and Whole Foods, have a large component of unskilled labour

- **"It is only for high-tech companies":** When we think about progressive organisations, we tend to think of high-tech companies in Silicon Valley. Technology organisations are indeed among the most advanced, thanks to the pioneering introduction of agile software development techniques, and there are many cases in point in that sector (Zappos, Valve, Netflix, Spotify, Neosoft, Gini, etc.), but examples proliferate in all kinds of industries. Take FAVI, a French company that has been using self-management since 1983 when Jean François Zobrist was appointed CEO. FAVI is as old-economy as it comes, manufacturing brass plumbing fixtures and gear forks for cars. It has more than 500 employees organised in 21 teams of 15 to 35 people called "mini-factories." Most of them are dedicated to a specific customer (the Volkswagen team, the Audi team, the Volvo team, etc.), or else they are support teams (engineering, quality, lab, administration, and sales support). They self-organise, and there are virtually no rules or procedures other than those that the teams decide upon themselves. *FAVI* was the only European producer able to survive Chinese competition. It generates double-digits margins and enjoys a 50% market share in automotive gearbox forks in Europe. The company pays salaries well above average and hasn't had a single order delivered late in over 25 years, nor any strikes. The book presents other examples from such different sectors as dry cleaning, education, movie theatres, health services, and hospitality.

- **"It is for small companies":** Implementing such revolutionary principles is undoubtedly easier in a small company, but there are also many successful examples in big companies. If Morning Star and FAVI are not big enough for you, the largest company I know is the Chinese giant Haier, the world's largest home appliance manufacturer, with global revenues of around $40 billion and over 70,000 employees. Its CEO and chairman, Zhang Ruimin, transformed the company from a near-bankrupt manufacturer of poor quality refrigerators to the world's largest white goods manufacturer. Haier is organised into an ecosystem of small, independent microenterprises (around 200+ customer-facing microenterprises and 3,800+ service and support microenterprises). Each microenterprise enjoys power over its decision-making, personnel selection, and profit distribution. The members of the microenterprises are self-employed and self-organised intrapreneurs.

- **"It can't be generalised":** False again. An entire industry, such as neighbourhood nursing in the Netherlands, has transitioned in less than ten years from Orange to Teal following the leading example of Buurtzorg. The Netherlands has a system that provides medical care at home with nurses. Patients get this care through local organisations. Buurtzorg was created by Jos de Blok in 2007, as a result of his dissatisfaction with the commercial and production-oriented home care model populated with caregivers who were overworked and demotivated. He had a vision of a patient-oriented model driven by a belief in "humanity over bureaucracy," with teams of nurses working in self-organised teams by neighbourhood. It all started with one group of four people in the small city of Almelo. Now it is the fastest-growing Dutch company, with more than 9,000 nurses in close to 900 autonomous teams, and 70,000 patients per year, providing more than half the district nursing in its home country. Government studies have repeatedly shown that Buurtzorg's patients are highly satisfied. Moreover, surveys of employees over several years indicate that the organisation has the happiest workforce of any Dutch company with more than 1,000 employees. The model is also cost-efficient. In the Netherlands, insurers pay for home care on an hourly basis, and on the average, Buurtzorg's nurses use only 40% of the care hours that are allocated per client, resulting in significant annualised savings by the government. The Dutch Government has selected Buurtzorg's model as a benchmark to be followed in the industry, and many other home care providers are already implementing this philosophy. Along the way, it has also applied the same model to "home help," where it employs a further 3,000 or so staff.

- **"It is for the US or Northern Europe":** Examples of vanguard organisations abound in the US and Northern Europe. It is quite understandable, as those countries are among the most socially and psychologically developed in the world. Most of the cases in this book come from those areas of the world and the rest of Europe; however, in my investigation, I have found examples in every corner of the world. The 3D Management Club of Conscious Organisations operates in Spain and Colombia, and one of the early pathfinders of the new management paradigm is Ricardo Semler's Semco, a Brazilian conglomerate that makes industrial machines, which shook the management world with its radical democratic practices described in the best-selling management classic *Maverick!* (1993). Ricardo Semler transformed the company that he inherited from his father in 1980, when he was only 21, from a conventional hierarchical model into a circular structure of small autonomous units, where shopfloor workers set their production targets and schedules, and even decide on their salaries. That transformation resulted in a growth of more than 900 per cent in the first decade, from a medium-sized company to market leadership. At its peak, Semco had around 5,000 employees[44].

- **"It is not for low-cost businesses":** If that's what you think, let me tell you about the very inventor of the low-cost concept, Southwest Airlines. Southwest Airlines is, without a doubt, one of the most successful companies in the history of commercial aviation. No other airline has run profitably for 44 years and counting. In 1971, it redefined the airline business with its low-cost strategy. That model has been replicated by many companies, giving rise to a type of company: the low-cost provider. Still, there are some things that the LUV Airline is not willing to sacrifice to reduce its costs: its exemplary customer service to more than 120 million passengers annually, the satisfaction of its 56,000 employees, and the exercise of values such as fun, love, and celebration. Today, Southwest is the third-largest North American airline and the nation's largest domestic air carrier. It is the first in the sector in customer satisfaction, productivity, safety, growth, and financial results. Post-bureaucratic organisations don't have higher costs than traditional ones. They might be higher in some areas but much lower in others.

---

[44] In 2001, Ricardo Semler started selling many of his Semco shares because he decided to apply his democratic vision in other environments such as consulting, schools, or a whole village. Semco Equipamentos, with around 50 employees, is the one remaining industrial company in his portfolio.

- **"You can't afford to be like that in highly competitive sectors":** The same cost concern, and wrong again. Dm-Drogerie Markt is a chain of retail stores headquartered in Karlsruhe, Germany that sells cosmetics, healthcare items, household products, and health food. In its industry sector, Dm-Drogerie Markt is Germany's largest retailer measured by revenues. They swept the former market leader, Schlecker, out of the market. The company is managed under principles of responsible autonomy and transparency and is an example of social responsibility. For its founder, Götz Werner, the wellbeing of employees is more important than the company's returns.

- **"It is not for public administrations":** Teal is not the colour that first comes to mind when we think about the culture of public organisations. Most of them are stuck in Amber; however, authors such as Gomez et al. (2018) have found evidence of Teal practices in some public administrations of the European Union. One of these pioneer cases is that of the Federal Public Service of Social Security (SPFSS) of Belgium. SPFSS was reorganised in teams, with the subsequent elimination of several levels of hierarchy. Employees make most of the decisions, organise their own work, and are evaluated for their results and not for their work time. The vast majority (81%) work part of their time (up to 3 days) from home. Offices have been replaced by common spaces that favour communication, creativity, and teamwork. From being one of the least demanded destinations (in 2002 only 18% of the new entrants wanted to work there), it is now one of the favourite destinations (in 2016 93% requested to join the SPFSS), and they register productivity increases consistent and superior to two digits (23% in 2009, the first year of transformation, 11% in 2010, 15% in 2011). Other services of the Belgian Government, such as the Federal Public Service of Mobility and Transport (SPFMT), followed in *SPFSS's* footsteps and are implementing a similar organisational model. Also, Erwin van Waeleghem, a police commissioner for the city of Leuven in Belgium, is doing a terrific job implementing Teal practices in police departments. The Netherlands is another hotspot of public administration innovation: The Service for the Protection of Children and Youth in Amsterdam, an organisation in the transition from a model based on the isolated actions of the different specialists, to a different one based on self-managed work teams, focused on the treatment of each individual case. It shows impressive results: the number of instances in which minors have to be removed from their families has decreased by 50%, they have demonstrated achievable annual savings of 30 million euros, in addition to being elected as the best public sector organisation in the Netherlands in 2015.

2.6. Case in Point: The ner Group

Many transformation stories come from threatened companies or industries. When the orthodox approach seems exhausted, experiments are given an opportunity. In 1991, Irizar, the one-century old Spanish coach manufacturer based in Guipuzcoa and part of the Mondragón Cooperative Corporation, was in technical bankruptcy. When Koldo Saratxaga became the new CEO (the third in one year), he took the democratic and participatory principles of Mondragón to the next level and focused on the assembly of luxury coaches (prior to that they had also produced urban buses).

In the 14 years Koldo led Irizar, the company grew 23.9% annually, from €24 million revenues to €310 million. Its innovative management model was recognised worldwide, winning, for example, the European Quality Prize in 2000, which is the most prestigious award in the Old Continent for organisational excellence. Today, Irizar is the leader of its sector in Spain, with a market share of over 40%, and is second in all of Europe. Its turnover exceeds €550 million a year, it has more than 3,000 employees, and it is one of the most awarded and recognised companies in Spain, with significant international expansion and impressive quality and productivity records.

Life for Koldo is structured in 7 year periods. Having completed a 2-periods tenure, he decided it was time to put his knowledge and experience at the disposal of as many organisations as possible. He set up a consulting business (K2K Emocionando) to implement what he defines as a "new style in relationships." The New Style of Relationships ("NER" is its acronym in Spanish) is a humanistic management approach based on principles such as total transparency, no hierarchies, self-management, equality, no redundancies, fair and equitable salary, and profit-sharing.

K2K leads processes of complete organisational transformation. It has taken on the CEO role in 28 companies and is supporting the existing CEO in 23 more. They have also carried out 18 partial processes. They develop their activities mostly in the Basque Country, although they are starting to work in other places.

Twenty-three out of its fifty-one clients are part of a network called The ner Group (usually written in lower case), quite an extraordinary partnership of organisations, united by the “New Style of Relations” as the key enabler of their success. They are sharing knowledge and relationships with society in an ethical and transparent manner, in order to achieve a fair and sustainable human development.

K2K Emocionando has two basic entry requirements for the organisations that want to join The ner Group. First is a total commitment from the ones at the top (and in some cases, other natural leaders, unions etc.). The CEO needs to fully agree that if he or she stands in the way of a successful transformation they can be replaced (as I mentioned earlier, in 28 of the companies K2K has taken over the role of CEO). Secondly, the decision must be democratic. The organisation closes for two days, and the employees visit other companies from The ner Group to speak with staff and to see how they work. Nobody from K2K Emocionando is present during those visits to ensure openness and honesty. Then, everyone votes anonymously in general assembly whether they want to go through the change process. K2K Emocionando only gets involved if more than 80% of the employees are in favour.

Today The ner Group is made up of 2,013 people (a 4% increase over the previous year), with a 317.3 million € turnover (6.5% higher than last year) and 29.8 million € Ebitda (17.8% increase). They export to more than 90 countries and manufacture in 7. As a group, they have created some internal cooperation tools, so they purchase together, collaborate in their internalisation processes, and bid for grants jointly. They have even created a banking pool, called the *Kutxa ner*, that has allowed members in a bad financial situation to obtain loans that they could otherwise not get in the financial market.

Some other indicators speak louder than all this praise I can give:

- The five industrial companies that had better results before starting the transformation process (Ampo, Ekin, Heroslam, Gashor, and Walter Pack), doubled their sales after the first two years. Their profits went up from 3.6% of sales to 15.5%, together with a staff increase of 12%.

- Out of the five industrial companies with worse results before starting the process (Royde, Zubiola, Logos, Lancor, and TTT Goiko), four were already profitable after only two years. They increased the turnover by 50%, and they went from losing 11.6% of turnover to gain 4.4%.
- The five largest service companies of the group (Lejarreta, Sarein, Trebeki, Estudio K, and Urtxintxa), after the first years of the transformation, managed to progress with results of just 1.8% of sales, to an increase of 7.8% with the same sales and with only a slight workforce reduction (as a result of retirements).
- Not a single person was fired for economic reasons in any of the companies in which the transformation process was carried out. That is a basic rule for K2K.
- The salary of the 10% that make more money has to be less than 2.5 times the 10% who earn less. The average salary of The ner Group companies is 27.4% higher than the average of the Basque Country and 41.1% higher than the average of Spain, and we are not taking into account the distribution of results at the end of the year (20% in cooperatives and 30% in the rest of societies).
- Absenteeism is 32.4% lower than the average in Spain, and the accident rate is seven times less.
- On average, 1 out of 5 people participates in the pilot teams, half of them being blue-collar workers.
- There are about six general assemblies a year per company.
- The average team size is five people.
- The presence of women in The ner Group is similar to the industry average in the Basque Country (around 18%), but 25% of the members of the pilot teams are women.
- Social contribution is an essential requirement to join The ner Group. Each organisation has to give 3% of its financial results to social projects and contribute 2% of the people´s time.

A recent development ratifies the enormous social impact of The ner Group. In 2018, the Council of Bizkaia gave K2K the assignment of implementing the New Style of Relationships in companies of the Enkarterri region. Enkarterri has 32,000 inhabitants, is the largest region in Euskadi and the birthplace of the Basque industry in the second half of the 19th century. The crisis was especially harsh there; the competitiveness of its traditional manufacturing companies was severely damaged, and the levels of unemployment had soared. The project aimed to strengthen the existing industry and thereby guarantee the sustainability of the region. A diagnosis and improvement plan was carried out in 19 organisations – nearly every company with more than 20 employees. Eleven of them, employing over 350 people altogether, are now part of the ner Group. Smaller companies were not forgotten: twelve companies of less than 20 people received a transformational workshop and personalised tutoring.

I consider The ner Group the most impressive example of transformation towards a Teal organisational culture in the world. It is just awe-inspiring that so many companies coming from fields as diverse as engineering, manufacturing, law, creativity, cybersecurity, and education, and a whole region of 32,000 people have decided to follow Koldo Saratxaga's vision and adopt the New Style of Relationships.

CHAPTER 3

3D MANAGEMENT

"Tao engenders One;
One engenders Two;
Two engenders Three;
Three engenders all things."
Lao-Tzu. Tao Te King

3.1. The 3D Organisation

The wait is finally at an end. The first two chapters set the stage for the moment you've been waiting for, the presentation of 3D Management.

If I had to choose the defining element of 3D Management, I would say first and foremost that it is an integral theory, then, I would add that it is humanistic, evolutionary, and socially responsible. Now let us take the time to review all those highlights:

Integral: 3D-Management is a distinctly integral theory. It appeared for the first time in 2004 in a book I published in Spanish (*D3D: Un Enfoque Integral de la Dirección de Empresas*), so it is, to the best of my knowledge, the pioneer theory of integral business. It is a Teal theory that shares an integral second-tier worldview with other leading-edge proposals such as the book *Reinventing Organizations* (Laloux, 2014), and *Holacracy* (Robertson, 2015). Those theories have been influenced by Integral Theory (*Reinventing Organizations* is premised on an application of SDI to an organisational context, and Wilber's holon theory inspired Holacracy), so they are integrally inspired and integrally informed. 3D Management goes one step further in its integrality. In addition to being integrally inspired, 3D Management is an integrally-built theory. First, this is because it was developed using a metatheory-building process that combined two large-scale methodologies as guiding resources:

metatriangulation[45] and AQAL[46]. Second, being based on AQAL and the Big-3 dimensions of human existence[47], it analyses organisational reality from as many perspectives, methodologies, types, lines, states, and stages as possible. As a result, it is a metatheory that offers a broader perspective by integrating all previous organisational knowledge in an integral, balanced, and non-marginalising framework. That makes 3D Management much more than a new methodology. It is a new epistemology. It does something that no other theory in the history of management has done before. If the traditional theory-building process aims to exclude other theories, 3D Management is a unifying framework that tries to include as many legitimate ones as possible. That is what metatheory means, a theory of theories. 3D Management is the result of an AQAL analysis of all management science and organisational theories (cf. 2.1) with the explicit aim of including all of their truths. To that end, it takes hundreds of models and theories and weaves them together in a coherent metatheoretical framework. Figuratively speaking its fundamental tool is the kaleidoscope, trying to make sense of the multiplicity of perspectives we can apply to the study of organisations from different fields, schools of thought, and levels of consciousness. My collaborator, Ricardo Martínez, invited the leader of an important Colombian organisation to join the Bogotá chapter of the 3D-Management Club of Conscious Organisations. He was not interested because he supported the conscious capitalism movement. But 3D Management does not want to compete with Conscious Capitalism or any other theory. Instead, its purpose is to connect the insights of many different theories and models (including, of course, Conscious Capitalism, and all the other post-bureaucratic theories) to create a more integrated conceptual system. Think of 3D Management as

---

[45] Metatriangulation is a qualitative research process developed by Gioia and Pitre and subsequently refined by Lewis and Grimes (1999) for building theories recognizing and combining various paradigms. Meta-triangulation identifies the underlying paradigms of different theories to develop new and more complex ones to explain the phenomenon of study. Its process includes three phases: groundwork, data analysis, and theory building.

[46] I don't want to get too academic in this book, so if you are interested in the whole metatheory-building process, you can refer to Robledo, M.A. (2014). "Building an integral metatheory of management." *European Management Journal*, *32*(4), 535-546.

[47] The Big Three is a concept employed by Ken Wilber to refer to the three major value spheres of subjectivity, intersubjectivity, and objectivity (see table 1). These three domains of reality are discernible in all major languages through pronouns that represent first-, second-, and third-person perspectives (I, We, and It/s).

an umbrella theory, a map of maps to navigate organisational complexity. It is like the operating system of your computer, which is compatible with lots of different software. In the same way, 3D Management can comfortably accommodate governance models such as Holacracy, "classical" Sociocracy or Sociocracy 3.0, agile or lean methodologies, certification systems like B corps or the Common Good Balance Sheet, or leading-edge theories such as Deliberately Developmental Organisations, Beyond Budgeting, or the For-purpose Enterprise.

Humanistic: The most common reason why organisations fail is the way people are treated. The basis of all humanistic philosophies is the recognition and respect for the dignity of people. That should be a guiding principle of any organisation. For the Greek philosopher Protagoras, man is the measure of all things, and Kant expressed the fundamental law of his "Practical Reason" as follows: "*Act so that you always take humanity as an end, and never use it as a medium.*" Instead, the capitalist system tends to consider people as merchandise and an instrument of the production system[48]. When we don't treat humans as ends, we are alienating them. Alienation is a term used by Marx to describe the state of a person separated from something to what should be united, or deprived of an essential right. Treating human beings as means is going against their dignity. Wages can't reduce people to commodities, as the machines in the fictional world of *The Matrix*, reduced humans to batteries. We are human beings, not human resources. 3D Management is a profoundly humanistic theory that unfolds people's potential and encourages them to flourish, grow, and find meaning.

Evolutionary: 3D Management holds an evolutionary view of human existence where individuals and collectives develop in predictable, sequential stages, transcending and including one another with increasing degrees of complexity, as we have seen illustrated in the SDI model. The conventional business model is built on premodern traditional and modern industrial rational structures influenced by Amber and Orange worldviews. The centre of developmental gravity of management is Orange, but the time has come to move up the spiral. There is a way out of the monological flatland of conventional business, and it is upwards. 3D Management is a Teal theory that aims to bring organisations to the vanguard of human evolution, the second-tier of development. As we have

[48] Incidentally, there is something fundamentally wrong with a system that considers money more important than people.

seen, a second-tier perspective honours and respects the previous value memes and takes them a step further. It recognises that different circumstances might evoke (or even require) responses from different stages. 3D Management embraces the instinct and intuition of Infrared, the rituality and sense of belonging of Magenta, the autonomy and strength of Red, the order and discipline of Amber, the efficiency and passion for improving of Orange, and the inclusiveness and social awareness of Green. At the same time, 3D Management promotes the vertical development of the members of the organisation as a necessary condition to create a Teal culture, becoming a conveyor belt of human and social transformation. In this way, business, being the most influential institution of the world, can play an essential role in raising global consciousness if, as 3D Management advocates, they commit to becoming practice fields for social change:

> *"People spend more of their time at their jobs than in any other waking activity. What is modeled at their places of employment has a profound impact on people's worldviews and behaviors, as well as on the larger cultural and systems. (...) Bringing Integral Theory to business and developing organizational leaders to become conscious leaders of change is more than just a good idea; it is a primary strategic lever for planetary transformation."* (Anderson 2013).

Socially responsible: Teal is a kosmocentric stage. Social responsibility is part of its nature. At this level of consciousness, the organisation follows moral principles not because society dictates them, or because of external incentives as rewards or punishments, but as a result of a thoughtful and independent decision. However, most of the writings about Teal organisations focus on internal practices. The Teal-organisations' movement is too self-centred, probably because it got carried away by the individualistic nature of this level of development. Self-management, self-organisation… Self is sufficiently covered, but what about the planet and society? Mathias Holmgren analysed the most accessed articles on the *Reinventing Organizations Wiki*[49] on July 9th, 2016. Topics such as the Teal paradigm, organisation structure, purpose and decision-making were the most popular ones, with more than 10,000 entries, followed by others such as compensation and incentives, job titles, role definition, project teams/task

---

[49] A volunteer-driven, self-governing Wiki, under the Creative Commons license, inspired by the book *Reinventing Organizations* (http://reinventingorganizationswiki.com). At the moment of Holgrem's study, the Wiki had been visited approximately 110,000 times.

forces, and self-management, in the range of 3000 to 6000 entries. Environmental and Social Management articles were the least-accessed ones with only 1302 entries.

Let's not forget that one of the strongest criticisms against the corporate world is its lack of social responsibility. That concern is one of the main reasons that brought us here in the first place. We are not happy with the conventional model of management, both from an internal point of view (culture, organisation, and people management) and from an external point of view (social responsibility, sustainability, and relationship with the stakeholders). Social engagement (and other related aspects such as environmental care, diversity, inclusion, and pluralism) is an exceptional contribution of the healthy Green meme, and it must gain even more strength in the Teal stage of development, the first genuinely kosmocentric one. My point is that environmental and social responsibility should be the *sine qua non* conditions for a theory to be considered integral, second tier, Yellow, or Teal (call it as you want). An integral organisation has to think not only of its own good but also of making the world a better place and creating a new model of integral social progress that is not just economic and material but also allows for a more harmonious development of both society and organisations.

Integral, humanistic, evolutionary, and socially responsible: that's 3D Management. If the purpose of a theory is progress toward greater truth, then, dare I say that 3D Management rings truer than any previous theory, because it is the first one in the history of management in the pursuit of an all-quadrant and all-level truth.

3.2. The Integral Management Triad

In Woody Allen's *"The Purple Rose of Cairo,"* Tom Baxter is a movie character who suddenly walks off the screen and into the real world. Liberated from his flat black-and-white world, he discovers a much more complex and richly-coloured three-dimensional reality.

Like Plato's prisoners, chained up in a cave forced to watch shadows projected on a wall, we have been led to believe organisational life is a one-dimensional reality where only profit matters and everything else is ancillary. There is a name for this reductionistic approach, and I explained it in the last chapter: lower-right absolutism. If you ask any entrepreneur why they set up their businesses, making money will be just one of the reasons, and often not the most important one.

It is about time we unchain organisations from their constraining assumptions. Management is not one-dimensional, as we have been led to believe. We need an integral approach so people can break free from their confinements and discover the real nature of work and management: a 3-dimensional reality more conscious, enlightened, and with broader goals than just making money.

A genuinely integral theory should consider, in an inclusive and non-marginalising way, all the different elements that structure organisational reality. As represented in the AQAL matrix (see table 1), the four dimensions of reality to be considered for genuinely integral management are the psychological, the behavioural, the cultural, and the social. The Right-Hand quadrants are objective, by definition, so that they can be grouped together in one single dimension. Therefore, the four quadrants correspond to the value spheres of subjectivity, intersubjectivity, and objectivity, which Wilber (1995, 2000b, 2006) calls the "Big Three" (table 5 fits the Big Three into the AQAL matrix). These three spheres can take many forms: aesthetics, morals, and science; consciousness, culture, and nature; mind, body, and soul; matter, life, and spirit; physiosphere, biosphere, and noosphere, to name a few[50]. In this case, I will use them as science, arts, and ethics.

Do you remember that in the introduction of this book, we reviewed the reasons that made the current management paradigm less and less suitable? Guess what. These reasons can be summarised in the Big Three categories of profit, people, and planet:

- Profit: Mainstream management is no longer responsive and agile enough to deal with frantic environmental changes. Its structures

[50] The Big Three are also present in the three major religions. In Christianity as the Holy Trinity of Father, Son, and Holy Spirit, in Buddhism as Buddha, Dharma, Sangha, and in Hinduism as the Triple Deity or Trimurti, in which the cosmic functions of creation, maintenance, and destruction are personified in Brahma, the creator, Vishnu, the preserver, and Shiva, the destroyer. If that sounds otherworldly to you, let me ground it by saying that Teletón Paraguay, an organisation that works in the rehabilitation of children and adolescents with disabilities, unconsciously incorporates those three symbolic Gods we need to take into account in our lives, by asking three questions in every meeting:

- What should we let die?
- What should we grow?
- What should we maintain?

are not lean and efficient enough to maximise productivity and profits.

- People: People are increasingly disengaged from a system based on distrust and control.
- Planet: A model exclusively focused on profit maximization, disregards sustainability, social and environmental responsibility, and ethics.

<table>
<tr><th></th><th>INTERIOR</th><th>EXTERIOR</th></tr>
<tr><td>INDIVIDUAL</td><td>First-person perspective
(Subjectivity)
ART
“I”</td><td rowspan="2">Third-person perspective
(Objectivity)
SCIENCE
“IT/S”</td></tr>
<tr><td>COLLECTIVE</td><td>Second-person perspective
(Intersubjectivity)
ETHICS
“WE”</td></tr>
</table>

Table 5: The four quadrants reduced to the Big Three (Wilber, 2000b).

These three domains of reality are discernible in all the main languages through pronouns that represent first, second, and third-person perspectives. 1st person is the *person speaking*, 2nd person is the person(s) being *spoken to*, and 3rd person is the person or thing being *spoken about.* A shortened version of this, as we will see, is “I, we/you, it/its”. The third person takes an objective perspective (“It/its’), the first person, a subjective individual one (“I”), and you and I, in communication, make up the “we” that represents the interior perspective of the collective in the first-person plural (“We”). The quadrants, therefore, correspond with “I,” “We,” “It/its.” Freinacht (2017c:315) adds to the analysis that the first-person view corresponds to our sense of self (how I view the “I” in the world), the second-person view to our ideas about right and wrong, or in other words, ethics and ideology (because it is about how I treat you), and the third-person corresponds to our ontology (how we view the world itself).

3D Management, or three-dimensional management, alludes to those three fundamental and irreducible dimensions[51]. It conceives an organisation as a unified three-dimensional reality. Although each will get a chapter of its own, let me first present an overview of the triad of integral management:

- **Science**: This dimension approaches management from a scientific viewpoint using mainly objective and quantitative measures and techniques. Its ultimate goal is to maximise the economic value of the organisation through quality, productivity, and profitability. To this end, the science of management has developed an arsenal of theories, systems, models, techniques, and technologies for planning, organising, and controlling organisations. The scientific dimension is central to the survival of the organisation.
- **Art**: Art takes us into the developmental dimension of management, one of transformation, creativity, imagination, intuition, emotions, aesthetics, design, fun, and passion. It is fuelled by growth and creativity as a result of our evolutionary drive, our innate need to get out of the comfort zone, and create novelty. Therefore, the purpose of the artistic dimension is the development of the organisation, its products, and its members. It aims to create a space of inspiration and expression for people and to develop the organisation through creativity, emotion, beauty, and learning.
- **Ethics**: Ethics is the moral dimension of management. It aims to guide the organisation through ethical principles and values such as honesty, social responsibility, and respect for the environment. From this perspective, the objective of an organisation must be to improve society and to contribute to the common good. Ethics is a sort of metadimension to which the others must be subordinated since it marks the limits of what is right and what is wrong, what should and what should not be done.

[51] Other models developed around the "Big Three" are Dolan and Garcia's (1997) management by values, which is based on the Platonic dimensions of praxis, ethics, and poietics, or Morris' (1997) that focuses on the Aristotelian dimensions of goodness, truth, beauty, and unity.

Each dimension is like a lens through which we view organisations. If we look at an organisation through a scientific lens, we will see systems, structures, and numbers (goals, objectives, roles, resources, processes, responsibilities, performance, policies and procedures, productivity, organigrams, and quantitative results). All objective and expressed in the third person. If we look through the artistic lens, we will see needs, feelings, ideas, values, fulfilment, motivation, enrichment, and commitment. All subjective and expressed in the first-person. Finally, if we look through the ethics lens, we will see responsibility, relationships, conflict, authority, coalitions, bargaining, culture, perspectives, language, and commitment. Intersubjective and second-person "we language".

You need to realise that none of these lenses is better than the others. The more lenses through which you view organisational reality, the better your perspective and decisions will be. The more aspects you take into account about an issue, the more accurate the analysis, and the more valid the conclusions.

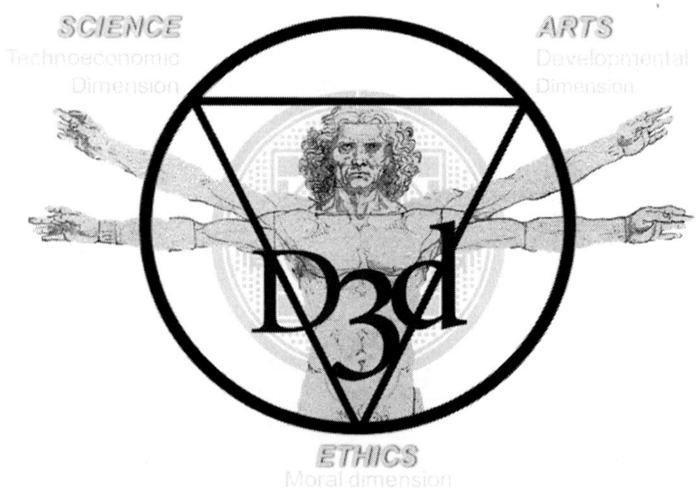

Figure 3: The 3D-Management triangle

The triad of science, arts, and ethics represent equally important phenomenological realities that work as an interconnected and interdependent organic whole. Science is necessary to know what, art to know how, and ethics to know why. This interrelated whole will work as a virtuous circle when every different dimension is given its rightful place and importance, or as a vicious circle when one is marginalised. For example, unethical behaviour might be penalised by consumers, resulting in bad financial results. When excessive focus on one dimension denies the importance, or even the existence, of the others, it unbalances the 3D-management triangle. Unfortunately, this is the case for most organisations, whose triangle is usually biased towards the scientific aspects of their practice, marginalising the other fundamental dimensions. The current business paradigm is primarily concerned with the "what" (performance and quantitative results), not so much with the how (how to improve or change the organisation), and very little with the why (the reasons we do what we do). We will see the consequences in the next section.

It goes without saying that the quadrants are conditioned by the levels. In other words, the 3D-Management triangle will take a different shape according to the average level of development of the organisation. Red and Orange organisations will give more importance to the scientific dimension, while the ethical dimension won't even exist in their map. Amber organisations, while still prioritising science, will grant more relative importance to ethics, but they will struggle with the artistic dimension, as they tend to be resistant to change. Finally, Green organisations recognise the importance of the previously marginalised dimensions of arts and ethics, sometimes even at the expense of science. Some Green organisations have an unbalanced triangle, where ethics (i.e., social issues) or art is the dominating dimension. Social enterprises, for example, pursue a social mission as their primary goal, but they will always have to engage in commercial activities to survive. The same happens to art. It is essential to give the art of management its rightful place in the agora, but no more than that. Just as Romanticism was a reaction against rationalism, certain gurus of the Green meme are trying to make the artistic dimension the dominant one, as a reaction against prevailing scientism. They believe they have found, in the domain of aesthetics, emotion, feeling, and creativity, the new talisman for organisational success. Members of the organisation become heroes of individual expression, and intuition and feelings are exalted over reason and intellect. The hegemony of the artistic dimension would be as limiting as the scientific one, only its sins would be different, including narcissism, rashness, and lack of rigour and systematisation. At the risk of repeating myself, I must insist on finding a balance between all three dimensions. An integral vision comes only after the recognition that all dimensions have to be equally acknowledged and balanced. Teal is the first level qualified to do that.

Let's examine the case of DeLuz y Compañía, a 13-year old Spanish restaurant group with operations in Santander and Madrid. It was created by two brothers, Carlos and Lucía Zamora, and has 160 employees. The company was founded on solid Green social values: 30% of its workers come from social exclusion, and diversity in age, gender, and sexual orientation of the workforce is one of its hallmarks, as well as work-life balance, in a sector that usually vilifies it. They have coined the term "agropolitans" to describe their philosophy: they work with 70% organic products and proximity of farmers, and healthy food is always present on their menus. Despite its social and environmental values, recognised by employees and customers alike (a demonstration of the strength of the ethical dimension), the company was facing problems. In retrospect, an integral analysis discloses that those problems were coming from the scientific and artistic dimensions, and that the issues with one had a ripple effect on the others. Regarding the scientific dimension, the economic results of 2016 and 2017 were worrisome as some restaurants were losing money. One of the reasons originated in the artistic dimension: A very rapid growth, with the opening of four new restaurants in two years, increased debt to unparalleled levels. Also, the scientific dimension had problems of its own, and in turn, that had consequences over the artistic dimension: The company was organised using a hierarchical structure that slowed decision making which crippled initiative and engagement. It was the portrait of a typical Green organisation with a very well developed ethical dimension and outbalanced scientific and artistic dimensions.

In 2018, inspired by Laloux and The ner Group, and with the support of Ouishare, they began a journey of transformation that is shifting them from Green to Teal. In less than two years, we can claim that DeLuz is a much more balanced company, with all the positive consequences it entails.

- The voice and ideas of all workers are now heard. Collaboration is increasing motivation, commitment, and engagement.
- The projects reach completion because they are chosen and co-created by the teams that will carry them out.
- Employees show increased versatility. Cleaners are working on a cost-reduction team and waiters devoting part of their time to a multidisciplinary task force focused on how to sell more in the restaurant.
- There are fewer criticisms with a less toxic environment because people are putting energy into collaborating on joint projects. When conflict appears, they have the tools to handle it.

- Communication has improved. Everyone is now connected with "Slack".
- Decision-making time has decreased.
- Transparency has increased. The financial results of the restaurants are shared every two months.
- Sales have gone up, and financial results have improved significantly.
- Following The ner Group's established practice, 30% of the profit is now shared among the workforce.
- Everyone wants to continue with the Teal-evolutionary journey. Employees are happier and are evolving as workers and as human beings.
- The restaurant group has started to reap the rewards of employees' initiatives. Examples abound, such as a waitress who has an engineering degree who has developed a project in eco-packaging; or a cleaner who decided to learn the use of a POS terminal to help reduce customers' wait time.

3.3. Differentiation of dimensions and scientific imperialism

One Ring to rule them all, One Ring to find them,
One Ring to bring them all and in the darkness bind them.
(*The Fellowship of the Ring*, J.R.R. Tolkien)

As Wilber brilliantly explains in his essential book "*The Marriage of Sense and Soul*" (1998: 11-14), in pre-modern cultures, the spheres of art, science, and morality were not differentiated. For Egyptian priests, medicine, music, and theology were the same thing. In those times, a patient could be prescribed songs as well as herbs. The underlying logic was that the remedies of medicine heal the body, while the soul, the nexus between body and spirit, must be tempered and nourished by music. Finally, the spirit was purified by the divine mysteries of theology. This belief lasted until the Renaissance and was one of the reasons why hospitals and infirmaries were part of abbeys and convents. It also empowered the Church permitting it to interfere in scientific affairs (such as forcing Galileo to renounce his heliocentric theories or burning Giordano Bruno, for his allegedly heretical ideas) or artistic ones (e.g. adding cloths to the once nude figures of Michelangelo's famed Sistine Chapel fresco).

For authors such as Habermas and Weber, what defines modernity is the differentiation of dimensions. Since the Enlightenment, the scope of action of the three spheres separated, each pursuing its own truths without interfering with the others. However, as Wilber notes in many of his works, such a positive and desirable event went too far and became dissociation, fragmentation, and alienation. In the same way, as in *"The Lord of the Rings"* Sauron created the One Ring to control the other Rings of Power and try to gain lordship over the Middle-earth, science colonised, dominated, and ended up annulling arts and ethics so that no different reality was accepted other than the one it revealed, consequently *"the worldview known as scientific materialism became the dominant official philosophy of the modern West"* (Wilber, 1998: 10). The other dimensions became illusory ("what is not measurable does not exist") or annoying ("feelings are bad for business," "business is amoral"). Disgraced and marginalised, they became "X files". Their only sin was to be "unscientific."

Our vision of the world went from being three-dimensional (with all the limitations that an unintegrated vision had in pre-modernity) to one-dimensional. If today many people have only a vague idea about wisdom or spirituality, and if science eclipses art and ethics, it is because we have forgotten that there are different forms of knowledge. Science is only one of them and not even the most sublime. Social progress was reinterpreted from an exclusively scientific perspective of objectivity and materialism, profits and efficiency, and our world fell into spiritual emptiness and superficiality. Modern society fell prey to materialism (and its numerous manifestations -consumerism, body cult, fashion victims- and associated pathologies -anorexia, bulimia, bigorexia, depressions-).

As I demonstrated in my AQAL analysis of organisation and management theories, scientific materialism is the underlying management paradigm (cf. 2.1). Science, in all its manifestations (economics, statistics, technology, finance, accounting, etc.), imposed its instrumental dictatorship and reduced organisations to only objectively verifiable truths. The influence of Comte's positivism[52] resulted in the aspiration to shape management science into a natural science (Bozesan, 2013; Robledo, 2013). "Management

---

[52] Auguste Comte was one of the main precursors and paladins of scientific materialism. Comte elaborated a structure of the evolution of the human spirit defined in his law of the three stages - theological, metaphysical, and scientific - with each stage being less primitive and more complete until the scientific stage crowned the process.

by numbers" reduced the Big Three to the Big One, a flatland of monological, empirical, analytic, positivistic "its." In Douglas Adams' classic radio series "*The Hitchhiker's Guide to the Galaxy,*" a computer is programmed to find the answer to the ultimate question of life and everything. After years of processing, the machine solemnly said: *"The answer is 42."* If that sounds silly, shouldn't it be equally simplistic when someone answers 42 to the question of how is the company doing? Let's face it, the exclusively scientific approach to management, based on a series of assumptions focused only on quantitative results, is appallingly shallow. The only reality it takes into consideration is the objective one. Everything boils down to the "bottom line" in all meanings of those words. The resulting technocratic organisations objectify everything around them, reducing management to a prosaic and instrumental reality that turns interiors into exteriors, subjects into objects, depth into surface, quality into quantity, wisdom into data, reputation into likes, and worth into money. Weber described it as the "iron cage" of rationality, which enriches us materially while impoverishing us spiritually.

I have said it before, but it can hardly be overstated: If we were to represent the management dimensions of most organisations according to their importance, it would look like an isosceles triangle, as they tend to be dominated by a scientific view of their practice. The result: purely materialistic companies with no heart or soul, full of logic but meaningless, overflowing with information but lacking in wisdom, focused on increasing profits at the expense of people, the planet, and everything else involved.

According to Wilber (1995), one of the direst consequences of the hegemony of the scientific dimension is that it reduced arts and ethics to what could be empirically described. In AQAL terms, it collapsed the Left quadrants to their correlates on the Right side. Precisely because there are correspondences between all four quadrants and their associated dimensions, this type of reductionism can be easily carried out. Let me quote Wilber's explanation (1995: 139-140):

> *"For example, I have a thought; a thought occurs to me. That's the given holon, which we will use as an example. For this holon, in the Upper-Right quadrant, there is a change in brain physiology, a change that can be described in completely objective terms (it-language): there was a release of norepinephrine between the neural synapses in the frontal cortex, accompanied by high-amplitude beta waves . . . and so on. All of which is true enough, and all of which is very important.*

> *But that is not how I experienced the thought, and I will never actually experience my thought in those terms. Instead, the thought had an interesting and important meaning to me, which I may or may not share with you. And even if you know what every single atom of my brain is doing, you will never know the actual details of my thought unless I tell you. That is the Upper-Left quadrant or aspect of this holon, this thought that occurred to me (and that is one of the many reasons why the Upper Left can never be reduced without remainder to the Upper Right; strong and general correlations and interactions, yes; detailed reduction, no).*
>
> *Parenthetically, this is why the brain, even though it is "inside" my organism, is still only the exterior of my being—the brain is still Upper-Right quadrant, still exterior. I can surgically cut open a human body and look at all the "insides," even down to the tissues and cells and molecules, but those are not the within or the interior, they are merely more surfaces, more exteriors that now can be seen. They are inside surfaces, not real interiors (which is why they are all listed on the Upper-Right quadrant; they are all the aspects of holons that can be empirically registered)."*

Wilber (1995: 138) sums it up as follows:

> *"In short, the Left was reduced to the Right, and thus interiors tended to get lost and flattened into mere exteriors. Interpretation, consciousness, and interior depth were converted (reduced) to exterior, objective, systems interaction - "I" and "we" were reduced to holistic "its"-."*

According to the monological gaze of scientific management, everything translates into a credit or debit on a balance sheet. Organisations have no within, no interior, no qualitative distinctions, and they can only be approached through an objectifying gaze. Community is reduced to teamwork, human beings to human resources, wisdom into data, and growth into market share. Consumers are merely statistical data, employee satisfaction becomes just an index, and ethics is diluted into compliance with standards such as SA 8000 or ISO 26000. I am not suggesting that you should not use those tools. They are useful, but it is as if you explain love as just being high on dopamine and low on serotonin: You only see the tip of a colossal iceberg.

The most unbalanced triangle I can think of is that of the infamous Valeant Pharmaceuticals. Using an unorthodox growth strategy, the drug company became a Wall Street favourite from 2010 until the beginning of its fall in 2014. Pharma companies grow basically on new product development, so they spend about 18% of revenue on R&D. For Valeant's CEO, Mike Pearson, R&D was just a waste of money. He reduced spending in this area to 3% and based all the company's growth on M&A (mergers and acquisitions). Valeant's primary source of growth was no longer developing new drugs, as everybody else does, instead, they focused on growing revenue by buying out new companies. In only four years, they bought nearly a hundred companies. Originating as an unknown Canadian company, they were about to become the biggest pharma company in the world. Their modus operandi went like this: they found a drug that had a monopoly, bought the company, fired the entire R&D department, and then they increased prices exponentially (from 300 to 5000% in the most extreme cases). Let's not forget we are referring to medicines, some of which were a matter of life or death for their users (e.g., heart medication or insulin for diabetes). In simple English, they were ripping people off by holding a gun to their head. For instance, they increased the price of one of the drugs most used to treat AIDS from $13 to $700, and there was no other medicine on the market of its kind. In one interview, Michael Pearson said it loud and clear: his primary responsibility was to Valeant shareholders, not helping the sick.

A little 3D Management is useful to analyse Valeant's case. Not doing research and not creating new drugs means marginalising the artistic dimension of learning and development. Decreasing R&D expenditure might generate financial value in the short term, but it will undoubtedly result in value destruction in the long term. Their predatory pricing strategies were unethical, and they used "phantom pharmacies" to be able to charge insurance companies those prices more easily, resulting in an accounting scandal that eventually was accused of fraud. Valeant represented an extreme case of scientific or right-hand absolutism. An isosceles triangle where only financial growth mattered. In July 2018, Valeant Pharmaceuticals International changed its name to Bausch Health Companies, in the hope that the reputation of its subsidiary Bausch & Lomb would allow for a fresh start to shed their past scandals.

If we want to avoid any dominance or unbalance, we need, just as in politics, separation of powers between our tripartite management dimensions. Each dimension is genuinely different and should be governed by its own rules. The modes of thinking and techniques used by science are totally different from the ones employed by arts or ethics (it is impossible, for example, to be creative using logical reasoning). Explaining with the eye of science, aspects of other areas such as motivation, social responsibility, fun, job pride, creativity, etc. is, in philosophical terms, a category error. Einstein gave the best definition of category error I have ever found: *"It would be possible to describe everything scientifically, but it would make no sense; it would be without meaning as if you described a Beethoven symphony as a variation of wave pressure."* In the movie *"Contact"* (Robert Zemeckis, 1997), based on the novel by the famous astronomer Carl Sagan, Dr Eleanor Arroway, the sceptic scientist played by Jodie Foster, says that she doesn't believe in God because there is no empirical evidence of its existence. She challenges Palmer Joss (Matthew McConaughey), theologian and spiritual advisor to the White House, to prove the existence of God. He contends that the things of the Spirit can't be seen with the eye of reason (a reference to Kant's famous argument that science can't prove the existence of God, because God is not an empirical object). He made his case asking her if she loved her father. "Yes, very much," she answers. "Prove it," he replies. How can we measure love? Certainly, not by how much we spend on a birthday gift. Science has its limits. It manifests what it is, and that's as far as it goes. Neuroscience reveals that the brain functions differently in ordinary states than in altered states of consciousness, but that does not explain whether a temporal lobe alteration is the result of union with God or schizophrenia.

We can find numerous category errors in economy and business. For example, economists, in their vain attempt to reduce the world to a few predictable rules, invented the principle of economic rationality, or simply the economic principle. Just a quick look at the stock market shows how wrong it is. Stock investors are far from being rational economic subjects. They behave more like out-of-control teenagers, capriciously falling in and out love with stocks. Whether we like it or not, we are not machines. A scientific perspective is sufficient to analyse a computer, but a person incorporates other aspects: perceptions, feelings, emotions, beliefs, values, etc. One more example is a branch of the economy, called environmental economics, whose purpose is to ascertain the economic valuation of the environment. Its mere existence bears witness to our quantitative blunder. It is regrettable that we need an economic assessment to protect the environment. Question: What is the economic value of a sunset on the beach with your loved one?

The theory of the multiple bottom lines shares the same Orange style of thinking. I don't need to say I'm in agreement of the concept, and I accept that it is helpful to measure the impact of a company on the environment and society because what you measure is, at the end of the day, what you are paying attention to. One way to change reality is to change what we measure, how we measure it, and why we measure it. Only when companies report on their social and environmental impact will we have responsible organisations. But not everything needs to be measured in order to do the right thing. It is tricky to evaluate the planet and people in the same terms as profits—that is, in monetary terms. The cost of an oil spill, for example, can't be reduced to cash. In AQAL terms, that is Lower-Right imperialism. As Albert Einstein once said, "Not everything that can be counted counts and not everything that counts can be counted".

The anti-capitalist movements portray corporations as a dark force that is the root of all evil. We have to admit they can be incredibly dangerous and destructive, but, in my opinion, corporations are not so much the forces of darkness as they are the forces of shallowness. Machado said that *"societies don't change until their gods change."* Money is the God of our (Orange) society and science its religion. The time for change has come. The myth of Prometheus symbolises the transition from a dualistic (first-tier) to an integral (second-tier) consciousness. According to Greek mythology, Prometheus stole the fire (symbol of the Spirit, creative power, and conscience) from the Gods to illuminate the Earth. Similarly, the integral vision of 3D Management brings the spiritual light to set organisations free from their rationalistic and materialistic prison.

The 3D Management model honours the complexity of management and organisations by turning the monological flatland of traditional management, dominated by the fragmenting assumptions of science, into a 3-dimensional reality, with a more multifaceted and inclusive vision. The scientific view and the values it encompasses (objectivity, efficiency, productivity, profit) are merely one aspect of the complex organisational reality that must peacefully coexist with the other dimensions. 3D-Management provides the conceptual framework to give its rightful place to every dimension and to recognise the relationships between them. Under its influence, organisational aspects like profitability, quality, spirituality, ethics, creativity, emotions, etc. are brought together, for the first time, into one integrative and coherent conceptual system. Indeed, other theories admit the importance of the different dimensions, and even focus on multiple "bottom lines," but they tend to subordinate them to the scientific objective of profit maximisation. 3D-Management goes beyond that, challenging common knowledge with a critique of the paradigm that currently drives management practice. Its integral gaze uncovers the distortions of the mainstream management ideology and the unbalanced forms of organisational activity its monistic approach produces. Ultimately, 3D Management advocates for a change of regime, in which the absolutist imperialism of science is replaced by a harmonic triumvirate that takes into account the perspectives of each dimension without any of them dominating the others.

3.4. The Big Three and the Fantastic Four

"One for all and all for one." (*The Three Musketeers*. Alexandre Dumas).

As Ken Wilber explains (1995: 16), from the time of Plato, the perennial philosophy has recognised that the Big Three *"were one continuous and interrelated manifestation of Spirit, one Great Chain of Being that reached in a perfectly unbroken or uninterrupted fashion from matter to life to soul to spirit."*

To avoid any imbalances in the management triad, we cannot contemplate its dimensions as isolated components, but as a whole. To do that, we need a fourth dimension which integrates the Big Three in an essential unit.

The Big Three are so big that they transform into the Fantastic Four. The fourth management dimension is the spiritual, that aspect of our nature that strives for unity. Its concern is the whole rather than the parts, and thus it aspires to join the three dimensions of management in one unified possibility. Accordingly, science, arts, and ethics are all integral expressions of spirit, and none of them can claim isolated authority; each is to be honoured in its respective task. The three of them should blend into an intimate, interdependent, and mutually reinforcing union that creates purpose, which gives direction and community, and provides internal cohesion. Just like the Three Musketeers found their maximum expression as a group with the incorporation of d'Artagnan, the spirit is the fourth musketeer of our management triad.

Thanks to the inclusion of the spiritual dimension, we can achieve real tridimensionality (i.e., more depth). The 3D Management triangle turns into a pyramid (as shown in figure 4) when we add the spiritual dimension at the apex, in recognition of the importance and integrative nature of that dimension.

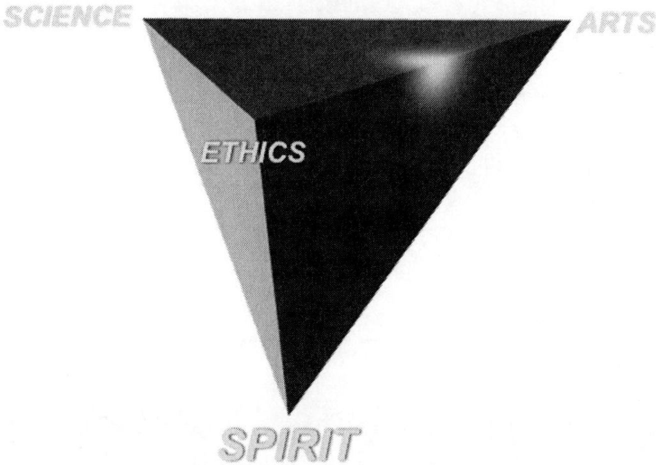

Figure 4: The 3D-Management pyramid.

Spirituality can be regarded as a fundamental human longing for wholeness and completion. Unity is the ultimate goal of the noetic or spiritual: the limitless integration between our thoughts and actions, our reason and emotions, ourselves and the others, business and the environment, the environment and the Universe (Zohar and Marshall, 2004). An ultimate unity that leads directly to wisdom.

The spiritual dimension reminds members of the organisation what is most important to them collectively, what they care most about, and what they stand for, or are up to, in the broader sense.

In the symbolist tradition, three is the number of spiritual syntheses, and the ternary is the number of the idea. Four is the number of minimal totality and rational organisation of the tangible realisations, and the quaternary is the number of the achievement of the idea. Therefore, I have chosen to represent graphically and symbolically 3D Management the quaternary driven by the ternary (figure 5). The sphere, which represents the spiritual dimension, means totality and perfection. Its place outside of the triangle conveys, with the idea of movement, the contradictions, and diversities of the angles and the sides.

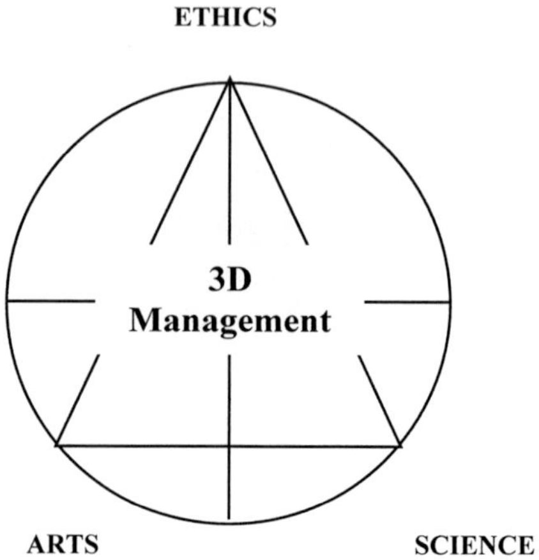

Figure 5: The symbolic representation of 3D Management.

3.5. The Pillars of 3D Management

3D management is a management philosophy, not a recipe. There is not a single way to be a 3D-Management organisation. Still, there are some fundamental principles to consider. As shown in figure 6, 3D-Management relies on four central tenets: integral purpose, total stakeholder orientation, integral leadership, and responsible autonomy and holarchy[53]. Same as it happened with the four dimensions of the theory, the four pillars are interconnected and mutually reinforcing.

[53] Those tenets are loosely inspired by the ones identified by Mackey and Sisodia (2013) for the Conscious Capitalism theory.

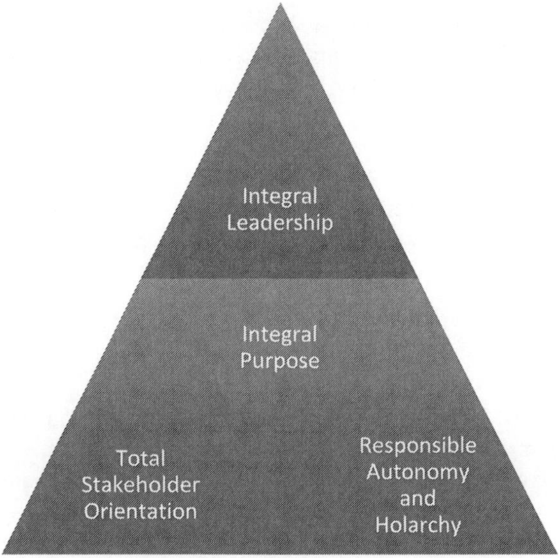

Figure 6: The four tenets of 3D Management

Integral Purpose: Any first-year management student will tell you that the purpose of business is to make money. Traditional management theory has spread the myth that the goal of business is profit maximisation. Everything else comes second to that. That statement is monological and reductionist since it only applies to the scientific dimension. 3D management organisations subscribe to a purpose that is different from, and goes beyond, making money. From the perspective of this integral theory, the purpose of business is still creating value, but in a holistic way. If we define value integrally, the concept incorporates other connotations in addition to the purely materialistic one of making a profit. An integral business should aim to simultaneously create multiple kinds of wealth or value (technical, economic, intellectual, aesthetic, emotional, experiential, social, cultural, ethical, environmental and spiritual, to name a few). The integration of them all, in a spiritual mission, gives an integral purpose to the organisation. A 3D-Management organisation seeks to maximise its value not just to their shareholders, but to society as well, through the achievement of a purpose that satisfies the needs of all stakeholders involved. Thus, value is multidimensionally redefined so that it contributes to the welfare and happiness of the highest possible number of people.

Responsible autonomy and holarchy: Self-management, democracy, and transparency are essential elements of 3D Management. Teal organisations like Zappos, Ouishare, or CineCiutat have no bosses and are organised into self-managed teams. Others like Semco or Buurtzorg go as far as to let their employees even decide on their salaries. These organisations use governance models such as Sociocracy 3.0 or Holacracy and have precise rules about how to function. However, getting rid of formal bosses does not mean hierarchy disappears. That is a common misunderstanding in this new tendency towards boss-less organisations. 3D Management resorts to integral theory to restore organisational depth and adopts a holarchical organisational structure that makes self-management and hierarchy fully compatible.

Integral Leadership: You can't have an integral organisation without integral leaders behind it. And when I'm saying leaders, I don't mean bosses, as I have explained in the previous tenet. Integral leaders strive to achieve the organisation's purpose, creating value for all stakeholders. One of the defining characteristics of integral leadership is the ability to balance and harmonise different dimensions and interests into a single project. In a purely integral fashion, it integrates the major styles of leadership based on the recognition that all of them will work with some of the people some of the time, but no single approach works with all types of people all of the time (Thomas, 2014). The power of Integral Leadership lies in transcending and including all the other styles, or schools, of leadership. As Thomas (2014) asserts: "*The promise of Integral Leadership is to know when, where and with whom a given leadership approach will reliably work (and when it will reliably fail).*" Integral leadership acknowledges all of the factors in a given situation, with a given person or group of people, and in a given organisation to know which approaches to draw upon, and always taking into consideration that the four dimensions of science, art, ethics, and spirit have to be balanced and combined inseparably in any action or decision. In particular, it requires a deep understanding of where people are (their needs, motivations, values, goals, capabilities, etc.) to interact in a way that is appropriate and helpful.

Total stakeholder orientation: Stakeholders[54] are all the people, groups, or organisations that have an interest or concern in an organisation.

---

[54] Sisodia et al. (2007: 12) came up with the acronym "SPICE" as a memory tool that identifies the five major stakeholders of modern corporations: Society

Stakeholder orientation has evolved together with the value memes. Red and Amber organisations only consider those in power. Orange organisations mostly care about shareholders and customers. Orange holds that for-profit companies should operate with a shareholder perspective, so that management's primary obligation is to maximise profits for investors. All these perspectives share an "either/or, win/lose" mindset. 3D Management favours a "both/and win/win" view. Viewing the interests of all the stakeholders as intertwined and interdependent is the way to respect the dignity of every one of them and actively align their interests in a balanced and non-marginalising way so that no single stakeholder group gains at the expense of the others. It is a philosophy that nurtures a reciprocating relation with all stakeholders, who are treated as partners. The key is to align the interests of the organisation with those of the different stakeholders. When that happens, meeting the needs of all parties is not difficult. All of them come first, whereby the requirements of all parties are satisfied. The result is a virtuous circle of value creation for everyone concerned.

3.6. Case in Point: CineCiutat

In 2012, the Renoir chain of cinemas announced that its art-house theatre in Palma de Mallorca, Spain, was turning the lights off. This time for good. That's all folks: One more theatre was going to disappear in the wake of several converging factors: the economic crisis, a disproportionate increase in taxes for cinema exhibition in Spain, the switch from 35mm film to digital, and the new and fierce competition of streaming services like Netflix, Amazon, and HBO. The Renoir was the only cinema in Mallorca where you could enjoy other kinds of movies different from the blockbusters, shown in their original language with subtitles.

However, this story was going to have a happy ending, just like in the movies. A small number of heroes, led by documentary producer Pedro Barbadillo, came to the rescue and started a social revolution. "Let's save the Renoir" was their call. Over 800 people gathered together with that goal in mind. They placed their hopes, confidence, and money into that vision and became members of the Xarxa Cinema Association, which would operate the cinema with Pedro as the president. Immediately, one hundred volunteers started working (yours truly included), and in less than

(communities, governments, NGOs), partners (suppliers, retailers…), investors, customers, and employees.

three months, the lights of the theatre were turned on again. The marquee of neon lights was making a new name dance: CineCiutat, a clever play on words between the Catalan nickname for the city Palma (Ciutat) spliced with Cinecittá, the legendary Italian film studio.

Like the phoenix, CineCiutat was reborn from its own ashes, turning a deadly crisis into a metamorphic opportunity. It has been more than seven years, and CineCiutat continues to offer the people of Mallorca theatrical content that otherwise might not be seen. Over the years, CineCiutat's membership model has proven to be a successful formula. It is so much more than simply locking customers into a regular payment system. We have developed a mutually beneficial, long-term relationship with our members, who have taken ownership and feel as though the cinema is theirs. We have built a community that shares common interests, many of whom actively work as volunteers.

However, CineCiutat had to face a second crisis only two years after its birth. The movie theatre was a typically Green organisation, operated under democratic principles. A Board of Directors (elected every two years by the assembly of members) was responsible for the governance of the project. The day-to-day running of the cinema was delegated to a general manager, who led a small permanent core of six employees, and an "ecosystem" of voluntary members, who worked temporarily and part-time in six working committees: Programming, Classic Reruns, Communications, Events, Education, and "Think Tank". Most of the decisions had to be made by consensus, which generated many problems and tensions. The decision-making process was long and painful, and no agreement was final. Many good initiatives of enthusiastic members were cut down by a lack of accord. I remember some hilarious, and even surrealistic, statements heard in CineCiutat's general assemblies, such as "Let's vote if we vote" or "I agree with your proposal, but I will support the other one for the sake of diversity." The strain that kind of culture exerted on effectiveness and connection to each other was too much to bear.

One of the most significant tensions the organisation suffered had to do with the 3D-Management dimensions of art and science. CineCiutat's positioning as an "arthouse cinema" set it apart from multiplex cinemas. Yet, at the same time, it still depended on profits to survive. The conflict between these two goals was a constant source of tension among the membership, who clustered into "idealists" and "pragmatists." Idealists conceived CineCiutat as a kind of film library whose billboard should advocate more radical, independently-produced, artsy and experimental movies. On the other hand, pragmatists took a contrary position that prioritised commercial values to make the numbers balance. Try to achieve consensus in that situation!

After a series of internal struggles that resulted in the announcement of elections, amid an operational block that lasted for six months, the turning point was the resignation of the general manager, Javier Pachón, a brilliant and visionary individual who grew tired of not being able to get anything done. But Javier couldn't simply let his baby die, so he returned to save the day supported by the former president and inspirer of the project, Pedro Barbadillo. He was aware of my model and was convinced that the only solution was to evolve from Green to Teal and to implement 3D Management. He ran for president, won the election with a brand-new board, and the transformation process was put into action.

3D Management is particularly suitable for an organisation like CineCiutat, which needs to find a perfect balance between its cultural aspirations (artistic dimension), its survival needs (scientific dimension), and its social and ethical vocation.

Our main organisational objective was to overcome the current paralysis and become an action-oriented organisation. CineCiutat adopted six organising principles:

1. Responsible autonomy: All members were given maximum independence in their areas of responsibility.
2. Self-organisation in work teams.
3. Participation and co-responsibility in decision making.
4. Decision-making based on consent, not on consensus.
5. Transparency.
6. Systematic and immediate resolution of conflicts.

The first step was to adopt a holacratic governance structure, so we turned the old committees into circles (see figure 7), which, as we will see later in the book, implied a move from heterarchy to holarchy. CineCiutat's second revolution was underway.

Circles are either permanent (e.g., operations, programming, or development) or temporary. The latter may fluctuate as members perceive the need for changes in the organisation. (e.g., a circle was created to organise the fifth-anniversary party, and once done, it dissolved).

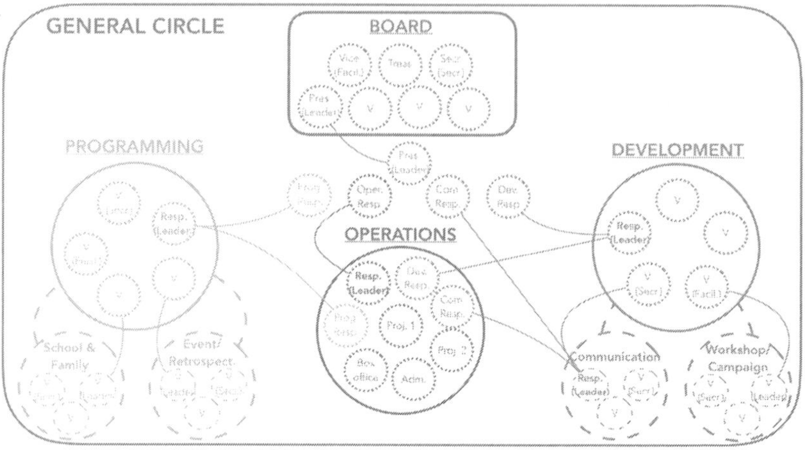

Figure 7: CineCiutat's structure.

Everyone's initiative is essential in an organisation with limited resources, as is the case of CineCiutat. Any worker or volunteer can propose projects or actions to a circle in a governance meeting. If approved, ideally he or she becomes the owner or leader, working as a freelancer, with full authority within its context. The circle where the project has been created becomes the internal customer of the owner of the project, who then acts as a self-managed internal supplier. If the person or the circle thinks he or she is not qualified to lead the initiative, either someone else is appointed as a leader, or the circle itself appoints a coach or somebody to report to, or consult with before making any significant advances. If the project cannot be carried out by only one person, it is also possible to create a new circle, with the support of the organisation.

Although the 3D management model is designed to find the right balance between its three constituent dimensions, if we wanted to weather the tensions between the economic and the artistic dimension, then we needed to define a shared organisational purpose to negotiate any differences. Using Open Space methodology, we invited all of the members to discuss their vision of the organisation. After receiving the qualitative, in-depth perspective of our more devoted members, we sent out a quantitative study, segmented by members (the association has around 1000), employees, and the board. The results of both studies helped clarify essential aspects such as:

- Finding the right balance between auteur and quality-commercial films, or experimental and conventional movies, and at the end of the day, between box office revenues and artistic ventures (science vs. art).
- Working out a healthy mix of first-run films and repertory.
- Defining the balance between traditional programming and special events.
- Finding out what genres our members prefer.
- Determining what kind of films they like[55].

The questionnaire also included questions about purpose and values, and, thanks to those responses, we were able to define our mission, vision, and values.

CineCiutat's purpose was defined as: *"CineCiutat is more than a cinema. It is a space to dream and share."* This statement encapsulates our challenge to make ourselves attractive and competitive in the face of the explosion of options for home viewing alongside the importance of communal physical experiences. We intended to do that by going above and beyond the traditional theatrical experience by finding new, innovative formulas to motivate people to leave their homes, thereby contributing to the ongoing vitality of moviegoing.

The association has a clear vision for the future: *"CineCiutat wants to be the hub, the meeting point for cultural, social, and environmental action through innovation, development, and citizen participation."*

Hence, our objectives:

- Offer cinematographic diversity
- Develop young and new audiences
- Explore multi-disciplinarity in the arts
- Provide an Innovation Lab between culture & tech
- Serve as a local and international Creative Hub
- Defend European values of equality & diversity
- Be a platform for social & environmental activism
- Promote citizen participation

---

[55] We devised an amusing "CineCiutat Index" for that purpose. Interviewees were requested to rank a long list of movies according to "how CineCiutat-like they were". This information is an excellent yardstick for the programming circle.

- Find responsible financial stability

And, in addition, a set of six fundamental values:

- We are culture.
- We are community.
- We are different.
- We are dreamers.
- We are participatory.
- We are conscience.

Seven years after its re-opening, CineCiutat is the main venue for all the film festivals that take place in Mallorca, it has received the Gold Medal from the City of Palma, it is the only Spanish Cinema that has moved to 100% renewable energy, and it has expanded beyond its walls, by bringing its programs to other towns in Mallorca with open-air projections. These are significant feats for a small and modest movie theatre which has become a European reference for independent cinemas, as a board member at CICAE, the International Confederation of Art Cinemas, and the only Spanish Cinema represented at Europa Cinema's Innovation Hub.

3.7. As above so below

The integral philosophy of 3D Management fundamentally redefines not only management as a whole, but each of its functions and disciplines. Each of the subsystems of an organisation equally has three managerial dimensions so that the model can be applied at that level too. It applies to operations, marketing, finance, human resources, etc. All of them have three independent and interrelated dimensions that must be balanced.

Just as an illustration, let's see how an integral approach to marketing would work. Like any other business discipline, marketing can be broken down into its constituent dimensions of science, arts, and ethics. Marketing is a science because of its use of the scientific method. As such, it includes a series of theories, models, and techniques (segmentation, market research, pricing, etc.). Art is also essential for such a creative discipline, especially in areas like product development and promotion. And finally, there is the ethics of marketing (with heated subjects such as pricing, sales, subliminal advertising, stereotyping and sex in advertising, invasion of privacy, electronic spam, deceptive advertising, etc.). When it comes to attracting customers, the principle is the same. We can appeal to reason (science), emotions (arts), morality (ethics) or spirituality:

- Rational marketing: The rational claim underlines the tangible and technical benefits of the product or service that beat the competition. The message focuses on demonstrating the superiority of the product or service in specific attributes such as price, quality, or performance through rational arguments, like scientific tests or statistics. It is among the most traditional methods of persuasion, and it is widely used in the promotion of industrial goods and high-quality products. In industrial goods, the rational argument is compelling because the potential buyer usually has excellent technical knowledge of the product and is accountable for the purchasing decisions. In consumer products, high price is a determining factor to make a rational choice, based on an informed decision and the comparison of alternatives.
- Emotional marketing: The objective of an emotional claim is to elicit some affective response that influences behaviour, be it positive (humour, love, pride, happiness) or negative (fear, guilt, shame). Research indicates that purely rational purchases have less and less weight, being gradually replaced by emotional factors such as the fundamental influence on consumer behaviour[56]. Advertisers know this very well, and more often they use emotional arguments (humour, feelings, stories, etc.) than rational ones. Harley Davidson is one of the best examples of a brand's emotional power. The company, founded in 1903 by Bill Harley and the Davidson brothers, sells much more than good bikes. Ever since the movie *Easy Rider* (1969) portrayed the lifestyle of bikers and made the American brand a cult phenomenon, the motivations for buying a Harley bike, or any of its related products (from clothing to jewellery, to themed restaurants), have little to do with reason - price, benefits, etc. - and much more with emotions - desire, passion, rebellion, etc. -. The Harley bike has become a legend inscribed in chrome letters, an object of desire, an icon of transgression, and a symbol of freedom. Its customers are enthusiastic apostles with tattoos of

[56] In our materialistic and superficial society, many people shop to express their individuality ("I shop therefore I am"), in a futile attempt to distinguish themselves from others by buying the same stuff.

the brand logo on their arms as a symbol of their eternal and unbreakable relationship with Harley Davidson.

- Social marketing: One of the traditional criticisms against marketing is that the satisfaction of individual needs is incompatible with long-term social good. We all know that there are products that may satisfy some immediate needs but have adverse side effects, from that cigarette as tasty as unhealthy to that car as fast as polluting. Social marketing tries to combine the satisfaction of the needs and interests of the individual with the contribution to the greater social good. It seeks to balance three things: the objectives of the company, customer satisfaction, and the common good. Real social marketing does not simply take a finished product and attach social value to it. The most effective social marketing is integral. Social considerations are taken into account from the very beginning to develop the product or service around its potential social value, benefitting the common good on as many levels as possible, from the choice of suppliers to the establishment of production specifications. When people realise that a company is making efforts to help the community, they will want to be associated with it and buy their goods and services. Companies usually position themselves in certain political, social, or environmental issues and even campaign for or against them, as is the case of Ben & Jerry's (gay marriage, the death penalty, etc.), or Patagonia, famous for its environmental activism. The downside is that together with followers, opponents are acquired, but who cares as long as you are standing for what is right. As Patagonia says, *"activism and advocacy are critical to achieving our mission. We'll always act, even if we lose some business along the way."*
- Spiritual Marketing: The spiritual is booming in a society as much in need of it as ours. It is an indication, in some cases, clumsy and opportunistic, that people are moving slowly to postmaterialistic values. The aim of real spiritual marketing is not to merely sell products or services, but also meaning and transformation. Spiritual marketing attempts to take customer relationships beyond mere transactions into a more profound level. Spiritual marketing does not need to deceive people to sell. At this level, there is no place for hypocrisy and cosmetic campaigns. It is no longer a matter of putting makeup on the brand to match what the customer wants or seducing the public with voluptuous models or hollow promises. It is about telling the

customer who you are and what you stand for, to establish a deep spiritual connection with them based on dialogue, mutual knowledge, and sharing the same values.

Finally, for a 3D-management company, marketing is not a separate activity but is integrally aligned with its purpose. As we see in Figure 8, the integral purpose (the essence of the company, the reason why it exists) shapes the corporate identity, which, in turn, determines the brand image in the market. For example, it wouldn't make sense that Southwest Airlines, known as the "Luv Airline" didn't treat employees well, or that Volvo plants didn't have proper safety conditions for their workers. The organisation must be able to define itself in a coherent and connected way. The smaller the discrepancy between how the company sees itself, how it would like to be seen, and how the market sees it, the better. Consequently, the company must have coherence between purpose and positioning. The internal must connect with the external. In 1986, one of the co-founders of Whole Foods Markets started selling cigarettes in one of the company's stores as an experiment. Although the initiative was profitable, when the CEO John Mackey discovered it, he asked his partner to discontinue, as it contradicted the healthy philosophy of the company. Whole Foods apologised and stopped selling cigarettes.

All in all, there must be congruency between values, objectives, and actions. For this reason, CineCiutat has an ethical code that defines which companies to work with. Conversely, whenever there is a conflict between values and profits, AES chooses its values even though doing so might result in diminished returns or foregone opportunities.

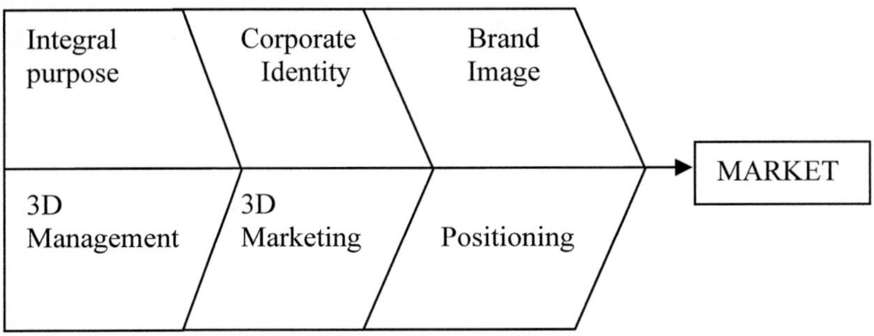

Figure 8: A 3D Marketing model

Scholars classify the evolution of marketing throughout the years in four stages according to the philosophy that dominated the discipline:

- Production philosophy: During the Industrial Revolution, the assumption was that consumers would favour products widely available and highly affordable. The focus was on the operation, regardless of the customer.
- Product philosophy (1900s-1930s): It assumes that consumers will choose products based on quality, performance, and innovative features. It also believes that the company knows best what is good for the consumer.
- Selling philosophy (1930s-1950s): The emergence of the selling philosophy was a result of the increase in competition which eventually led to an increase in customer choice. The principal task of marketing is to persuade the customer to buy. The idea was that the company could sell any product with the use of these selling techniques.
- Marketing Philosophy (from the 1950s): The starting point for marketing is the customer needs and wants, and no longer aggressive selling. The customer is king, and the objective is the satisfaction and the loyalty of the customer.

This classification can easily be related to SDI. The two first stages are reminiscent of an Amber worldview, while the last two inherit the Orange value meme. Some authors add a further stage in the 1970s, the societal marketing philosophy (that I just explained), which is typically Green.

Now, what would a Teal marketing philosophy look like? I suggest that the next stage of marketing evolution is a *stakeholder philosophy*, which is based on the precept that the customer is no longer the only king. The throne will have to be shared with the rest of the stakeholders. Put differently, every stakeholder should be treated as a customer, to satisfy all needs and wants. Customer centricity remains as essential as ever, but the circle of "customers" widens to embrace all stakeholders. Thus, members of the organisation are internal customers (a central concept in 3D Management, as we will see), the planet also becomes a customer whose needs have to be served, and so forth. Groundbreaking? Of course.

3.8. The Real Teal

In 2016, I attended a Teal-organisation's workshop organised by Enlivening Edge at the 2nd Integral European Conference in Hungary, an event not to be missed for all the integral community. One of the participants talked about a self-managed organisation whose purpose was maximising profits. In her opinion, the company fulfilled all the conditions to be Teal. I can't disagree more. Teal is a kosmocentric stage, and a Teal purpose can't be as reductionist as that. Laloux clearly states that the purpose of a Teal organisation goes beyond profit. Making money is just a means to an end, and that end is purpose. Having said that, I can understand her confusion. Although Laloux rejects profits as an ultimate purpose, he does not specify what an appropriate purpose would be. That woman's mistake would have been much more unlikely had she been familiar with 3D Management as it clearly defines a hierarchy of dimensions with the objectives of the scientific dimension (maximising profit), artistic dimension (development), and ethical dimension (making a better world) being just as instrumental as the final objective of the spiritual dimension, which is none other than the purpose of the organisation. Ultimately this purpose is spiritual in nature, i.e., meaningful and transcendental. As we will see in chapter 7, 3D-Management's integral purpose requires it to transcend and include the objectives of the other dimensions.

This is just an example of the many misunderstandings I have encountered concerning what a Teal organisation is or should be. In most cases, they are derived from a lack of knowledge of Laloux's theory, but in other cases, they are the consequence of shortcomings and imprecisions that would need to be addressed.

Please, don't get me wrong. It is not my intention to criticise the book at all, only to contribute to the development of Teal organisations. In my opinion, *Reinventing Organizations* is one of the best management books ever written. It is insightful, groundbreaking, practical, well researched, and compellingly written. It has single-handedly created a movement of Teal organisations based, as we saw, on its description of the three innovations of this new paradigm: evolutionary purpose, wholeness, and self-management.

Now that I have stated my good intentions, I must confess that I have some issues with the famous three criteria. Actually, not with them, but with the idea of using them as a checklist to qualify an organisation as

Teal. I also don't think that was how Laloux intended the three criteria to be used. He only identified some common traits in the companies he studied, but I don't think he wanted them to become the "Three Commandments of a Teal Organisation", as many people may think of them. It would be like saying that to be a top-ten-tennis player you must necessarily have a big serve. Most of the players that make it to the top of the ATP ranking do have big serves, but not all of them. Nadal is the most recent prominent case. To return to our case in point, we have been discussing how imprecise it can be to label a person as Teal. Defining an organisation as Teal is even more complicated. There is no procedure or list of instructions to follow to become Teal, and the book *Reinventing Organizations* certainly does not intend to be an implementation manual. If we address the three features, we will see they are not Teal breakthroughs in a strict sense, and that they may be either incomplete or improvable.

Let's take self-management first. Needless to say, I am a big fan of the concept. I teach it as a professor, I use it as a practitioner, I recommend it as a consultant, but I don't think every Teal organisation should necessarily use it. Imagine you have a mostly Red-centred workforce. Would you implement a self-management model there? Self-management requires responsible autonomy, and that is not one of the virtues of the Red mindset. In the case of rejecting the option of self-management, is the organisation automatically ineligible for the Teal qualification?

Furthermore, I find it questionable to consider self-management a Teal breakthrough. To be fair, it was the Orange meme that invented self-management. The first experiments with autonomous workgroups and self-managing teams were in the seventies in the UK (e.g., the Longwall coal mining study by the Tavistock Institute) and in the United States (e.g., the Topeka Gaines dog food plant experience), where these were carried out by Orange-centred companies. The substantial productivity gains and cost savings of self-management identify them as a good practice. In the late 80s and early 90s, self-management was used by pioneering Orange organisations such as Saab, Volvo, Johnsonville Sausage, General Mills, and Oticon, and even such big companies as General Electric, HP, 3M, Airbus, Xerox, and Monsanto experimented with the approach in their quest for productivity and profits. Later, "lean manufacturing" (as developed by Japanese companies like Toyota and Honda) included self-organisation as one of its fundamental principles. Those practices were largely responsible for the salvation of companies as notable as Harley Davidson. Harley Davidson's turnaround from nearing extinction to remarkable success was led by former CEO Rich Teerlink using "lean" manufacturing strategies and changing the structure from a command and control, top-down management style, to one of autonomous cross-functional circles. Software developers were also self-organising pioneers with their Agile and Scrum methodologies developed initially by people like Jeff Sutherland and Ken Schwaber[57]. One of the main principles of Agile philosophy is to organise into small, autonomous teams, working in short cycles, on small batches, and getting continuous feedback from the customer. Agile has expanded beyond software development, scaling up company-wide to become a full-fledged management philosophy, applicable to any area and sector. Its increasing popularity is helping to introduce new theories derived from more advanced value memes, for example, Jurgen Apelo's *Management 3.0* (2011). Actually, most theories in the transition from Green to Teal or even directly operating from Teal, like Sociocracy 3.0 or Holacracy, are very much influenced by Agile principles. More importantly, I consider Agile to be like a Trojan horse that is paving the way by introducing those vanguard theories. Obviously, when Laloux put forward self-management as a distinctive Teal feature, he referred to SMOs, i.e., organisations that apply self-management not only at the team level, as it occurred in most of the examples mentioned above, but functioning as the central governance system throughout the organisation. Even so, self-management has a long-standing tradition in Green organisations, such as intentional communities and the like. It is a fundamental principle of governance systems such as classical Sociocracy, and there are many sociocratic SMOs out there operating from Green. Granted, self-management finds its perfect soil in Teal organisations, but the practice has a too-long history to claim it as a Teal breakthrough.

Let's talk about purpose now. As I have mentioned before, in my opinion, Laloux defined purpose somewhat vaguely. As I see it, a Teal purpose should be evolutionary, as Laloux claims, but I would add that it needs to be integral and spiritual. More on that in the next chapter.

Last but not least, "wholeness" is given a turn. Wholeness is a distinctly Teal feature, but Laloux's perspective on it is only partial. His definition of wholeness is "the capacity to bring all of ourselves to work". Again, a Green-centred individual would be quite comfortable with that description of wholeness, and many Green organisations have made significant

---

[57] Agile advocates for small, autonomous teams, working in short cycles, and small batches.

inroads to allow individuals to show up more fully; however, the concept should include not only the individual, but the collective dimension. When an organisation cultivates wholeness not only individually, but also as a corporate philosophy, it becomes truly integral.

So, what is a Teal organisation, again? In my opinion, a Teal organisation is one that has an integral approach to management. An integral vision is what is required in order to make the grade and ultimately become Teal. Being integral means using an all-quadrant, all-level approach. Being all-quadrant means giving equal consideration to each of the quadrants or dimensions of management, as 3D Management does. A Teal organisation should be equally concerned with the productivity and profitability (science), with the development of the organisation and its members (arts), and with its social responsibility and contribution to the common good (ethics). Above all, a Teal organisation should be a community with an integral purpose (spirit). Being all-level means having an evolutionary view, embracing development as an organisational objective (in all its facets, including states, stages, and shadow), and at the same time, respecting and aspiring to a healthy integration of all the different levels of the first tier focusing on taking advantage of their functionalities. As Dawlabani says (2013:173):

> *"Yellow [teal] is informed by the dynamics of all the first tier-level systems and treats them as subsystems to its own superordinate goal. When designing functional solutions from Yellow [teal], all the other levels contribute in a 'natural design' that in and by themselves begin to shift individual behaviour and cultural values."*

A Teal organisation has to make room for the healthy expression and the contributions of all the previous levels. The resiliency and capacity to take risks of Red, the order of Amber, the competitiveness and innovative spirit of Orange, and the inclusiveness and plurality of Green. It would be even desirable to have different dominant levels in different areas of the organisation. For example, the accounting area can work very well-grounded in Amber, or the sales team could use a healthy Orange anchor. Let me repeat: Integral is the real Teal and 3D Management its guiding model.

Finally, being a truly Teal organisation requires most of its members to own the stage. It is impossible to achieve integral depth in any group where the majority of those individuals are not themselves at Teal or beyond. Having said that, a Teal organisation should make every effort to integrate everyone, regardless of their developmental altitude. It is elitist, unrealistic, and even unethical to include just the "developed ones." In a controversial comment, Kofman (2002) suggested that somebody that falls below the average or defining level of development of an organisation should not be considered a full member of it. The moral implications of that statement are, in my opinion, dangerous. I fully agree with Edwards (2002a) that Kofman's assumption implies that babies/toddlers are not full holonic members of their families, children and adolescents are not complete members of society, or people with intellectual disabilities are not valid members of the wider community. It is as crazy as not recognising an apprentice as a member of the organisation just because he has not the required skills. Edwards finally remarks:

> *"The developmental success of all healthy societies has been made possible by the inclusion of previously unrecognised and undervalued members of society. The history of social and cultural development tells us that the exclusion of individuals from social and community on the basis of a perceived lack of some fundamental quality is a sure recipe for evolutionary stagnation. Development, in all spheres of life, rests on a basis of diversity, and Integral theory recognises that deeply in the multidimensionality of its psychological and social modelling."*

We are already seeing how the combination of people from different generations (X, Y, and Z) in every organisation is growing. Each of these generations has a different gravitational pull, so an organisation will be increasingly a cacophony of voices, each with different meaning-making frameworks. This trend will be accentuated in the future because of increasing life spans and new notions of retirement. Obviously, start-ups will have the freedom to recruit only individuals operating from Teal, but that would be the exception, not the rule. For the majority of organisations, Teal will be a philosophy to aspire to, but not the average stage of its members. Joachim Galuska, the founder of Heiligenfeld Clinic, a transpersonally and integrally based psychosomatic hospital in Germany shares my point of view, as he said in his keynote speech at the 2018 Integral European Conference: *"Teal is not real. It's an ideal"*. There is something fundamentally wrong if the primary principles of the Teal worldview are betrayed on the path to becoming a Teal organisation.

The Integral Person

> *"You do the little job you're trained to do. Pull a lever. Push a button. You don't understand any of it, and then you just die."* Chuck Palahniuk, *Fight Club*

Some books are transformative. I hope reading this one will be, at least for some of you, the beginning of something. Integral Theory gives us the tools to undertake an evolutionary journey to wake up, grow up, clean up, and finally, show up as true leaders because you cannot be an integral leader if you are split and incomplete.

Frank L. Baum's classic, "The Wizard of Oz", is an accurate metaphor of our fragmented lives. It tells the story of four incomplete individuals (the Tin Man does not have a heart, the Lion lacks courage, and the Scarecrow needs a brain) that band together with a lost girl, by the name of Dorothy, in a cathartic journey to overcome their limitations and become whole again. Once they get to the Emerald City to meet the wonderful Wizard of Oz, Dorothy's dog Toto draws a curtain away (analogy for the truth) and reveals that he is only a little old man. But by now, they no longer need a power figure to solve their problems. On their own, the Lion finds his courage, the Scarecrow his brain, the Tin Man his heart, and Dorothy finally finds her way back home (the path of self-acceptance and self-esteem).

The citadel of being is a complex and multidimensional whole. In the seventeenth century, the great mathematician and scientist, Blaise Pascal, suggested three orders of reality: the physical realm, or order of the body, the intellectual realm, or order of the mind, and the spiritual realm, or order of the heart. All too often, we live in only one or two of these realms and neglect the others, thereby giving up a fuller life. When we inhabit the physical realm, we only care about material things. When we live in our minds, concepts and ideas are the only things that matter. The kingdom that we most easily neglect, according to Pascal, is the realm of the spiritual. He considered it the most important one because it is where the source of happiness lies. Those three realms are but a version of the Big Three dimensions of existence. Body, mind, and soul for an individual; science, arts, and ethics for an organisation.

The millennial Chi principle of Chinese philosophy holds that the three orders form a unity. The Big Three turn into the Fantastic Four, the fourth dimension being the spiritual one, which makes possible the integration of the former. Our nature (what Ken Wilber refers to as the "Great Chain of Being") is thus composed of spirit, soul, mind, and body. Therefore, there is a 3D Management of the person, which integrates all the spheres of our being - biological, psychological, relational, and noetic, or body, mind, heart, and spirit - for a balanced existence and harmonious development. A person without a body is a ghost, without a mind brainless, without a soul a zombie. For eight years now, I have used this approach in a Management Skills course I teach at the University of the Balearics. It draws on Integral Life Practice (Wilber et al. 2008) as a frame of reference. The framework of body, mind, soul, and shadow allows me to include, together with the classical topics (leadership, negotiation, decision-making, teamwork, etc. that, incidentally, always get the integral "touch" from me), more unusual contents and techniques such as AQAL, SDI, Voice Dialog, meditation, shadow work, Circling, and Non-Violent Communication, for this kind of course. It is the only course covering these topics that business and tourism management students get in their entire degree programme, and that's why they love it. After crossing a flatland of right-hand scientific courses, it is quite a discovery for them to find an integral oasis that takes into account every dimension of their development.

Speaking about oases, allow me to introduce you to a wonderful one in the healthcare business: Heiligenfeld GmbH, in Bad Kissingen, is a private group of hospitals devoted to the treatment of psychosomatic and somatic disorders. Its approach to therapy and management is deeply integral. Since its foundation in 1990, it has developed an alternative style of healthcare, based on holistic and humanistic concepts, combined with scientific and economic efficiency. Its therapeutic principles encompass body, soul, mind and spirit, social relationships, and professional techniques. The same all-encompassing philosophy is applied to the mental, physical, and spiritual wellbeing of its more than 600 employees.

Our way of life is profoundly unbalanced and dominated by the right-hand scientific dimension. As influential philosopher Kwame Anthony Appiah (2011) contends, we concentrate on reasons for doing and having (materialistic) while neglecting reasons for feeling (sentimental) and being (existential). We can see that in table 6. As we divide our life into parcels, our professional life is oriented towards the external world of doing (as analysed by the scientific dimension), and we relegate feeling (addressed by the artistic dimension), relating (ethical dimension), or being (the spiritual dimension) to the darkest corner of ourselves. Ultimately, very few people bring all of themselves to work. When we get to the office every morning, we hang our heart and our soul next to our coat, to pick them up back when we exit.

Everything that is marginalised in the workplace tends to emerge in private. Not only positive emotions, such as love and affection but also negative ones. Much too often we unload all the stress and bad moods accumulated during the day on our family. Creativity is also kept away until we get home, where we paint, write, or cook with great dedication and passion. Finally, in this private sphere, we are governed by irreproachable moral criteria, we participate in altruistic social causes, or we find a space for the development of our spirituality. We are changing masks all the time. Truly schizophrenic!

	INTERIOR	EXTERIOR
INDIVIDUAL	**"I"** ART **Thinking and Feeling**	**IT(S)** SCIENCE **Doing**
COLLECTIVE	**"WE"** ETHICS **Relating**	

Table 6: Life orientations and the four quadrants.

As desirable as it sounds, engaging more women into CEO positions is not the right objective either. The really progressive goal, if we want a more equitable world, is to get rid of CEOs altogether, regardless of their gender. Not just for moral reasons, but also for health reasons. What is the portrait of a CEO? Male, white, mid-sixties, filthy rich, who has everything money can buy but works an average of 15 hours a day (maybe 12 on weekends), has not taken a vacation in 20 years, spends most of his life in airports, planes, and anonymous hotels, thus he hardly knows his children and he certainly does not spend enough time with them. It is a big "but" that most people seldom take into account when they picture this life of the rich. Not for me, thanks! To live like that, one would have to be wired in a very particular way. Some people are like that, of course, and most of them are men. In some cases, because of the infamous glass ceiling, but in most cases, many women seem to know better and are not willing to make this kind of sacrifice, no matter what they receive in exchange. They choose a more balanced life, like Dutch women, who are the ones in the world that most often opt for part-time contracts, despite all of the Government incentives that encourage them to work full time.

The great paradox is that work is the dominant area of our lives, but it is the one we least enjoy. People work more and more hours, often to the detriment of other activities. How many people sacrifice love for a career? How many women decide not to have children because that would be an obstacle to their professional development? A study by Fast Company magazine found that 91% of the 1,096 managers interviewed would like to have more time for themselves and their families, but when given a choice, 83% preferred a $10,000 salary increase to an additional hour each day with their families. Despite all the sacrifices made to boost our professional life, we never stop complaining about it. For most people, work has lost its substantive character to merely become instrumental. The divine punishment *"By the sweat of your face you shall eat bread"* has acquired its full dimension in our times. Most people see their job as a necessary evil they have to put up with to make money. It is a job, and you are not supposed to love it. Fun is for our leisure time. In fact, free time can only be understood in opposition to "slave time." Remember that for the Orange mindset, success means earning as much as you can, but not necessarily enjoying what you do.

Work has been commodified in strictly material terms. In our materialistic world, working means selling away time for money. People work hard to earn money and indulge in needless gratifications that they don't have the time to enjoy because they work too hard to make money to buy needless gratifications that they don't have time to enjoy because they work too hard to... That's how they live, trapped in this vicious cycle until they die. We have built a dispirited society in which many are unemployed, and others are over-employed. The price we pay is immeasurable. Stress, depression, and spiritual emptiness are the main illnesses of our times, and the system we have created can only stick temporary patches on that quickly wear off. Are your working days empty? So, live for nights of partying and clubbing. Are you mildly depressed? We've got a pill for that. Are you over-stressed? Take a holiday. Don't have time for your family? Download our new app so you can contact them 24/7 while you are away. So much of our economy works on these mechanisms of repression and distraction. Surely, as artificial intelligence advances, we will find new partial solutions. We will carry biomarkers that detect our real-time cortisol levels (indicating stress) and headsets that guide us to a calmer state. We will return each day to a smart home that, using facial recognition and other sensors, will know how we feel as soon as we walk through the door. Our home will provide us with the sounds, smells, food, and words that a loved one might provide, but doesn't. What a contradictory world. Computers get smarter by the minute, while humans get dumber.

We must understand our life as a unified whole, especially when the traditional distinction between our work and private lives has become so blurred. Work is no longer a physical place or a process that ends after 40 hours per week. That fact has not yet been understood by many companies that still have time clocks to control people and pay them for the time they are daydreaming or surfing the Internet, but don't compute the time a person is working outside the office or simply thinking about work. If we could compare the losses from physical absenteeism with those that are the result of mental absenteeism (i.e., workers daydreaming) or spiritual absenteeism (i.e., when they are not involved or committed), what would be the most important one? Employee engagement can't be bought or rented; it can only be conquered. We are not built with independent Lego pieces. Everything in us is interconnected: family problems affect work performance, the body changes the mind (a back pain can put us in an unbearable mood), the mind to the body (a depression affects the immune system), the spirit to the body (meditative states reduce heart rate and breathing), etc. Our life has got to be whole and balanced.

Consequently, we need to understand our wellbeing as a multidimensional task. Material wellbeing will be achieved with a well-paid job, physical exercise and adequate food; mental wellbeing will have an intellectual component and an emotional one; moral wellbeing will be achieved if we live according to our values. Finally, spiritual welfare will be directly related to our ability to experience and integrate meaning and purpose, and live according to our True Self. Well-rounded individuals balance the three dimensions and manage to integrate them with the spiritual dimension, the dimension of being.

Laloux (2014) pinpoints that our longing for wholeness is at odds with the separation that most existing workplaces foster: *"Vocabulary we use is often revealing: in organisations, we often speak about "work-life balance" a notion that shows how little life is left in work when we have separated ourselves from so much that truly matters."*

For those whose centre of gravity is Green or Teal, this schizophrenic way of life becomes unbearable, and often they end up leaving their organisations. They need to emancipate themselves from those suffocating environments and bring wholeness to their lives. People "going Teal" enjoy bringing the whole of who they are to work, instead of the mask of a narrow, "professional self." (Pór, 2015). They no longer want to live a divided life. They want to bring their whole selves to work.

Once I read a Hasidic tale in which a man, who after many tribulations had prospered, went to the best tailor in town to have his first bespoke suit made. Days later, when the tailor finished it, the man tried it on. The colour and the fabric were beautiful, but the right sleeve was too long, the left leg was too short, and the shoulders were cut asymmetrically. "Don't worry," said the tailor, and he began to guide the man to contort his body in the strangest way for the suit to fit. After paying the bill, the man left the tailor shop wearing his expensive suit. Two older women saw him walking down the street, limping and deformed. "Poor fellow," one of them sighed. “Yes,” said the other, “but that's a lovely suit he's wearing."

Are you wearing a suit that doesn't fit? Have you given up on other essential facets of your life by working too hard? Are you following your dharma (your vocation or inner voice)? Are you connected to your internal purpose at work — to a job that matters to you, and makes the world a better place? Mackey and Sisodia (2013: 87) differentiate between job, career, and calling. If it is just a job, it is a simple transaction where you put in a certain number of hours a week in exchange for a salary and set of benefits. A career offers opportunities to attain higher levels of responsibility and reward by doing more than the bare minimum necessary to keep the job. Finally, a calling is a vocation, something so meaningful that you would continue doing it even if you won the lottery.

In 2006, district nurse Jos de Blok felt he was not living up to the vocation that had brought him to be a nurse. He was utterly frustrated with what neighbourhood nursing had become in the Netherlands (not that other places are different): a profit-oriented, production-focused, dehumanised business. Subsequently, he founded Buurtzorg with a vision of what community healthcare should be. Buurtzorg actually means neighbourhood care, and it was established to recover the person-centred relationships of caregivers and their clients. Its purpose is to help sick and elderly patients live productive, meaningful, and autonomous lives, to whatever degree is possible.

Teal wants to close the gap between our professional self and our real self. Teal organisations invite the whole person into the workplace. They encourage their members to be authentic, to be open, to talk about personal issues, to show vulnerability.

CHAPTER 4

SCIENCE:
MAXIMISING VALUE THROUGH QUALITY, PRODUCTIVITY, AGILITY, AND FINANCE

"In our culture, the notions of "science," "rationality," "objectivity," and "truth" are welded together. It is thought that science offers the "hard" and "objective" truth: truth as correspondence with reality. (...) We tend to identify the search for "objective truth" with the use of reason, and we consider the natural sciences as the paradigm of rationality. We also conceive rationality as something that consists of following the procedures set beforehand, to follow a "methodical" procedure. Thus, we tend to use the terms "methodical," "rational," "scientific," and "objective" as synonyms.

Concerns about "cognitive status" and "objectivity" are characteristic of a secularized culture in which the scientist replaces the priest. Now the scientist is regarded as the person who keeps humanity in touch with something that is beyond itself." (Richard Rorty)

4.1. The Nature of the Beast

"In the past, man has been first; in the future, the system must be first."
Frederick Taylor (1911:2)

As Nietzsche stated, science is the religion of modernity. Our society holds it in such high esteem that when something receives the qualification of "scientific," it acquires credibility and authority almost beyond doubt. Many people are convinced that science and technology are the miraculous solutions for all the predicaments of our world. Science will save us from climate change, hunger, poverty, and extinction. It is the same kind of magical thinking as believing that an almighty anthropomorphic God will be the One to save us.

Organisations, as a manifestation of modernity, have been under the influence of science from Comte to present time. As I demonstrated in chapter 2, science is the hegemonic dimension of management. It is no accident that the dominant management model based on the division of labour and command-and-control structures was initially called Scientific Management. It is so important that all business faculties go out of their way to prove that the discipline they research and teach is scientific. Indeed, management science has an organized body of knowledge and certain universal truths, consistently tested and verified, which have resulted in a complete array of theories, systems, models, techniques, and technologies for managing organisations.

The paradox is that management practice is mostly unscientific. It is much more fad-based than fact-based. Just think how many models and technologies become fashionable without a shred of evidence of their value. In that respect, scholars could have something important to say, but first, they should leave the ivory towers where most of them remain secluded, doing endogamic research in which the tools (quantitative methods, in this case) are more important than the ends. As they say, "when you have a hammer…" Try to build something of value with only a hammer. No wonder that much of the research published has an extremely sophisticated econometric methodology (yes, management researchers have really cool sticks, and they know how to use them), and terribly obvious and shallow findings (I could give some examples of results published in top academic journals, but I do not wish to embarrass anyone). It is no wonder they are left unread.

I know I am not making a lot of friends with my digressions, so perhaps I'll get back to the point. The goal of science is the truth. Not in vain, the word comes from the Latin "scire," which means "to know." Science assumes the existence of universal rules of behaviour or functioning. The scientific method, based on values such as abstraction, generality, empirical evidence, ethical neutrality, and objectivity, has been developed to discover the truths or laws that govern reality. A process is followed, beginning with the establishment of facts and the identification of critical problems, and concluding with the objective application and evaluation of possible solutions following inductive and deductive procedures. The dream of all physicists is to discover a natural law that explains everything. Likewise, from the times of Frederick Taylor to the present day, management science shares the same dream: Find the law that defines the complex network of interrelations that take place in an organisation to determine its optimal functioning, and make it so simple that it can be printed on a sticker. Weber (1961) believed to have found it in bureaucracy, a model of efficiency and rationality *"in which there are no mysterious incalculable forces, but everything can be controlled by calculation."*

Postmodernism's harsh critique of science attempted to cut out the legs from under the privileged pedestal where it still stands. Nietzsche, Kuhn, and Feyerabend, followed by many other postmodern thinkers, questioned the firmly established axioms of objectivity and rationality of the scientific method. Their point was that science is based as much on rational and objective criteria as on emotional and cultural ones. For them, scientific knowledge, far from being objective, reflects and encodes the dominant ideologies and power relations of the culture that engenders it. Their devastating conclusions were that the scientific discourse is self-referential, and it does not deserve a privileged epistemological status over other social beliefs.

Consider scientific management, the foundational organisational theory authored by Frederick Taylor, who called it "scientific" because he claimed it to be the fruit of objectivity and rationality. Further analysis reveals that the method was primarily a reflection of his personality. Taylor was a control freak, with an obsessive-compulsive character. He meticulously programmed every aspect of his life and executed it with martial rigidity, to the extent that he even counted the steps of his morning walks.

Heidegger argued that the reason that science is so foolish is that it offers certainties. It is a mistake to believe, for example, that accounting objectively reflects an external truth. Accounting is an interpretive tool, not a mirror of a hypothetical reality. It is closer to painting than photography. Once, Picasso was commissioned with the portrait of a woman. When her husband saw the result, he was furious. *"It doesn't look anything like my wife,"* he shouted while showing a picture of his wife. Picasso, displaying his unparalleled genius, remarked: *"Is this your wife? How small!"*

In integral theory terms, what postmodernism demonstrates is that science has four quadrants (or three dimensions). It has the objective dimension of the modern worldview and also the subjective and intersubjective ones that the postmodernists added.

In Stephen Soderbergh's version of Stanislaw Lem's science fiction classic "Solaris" (2002), there is a statement that perfectly describes the nature of managerial decisions: *"There are no answers, only options."* It is what I always tell my students when they ask for the right answer to a case study. Business Administration is a multidisciplinary, diverse, fragmented, complex, and plural field of knowledge that cannot be reduced to the mechanical application of theoretical models to objective realities that are waiting to be observed.

It is a mistake to believe in science blindly and dogmatically, but it is even worse to reject its legitimacy. Wilber notes (1998: 23) that one of the main errors of postmodernism is to try and reduce science to poetry. Science is a form of privileged discourse because it is based on solid epistemological principles dating back at least to the seventeenth century (e.g., distrust of *a priori* arguments, revelation, sacred texts, and arguments of authority). Besides, the accumulated experience of three centuries of scientific practice provides some very valid methodological principles (e.g., repeating experiments, using controls, etc.). Without scientific rigour, management loses all its credibility. You can't convince potential customers or investors with only slogans. They want facts and evidence. Nor can you run a company based on hunches or acts of faith.

The scientific method is essential for Netflix. Gibson Biddle (2018), former VP, tells how its CEO, Reed Hastings, built a culture of customer obsession based on extensive consumer knowledge through the use of the scientific method and thousands of experiments. The research techniques Biddle boosted were:

- Data analysis to form hypotheses about past and current customer behaviour.
- Qualitative research — focus groups, one-on-ones, usability — to find out how people think and react to Netflix's initiatives.
- Surveys to capture who the customer is and how to think about the company — by demographics, competitive product usage, entertainment preferences, etc.
- A/B testing the hypotheses formed via the above inputs to see what worked.

The "Let's test it!" mentality improves consumer insight and accelerates learning that results in the development of stronger hypotheses about what delights customers. Those methodologies go well beyond the standard analysis of what customers say. This discloses unanticipated, future needs through a mix of research techniques that put the customer in the spotlight so that the product can be seen through their eyes.

As Aristotle defended, virtue is always in the middle. 3D Management weights the strengths and limitations of science equally, to give it its proper place in the management triad so that a more integral and balanced understanding of the organisation can be gained. Under no circumstances, does it reject the importance of science as a legitimate component of the management trinity/quaternity: Without theories and models, without techniques and technology, without procedures and guidelines, without checklists and tests, without statistics and controls, without accounting and audits, a company cannot function. It is as simple as that.

Nevertheless, management science needs to be profoundly re-evaluated in these uncertain times. We need to question many bedrock core ideas if we want to have organisations that are more nimble and responsive. Bogsnes offers a list (2016: xviii):

> *"The main purpose is liberation from dictatorship, micromanagement, number worshipping, bureaucracy. calendar periods, secrecy, sticks and carrots, and all the other management myths about what is best for achieving great performance in teams and organizations."*

3D Management redefines all traditional functions of scientific management. Organising by replacing traditional hierarchical structures with self-managed holarchies, controlling by transcending conventional budgeting methods, and planning by reinventing strategic management. Say you want a revolution? *Voilà*. Served on a silver platter.

4.2. The Boss is Dead. Long Live Anarchy

> *"The roots of the word 'anarchy' are 'an archos,' 'no leaders,' which is not really about the kind of chaos that most people imagine when the word 'anarchy' is mentioned. I think that anarchy is, to the contrary, about taking personal responsibility for yourself."* Alan Moore.

FAVI is a metal manufacturer and supplier of mechanical parts for various industries, especially the automotive industry. When the now-retired Jean François Zobrist became CEO in 1983, he radically changed the way FAVI was managed. According to Carney and Getz (2016: 14), the company was organised following Theory X's assumptions[58]: a structure of bosses to tell workers what to do, as if they were children, systems and supervisors to control the work, as if they were slackers, and detailed rules

[58] See footnote 34 for a description of the theory.

and procedures, as if they were stupid. Zobrist had a different set of beliefs about human nature, more in line with Theory Y's premises: "*Men are good. There are maybe 2-3% of people who don't work with integrity, but we treat the other 97% as if they had no integrity (and need to be controlled, ask for permission for everything...). And then they stop being integer.*"

Shortly after being appointed CEO of FAVI, while wandering around the supply closet, Zobrist had a revealing experience:

> *"There he saw an employee, Alfred, waiting in front of the closed window. "What are you waiting for?" Zobrist asked. "I came to exchange my gloves," Alfred replied. He hastened to add, "I have a slip from my boss and my old gloves." And so Zobrist learned the policy: When a worker wore out his gloves, he would show them to the head of the workshop, who would give him a slip for exchange. He would then cross the workshop floor -chatting with others and perhaps visiting the bathroom-, before ringing the supply closet's bell, waiting for the keeper, and giving him the slip and the old gloves. At that point, he could get his new gloves and go back to work. The process could easily take a good ten minutes—assuming the closet keeper was present and answered the bell promptly. So, Zobrist posed a question to the accounting department, which informed him that it cost FAVI the equivalent of one hundred dollars an hour to run the equipment on which Alfred worked. That worked out to more than fifteen dollars lost every time a pair of gloves needed to be exchanged—nearly twice what the gloves themselves cost. The real cost of the gloves to FAVI was so high that if they were freely distributed, the company would actually save money, even if some workers took home an extra pair for their gardening every now and then. Of course, as in most companies, accounting had a line item for glove purchases but kept no track of the productivity lost to glove policing. In reality, FAVI was losing thousands of dollars by keeping the gloves under lock and key, Zobrist discovered, but on the official ledger, it would be recorded as a gain. And the gloves were only the beginning. The more he looked around, the more of these bureaucratic false economies he discovered." (Carney and Getz, 2016: 14-16)*

Jean François Zobrist decided to introduce a management system true to his values. He told his managers: "*We don't tell people what to do anymore, but we lead. We don't reward or reprimand, but we lead by example. We don't control, but we help the people to measure their own results.*"

Just before Christmas, he convened a company-wide meeting, and he gave the following speech:

> *"It has been nine months that I have been among you. During these nine months, I have observed you and seen people of great courage, great professionals who love their job but who are prevented from working efficiently. I have arrived at the conclusion that people of your qualities need neither carrots nor sticks"*
>
> *Carrots and sticks are unworthy of professionals, which you are. That's why, once you come back from Christmas, the time clocks will be dismantled. There will be no time clocks because you're not paid to make hours, but products, and good products. That's why the bell will also be gone. There won't be bonuses anymore either. [Instead,] we'll take the average bonus everyone received over the past two years and will add it to your salaries. There are no thieves among you, so the doors of the supply closets will be removed. We'll put up a board and a pen, and everyone will mark what he took -no names- so we can reorder supplies at the appropriate time... There won't be any paid drink dispensers, but for each workshop, we'll provide two free cold water dispensers with syrups and two coffee dispensers. The adjustable wrenches are out. Each machine will have its own complete set of maintenance tools. And to allow everyone to equip himself as he desires, every employee will have a budget of up to $100 to buy whatever he wants – on the condition that it is related to his work." (Carney and Getz, 2016: 119).*

Thus, he got rid of procedure manuals, middle management (supervisors were moved to other roles while leaving their salaries intact), central operating committees, time clocks (Zobrist believed that employees *"should work to make products, not hours")*, and he unlocked all supply cabinets and tool cribs. More importantly, he re-organised the factory into self-management teams of 20 to 35 operators, headed by a democratically elected leader. Each workgroup served a particular customer and product, so they became intimately involved with the clients. The team was responsible for every aspect of its own business, from budgeting and purchasing, to hiring and training, and obviously, manufacturing.

Thanks to this turnaround, FAVI has not only been able to survive the Chinese competition that eliminated all the rest of European companies, but it became a European leader —half of all cars built in the old continent contain gearbox forks from FAVI— it even exports parts to China.

FAVI's case confronts two basic organisational structures: Top-down control and self-management. The former has been the default regulatory mode in families, businesses, and nations, for centuries. It is based on the idea of command and control of a single person, supported by lesser rulers. Traditional hierarchical management, as we have seen, is rooted in

Theory X's assumption that people are inherently lazy. Then, it is only natural to adopt a police model of repression. If you think about it, not trusting anyone because you are the only responsible person, doesn't make much sense. Even if the assumption was correct, then a terrible job of recruiting others was done. According to Gordon Forward, former director of Chaparral Steel, a Theory-X style of managing addresses only 3% of your people. This 3% management method defines and introduces rules and constraints that apply to everyone, in order to control the small number of people that actually cause the problem. Such as, forcing employees to take the train instead of their own vehicle or creating strict procedures to control office supplies because there had been an employee who abused the system. Managing for the 3% contributes to the disengagement of the other 97% who feel they are treated with suspicion and crushed by the straitjacket of restrictive company rules[59].

Top-down control is based on an anthropomorphic metaphor that divides the organisation between mind and body. We even call those on top "heads" (as in the head of the organisation, or the heads of department). They do all the thinking and decision making, and the hands just follow orders. Mintzberg (1994) describes it as a system based on separation: *"If the system is the thinker, thinking must be separated from action, strategy from operation, thinkers from executioners."* The latter are paid to work, not to think, which made Henry Ford complain: *"Why do I have to pay for the entire human being if all I want are the hands?"* Organisations that operate like this have lots of muscle but not many brains. Thinkers are locked in their towers of glass to make decisions, isolated from the operational level and the customers. Jack Welch once defined hierarchical organisations as places in which everyone has their face towards the CEO and their ass toward the customer. The last straw is that the higher the rank of the decision-maker, the fewer people there are who can challenge him or her. Hence Gary Hamel's warning (2011): *"Give someone monarch-like authority, and sooner or later there will be a royal screwup."*

The illiterate workforces of the past made centralised authority inevitable. Nowadays, with a much more qualified working population and increasingly

[59] At Chaparral Steel employees are free to choose their break and meal times and their duration. There is no minimum working time requirement. Plus, there is no visible hierarchy thanks to the elimination of executive benefits (reserved parking spaces, separate entrances to changing rooms, etc.). Raises and bonuses are proportional to the skills demonstrated.

complex problems, the chain of command only slows down decision making, increases the risk of bad choices, and often disenfranchises employees. According to Denning, it is the root cause of our organisations becoming less and less productive, thereby going out of business faster than ever before:

> *"The performance of these workplaces is suboptimal, but not because workers are unwilling or because managers are lackadaisical. Everyone is working hard. Yet the workers feel used. The managers feel just as much victims as the workers. And the customers end up getting the short end of the stick. Whether the participants realize it or not, these workplaces are quietly dying" (Denning, 2010: 20)*

Despite all these deficiencies, hierarchy is still generally considered a necessary evil and remains the hegemonic organising structure. In the Star Wars movies, the Death Star is the central hub of the Empire. All that the rebel forces have to do is to destroy it in order to restore freedom to the galaxy. But the Empire doesn't seem to learn from its mistakes, and they build one Death Star after another. This lack of creativity is only comparable to the predictability of the plot. The same thing happens with hierarchy. People seem to believe that, in its absence, mayhem will ensue, costs will run amok, employees will ransack all office stationery, and the board room will be used for company-wide bacchanals.

Beyond this apocalyptical scenario (which, perhaps doesn't sound so horrible for some, and like an ordinary day at the office, for others), more options can be found. There is a better alternative to top-down control and it is called self-management. Self-management or responsible autonomy, to use Gerard Fairtlough's terminology, is an organisational model where *"an individual or a group has the autonomy*[60] *to decide what to do but is accountable for the outcome of the decision."* (Fairtlough 2005: 24).

Bogsnes (2016: 58) explains the difference between the two with the metaphor of traffic control. If you want to manage traffic at an intersection, you can use a traffic light or a roundabout. Drivers can only follow the traffic light's fixed rules that come from above. On the contrary, in a roundabout, drivers are in control, and they apply real-time information to guide their decisions. A roundabout is a self-regulating system that is much more efficient because it is based on decision making at the right level (close to the situation) and at the right time (as late as

[60] Note that the Greek etymology of autonomy means self-governing.

possible) in an environment of cooperation, courtesy, and shared agreement (like the “every second car” principle). Incidentally, if you want to experience self-organisation taken to its limit, try and drive a car in the streets of Delhi. It does work (sort of).

Self-managing organisations (SMOs) can be defined as *“those that radically decentralize authority in a formal and systematic way throughout the organisation”* (Lee and Edmondson, 2017). SMOs apply self-management not just at a team level but as an organisation-wide principle. The core element is *distributed control*, i.e., one that gets rid of central authority and reporting relationships. In short, there are no bosses. For some people, a world without bosses might look like paradise; for others, it sounds like anarchy and chaos. You may well be correct about the anarchy, but not about the chaos. Anarchy in Greek means "without bosses" but not necessarily "without order." Many organisations have gotten rid of the seemingly indispensable figure of the boss and have demonstrated that work can be accomplished much better if they are eliminated. Anarchy is not when no one is in charge, but when everybody is. I've been self-managing for most of my professional life. Although universities have mostly Amber cultures, they usually give professors a great deal of freedom and flexibility, putting minimal constraints on how they manage their work. And believe me, universities can be criticised for many things, but not for being chaotic.

Those with a conservative bent will consider self-management something that goes against the laws of God and Nature, if not a strategy to reinstate communism. The incoherence of this position is manifest. First of all, how can they defend self-organised free markets tooth and nail, and yet be against SMOs? Secondly, I don’t know about God, but self-organisation is decidedly not contrary to Nature. If you analyse a flock of starlings, your digestive system, or the creation of the Universe, then you will soon realise that self-organisation is the way of Nature. It is the way of your body, and it is the way of your life, in every area except work. Nature is doing an excellent job on its own, your body as well, and most of us are managing our adult lives fairly decently without having anyone telling us what to do. Why should it be any different at work? Thus, Jurgen Appelo does not regard self-organisation as a management best practice. Self-organisation cannot be a best practice, because it is the default practise of any dynamic system. Everything in an organisation that managers don’t or can’t control (from spontaneous lunch meetings to office romances) self-organises:

> *"The funny thing is that many people think command-and-control has always been the norm and that self-organizing teams are a new and interesting concept. But that's just common "simple-mindedness" again. Self-organization is the formation of things without top-down direction, and it pervades the universe. Conscious command-and-control (imposed order) was invented 13.7 billion years after self-organization, by humans, in their attempts to protect what they believe is valuable. Self-organization is the norm. And command and control is the special case." (Appelo 2011: 102)*

If there were any advantages to central control, Appelo continues, Nature wouldn't use distributed control as the main design philosophy of organisms. It doesn't because it is a worse alternative. For instance, if a central authority controlled my immune system, it would be much easier for viruses to dismantle it.

Self-management gives freedom to people. Following Theory Y, it assumes that when individuals have the right information, incentives, tools, and accountabilities, they can mostly manage themselves. Olivier Gesbert, the owner of Pressto Peru, believed in people, but everything around him seemed to prove him wrong. In 1998, just one year after landing in Peru with his wife and two children, Olivier opened his first dry cleaning and laundry shop as a franchisee of the leading Spanish chain Pressto. To begin with, at that time, the polls noted that 95% of Peruvians distrusted their compatriots. But it was his personal experience that gave him every reason to stick to a hierarchical management model. In 2003, -after a successful expansion that enabled him to reach 13 stores, there was a failed attempt to kidnap his two children, followed by death threats. He decided to go back to France taking his entire family. However, managing the business from abroad proved to be very difficult. Although sales were growing, revenue was declining caused by widespread theft at virtually every level of the business. After his two partners sold their shares in 2007, Olivier had to return to keep the company afloat. He did this, but eight of the shops had to be closed. In 2014, just when things seemed to be normalising, his father became terminally ill. Olivier was afraid that, if he went away again, he would end up losing the business. He really had no choice as it was unthinkable for him not to be by his father's side. "What would my father do in this situation?" he thought. His father had raised him with the solid value of trust, and he had not been following it. Desperate times called for desperate measures, so he decided to be true to his convictions and took a leap of faith. To make a long story short, as a legacy to his father, and inspired by French examples such as FAVI, Michelin, and Isaac Getz's model (Carney and Getz, 2016), Olivier

Gesbert started the process of "liberating" Pressto. Gradually, Pressto eliminated most of the control mechanisms over workers who then self-organised into autonomous circles based on some sociocratic patterns. They took responsibility for their own schedules and work, recruitment and selection, and many other tasks, including electing the general manager.

A turning point happened when they got rid of the security guards at the exits of the shops. It was a difficult step, as thievery of customers' garments had not been uncommon, but when you trust people, you must demonstrate it completely. Not checking people's bags as they left the properties was a visible measure that increased the feeling of trust. And more importantly, the incidence of stolen properties decreased. As I mentioned, trust was a scarce resource in Peru, and as such, it is highly valued. Offenders were denounced by their own colleagues and peer pressure made them leave the company. As Olivier Gesbert told me, having 100 employees who are committed is much better than having a guard at the gate.

Even the organisation's purpose was co-created with everyone's participation. An employee suggested the idea of treating the client's garments as if they were their own. This idea was enthusiastically accepted, which, according to Olivier, would have been difficult had it been his idea. In only two years, staff turnover rate and absenteeism were cut in half. Productivity per person increased by 29%. Reimbursement for damaged clothing declined in the same proportion. The teams in each store became increasingly independent and responsible, not only for their sales but also for the cost control of each production unit, attaining incredible savings. Sales increased despite the closure of 3 of 25 stores (a decision that was made by employees). Overall, the Pressto laundry chain has tripled its profits in the last three years.

The idea of freedom is a fundamental tenet of modern society. A workplace based on freedom is a better fit for our current life conditions than one based on command and control. Business is, arguably, the least democratic current social institution, and one that offers the least amount of freedom. Why do we have to surrender such a fundamental right in the workplace? Not only it is unfair, but it also doesn't make good business sense. As early as 1924, William L. McKnight, CEO of 3M remarked: *"If you put fences around people, you get sheep. Give people the room they need".* If you want to unleash people's potential, you must liberate them. Given a choice between working for a company where you are timed when you go to the loo, or work for an SMO with no time clocks and where members who work overtime enter their own hours with no further control, which one would you prefer? In the past, workers tolerated tyranny in return for economic security, but today the promise of security is not enough; people are much more demanding in what they expect from their jobs. Simply put, the younger generations, millennials[61] and digital natives, will not work in bureaucratic and hierarchical organisations. They have been born in democratic countries, they have been raised in non-authoritarian families, they have grown up with social networking, they live in a world of open source[62] and creative commons, they can interact with and influence their favourite brands through Facebook, Twitter, or Instagram. Having a say is a defining element of who they are, and they expect to have that right at work too. The most educated and talented people want more than just a paycheck from work, and they refuse to waste their lives in jobs where they sit at desks doing what they are told. They want stimulating work, where they can learn, grow, make a difference, and have fun. They want to work in free, open, empowering, creative organisations where they can be fully human.

In summary, the main practical reason for self-management is that most of us have reached a stage of development where we can manage ourselves. The person doing the work is the one who can best decide how, when, where, and why work gets done. We don't need people staring over our shoulders and micromanaging us. Let’s go back to Peru for a moment. The minimum wage in the country is $300 per month. Even though Pressto pays above the average, many of the salaries are not far from that amount. Would you be able to maintain a family with that? No manager could do better than these people who create miracles with so few resources. They definitely don’t need a boss.

---

[61] Ganescu (2017: 6) identifies the most important values of the millennial generation:

- They are not interested in a traditional career ladder; they have a greater need for self-expression and personal growth.
- They are not looking for work-life balance. They want a fulfilling life.
- They have less respect for authority and hierarchies.
- They care about the world, and they want to make it a better place.
- They want to contribute their best in a company that won’t suffocate their drive and creativity.

[62] Linux, Wikipedia, Bitcoin, and most of the software running the World Wide Web are the products of self-organized work. Linux, in particular, has more than 100,000 volunteer and self-managed contributors.

Additionally, you can't get the kind of entrepreneurial and innovative spirit necessary to thrive in the 21st-century business environment bound by rigid hierarchies. A traditionally hierarchical work system tends to stifle workers' contributions with unnecessary control mechanisms and red tape. We need a management model collaboratively organised rather than centrally controlled. The Responsive.org manifesto describes it brilliantly:

> *"In the past, a limited number of people held the power and understanding necessary to steer the organization and its public image. Control was forced through centralized, top-down decision-making. Corporate Communications, IT departments, and rigid processes controlled what people said and did. The higher up the pyramid you were, the more power you had. This makes sense in a world where a select few people are most likely to have the knowledge and experience necessary to make the best decisions.*
>
> *Today, that is no longer the case. Circumstances and markets change rapidly as information flows faster. Now the people with the best insight and decision-making ability are often people closest to the customers, on the front line, or even 'outside' the typical organizational boundaries. Rather than controlling through process and hierarchy, you achieve better results by inspiring and empowering people at the edges to pursue the work as they see fit – strategically, structurally, and tactically."*

Daniel Tenner, the co-founder of GrantTree, a London-based company helping startups to access government funding, stresses its importance:

> *"One of the reasons you want to do self-management from a commercial perspective is that the people who are dealing with clients have all the power they need to do the right thing. When you are B2C you do this by putting all the power in the hands of the call center staff. You don't stymie them with scripts and processes; you get them to "own the work."* ("*GrantTree's Journey Towards Self-Management*" 2018)

Companies like that have a significant edge. They have people engaged with the purpose of the organisation, solving problems no one asked them to, and doing more than what is required.

Modern technology further enables adoption of self-management. Today, we can work anywhere. There is no need to go to the office or work at fixed hours. The unprecedented coronavirus crisis has been a full-scale trial-by-fire that has proven that teleworking is much more than a residual modality of work. In a world where everyone is connected 24/7 and can reply to work e-mails even on the weekends, the old notion of a prescribed 9-to-5 workday or a three-weeks-off vacation policy has become pointless.

Remote and flexible working conditions attract and retain talent. This has increased dramatically thanks to digital connectivity, and this trend is likely only to grow. Simultaneously, our ability to self-organise has increased, collaborating more easily across internal and external organisational boundaries. It is no longer true that the most effective way to coordinate people is with a manager. Working within a network allows us to organise ourselves much better, with many different kinds of connections, and increased autonomy.

Finally, when the pyramid is dismantled, much of the poison drains out of the organisation. In a self-managed organisation, there are no bosses to please and no adversaries to elbow aside. The competition for advancement disappears, which means the end of a significant amount of politicking and rivalries because people are not competing anymore for the scarce commodity called promotion.

As a summary, table 7 shows an integral analysis of the benefits of self-management using AQAL's four quadrants:

	INTERIOR	EXTERIOR
INDIVIDUAL	Perception of greater ownership Higher motivation Higher commitment Higher satisfaction Increased responsibility	Decreased absenteeism Stress reduction
COLLECTIVE	Reduced interpersonal conflicts Increased sense of community	Cost reduction Increased productivity Decreased turnover Increased quality Increased innovation

Table 7: Four-Quadrant analysis of the benefits of self-management (compiled by the author based on literature review and own experience).

4.3. The Responsible Autonomy of Self-Management

"I know you're out there. I can feel you now. I know that you're afraid. You're afraid of us. You're afraid of change. I don't know the future. I didn't come here to tell you how this is going to end. I came here to tell you how it is going to begin. I'm going to hang up this phone, and then I'm going to show these people what you don't want them to see. I'm going to

> *show them a world without you, a world without rules and controls, without borders or boundaries, a world where anything is possible. Where we go from there, is a choice I leave to you." The Matrix* (1999). The Wachowski Sisters.

The traditional organisational model works under the assumption that managing should be carried out by a superior class of formally appointed individuals who always have the answer and the last word. If we study formal hierarchy from a Transactional Analysis perspective, we notice that most of the relationships across levels are from parent to child, with the result of maintaining many people in the dependent child role. It is profoundly contradictory that most organisations go out of their way to recruit the most intelligent, innovative, talented people, and once they get them, they are treated like children. On the contrary, self-management replaces parent-to-child patterns for adult-to-adult. They regard everyone as mature human beings capable of taking an independent stance:

> *"With freedom comes responsibility: you can no longer throw problems, harsh decisions, or difficult calls up the hierarchy and let your bosses take care of it. You can't take refuge in blame, apathy, or resentfulness. Everybody needs to grow up and take full responsibility for their thoughts and actions."* (Laloux 2014: 137)

Traditional organisations have old-fashioned paternalistic systems to control things like expenses, travel, and gifts. They create complicated procedures around these and have departments that verify their compliance. Companies like Netflix think differently. There are virtually no controls, and the general policy is one-sentence long: *Act in Netflix's best interest.* When it comes to timetables, as most of us have experienced, conventional organisations have fixed working hours and limited holidays. The rationale is that people are a set of hands or brains hired from 9 to 5. On the contrary, Netflix has an unlimited time-off policy, meaning it is entirely up to the employee to decide how many hours to work, how many days to go on holiday, or how long a parental leave should be[63]. There is no need to ask for prior approval with the only constraint being that their absence won't damage the business. Opposite to what Theory X-ers would think, Appelo (2016:128) reports that companies with these kinds of policies, such as the Motley Fool, Workday, and Evernote, have found that people take less time off than they should. Some companies have been

---

[63] Working hard is not how they measure contribution at Netflix. They believe in working smarter.

forced to advise a minimum amount of vacation per employee. They had a similar experience at Semco when employees started to set their own targets. They were higher than those that managers set, and more often they were exceeded.

Valve Corporation is a video game developer, publisher, and digital distribution company famous for the software distribution platform Steam (with more than 90 million active users monthly) and first-person shooters that are among my favourite video games of all time, like *Half-Life* and *Counter-Strike.* Valve[64] does not hire people to fill a specific job description, but instead to contribute in the best possible way. All desks have wheels to give people full autonomy and flexibility to move around freely and choose where they would like to work. Thus, employees vote with their feet on the projects they prefer, and they determine the games the company develops. People move their locations so frequently that the company had to create a tracking app to allow peers to find each other[65].

Companies like Google made headlines because they had people allocate 20% of their time to self-directed projects. At Valve, the percentage of self-allocated time is 100%. People don't join projects because they are told to, but because they choose to be part of a cabal. Cabal is their jargon for a multidisciplinary, self-organised, temporary project team born to get a product or large feature market-ready. They are usually 8 to 12 members and usually include an expert from every functional area (programming, art, etc.). The leader's role is primarily to act as a clearinghouse of information, keeping the overall project in mind so that members of the cabal can verify any decisions with them. As they say at Valve: *"The leads serve the team, while acting as centers for the teams."*

Getting rid of all the bosses has the immediate consequence of promoting everybody to a managerial position. Management becomes everyone's

---

[64] If you are interested, you can retrieve Valve's employee manual at https://steamcdn-a.akamaihd.net/apps/valve/Valve_NewEmployeeHandbook.pdf

[65] Oticon, a Danish manufacturer of hearing devices, must have been a reference for Valve's model. Its CEO Lars Kolind implemented in 1990 a new style of management he called "the spaghetti organisation" that has many points in common with what Valve does. It was based on self-managing project teams, no job titles, and an entirely open-plan physical layout with no desks. Oticon remains a classic transformation story because the company went from near-bankruptcy to become the second-largest company in its industry. When Lars Kolind left the company in 1998 they changed to a more conventional version of the model.

business. When Gary Hamel (2011) said he was impressed that Morning Star had learned how to manage without managers, founder Chris Rufer corrected him:

> *"Everyone's a manager here," he said. "We are manager rich. The job of managing includes planning, organizing, directing, staffing, and controlling, and everyone at Morning Star is expected to do all these things. Everyone is a manager of their own mission. They are managers of the agreements they make with colleagues, they are managers of the resources they need to get the job done, and they are managers who hold their colleagues accountable."*

A common misperception of self-management is that it is similar to empowerment. If subordinates can be empowered it is because they have been disempowered in the first place, as Zappo's CEO, Tony Hsieh explains in an e-mail he wrote to his employees[66]:

> *"Many organizations today claim to be empowering. But note the painful irony in that statement. If employees need to be empowered, it is because the system's very design concentrates power at the top and makes people at the lower rungs essentially powerless, unless leaders are generous enough to share some of their power."*

Borrowing Kirkpatrick's (2011) seminal book title, self-management goes well beyond empowerment. In an organisation built on the principles of self-management, such as Morning Star -the company Kirkpatrick mostly based his book on-, individuals aren't given power by the higher-ups; they simply have it:

> *"The term "employee empowerment" implies that one person is transferring power to another person. In the real world, what is given can be taken away. In self-management, colleagues already have all the power they need to make anything happen they want to have happened from the moment they start work. Self-management is beyond empowerment. Self-management is power itself".* (Kirkpatrick 2011: 72)

And he emphasises (2011: 67):

> *"In an environment of freedom, you know how to do your own job better than anyone else, and you should be free to make it better. In an environment of freedom, you should be able to talk to anyone in the*

---

[66] https://www.consciousculturegroup.com/zappos-and-Holacracy-ceo-memo-to-employees/

> *enterprise about anything having to do with the enterprise. In an environment of freedom, there should be absolutely no barriers to pursuing your mission and the mission of the enterprise to the best of your ability. And finally, in a free environment, there should be no barriers to any of you becoming whatever you wish to be."*

Self-management brings about a new orientation to power, defined by Freinacht (2017c:119) as transpersonal power: *"Not the power of self over others; rather, the power of selves and others, the power to self-organize in complex fashions."* As Laloux underlines (2014:136), not everybody has the same level of power, but everyone can be powerful. The scope of influence of a cashier will be more limited than the one of a product designer, and yet the cashier will have the same amount of power to do the job as the latter.

In a self-organised environment, it is especially important to make sure that all the necessary activities are carried out, even the uninteresting or unpleasant ones. Although the ultimate control comes from within, freedom must be balanced with responsibilities. Having no bosses does not mean there are no rules or control mechanisms. Self-management is not equivalent to no boundaries. Regulations, duties, and other people create limits. A self-organising flock of starlings has unambiguous rules of flying based on keeping distance from your neighbours (short-range repulsion), alignment to follow the same direction, and cohesion to stay with the group (long-range attraction). With these three simple rules, the flock moves in a precise and complex way. Likewise, self-managing organisations have strict rules on how to get work done, including how the organisation is structured, how decisions are made, how tasks are defined and distributed, how conflicts are resolved, how salaries are set, how people are recruited, etc. In my opinion, they have even more structured rules than traditional organisations.

All these rules and accountabilities need to be widely understood, transparent, legitimized, and shared from the start. For this reason, governance models like Holacracy utilise highly formalised and impersonal forms of management vested in formally-defined roles and responsibilities (Lee and Edmondson, 2017). Brian Robertson (2015: 64) quotes David Allen to justify the rules and structure of Holacracy (and, as an extension, of other governance systems for self-organisation):

> *"There is no freedom without discipline, no vision without a form... if they were no lines painted on the road, you wouldn't be free to let your mind wander and be creative while you drive. You'd be too busy hoping no one*

hits you, but if there were too many lanes and restrictions and rules, you'd have traffic moving much slower than it should, as everyone was trying to pay attention to the right place to be."

Richard Sheridan, CEO of Menlo Innovations, says you can only create freedom through tyranny:

> *"It is true that we have created a joyful place and people love working here, and they are fully engaged. And yet it is also true that we have introduced tyranny by removing ambiguity from the workplace. In our world, people know who they are working with and who they are working for. They know what they are working on, and they know what order they are going to work on it. That's the tyranny part. Once that's established, the freedom part kicks in. I say, 'You are now free to pursue the work that you love without anyone hanging over your shoulder, cutting in, and asking what you are working on and how it is going."* (Denning 2018: 39).

In that sense, Bernstein et al. (2016) rightfully label self-managing systems as bureaucracy 2.0:

> *"The new forms resist hierarchical constraints—but in some ways, contrary to popular arguments, they resemble bureaucracy as sociologist Max Weber defined it in the early 1900s. Bureaucracy vested authority in depersonalized rules and roles rather than in status, class, or wealth. The idea was to liberate individuals from the dictatorial rule of whimsical bosses. Self-managing systems aim to accomplish the same thing, with less rigidity."*

In such an environment, it is probably more difficult to fail at your responsibilities because of peer pressure and transparency. Self-managed organisations have changed boss or rule-driven compliance for peer-reviewed accountability in a context of shared responsibility for shared goals. Accountability is to the customer and the team, not to a boss. Imagine a football player that stops running in the middle of a game. It would not be the coach that was the first one to rebuke him, but his teammates. Peer feedback thus becomes the primary performance measure. If traditional organisations have a central control system, SMOs have a distributed control system based on situational pressure. The fact is that group pressure is a much more effective control method than the iron hand of a boss. What makes us conform is what Frank and Pettit (2018) call the "esteem motive." As they define it, all of us tend to conform reliably to socially endorsed standards given the existence of an attraction to esteem and an aversion to disesteem. When we score high in the eyes of the others, we win respect for being a reliable or robust source of good work. Research solidly shows that the esteem motive *"plays an important part in driving people's actions, in shaping their adjustments to the action of others, and of course in determining their responses to the aggregate effects of such actions and adjustments, overall"* (Frank and Pettit, 2018: 232). Technology plays a vital role in enabling peer control on a large scale. For example, apps like Knozen have been designed to rate co-workers anonymously.

In 3D Management, control and accountability are based on the concept of the internal customer. An internal customer is anyone in the organisation who depends on another to fulfil their job responsibilities. The internal customer needs should be identified so that they are satisfied, the same as if he or she was a client. Every person's set of commitments to their internal customers are unambiguously specified, and he/she has to fulfil them. Whereas in the traditional system you report to one boss, here nobody is your boss and, at the same time, you are fully accountable to many colleagues. In a way, every internal customer is your boss, as it relates to the commitments you have. This way, authority and responsibility are as close to the (internal or external) customer as possible, and there is no gap between them. Individual performance should be transparent and shared with everyone. In such a system, process definition is of paramount importance. Process maps and flow charts need to be defined to ensure full accountability.

In CineCiutat, for example, every member of the organisation has an individual purpose aligned with the enterprise's purpose, and we have identified all the processes every role is responsible for, the internal customers they work with, and the accountabilities and measures of performance (KPIs) they are expected to deliver.

Similarly, every employee at Morning Star (the world's largest tomato processing company in the world) is responsible for drawing up a personal mission statement that outlines how he or she will contribute to the company's purpose. Even though employees have a great deal of autonomy, they can't do whatever they want. They are obliged to fulfil their commitments to other associates of the company (their internal customers), and everything they do must conform to the company's mission statement, the only recognised boss at Morning Star. One of the critical self-management tools of Morning Star is the CLOU. CLOU (pronounced "clue") stands for Colleague Letter of Understanding and is an accountability agreement between colleagues declaring each individual's commercial mission, business process responsibilities, scope of decision, authority, performance measures (called "stepping stones" at Morning Star), and the reporting intervals for each metric. Every year each person negotiates it with the associates affected by his or her work (internal customers, in 3D-Management jargon). A typical Morning Star colleague will likely have about 6 or 7 CLOU signatories. Altogether, the CLOUs spell out all formal relationships among Morning Star's full-time employees and all relevant performance metrics. The CLOU clearly defines the work schedule commitment (for example, 40-45 hours off-season, and 50-55 in high season), and is stored in the company's intranet, available for everyone to see. At the end of the year, employees receive feedback from their internal customers, and in January, every business unit has to defend its annual performance. Team members have to justify their use of the company's resources, acknowledge shortfalls, and prepare plans for improvement.

As Kirkpatrick notes (2011: 133), relationships at Morning Star are thus governed by a set of principles that require several commitments: First, to the mission of the company; second, to the individual goals specified in the CLOU; and third, colleagues agree to accept personal responsibility and take initiative. Ultimately, Morning Star's employees have total responsibility (Kirkpatrick 2011: 132). While each colleague is identified with specific business processes, no one is allowed to ignore a known issue. The phrase "that's not my job" is incompatible with this system, and they have an affirmative obligation to report a problem that enters their field of vision to other pertinent colleagues. It is a matter of professional shame, even ostracism, failing to do that (including not to report on somebody who has done something wrong).

Likewise, an interesting tool has been developed at W.L. Gore, called the credibility bucket, to keep track of individual responsibilities, and ensure that everyone fulfils their commitments. According to this metaphor, every time an associate keeps a promise or helps an associate, a drop of water goes into the bucket whereby trust accumulates. Failure to do so, pokes a hole in the bucket, your credibility drains out, and with it, your capacity to work effectively with other associates.

The advice process is a decision-making method typical of self-managed organisations such as AES, W.L. Gore, or IDEO, designed to make sure freedom is used responsibly. Here is how it works: Before making a decision, the decision-maker should consult directly with the colleagues who will be affected and, if necessary, with people considered experts in the matter. In Holacracy, this is known as "going role to role." The advice received must be taken into consideration but is not binding. This way, anyone can make any decision, as long as they consult with those affected as well as any required experts while respecting the principles, values, and the purpose of the organisation.

Despite all those mechanisms, ultimately the power resides in the person. A Teal organisation is managed by values, not by rules (as Amber does). Rules are a consequence of values. Those are translated into internal and external standards of conduct, so that *"values provide a framework within which each member of the organisation can operate with responsible freedom"* (Barrett 2003: 107). It is values, rather than control mechanisms, that ensure consistency of behaviour and alignment with the organisation's purpose. In the case of Holacracy, its Constitution[67] refers expressly to the capacity for "individual action" (defined by Brian Robertson as *"a rule about how to break the rules"*). The individual action rule states that you are authorised to act outside the bounds of your formal authority, and that shall not be considered a violation of the Constitution as long as (a) you are acting in good faith to serve the purpose or accountabilities of your role within the organisation, or of the overall organisation itself, (b) you believe the action will resolve or prevent more tension for the organisation than it might likely create, (c) the act does not compromise the organisation's resources or other assets beyond what you are otherwise authorised to commit or spend, (d) you are unable to delay the action long enough to request permission customarily required. If you take individual action then you have the duty to inform the teammates affected, also to resolve any tension created, and if you repeatedly take the same action, then you must find a solution to stop acting outside of the formal structure.

With such a system, you have to allow time and space for communication to happen. Loomio is an open-source platform cooperative that offers free online software for collaborative decision-making. It emerged as a tool to be used by the Occupy Movement in New Zealand, and its prototype was launched in 2012. As one of its co-founders, Richard Bartlett (2016), explains, Loomio has different time scales for communication to happen:

- Daily: the whole team checks in every morning for 10 minutes: What did you do yesterday? What are you doing today? What

[67] Holacracy Constitution v4.1 (retrieved from https://www.Holacracy.org/wp-content/uploads/2015/07/Holacracy-Constitution-v4.1.pdf)

support do you need? What are you doing for your wellbeing today? This generates accountability, support, agility, and focus.
- Fortnightly: They start by committing to what work they will deliver over the next two weeks. Then, they reflect on what they learned and what they will do differently next time.
- Quarterly: They create focus by setting three or four measurable objectives that everyone is working towards.

Having these rhythms helps to maintain agility without pivoting every 5 minutes. You can agree on a course of action over three months, and fine-tune your direction every day. The organisational structure evolves every two weeks, and everyone on the team has access to changing it.

Feedback is also critical. Valve Corporation has a framework on how to give feedback to each other. Every year, a set of people, that changes each time, interviews everyone in the company, asking whom each person has worked with and how the experience with them has been. The purpose of this exercise is to provide people with information that will help them grow. The feedback is then gathered, collated, and delivered to each reviewee anonymously. Outside of these formalised peer reviews, the company expects that everyone will gather input from those around them whenever they need to, outside the constraints of the official report.

All things said and done, if the main reason many organisations are holding on to hierarchical structures is not to lose control, then the self-management alternative is a much better one. Metamodern thinker Hanzi Freinacht (2019: 71) presents in his new book *Nordic Ideology*, a developmental view of how social order mechanisms evolve from more straightforward autocratic methods to more sophisticated and inconspicuous ones. He presents a social rule that can be easily applied to organisational contexts, *the rule of increasing intimacy of control*, according to which, more complex societies have more intimate mechanisms of control. Hanzi ascertains: *"The issue is not to avoid control, but to avoid bad, unscientific, corrupt or despotic control."* Just as the control mechanisms of a dictatorship are more visible but less effective than those of the modern welfare state, the gross and fear-based control mechanisms of a Red-centred boss are less effective than those of an Amber bureaucracy; which in turn, are less effective than those of a meritocratic Orange organisation; which is bettered by the culture of empowerment and participation of a Green organisation; which can't compete with the peer-based, intimate control of a Teal SMO. Teal organisations have more integrated cultures, and people are freer and can demonstrate who they truly are, showing the subtler, more profound, and complex forms of social integration. However, despite the fact that the social order of a Teal organisation is more emancipating, giving more rights and freedom to the individual, it is not free from oppression. Albeit on a higher and subtler level, some are bound to feel pressured, surveyed, and manipulated by the high degree of involvement demanded, the greater transparency created, and the interest in the other facets of the person, such as the emotional and spiritual ones (it is not by chance that those who have trouble fitting often compare postconventional organisations to sects).

4.4. Governance Structures for Self-Management.

"Ok. You convinced me, but how do I go about it?" If that's what you are asking yourself, don't worry. There is no need to reinvent the wheel. There are many pioneering companies such as Buurtzorg, Morning Star, The ner Group, or FAVI, whose homegrown models are excellent benchmarks. Even better, in my opinion, is to use a well-established governance method, such as Holacracy or Sociocracy, as your blueprint. The metatheoretical framework of 3D Management is compatible with any of them[68]. For reasons of space, I won't explain them in too much detail at this time. Some excellent books and courses do. However, I will try to give a small taste of each of them.

Sociocracy was the first to be created. Etymologically, it means government by its partners or members. It is a method of collaborative governance based on effective organisation, distributed authority, and inclusive decision-making. In 1926, Kees Boeke, inspired by Quaker principles of consent, established the first sociocracy in his school. Later on in the 1970s, his former student, Gerard Endenburg, implemented it in his electronics company in the Netherlands, and inspired by cybernetics, systems theory, and other self disciplines, evolved it further. He was the one who laid out the fundamental principles of sociocracy: People organised in semi-autonomous circles connected by a double link of representatives, using consent as the decision-making principle (more on that later). Nowadays, Sociocracy is widely used throughout the world in

[68] This is what makes a metamodel like 3D Management useful. Being a model of models, it can accommodate within its framework the highest possible number of legitimate models, be it classical Sociocracy, Sociocracy 3.0, Holacracy, or on another front, B Corps or the Balance of the Common Good.

companies, non-profits, ecovillages, and intentional communities. In the Netherlands, it even has a societal form status.

In 2014, the Sociocracy 3.0 Movement was started by Bernhard Bockelbrink and James Priest (the third co-developer, Liliana David joined soon after) with the mission to make Sociocracy available to as many organisations as possible and integrate it with lean and agile thinking. Sociocracy 3.0 (S3) is a principles-based framework of patterns and practices that includes:

(1) An organisational structure based on groups of people structured in circles with double-links (i.e., people from each circle that represent and carry the information between the two circles) to make sure that information travels effectively into both directions.
(2) A set of tools and patterns[69] for decision making, selection of members and proposals, conflict management, etc.

One of the beauties of S3 is that it is free and open. The S3 Movement wants to make S3 available and applicable to as many organisations as possible, so they provide plenty of resources under a Creative Commons Free Culture License. Just go to https://Sociocracy30.org. Everything can be found there. It is also extremely flexible, so you choose only the elements that you need and discard the rest.

Enter Holacracy. Initially developed by Ternary, the software company created by Brian Robertson, Holacracy is a refinement of Sociocracy. Its name derives from the root word coined in 1967 by Arthur Koestler "holarchy" (a concept I will fully explain in the upcoming section). Holacracy means governance by the organisational entity itself (the holarchy). It is not governance by the people within the organisation (as in Sociocracy), or by those who own the organisation (as in traditional hierarchical systems), but by the organisation's own "free will." My good friend Dennis Wittrock (a well-known name in the European integral scene, co-founder of the Integral European Conference, and now a partner at Encode.org), summarised it to me as follows: *"Sociocracy is the governance of the people, by the people, for the people. Holacracy is the governance of the organisation, by the people, for the purpose."*

[69] Sociocracy's definition of a pattern is a template for successfully navigating a specific context.

Holacracy is the structure of choice of more than a thousand companies including Zappos (the largest company so far to implement this system), Encode.org, GrantTree, Dwarfs and Giants, Mercedes-Benz.io, Teleton Paraguay, David Allen Company, Hypoport AG, and Enlivening Edge, just to name a few. The first step required is that the CEO formally ratifies a document called "The Constitution," that explicitly codifies the rules of Holacracy (available at Holacracy.org/constitution), and cedes his or her power in favour of the new governance process. As Robertson (2015: 26) explains: *"Holacracy thus takes some of the organizational design functions that traditionally reside with a CEO or executive team and places them into processes that are enacted throughout the organization with everyone's participation."*

As I will explain later, Holacracy's governance structure is based on a nested hierarchy of roles and circles. Every role comes with a purpose, one or more domains to control, and several accountabilities to respond to. The day to day running of the system is based on tactical meetings and governance meetings. Tactical meetings are typically held weekly to provide fast-pace forums for a circle to discuss operational issues, give and get updates on projects, and ask for help when needed. Governance meetings usually happen monthly, to refine the operating structure of the circle, including:

- Creating, amending, or removing roles within the circle.
- Creating, amending, or removing policies of such a circle.
- Electing members to specific roles for the circle (facilitator, secretary, and rep link).
- Creating, amending, or dissolving sub-circles.

In the beginning, the rules of Holacracy might seem cumbersome, but once you get the knack of it, they are incredibly efficient. You wouldn't believe how many hours of tiresome meetings I have saved since I started using them. I am not the only one; it is also the experience of most organisations running Holacracy. For example, GrantTree moved from only being able to make one big decision a month to making lots of smaller incremental changes each week. Also, the government agency Washington Technology Solutions (WaTech) reports improved team performance in all metrics (De Angelo, 2016). In particular, the empowerment metric reached a level of about 90%, a 50% increase from the 60% measured at the beginning of the experience. The processing speed of operational issues also plateaued at about an average of two minutes to raise, discuss, and decide on an action, a significant improvement from the original 20 minutes. They regularly process 20-24 issues in a one-hour tactical meeting.

4.5. The Hierarchy of Anarchy[70]

"Eve: All this riot and uproar, V... is this Anarchy? Is this the Land of Do-As-You-Please?

V: No. This is only the land of take-what-you-want. Anarchy means "without leaders," not "without order." With anarchy comes an age or ordnung, of true order, which is to say voluntary order... this age of ordnung will begin when the mad and incoherent cycle of verwirrung that these bulletins reveal has run its course... This is not anarchy, Eve. This is chaos." (Alan Moore, *V for Vendetta.*)

The Magenta level of development invented hierarchy resting on the authority of the elders. Red established the hierarchy of force. For the Amber worldview, the natural order of things is hierarchical; some are up, and some are down, and that's just the way it is. Finally, for the Orange altitude, hierarchy is a result of your achievements and a symbol of status. If Red, Amber, and Orange organisations have a hierarchical ontology, Green is unreservedly anti-hierarchies, reaching such extremes that some Green organisations got rid of them and replaced them with heterarchies. A heterarchy is a system whose elements are unranked (non-hierarchical). As well-intentioned as it may be, it is profoundly impractical. In most cases, this new state of affairs turns organisations into an inoperative flatland of inefficiency, demotivation, and endless decision making. The root cause of the problem is the assumption, especially among people that gravitate towards the Green altitude, that hierarchies are inherently evil. Postmodernism wrongly believes that all hierarchies or value rankings are oppressive and marginalising. In actuality, Nature is made up of hierarchies. Every complex organism is a hierarchy of parts, each part being a whole on its own but, at the same time, combining into something more.

Arthur Koestler (1967:48) coined the term *holon* to describe an entity that is simultaneously a whole in itself and a part of a larger whole. Subsequently, a holarchy describes an order where each higher level is more whole than the previous levels: *"A normal hierarchy, then, is simply*

---

[70] An earlier version of this section was published in the Integral Leadership Journal. See Robledo (2018b)

an order of increasing holons, representing an increase in wholeness and integrative capacity" (Wilber 1995: 26). For example, atoms make up molecules, molecules make up cells, cells make up organs, and organs make up complex living organisms. If hierarchies were as bad as the Green meme believes, Nature wouldn't use them as a fundamental organising principle. Wilber elaborates his explanation:

> *"To be a part of a larger whole means that the whole supplies a principle (or some sort of glue) not found in the isolated parts alone, and this principle allows the parts to join, to link together, to have something in common, to be connected, in ways that they simply could not be on their own.*
>
> *Hierarchy, then, converts heaps into wholes, disjointed fragments into networks of mutual interaction. When it is said that "the whole is greater than the sum of its parts," the "greater" means "hierarchy." It doesn't mean fascist domination; it means a higher (or deeper) commonality that joins isolated strands into an actual web that joins molecules into a cell, or cells into an organism."* (Wilber 1995: 26)

Certainly, hierarchies can go wrong when the higher levels dominate, or even repress and alienate, the lower levels. This is where some Wilberism is useful. He differentiates between dominator hierarchies and actualisation hierarchies. In a domination hierarchy, one part tries to dominate the whole by force or threat of force, de-emphasizing communion in favour of control. The traditional hierarchical organisational structure is a domination hierarchy where the boss is the part that tries to control the whole. A dominance hierarchy is indeed oppressive (the caste system being a typical example), and most organisations fall into this category. So, I'll make myself clear: formal hierarchies are pathological, and we have to get rid of them. Plain and simple.

Nevertheless, most forms of hierarchy are what Wilber calls actualisation hierarchies or growth hierarchies, and they are useful and necessary. While dominance hierarchies are instruments of oppression, growth hierarchies are instruments of progress because they maximise the potentials of the whole. They gently bring together separate and fragmented elements just as letters combine into words, words combine into sentences, and sentences are the blocks that make this book possible. In natural organisational hierarchies, status and influence are derived from contribution and expertise, rather than position.

Heterarchy is not the solution to domination hierarchies. On the contrary, it creates more problems than it solves: *"Heterarchy, in and by itself, is merely differentiation without integration, disjointed parts recognizing no common and deeper purpose or organisation: heaps, not wholes."* (Wilber 2001: 29). Anybody who has dealt with a heterarchical system based on consensus has seen the problems and inefficiencies it creates. Any person can boycott or block decision making, which effectively turns this kind of organisations into *de facto* "vetocracies." A successful meeting is one where everybody has a chance to share their feelings, even if no conclusion is reached. Have you been in one of those endless sessions where everything has to be co-created by the group? (excuse me if I'm yawning). It doesn't even matter if the leading experts on the topic are present; no recognition will be given that their view is superior to the others' because that goes against Green principles. Don't forget that, for the Green value meme, efficiency is less important than the community. In fact, Wilber (1995: 31-32) considers heterarchy as pathological as domination hierarchies, and a pathology is not cured by replacing it with another one:

> *"On the other hand, in pathological heterarchy, individual holons lose their distinctive value and identity in a communal fusion and meltdown. This holon doesn't assume it is both a whole and a part, it assumes it is a part, period. It becomes only instrumental to some other use; it is merely a strand in the web; it has no intrinsic value.*
>
> *Thus, pathological heterarchy means not union but fusion; not integration but indissociation; not relating but dissolving. All values become equalized and homogenized in a flatland devoid of individual values or identities; nothing can be said to be deeper or higher or better in any meaningful sense; all values vanish into a herd mentality of the bland leading the bland.*
>
> *Whereas pathological hierarchy is a type of ontological fascism (with the one dominating the many), pathological heterarchy is a type of ontological totalitarianism (with the many dominating the one)."*

When a hierarchy becomes pathological and turns into a dominator hierarchy, the cure is not getting rid of it and substituting it with a heterarchy as postmoderns are inclined to do. When that is done, the baby is just being thrown out with the bathwater. An organisation will only be healed by getting rid of the oppressive holons that have usurped their position in the overall system by abusing their power in the hierarchy (the formal boss, in this case) so that the holarchy itself can return to harmony.

All in all, for 3D Management, a hierarchical order is something natural and unavoidable. Hierarchy is the fundamental structural principle of the organisation[71]. The organisation is a totality whose parts are integrated into a hierarchical whole. If you don't define hierarchies in advance, they will spring up spontaneously and organically based on expertise, interest, or willingness to step in. Leadership is thus dynamic, and it naturally emerges where it is needed. A team recognises leaders for their knowledge or experience, or for being good coordinators. Authority shifts accordingly. One accumulates authority by demonstrating expertise, helping peers, and adding value. Sociocrats use to say that everyone's voice has equal value, but not equal influence. That means that a person can act as the leader of a team for a particular project, and be a follower in a different context. Power and authority are not attached to a position. The static form of hierarchy traditionally represented in the organisational chart disappears. As a result, lots of natural, dynamic hierarchies are built from the bottom up based on influence, not position. I agree with Laloux

---

[71] At this point, an understanding of the etymology and origins of the term hierarchy is most revealing. Hierarchy is the "ranked organisation of persons or things" and it comes from the Greek *hierarkhia* (*hieros* means sacred and *arkhein* to lead, rule or order). The term was introduced by Christian theologian and Neoplatonic philosopher Dionysius the Areopagite (late 5th to early 6th century). His definition was: *"Hierarchy is a sacred order, knowledge and activity, which is being assimilated to likeness with God as much as possible."* He described a Celestial hierarchy comprised of three divisions of the nine orders of angels, with Seraphims and Cherubims at the top and Archangels and Angels at the bottom, a way of divine knowledge through a progression of the Divine Names. Hierarchy is supposed to enable beings to be as alike as possible to God and to be at one with Him. Union with God is fully realized in all stages of the ladder, through a double movement of Ascent and Descent. The former manifests divinity to all beings and the latter rises toward deification. The law of inclusion and manifestation organizes the created hierarchies. If there is an element that maintains a more specific activity, it includes all the other activities which are more general. So, every higher level not only exceeds, but it also includes all the lower levels, and this makes it superior to any other. Thus, Being is higher than Life, because it includes all beings and "extends farther." On the contrary, Life extends only to living things. Also, Life is superior to Wisdom, since, in the latter, there are only logical living beings. Therefore, the developmental principle of evolutionary psychology and integral theory where a whole becomes a part of a larger whole at the next stage, unfolding and enfolding the former, is already present in Dionysius' system. The problem began when the Catholic Church translated these celestial orders into political orders of power (with the Pope at the top, and then the archbishops, bishops, priests, and deacons).

(2104: 135) when he points out: *"it can be argued that there is more management and more leadership happening at any time in Teal Organisations despite, or rather precisely because of, the absence of ultimate managers."*

The fundamental challenge of self-management is to provide the autonomy each holon requires to self-organise without the higher holon losing control and the lower holon reducing its responsibility. The solution comes by combining heterarchy with hierarchy. The hierarchy of levels is respected, but the elements within any given level operate by heterarchy:

> *"That is, no one element seems to be especially more important or more dominant, and each contributes more or less equally to the health of the whole level (so-called "bootstrapping"). But a higher-order whole, of which this lower-order whole is a part, can exert an overriding influence on each of its components. Again, when you decide to move your arm, your mind—a higher-order holistic organization—exerts influence over all the cells in your arm, which are lower-order wholes, but not vice versa: a cell in your arm can't decide to move the whole arm—the tail does not wag the dog." (Wilber 1995: 28)*

Within each level, heterarchy; between each level, hierarchy. That is the fundamental organising principle of an integral holarchy. It is the only organising system that rightly integrates hierarchy with heterarchy. The higher holon (e.g., a circle) has decision making power over the lower, and the lower one is subordinated to the more senior.

To sum up: self-management does not make organisations flat, as many people wrongly believe, but full of depth, as Freeman (2015) clarifies: "*The goal of self-management is not to make everyone equal, to have everyone having the same say on all the questions. It is really the opposite. It is to have natural hierarchies, and to have lots of natural hierarchies.*" Thanks to integral theory, organisations recover their depth, and "higher" ceases to be a dirty word but a natural and desirable condition of a holarchy.

We are much too used to picturing hierarchies linearly, like rungs on a ladder. That is the way a traditional organisational chart envisions its different levels. For Wilber, those images fail to do justice to the complex interrelations they try to describe:

> *"Thus, the common charge that all hierarchies are "linear" completely misses the point. Stages of growth in any system can, of course, be written down in a "linear" order, just as we can write down: acorn, seedling,*

> *oak; but to accuse the oak of therefore being linear is silly. As we will see, the stages of growth are not haphazard or random but occur in some sort of pattern, but to call this pattern "linear" does not at all imply that the processes themselves are a rigidly one-way street; they are interdependent and complexly interactive. So we can use the metaphors of "levels" or "ladders" or "strata" only if we exercise a little imagination in understanding the complexity that is actually involved." (Wilber 1995: 27)*

He prefers to picture them in 3D as a series of concentric spheres, much more like Chinese boxes, where every new box transcends and includes the previous one. As Forrest Gump would describe it, an organisation following this structural pattern is like a box of chocolates; each chocolate is made up of different ingredients of the same importance (e.g., hazelnut pieces), and each of these ingredients includes other various parts.

The traditional hierarchy goes from individuals to teams, to departments, to SBUs, to divisions, to corporations. A holarchical structure is organised in circles: "*A holarchy is a series of nested holons that goes all the way up from roles to circles to broader circles until the biggest circle that contains the entire organization*[72]*.*" (Robertson 2015:26). As its name implies, Holacracy, inspired by integral theory, is based on a holarchical structure. However, this model considers human beings not as a constitutive element of the organisational holon, but as separate autonomous entities that only participate in its functions through the roles they perform. In essence, holacracy differentiates people from the roles they fill, so a person is a "member" of the organisational holarchy, not a part of it. That is, people are not roles; they just take on these roles. The organisation is the relational space in which they find a common affiliation.

Holacracy was created to solve many of the problems that the traditional model generated. Decoupling people and organisation is one of the solutions they offer. It is a fundamental departure from the orthodox notion of an organisation as a collective of people coming together to do work geared towards a common objective. For Holacracy, an organisation is not a collective of individuals; it is something separate from them. As Holacracy defines it, an organisation is an autopoietic system (i.e., a self-organising system) that senses and responds to whatever is needed to express purposeful work. The organisation structures its constituent holons

[72] At Zappos, for example, the general company circle has 18 subcircles.

(roles and self-organising circles), establishing the relationships and the degrees of dependence and interaction to achieve the intended purpose. It is a holarchy with no people, just work and roles. It includes only the interactions of their members, not the members themselves. I know it goes against conventional wisdom, so let me repeat it once more: roles –not people- are the most basic building blocks (the smaller holons) in the holacratic system. The structure is thus defined by the roles the organisation needs to pursue its purpose, without reference to the particular individuals in the organisation. It is a functional chart, not a power chart. After roles, the next holon in the holarchy is a circle, which is not a group of people, but a group of roles. The people come in later, to enact or energise those roles, and they can perform different roles in different circles. You can serve the role of receptionist and, at the same time, take care of Twitter communications. For example, Carmen Duque takes care of administration at CineCiutat, but recently she took on a brand new and totally unrelated role. As she is an accomplished practitioner of yoga and meditation, now she facilitates sessions for her colleagues.

At this point, I think it is important to analyse, with AQAL lenses, this new and radical conception. In a conversation I had with Tom Thomison[73] 8co-founder, together with Brian Robertson, of HolacracyOne, and now a founding partner at Encode.org, a consulting company specialised in implementing self-management, he described a holacratic organisation, in integral theory terms, as a dominant monad that has an evolutionary purpose that is discovered through a self-organising system that, in his own words, "senses into the environment." Such a definition leaves no doubt that for Holacracy, an organisation as a senior holon or holonic system (i.e., as a whole) is an individual holon, not a social one. What does it mean? Integral Theory makes the distinction between individual and social holons. As defined by Kofman (2002), individual holons have a subjective awareness or dominant monad (an "I" or consciousness), while social holons don't have localised interiority or consciousness; they have intersubjectivity, non-localised consciousness or dominant mode of discourse (a "We"/"Its"). In short, as Wilber says (1995), *"social holons emerge while individual holons commune."* There is not a social collective inside the holacratic system, but just a collection of roles energised by

[73] In fact, I had a fascinating series of talks with Tom, Christiane Seuchs-Seuler, and Dennis Wittrock, all partners at Encode.org, Holacracy experts, and integrally informed. Their help was invaluable to help me go beyond the surface and understand the ontology of holacracy.

humans. One thing is the role (which is considered a holon), and another one is the role filler (who contributes to the organisation by taking on specific roles but is not a constituent holon).

That is a fundamental difference not only between Holacracy and conventional organisational theory but between Holacracy and Sociocracy. Sociocracy considers itself a social technology. Sociocracy and Sociocracy 3.0 are eminently social systems that have been created to help a group of humans to express purposeful work in the world. Ergo, they conceptualise organisations as social holons. In fact, before my talks with Tom, that was my point of view[74], in accordance, I would dare to say, to standard integral theory, based on the Wilber/Kofman model of holons (Kofman, 2002). Instead, for Holacracy, organisations are individual holons, and they qualify as such, insofar as they reliably pursue determinate purposes, they represent themselves in such terms, and they establish ongoing relationships with different kinds of stakeholders. In light of the above, we can conclude that organisations show consciousness. Holacracy agrees more with Edward's Integral Holonics framework (2002b) shown in figure 9, than with Wilber[75].

[74] I have to confess that it took me some time to conceive an organisation as an individual holon. I finally did it thanks to the generosity of Tom Thomison, the mastermind (together with Brian Robertson) behind Holacracy. Tom likes to define himself as a doer, but I consider him one of the most brilliant organisational thinkers out there. By the way, he knows his Integral Theory from top to bottom.

[75] If you want to go further, I strongly recommend you to read Mark Edwards' seven-part series of articles "Through AQAL eyes" (2002a, 2002b, 2003). Edwards is, in my opinion, one of the best integral theorists alive. His contribution goes beyond the usual application of Integral Theory in a particular field (in his case, organisation theory) since he has made substantial contributions to the theory itself, as this is the case.

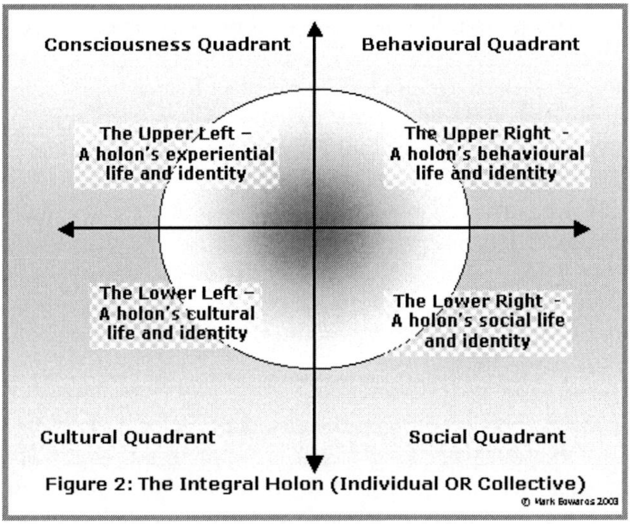

Figure 9: The Integral holonic framework (Edwards, 2003)

Now, let's break down Holacracy's concept of organisations as individual holons in its four constituent quadrants:

- UR: It includes all the concrete expressions and creations of the organisation, what in integral theory terms is known as the artefacts[76], the things that the organisation creates in the world (products, services, specific projects, actions, measurements).
- LR: The systems quadrant covers all the business processes, workflows, supply chains, customer relationship management systems, EMS systems, etc. that the organisation generates.
- UL: The consciousness quadrant. Individual holons, unlike social ones, have a consciousness. Conscious organisations? Tom's reply is a resounding yes. For him, roles are interiors with awareness. That consciousness is introduced by the role filler, who is not showing up personally, but in a role, and uses his capacity and his best sense of what is needed to express work. Roles, being composite structures of the role that is defined and

[76] *"An artifact is an entity created by a holon; its pattern (structure and function) is derived from the holon's agency."* (Kofman, 2002). Artefacts have no interiors.

the role filler filling it, are then alive and have a consciousness. Humans show up to energise roles and interpret how to express the work they require. Individuals tap themselves as role fillers to serve a purpose they care about, they sense and respond to the needs of their roles and the purpose of the organisation.

- LL: Roles can be energised by humans, systems, or even software. They interact with each other and create a culture. That is where actual organisational values are encoded. Remember: It is not the culture of the people; it is the culture of the roles. Thomison considers corporate culture, as it has been traditionally defined, a total misnomer because it referred to the people, not to the organisation.

As a consequence of eliminating the personal factor, holacracy has been accused of being mechanistic and even dehumanising. In my opinion, all those criticisms denote a profound misunderstanding of the model. The creator of Holacracy, Brian Robertson, said in a Facebook conversation we had: *"Holacracy enables the humanity in our relationships by giving us another method for dealing with the mechanical work needs."* It is mechanical for the right reason, pointed by David Allen: *"If you don't mechanicalize the mechanical, you'll mechanicalize your human relationships."* The traditional model treated people as cogs in a machine. Holacracy has solved the problem by decoupling them from the roles they energise. Individuals have a relationship with the organisation, but they are not a part of it, so the organisation cannot control them. Being a participating member is quite different from being a disposable component of a system. That is, in part, what gave rise to Holacracy as an operational practice to change one power system for another, that is, to swap management hierarchy for a distributed authority system. Thinking in terms of roles is extremely liberating and empowering for the people. Philosophically it does not equate the person to the job. You are not an accountant; you are not a machine operator; you are not a flight attendant. You just happen to be performing those roles. It reminds me of the difference we have in Spanish (and in other Latin languages) between "ser" and "estar" (both meaning "to be"). "Ser" is a permanent condition and "estar" is temporary. So, you are not a doctor; you are temporarily doing that kind of job. You are a field of possibilities, and you shouldn't identify with any limiting view of yourself. Holacracy opens up this field of possibilities for you, unlike the traditional organisational structure that imprisoned people in boxes. It is a paradise for Teal-centred people that usually have a very varied set of interests (one person might be a software programmer, but also an accomplished musician, a Zen practitioner, and an environmental activist).

The concept of a position that contains a more or less static set of functions and skills, defined in a job description, freezes the job. Nowadays, most organisations need flexibility and broad categories of work, so people have to assume roles that vary widely over time. Generalists with the capacity to move from role to role and adapt to changing requirements are far more valuable nowadays than specialists who, if needed, can be hired as consultants.

In Teal organisations, job assignments and roles are no longer engraved in stone as they used to be, and they change often. Look at Morning Star, a true pioneer of self-management. No one in the company has a title, so employees get the opportunity to do what they are good at, take on multiple roles, and pick up responsibilities based on their talents and experience. As a result, people have broader and more complicated functions than they would have elsewhere. In the same way, Finext, a network of consultancy companies in the Netherlands, is organised around experts with no job titles who share their knowledge and expertise in self-managing teams (de Bree and Stockman 2013:198). They act as intrapreneurs that commit themselves based on passion and talent for one or more projects. Finally, Edward Jones, a financial services firm, headquartered in Des Peres, Missouri, follows a philosophy called responsibility based management (in short RBM) that helps associates focus their work and link their contributions to the firm's objectives. They don't have job descriptions but instead, they write responsibility statements that define their goals and how are they going to measure their achievements, available for everyone in the company to see.

While researching for this book, I stumbled upon a text written by Tom Thomison. It described how Holacracy differentiates and holds appropriate boundaries between four "spaces" that always coexist but are inevitably fused within conventional organisations (Compagne, 2014):

- Role space: This space is unique to Holacracy as role relationships are a new organisational realm delineated by Holacracy. Roles are entities with accountabilities and power differentiated from the people that fill them. As authority is distributed among roles, role-fillers sometimes act as leaders and, at other times, as followers. It is here that feedback is channelled from reality, to define and refine roles, and process tensions that help evolve the organisation.

- Organisation space: The ritual, formalised, and structured space of meeting practices (as we have seen, they can be of tactical or governance nature). This is the sacred space of the organisation, and it is focused on the purpose. It is not about humans, and, from this point of view, it is deeply impersonal.
- Tribe space: The space of shared contexts, interests, and meaning-making. In short, community and culture. In conventional organisations, work gets done through the tribe, by influencing or shaping it in a certain way, and by conveying work expectations and leveraging organisational authority. For Holacracy, organisational work contaminates tribe space. This space is just about people sharing interests. No work is done, and no authority shows up. Tribe space is free of the organisational context and its implicit burdens.
- Personal space (or soul space): Thanks to the clear distinction between spaces, individual sovereignty is profoundly honoured. With the organisation having no control over you personally, you are free to choose whom you engage with and how you show up. Personal relationships are never forced since the work is done and clearly defined via roles. Organisational power does not come into play within this space.

I immediately realised that those spaces are equivalent to AQAL's four-quadrants. Table 8 shows the four quadrants of AQAL as a theory of everything. As applied to an organisation, understood in its broadest possible sense, the Left-Hand quadrants represent the interior dimension and it goes from the individual subjective (personal) space that corresponds to the intentions of the individuals, to the organisational culture including its subcultures (i.e., the tribe space). In their turn, the Right-Hand quadrants represent the exterior of the organisation and go from the role space to the organisational space, which is the result of working together role-to-role and governing those roles for the sake of the purpose.

	INTERIOR	EXTERIOR
INDIVIDUAL	INTENTIONAL Personal Space	BEHAVIOURAL Role Space
COLLECTIVE	CULTURAL Tribe Space	SOCIAL Organisational Space

Table 8: Quadrants of development of an organisation and Holacracy's spaces.

The separation that Holacracy introduces between the context of the organisation and the context of the people is very healthy, as it allows all of them to coexist without anyone dominating the others. *"Holacracy is all about Role and Organizational spaces. Of course, Personal and Tribe spaces are also present in parallel, but Holacracy lets them be—not out of disdain, but out of respect: they are too sacred for the organization to govern."* (Compagne, 2014). Traditional organisations tend to lump together the personal and the professional. Holacracy clearly distinguishes between person and role. The problems that may arise are between roles, not between people, and there are processes to address them; thereby keeping personal relationships independent of work-related issues.

Evolution@work, an organisation co-founded by Christiane Seuhs-Schoeler (also a partner at Encode.org), developed Tom Thomison's model, worded it in a slightly different way (see figure 10), and created the Language of Spaces, a groundbreaking methodology that focuses on developing and integrating the people context that Holacracy is not addressing.

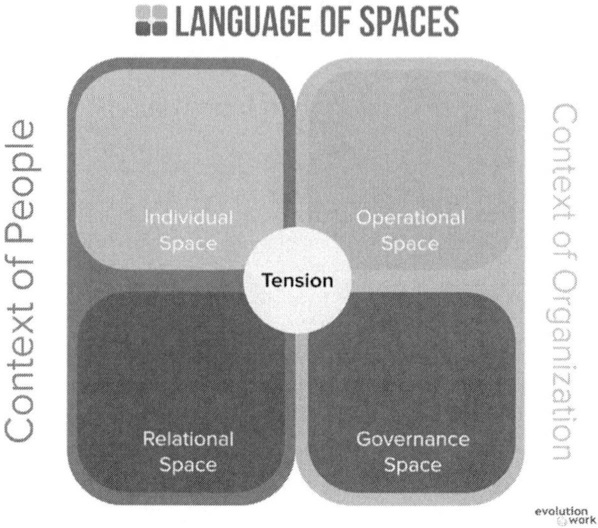

Figure 10: The Language of Spaces (reproduced with permission of Evolution@work)

4.6. Decision Making

> *"What is an anarchist? One who, choosing, accepts the responsibility of choice."* Ursula K. Le Guin.

Hierarchy is characterised by centralised decision-making. Leaving decision making to an elite of bosses is neither engaging nor effective. The alternative is a democratic system, where each worker has one vote, and we can go for unanimity or majority decision. That's the way many Green organisations operate, including many associations, cooperatives, and communities of intention. The Mondragón Cooperative Corporation (MCC), founded by a Jesuit priest in 1956, can be considered the world leader in cooperatives. MCC currently employs over a hundred thousand people, being the biggest business group in the Basque country and the eighth in Spain. Mondragón operates in the finance, manufacturing, and retail sectors. Also, it has a University and various Research & Development centres. It was created by and for workers, who are the joint owners of the firm. The cooperative organises itself through elected councils based on the principle of subsidiarity, which implies that the higher levels of the corporation can't carry out tasks that could be done at a lower level, and the structure as a whole is incapable of acting if those below are opposed (for an in-depth description of MCC's structure and operating principles see Forcadell, 2005). Other pioneering companies, such as Semco, follow this same principle. Everybody at Semco has the right to vote on important decisions. Semler (1993) remembers they were considering moving to a new factory, and they closed one day so the employees could inspect the three alternative locations to make an informed decision. Using majority vote for essential decisions makes sense, but can this be used as a general operating principle? Giving everyone an equal voice is appealing, but it is not the most effective decision-making process. Bringing about consensus among large groups of people is extremely time-consuming and sometimes impossible. More often than not, it degenerates into frustration and paralysis. As if that was not bad enough, Laloux (2014: 103) highlights a further flaw: It dilutes responsibility:

> *"The original proposer is often frustrated that the group watered down her idea beyond recognition; she might well be the last one to champion the decision made by the group. For that reason, many decisions never get implemented or are done so only half-heartedly."*

Teal organisations replace consensus with consent. Consent-based decision-making retains the participative and democratic nature that next-stage organisations demand, but is far more efficient. Sociocracy invented consent decision-making, but other governance models like Sociocracy 3.0 and Holacracy, also adopted it. It works like this: when the member of a circle presents a proposal, everyone else must consent to have it approved[77]. A consent decision is not one that you agree completely with, but one that you can live with (or tolerate). Consent, in short, is just the absence of objections. If the standard question for consensus is if everyone is in favour of the proposal, for consent it is if anyone has any reasonable objection. In Sociocracy 3.0, the members give consent (i.e., pass) to a proposal if it helps the circle carry out its purpose or drive. They oppose if it prevents the circle or the organisation from carrying out its objective in any way, or if it will prevent an individual from carrying out its function or tasks in the circle. Those are the only instances where one can object to a proposal. Holacracy is pretty much the same thing, and the facilitator asks a straightforward question: "do you see any reasons why adopting

[77] In general, Holacracy and Sociocracy only allow individuals to make proposals in circles to which they belong.

this proposal would cause harm or move us backwards?" A proposal does not have to be perfect, but simply "good enough for now," or "safe enough to try," as sociocrats put it. If so, the proposal is approved, but you can always revisit it in the future to make it better or change it. On the contrary, if someone believes the proposal will interfere with the objective of the circle or it does not allow for effectively fulfilling the role or tasks of someone, then the person will object and explain why. For a proposal to be adopted, no one must have a principled objection in the round of consent. When one or more people object, the facilitator suggests the possibility of modifying the proposal. Then the facilitator conducts another round of consent. The process can be repeated several times until there are no more objections. That means that a proposal cannot be blocked; it can only be challenged and then modified. If no one can change a proposal to meet an objection - because it is inadequate or poorly designed - it could be abandoned or referred to a larger circle or special resolution circle. In sum, consent decision-making is an action-oriented process that still provides safety mechanisms to stop potentially damaging proposals.

4.7. Case in point: Decision making at Ouishare[78]

Ouishare is an international network of peers with the vision of transforming the world through sharing and using technology to do business in a more open, collaborative, and horizontal way. Ouishare has about 1,500 active members organised in 30 sub-communities in more than 20 cities around the world developing projects at a local and regional scale to make a positive impact on society.

The founders of Ouishare conceived the organisation as a collective of in(ter)dependent individuals who gather together in a collective project to imagine the future of work and society. Ouishare was born on strong ideals: a self-managed organisation where everyone is autonomous and free to participate in the collective decision-making process.

In Ouishare, all the responsibility falls on the individual. He or she chooses how and when to contribute, what to learn, with whom to work, etc. Such a philosophy is not for everyone and many people who had joined the organisation, waiting for someone to tell them what to do, left

[78] This case was prepared with the invaluable support of Ana Manzanedo, from Ouishare.

within six months. Responsibility (and therefore, power) is fluid, and it varies according to contribution and reputation. The more you contribute, the higher the perception of commitment to the organisation and the greater the trust and reputation.

Ouishare is structured around three levels of involvement. Moving from one to another is always the result of personal initiative:

- Supporting Members: This is the entry-level within the community. Supporting members are people who identify themselves with the OuiShare mission, values, and culture and are willing to join the community, but they don't have the time nor the possibility to contribute actively.
- Active Members are individuals who actively contribute to community activities, such as events, projects, or online discussions.
- Connectors are the highly engaged members that are community and project leaders. They participate in the creation of the strategy and take part in decision-making processes. Those members who want to become connectors must write a letter of intent and get the support of 3 connectors. As the organisation needs to make quick decisions (e.g., allocate a budget for an event, remuneration of a person, etc.), in 2018 the community entrusted this group of selected individuals with the responsibility of making daily decisions while they put in place safeguards to ensure that governance remained shared. Currently, only strategic decisions that require an in-depth knowledge of the organisation (related to governance, budget, and the brand) are made in a closed group, and they are just 10% of the total.

Trust in a strong, shared culture allows Ouishare to guide its decision-making process following three general principles. These principles try to promote a nimble and inclusive decision making, encouraging discussion, and avoiding voting:

1. Subsidiarity and Autonomy: Naturally, Ouishare changed focus very early on from "global strategy" to local autonomy. All OuiShare local communities and projects are autonomous. They define their road map and rules, as long as they respect the shared values and governance principles. Once a year, each local

community defines its activities and budget[79]. Their only obligation towards the organisation is to contribute 10% of the structure costs to their local OuiShare non-profit. They should, however, ask for feedback and advice from the rest of the community when they feel a decision could significantly impact the organisation as a whole, both financially and from a branding perspective. Depending on the context, the opinion of some people has more weight than that of others. They rely on the connectors to make the call when this is the case. Until a person who is considered key gives advice, the decision-making process is not closed.

2. The "3-Connector-Rule": This principle says that all day-to-day decisions (that are not project-related, e.g., a OuiShare meetup in a new city, or any new OuiShare project) without considerable impact on budget or the brand can be made by any three connectors together. This principle relates directly to OuiShare's nature as a do-ocracy, which means that by default, those who do the work have legitimacy and also take responsibility for it.

3. Only vote when necessary: Voting divides a group into winners and losers. That's not good for a collaborative environment and often slows things down. In OuiShare, they choose to discuss topics collectively (in person and online), but they only vote when it is absolutely necessary. The tools they use to make decisions are meant to enable discussions to take place in a transparent and agile way without forcing votes on all points. Only when an aspect emerges that clearly needs a decision is an election held. The online voting process applies a version of consent-based decision-making, called *lazy consent*, which means that you don't need a specific percentage of people to vote on a matter for the result to be valid. The voting process usually lasts a series of days, depending on the urgency. Once the period is closed, the position of those who didn't vote is interpreted as consent (not opposition). In other words, silence is equivalent to supporting a decision. Remember

[79] In 2017 they started to use Cobudget (mainly in Ouishare Spain), a tool developed by Enspiral, through which they allocate funds in a collaborative and transparent manner. It works as an internal crowdfunding platform, where any member of the community can propose an internal improvement project and obtain financing for its realisation. Each donor has a "personal moneybox" where the funds are accumulated and then distributed among the different projects that are proposed throughout the year.

they are using consent, not consensus, meaning that they don't try to seek agreement but to ensure that there is no opposition. If you vote yes, it doesn't mean you necessarily agree, only that you can live with the decision, and don't veto it. In OuiShare, formal decisions are made using a software tool called Loomio, which helps groups make collective decisions using constructive deliberation. The process follows the principle that diverse perspectives can be synthesised to achieve better solutions that work for more people. While other online and offline channels used to enrich input into a decision are strongly encouraged, the results on Loomio are considered the official outcome. This way, they can keep a clear record, and ensure that everyone who desires to participate in a given decision-making process has the opportunity to do so. However, not every Loomio proposal constitutes a formal decision. Some of them are meant to gauge interest or share information.

Decision Type	Passing Criteria	Minimum time frame for voting	Description
Standard Decision	As long as 3 Connectors agree	None	Any day-to-day decision that does not have a significant impact on the OuiShare brand and budget. For example, organising a meetup in a city.
Use of the OuiShare Brand	As long as there are no blocks	Five working days on Loomio	For example, associating an external project, event or organisation with the brand and promoting it on our communication channels.
Strategic Decisions	As long as there are no blocks	Five working days on Loomio	For example, partnering with other organisations, applying for an EU project, or moving to a new office.

Budget Decisions	Passing Criteria	Minimum time frame	Description
> 300 €	The decision of each local communities' financial steward(s)	None	Examples of uses of such budgets are travel costs, event tickets, office costs, etc. The financial steward is responsible for knowing the current status of finances to make this decision.
> 2000 €	As long as there are no blocks	Three working days on Loomio	The decision is made in the local community whose budget is in question.
< 2000 €	As long as there are no blocks	Five working days on Loomio	The decision is made in the local community whose budget is in question.
Annual budget for local commons	Depends on the local community, see decision making principle #1	Validated once a year in November on Loomio for the budget of the following year	Operational costs of local OuiShare entities and their communities.
Annual budget for global commons	Each local community votes with money via the collaborative funding tool Cobudget	November - December for funding the budget of the following year	Global operational costs.

Table 10: Decision types at Ouishare (source: https://handbook.ouishare.net/governance-and-decision-making/decision-making)

4.8. Implementation Issues

Becoming an SMO is challenging. It is much more than a change from, say, a divisional to a matrix structure. It is a paradigm shift. Thus, you might be asking yourself: Is every company ready for self-management? Unfortunately, the answer is no. Self-management is not for everyone, mainly because responsibility is not something you can give if people don't want it. After an entire life within command-and-control structures, many people are not ready or willing to be liberated from the old power structures. That can be especially true for managers. Paul Green Jr., head of the Morning Star's Self-Management Institute, estimates that close to 50 per cent of the people who held senior positions in other organisations left Morning Star (Laloux 2014:176). Neither is it for those who won't take responsibility or who need to be told what to do, nor for control freaks, chronic complainers, distrustful, dishonest, or inflexible people.

Zappos is an online shoe and clothing retailer famous for its excellent customer service and for being the largest holacratic organisation to date. When its CEO, Tony Hsieh, decided to implement Holacracy, he wanted to identify the misfits as early as possible, so he offered severance packages of at least three months[80] (and up to three months of reimbursement for benefits) to anyone who felt uncomfortable with self-management and Holacracy. 18% took it, and 6% did it because of Holacracy. Now when Zappos hires new employees, it puts them through an intensive four-week training program. After the first week, the newbies are asked if they want to quit, and the company pays for the month, plus a $2,000 bonus. Only 2% to 3% of people take the resignation offer.

In my opinion, if many people in your organisation are against self-management, it is better to drop the idea altogether. Effective self-management is difficult and requires a high level of development and a varied set of personal and interpersonal skills. If the majority of the workforce is operating from Red or Amber principles, it is recommended not to implement self-management. In particular, self-management is not for the Reds. They are just not ready for it, and they will constantly try to play the system to their advantage. If they are in the minority, they can be kept at bay with an internal-customer system, and eventually, their own colleagues will end up pushing them to leave. Self-management also goes

[80] The offer was one month for every year worked in the case of employees that had been with the company four or more years.

directly against the nature of the core beliefs of Amber-centred people. They prefer very well defined rules, paternalistic leaders that offer clear limits and guidance, and value order over freedom. However, with Amber, there is a higher probability of success. My message to them would be, we are getting rid of bosses, but not rules, and then communicate clearly the new set of rules to make them feel secure: This is the new organisational structure, this is how we are going to make decisions, this is how we are going to assign jobs, this is how we deal with conflict, this is how we are going to manage meetings, etc. Just give them the Holacracy Constitution and tell them, "this is your new Bible." It is crucial to let them know they are not going to be forced to make more decisions than before. They can do it, but only if they want to, and only when they feel ready for it. The situation improves as we get higher up the spiral. Orange is the first level that shows enough maturity for self-management. From that stage onwards, bosses usually hinder the potential of employees, and self-management is the best option.

3D Management manages by colours. It takes into consideration altitudes as part of its integral approach to management and communication and meets everybody where they are. The idea is to language the message to address as many levels as possible, and then, customise the implementation according to their needs and expectations. In simplistic terms, it would be something like this:

- For Red: Don't try self-management with them if you don't want to trigger Armageddon.
- For Amber: Behold the new Tables of the Law. Follow them and respect them. Just be a good soldier. It is the moral and righteous way to go.
- For Orange: This is the cutting edge. The key to competitive advantage. A proven technology that all the cool organisations are successfully implementing. We are going to be more productive, agile, and profitable. And yes, we will make tons of money.
- For Green: This participatory system will bring harmony to the organisation. Every voice will be heard, and we will all feel as one. It will help us develop and make a better world together. There will be plenty of opportunities for hugging, chanting, and meditating.
- For Teal and beyond: Come on, you are the people of the future, the Anointed Ones. You can see the big picture. I don't need to explain it to you.

There are intermediate solutions if you don't want or can't go all the way from the very beginning. Whole Foods, has a mixed structure with its central services organised according to a traditional, albeit empowered, hierarchical structure and its more than 300 stores operating as self-governing units. Each store consists of roughly eight self-managing units, such as produce, seafood, and check-out.

Appelo (2011:127-8) distinguishes seven levels of distribution of authority:

1. Tell: You make all the decisions and just announce them to your people when necessary.
2. Sell: You make decisions, but you attempt to gain commitment from workers by selling your idea to them.
3. Consult: You invite and wait for input from workers, but it is you who is making the decision.
4. Agree: You welcome workers to join in a discussion and to reach consensus as a group. Every voice is equal, including yours.
5. Advise: You attempt to influence workers by telling them what your opinion is, but ultimately, you leave it up to them to decide.
6. Inquire: You let the team decide first and suggest that it would be nice but not necessary if they can convince you afterwards.
7. Delegate: You leave it entirely up to the team to deal with the matter.

As Kaltenecker and Hundermarkhere (2014) clarify, self-organisation is an umbrella term encompassing various options depending on the extent of a team's control and authority over each of the following four functions that must be fulfilled by any organisational unit:

- Setting directions, i.e., specifying its objectives, purpose, or mission;
- Designing the team and the required organisational support, i.e., structuring tasks, deciding who will do what, establishing work standards, and ensuring teams members have the resources and support they need;
- Monitoring and managing the work process, i.e., gathering and analysing how work is proceeding and initiating corrective action if necessary;
- Executing the work itself.

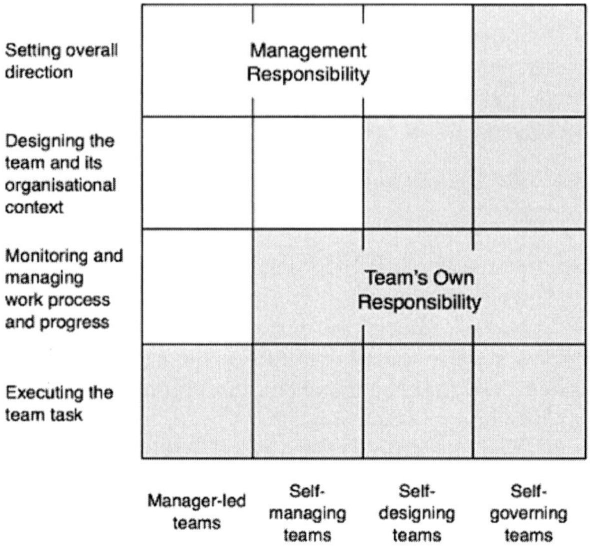

Figure 11: Authority Matrix (Kaltenecker and Hundermarkhere, 2014)

By distributing these core functions to the responsibility areas of either management or team, Hackman (2011) designs an authority matrix to distinguish four organisational levels with hierarchy and self-management at its extremes and two other intermediate options (see Figure 11):

- Manager-led teams where the team members execute the tasks under the management of a boss. This is the conventional organisational model based on hierarchies of dominion.
- Self-managing teams are not just in charge of task execution but also for managing their progress. An example would be Kanban teams in agile environments.
- Self-designing teams give members the authority to modify the design of their team and/or aspects of the organisational context in which they operate. Most real management teams are in this position as well as some scrum teams, especially when Lean/Agile is scaled. Concrete examples are pods in Podularity, Spotify's squads, chapters, and guilds, Valve's cabals, etc.

- Self-governing teams have responsibility for all four core functions as shown by SMOs, corporate boards of directors, worker cooperatives, and start-ups[81].

Ultimately, self-management is about freedom, so let the people decide. At Heiligenfeld, employees can choose if they even want to have a leader.

Any way you do it, implementing self-management is complicated and demanding. Even though the payoffs might be dramatic, it is a significant paradigm shift with tremendous challenges, especially in the beginning. People have to take responsibility for their actions and be exposed to inconvenient truths as there is no manager to hide behind.

Obviously, introducing self-management into a greenfield site is the most comfortable option and has more chances at success than changing an established system, but in any case, it would be somewhat naive to pretend that implementing self-management is going to be an easy undertaking and not everyone is going to welcome it with open arms. Resistance and turnover have to be anticipated. Provisions have to be made to deal with the concerns of those who are reluctant or hesitant, but it shouldn't be pushed onto anyone. Managers, supervisors, and people in staff functions might feel as if they are the big losers. They will probably resist having to perform tasks that they view beneath their status and perceive the greater prominence of other workers as a threat. Zappos managed the situation by keeping the salary of all former managers intact even though their day-to-day work changed radically. A new circle called "Reinventing Yourself" was created to help adapt to new roles, in an attempt to make a good match to existing passions, skills, and experience. Another prudent measure would be to guarantee that no one will lose their job[82]. Still, some may be incapable or unwilling to adapt to these changes, and they often choose to leave for a more traditional employer.

One of the biggest and most common mistakes in implementing self-management is to believe that the process should self-manage itself

---

[81] Most start-ups work naturally as SMOs -a multi-skilled team focused on a common purpose. Only as they grow, do they change to "conventional" organisational structures.

[82] Actually, firing is rare in a Teal organisation. If you are your own boss, nobody can fire you. In extreme cases, and only when the options of the conflict-resolution process are exhausted, you can be asked to leave.

without any planning, training, or a clear change in strategy. GrantTree learned it the hard way:

> *"Our assumption that "if you remove management, self-management will flourish" was dead wrong. If you just remove management, then there is just "no management." To have self-management, you actually need a helpful structure to enable people to do the work in addition to their day to day work. Otherwise, it simply doesn't get done."* ("*GrantTree's Journey Towards Self-Management,*" 2018).

Experts like Manz and Sims (1995: 114) recommend putting into place structures for guiding and designing the change effort; for example, a steering committee or a design team. It might be useful to have transition periods where each team still has a manager. As the organisation matures, they will gradually disappear. In larger companies, it is possible and even advisable to start with a pilot in one department or division before the organisation goes all in. That's what Zappos did. Tony Hsieh decided to pilot Holacracy in a small department. After the success of this experiment in 2013, he carried on to implement it throughout the company, so they created an implementation circle to oversee the broader roll out and train facilitators.

Training is also of the utmost importance, as added responsibilities and autonomy means that both the technical and behavioural skills repertoire must grow. You cannot give total responsibility without providing the means to assume it. Courses on self-leadership, negotiation, conflict resolution, and communication are essential (for the latter, I recommend methodologies such as Non-Violent Communication, Crucial Conversations, or Deep Democracy). Even more important than technical knowledge is to have the necessary values to support the idea of self-management.

4.9. Case in point: W.L. Gore

W.L. Gore is most famous for Gore-Tex, a breathable, and yet waterproof fabric recently included by the Royal Academy of Engineering in a list of the seven technological wonders of the world. Gore is also a pioneer of freedom in the workplace. It has been operating on self-organising principles since its founding in the late 1950s. The flat structure of Gore was defined initially by Bill Gore as a lattice organisation or a horizontal network of peers. It has the following characteristics:

1. Communication is direct from person to person with no intermediary

2. There is no fixed or assigned authority
3. There are no bosses, only sponsors
4. Leadership is natural, and it is defined by followership
5. Objectives are set by those who must make them happen
6. Tasks and functions are organised through commitments

Everyone in the organisation is an associate. The lattice allows associates to interact directly without having to go through a formal chain of command. Orientation and training to deal with the high levels of autonomy are essential. Every associate at Gore, new or veteran, has a sponsor. Before a person can be hired, an associate must agree to be the new employee's sponsor. The role of a sponsor is very different from the role of a traditional supervisor. Sponsors are cicerones, mentors, and coaches, responsible for tracking the new associates' progress and assisting them as needed. After six months, the sponsor will generally give a verbal evaluation and a written evaluation after 12 months. Typically, sponsors are responsible for about five associates at a time.

Each division and all associates have their own mission statements. More importantly, associates follow Gore's four guiding principles which enable them to work more effectively while growing as professionals and individuals:

1. *Freedom*: They encourage, help, and allow people to grow in knowledge, skill, responsibility, and range of activities. They believe that associates will exceed expectations when given the freedom to do so.
2. *Fairness*: Everyone at Gore sincerely tries to be fair with each other, suppliers, customers, and anyone else with whom they do business.
3. *Commitment:* Each associate makes his or her own commitments and keeps them.
4. *Waterline*: As a rule of thumb, the advice process is guided by a US Navy analogy called the "waterline principle." A hole above the waterline posits little danger while a hole below the waterline might sink the boat. Associates are encouraged to make autonomous decisions as long as the risk does not threaten the survival of the organisation. If there is a threat to affect the reputation or financial stability of the company, they need to consult with other associates before making the decision.

At W.L. Gore they don't believe in large organisational units because they destroy community and they often lead to groupthink. W.L. Gore sums up its expansion strategy in the sentence "get big by staying small." No Factory can exceed 200 employees to maintain familiarity and to keep communication fluid.

4.10. Control beyond Budgeting

According to Bogsnes (2016: 22), when managers are asked about their most significant concern in abandoning traditional management practices, invariably, they answer "losing control". Control is necessary, but not all types are beneficial:

> *"There is some control we want to keep, and some control we want to get rid of. We still want to understand where we have been and where we are, through quality accounting and reporting. We still need effective processes with no waste and order in the house. We still need to understand when we are performing well and when we are not, and what might lie ahead if this is possible and useful to predict (...)*
>
> *There are, however, two other types of control that we want much less off. The first one is too much controlling of what people shall and shall not do through detailed budgets, tight mandates, detailed job descriptions, rigid organizational structures, smartly constructed monitor schemes, and all other Theory X-driven control mechanisms. Some of these controls might seem real and effective but are often nothing but illusions of control. People are smart, and any system can be gamed if people want to (...)*
>
> *The second type of control we need less of is maybe an even bigger illusion. It is the perceived control of the future, the one we think we get if we only have enough details in our plans and forecast."*

Traditional budgeting is a remnant of the predict-and-control mindset. The customary annual operating budget is a management tool first introduced by Alfred Sloan at General Motors nearly a century ago. For various reasons, people as qualified as Robert Kaplan consider it an anachronism (Bogsnes 2016: 2):

- It encourages rigid planning and a lack of flexibility.
- It is a very time-consuming process.
- It provides just an illusion of control.
- Decisions about activities, projects, and spending are made too early. It prevents the right things from getting done if

they are not in the budget, and at the same time, it leads to the wrong things being done because they are in the budget.
- It often leads to a non-optimal use of scarce resources. A cost budget defines the maximum you can spend, but that ceiling works just as well and often better as a floor for the same cost. Spending too much is terrible, but spending too little is not good either. So, everybody spends every single cent of the budget.
- It stimulates unethical behaviours like gaming, lowballing, and hidden agendas.
- Decisions are taken too high up as a result of a lack of autonomy.

Beyond Budgeting is a new way of budgeting, but also, a holistic approach to strategic management, business planning, target setting, forecasting, and performance management based on financial and non-financial key performance indicators[83]. The Beyond Budgeting round table was developed in Great Britain in 1998. It is not about ignoring the need for proper cost management; on the contrary, it is about better cost management and better optimisation of scarce resources than the traditional budget offers (Bogsnes 2016: 22). Beyond Budgeting tries to overcome the limitations of conventional approaches and to transform finance's historical role of reporting and controlling into a new position more empowered and adaptive based on:

- Replacing annual budgeting by rolling budgets, produced on a quarterly or monthly basis, or dynamic forecasting with no fixed predefined frequency or time horizon. Units update their forecasts when events occur or new information becomes available (external forecasting), or when an action is taken that will have a forecast impact (internal forecasting), which should result in a timelier allocation of resources.
- Rolling forecasts that embrace KPIs based on the balanced scorecard and linked to the organisation strategy and performance measures.

[83] Though I am underlining the financial aspects, Beyond Budgeting goes beyond getting rid of the traditional budget. It is about moving from command-and-control management and radically transforming organisations as a whole.

- Activity-based costing: By identifying the drivers behind the activity cost, they can be allocated to the products and customers generating these costs.
- Benchmarking: It is incorporated in the budget by linking managers' targets to external benchmarks instead of past performance.

4.11. Integral Performance

A business needs to sustain superior performance over time, but financial results are only one part of the story. Integral organisations look at performance with a broad set of criteria. Anyhow, don't feel guilty if the Orange in you is crying out loud: "This is all very nice, but give me the numbers." Some studies have demonstrated how vanguard businesses outperform conventional ones, even financially. The book *"Firms of Endearment"* (Sisodia et al. 2007) illustrates how conscious companies that work to 'endear' themselves to all stakeholders outperform those that don't. As Table 9 indicates, the 18 companies analysed (including BMW, Johnson & Johnson, Whole Foods, and Southwest Airlines) defeated the market in all time frames, ranging from three years to 15 years. The "endearing companies" (those that secure the emotional loyalty of all their stakeholders) even beat the Good to Great firms[84] (Collins, 2001) over the 10 and 15 years periods'. They demonstrated a 1025% cumulative return over ten years, compared to 316% for *Good to Great* companies and 122% for S&P 500 companies. A further advantage pinpointed by Sisodia et al. (2007: 127) is that while the life expectancy of mainstream companies is dropping year after year, endearing companies tend to be more enduring.

---

[84] *Good to Great* is a book written by James Collins that presents the results of his landmark study that tried to identify the universal distinguishing characteristics that cause a company to go from good to great. Collins and his research team identified a set of 11 companies that made the leap to great results and sustained those results for at least fifteen years. Those good-to-great companies generated cumulative stock returns that beat the general stock market by an average of seven times in fifteen years, better than twice the results delivered by a composite index of the world's greatest companies.

Cumulative Performance	15 Years	10 Years	5 Years	3 Years
US FoEs	1681.11%	409.66%	151.34%	83.37%
International FoEs	1180.17%	512.04%	153.83%	47.00%
Good to Great	262.91%	175.80%	158.45%	221.81%
S&P 500	117.64%	107.03%	60.87%	57.00%

Table 9. Financial performance of FoEs vs. Good to Great and S&P 500 companies (Sisodia et al. 2007).

Simpson et al. (2013) replicated the study gathering data until 2013 and found again that the 18 publicly traded companies, as a portfolio, were a much better investment with an average 15-year performance of 83.4% compared to a gain of the S&P 500 of 47% over the same time.

Finally, Bozesan (2013) compared those companies to a set of integrally-acting businesses (including Stoneyfield Farms, REI, Puma, or Whole Foods). They were even more financially successful than FoEs, which already were three times more successful than *Good to Great* companies. Whole Foods is a remarkable case since over a period of 10 years it returned 1,800% to its investors (Sisodia et al., 2007) and outperformed all of its competitors significantly.

Other studies cast similar results. Since 1997, The Great Place to Work Institute, in partnership with Fortune Magazine, has produced a ranking of the hundred best companies to work for. The firms in the list tripled the returns of the S&P 500 index in 15 years (10.32% vs. 3.71%) (Mackey and Sisodia 2013: 279).

If we focus on the ethical dimension, there is an organisation called Exosphere that produces a list of the world's most ethical companies. The list includes about 100 companies that outperform the Standard & Poor 500 every year since the creation of the program in 2007 by an average of 7.3% annually. These companies have been found to enjoy superior brand reputation, higher customer loyalty, and lower team member turnover (Mackey and Sisodia 2013: 280). Another example is the LAMP index, created by investment advisor and author Jay Bragdon. It screens companies that operate with integrity, value their employees, and follow the principles of nature. Just before the crisis started to have its effects, in 2009, Global LAMP Index companies returned 44.56 per cent, far surpassing the S&P 500 (+26.46 per cent) and the MSCI World Index (+28.01 per cent). Over the past decade, Global LAMP Index companies made 98.03 per cent, while other benchmark companies collectively lost money.

To the amazement of many, the more companies focus on something beyond money, the more money they make. It makes perfect sense. More and more customers are interested in developing closer relationships with organisations whose purpose and values align with their own. Teal organisations have a better chance of getting customers emotionally linked with the organisation and its values. My favourite example is CineCiutat, the Mallorca-based arthouse membership cinema. To my amazement, many of its members tell me that they would never go to another cinema in Mallorca, no matter what movie they show. They consider CineCiutat their own, and they would never betray it for another. Apart from that, there is simply no comparison between the high degree of employee engagement of these organisations and the depressing results conventional organisations get at the Gallup's Global Workplace Report. Among the best-managed companies in Gallup's database, as many as 70% of employees are engaged, an indication of the high level of psychological ownership those companies achieve. They estimate that companies that successfully engage their employees experience a 240% boost in performance, as compared with companies that don't. SAP AG, the world's leading provider of business software, headquartered in Germany, estimates that a 1% change in employee engagement would have an impact of 35 to 45 million euros for SAP's operating profit.

Mackey and Sisodia (2013: 283-284) aptly summarise why these businesses deliver superior financial results as opposed to their money-obsessed, employee-disengaging competitors:

> *"These companies generate very high levels of sales because they excel at creating value for customers; they willingly operate with lower gross margins than they are capable of yet they achieve higher net margins than their traditional counterparts. Over time, conscious businesses develop sterling reputations and grow faster. They attract more loyal customers, committed team members, higher-quality suppliers, and generate greater community goodwill. All of this also helps these firms earn more and receive higher valuations relative to their earnings."*

CHAPTER 5

ARTS: DEVELOPING PEOPLE, PRODUCTS, AND THE ORGANISATION

> *"Business is far more than a profit machine. It is a vehicle for self-expression, for dreaming about creating the future we desire, for accomplishing together what we can't do alone, for creating extraordinary amounts of value of many kinds for everyone a business touches.*
>
> *Business is a powerful instrument that we must use to serve the noble cause of greater human and planetary flourishing."* Chapman and Sisodia, 2015: 241.

5.1. The Company as a Work of Art

> *"Practicing an art, no matter how well or badly, is a way to make your soul grow."* Kurt Vonnegut.

The voice of art is relatively weak in a world that mostly accepts the authority of science and reason. Nietzsche requested more poetry and imagination as the only way to adapt to the continuous changes in the environment. Business problems don't persist because leaders don't know management science, but because its tools are insufficient. Science is extraordinarily efficient in solving simple questions, but not when dealing with a VUCA world of challenging issues and relentless change. The exclusively scientific view of management treats a complex system such as an organisation, as a complicated system. A human-based, uncertain, and unpredictable system can't possibly be managed like clockwork, and can't be conceived through non-ambiguous cause-and-effect chains.

Management is a practice, and as such, it has a strong artistic component. The business world is the territory of the unsure, the unforeseeable, and the indefinite. Given this overwhelming lack of certainty, maps and instruction manuals have a limited utility. Science, at best, can present a consistent set of alternatives, but ultimately decision-making is an art. Of course, management should draw on all of the organised body of knowledge we call science, but decision-making, creativity, and human relations are beyond logic.

Science is the dimension of the present. It helps to understand the rules of the current paradigm and to devise methods to work within its limits. But art is the ideal dimension to navigate into the future, the one that is better suited to deal with the unknown, the indecisive, and the unresolved.

The artistic dimension is a generative dimension that works toward the betterment of the organisation, its products or services, stakeholders, and ultimately society as a whole. Growth could be another term to describe it, but I'm not going to use it, as growth is one of the main aspirations of Orange organisations, so more often than not, the word is associated with size and profit. I prefer to talk about development, which is not as biased towards material growth. Hence, the purpose of the artistic dimension is the development of the organisation and all its stakeholders, especially its members. For the development of the organisation and its products and services, we need innovation, which is the result of imagination, intuition, design, and creativity. The artistic dimension also strives to increase the collective intelligence and consciousness of all stakeholders. Our institutions are but a reflection of ourselves, for we do things in our own image. The only way to create integral organisations is to develop people to integral levels of development. 3D Management's conception of development is much more comprehensive than that of traditional organisations. It encompasses not only horizontal development, i.e., acquiring new skills and capabilities within the current frame of reference, but also, as we will see, growing into higher altitudes of consciousness and mastering ever higher and better states of mind.

On another level, art incorporates an aesthetic and emotional component that, as Aristotle well knew, aspires to the creation of beauty. Beauty is a mighty word sadly absent from management jargon. Imagine if we approached organisations with an artist's mindset. A real artist is never satisfied with good enough. Think about the standards a company could reach if it looked for beauty rather than just quality in its products, services, and processes.

There are many different forms of beauty in the world. A woman may think of an attractive man, a golfer about a perfect swing, a musician about a captivating song, a salesperson about a well-constructed argument. As

Confucius once said: *"Everything has its beauty, but not everyone sees it."* Organisations should not only be coldly analysed in terms of bottom-line results, but also in terms of passion, emotion, and beauty. There is beauty in a well-designed product, a job well done, an original idea, a compelling ad. Most people see their work as something prosaic and don't savour the beauty of it. If we manage to perceive the aesthetic dimension of work, we will have taken a big step in the path of personal fulfilment. *"The work can be seen as a symphony, a jam session, a dance or a theatrical performance, as a show, in short. We must encourage people who work with us to think of their employment as an art, regardless of what the job is "* (Morris, 1997). Even the most routine work has the necessary ingredients for the expression of our true artistic nature. Martin Luther King said, *"If you have to sweep streets, you should sweep like Michelangelo painted, or Beethoven composed music, or Shakespeare wrote poetry."* Also, C.D. Warner wrote: *"A great artist can paint a great work on a small canvas."* Imagine David Lynch in a world where filmmaking didn't exist. What would Messi do without football? Whatever would have happened to Roger Federer or Martina Navratilova if tennis had not been invented? Think of Juliette Binoche or Javier Bardem without acting, Marie Curie without science, or Nietzsche without philosophy. Picture Velázquez without painting, Björk without music, or Richard Branson without enterprises. Humans fully develop their potential in structured activities. Business is one of them. That is its beauty. A kind of beauty that Morris (1997) presents in this captivating way:

> *"The best businesses are beautiful structures within which human beings work, develop and flourish. (..) The beauty of business is the beauty of what can be and what should be. And this is the art of business: the art of creating structures in which human associations can grow and live well. "*

What am I talking about? Turning the cages that organisations are today into chrysalis where people grow, develop, and flourish. I'm talking about the end of artisans and human resources. I'm talking about workers as self-managed artists. I'm talking about processes, products, and services not as mere commodities or outputs, but as works of art. The organisation that conveys that vision won't have to worry about employee motivation anymore.

Even before he started to work, Michelangelo claimed he could see the sculpture within the marble block. Can you see the beauty of your organisation underneath its current coarse appearance? Now, you have to chisel away what is superfluous.

5.2. Case in Point: Knowmads Business School[85]

One of the cutting-edge examples of people development, together with customer involvement, is the Knowmads Business School. In June 2009, Pieter Spinder and three other colleagues, inspired by the knowmad[86] concept developed by Daryl Goodrich and John Moravec, planted the seeds of the Knowmads Business School in Amsterdam. They had worked in university education and they all agreed that the traditional business degree, with a pre-defined curriculum that lasts a fixed period of time, seemed awkward and outdated.

Knowmads is a 6-month, non-formal, creative business program, focused on self-development and entrepreneurship, targeting young professionals who want to make a positive difference in the world. The program challenges participants to co-design, with the support of the Knowmads' staff, their own curriculum and create actionable projects around various assignments for partnering organisations.

The program focuses on personal development, leadership, entrepreneurship, and learning by doing. It has a few core workshops and tools such as Deep Democracy, Non-Violent Communication, Business Model Canvas, The Start-up Wheel, Theory U, Chaordic Stepping Stones, sales, marketing, and project management.

It all starts with a single question. In the first week, participants are asked to formulate why they came to Knowmads. This so-called Individual Learning Question becomes the guiding focus that accompanies them throughout the rest of the course. In addition, the program poses five driving questions related to the participant's strengths and motivations that serve as subject areas and provide an inside-out approach:

1. Who am I? Personal development.
2. In what world do I want to live? Social innovation and sustainability.
3. What do I want to contribute/change? Personal leadership.

---

[85] This case study was prepared based on personal conversations with Pieter Spinder, the case study he wrote for the book *Knowmad Society* (2013) and the organisation's web page (www.knowmads.nl)

[86] Moravec defines a knowmad as a nomadic knowledge worker, a creative, resourceful, and innovative person who can work with almost anyone, anytime, anywhere.

4. How can I best organise to get it done? Entrepreneurship and new business design.
5. How do I bring it to the world? Marketing and creativity.

Self-organisation is an essential element of the Knowmads philosophy. They don't believe in tests, marks, rights, or wrongs, as they don't see them anywhere in real life. Students make decisions, set their personal goals, and thus have their own successes and failures.

They don't approach students as empty buckets to be filled with knowledge. They treat them as young professionals ready to work and co-create with partnering companies and institutions. Pieter Spinder always says that Knowmads is not a dress rehearsal. Hence, unlike most business schools, they don't use case studies. They work on real assignments (4 per year) to generate real value and even "earning while learning." The partnering company delivers a challenge, and the students have to create a working plan which includes a financial proposal for services. Once the partner accepts the project, the tribe (that's what each cohort of students is called) starts working while being coached by The Knowmads staff. In addition to the program, students are free to work on their own projects and businesses. After the one-year programme, the students can stay at the school to incubate their own business (coached by Knowmads staff) in the Knowmads Greenhouse.

As a reflection of its nomadic philosophy, the Knowmads Business School has created extensions that offer shorter programmes in Hanoi, Argentina, and Bogotá.

Knowmads Business School rests outside of the educational system, so they cannot award official diplomas, but Pieter Spinder told me you could get a really cool tattoo instead.

5.3. Stairway to Heaven: Integral Organisational Development

"And he dreamed, and behold a ladder set up on the earth, and the top of it reached to heaven; and behold the angels of God ascending and descending on it." (Genesis 28:12)

"Most businesses use people to build products and make money; we use our products to build people." Bob Chapman, CEO of Barry-Wehmiller (Chapman and Sisodia, 2015:123).

The conservative tendency of a culture striving to perpetuate itself can quickly change into deadening immobility. Only an organisation light on its feet is in a position to adapt to the unexpected. When everything has to be controlled, when the unknown is not allowed to exist, the creative, exploratory process that renews the organisation can no longer manifest itself, and the organisation drifts towards decay.

Organisational Development (OD) is a well-established field dedicated to improving organisational growth and individual development. A classic definition of the term, valid for the Teal paradigm is the following:

> *"Organization Development is the attempt to influence the members of an organization to expand their candidness with each other about their views of the organization and their experience in it and to take greater responsibility for their own actions as organization members. The assumption behind Organization Development is that when people pursue both of these objectives simultaneously, they are likely to discover new ways of working together that they experience as more effective for achieving their own and their shared (organizational) goals. And that when this does not happen, such activity helps them to understand why and to make meaningful choices about what to do in light of this understanding."* (Neilsen, T. 1984: 2-3).

The objective of OD is transforming organisations through the alignment of strategy, structure, culture, processes, and people. Even though each of these areas is a combination of science, arts, and ethics, some, such as coaching, leadership, human development, change management, or culture, have a strong focus on "soft" factors. Others such as strategic management, organisational design, and structure or process management require more "hard" scientific techniques (that is why we talk about organisational structure and design in the last chapter). The kind of OD I will focus on in this chapter relies more on the artistic dimension, meaning it is based on soft factors of individual and cultural transformation, which are more liquid and dynamic in nature.

Companies invest vast amounts of money each year in change programs. Product lines are renewed more and more quickly. Technologies follow each other at an unparalleled rate. Organisations shouldn't get carried away by this change frenzy. They need to distinguish between what needs to be more permanent (their values, culture, and purpose) and what does not (their operational strategies and practices that must adapt to changes in a VUCA environment). Despite this obsession for change, most programs either fail or fall short from their stated objectives. Many companies back off soon after they start implementing a new change programme or simply initiate a makeover that only scratches the surface leaving the culture and philosophy of the company intact. Change only affects the external right-hand quadrants, which is the territory of the scientific dimension, while the internal dimensions of needs, motivations, beliefs, culture, and values remain the same. They approach change superficially, not as real transformation. The difference in degree between both concepts is significant. As Barrett (2001: 13) explains, change is a different way of doing, whereas transformation is a different way of being.

I have met some organisations that define themselves as Teal, but they are so only on the surface. They speak Teal, they apply some Teal practices, but it is skin deep, they don't fully own the level. Going Teal is not about implementing some tools. It is about embodying the Teal consciousness. Change is only internalised as it affects our values and beliefs. Real change must be transformational and integral. It requires changing the paradigms and ideas that make up the old structures.

Most organisations and people, often unconsciously, are not willing to go that far. In fact, the main reason that change programmes fail is resistance. As we have seen, a worldview determines how each person perceives reality and how she/he subsequently behaves. The moment we create a way of seeing things, we are also creating ways of not seeing other things. We become prisoners of our ideas, similar to the deluded prisoner in a Hindu story: every time he saw someone on the other side of the bars, he burst out laughing. The guard, puzzled, asked him what he was laughing at, and he replied: *"I laugh at all those losers trapped behind these bars."* It is a cage of our own making, and we are not even aware of it. As George Sterling once said: *"A prison becomes a home when you have the key."* Watching movies like *The Sixth Sense* is an excellent way to realise how easily we get stuck in ill-judged ways of seeing things. The surprise ending is like a whack to the head that makes us reinterpret everything we assumed to be true.

The propensity to become locked into certain modes of thought is a consequence of how our brain works. Paradoxically, as Edward de Bono contends, the primary purpose of thinking is to avoid thinking. The mind is a self-organising information system that makes sense of external confusion by collecting and organising information into patterns. When the mind recognises one, connects with it, and then stops thinking. It is like tuning a radio station, you look for a particular signal, and once you find it, you quit searching. For example, when we learn how to type, it takes tremendous mental effort, but once we master the technique, we do it almost automatically, so we can dedicate our energy to other purposes. Admittedly, this is a handy evolutionary feature that makes life much more comfortable but is also a double-edged sword.

If the world is becoming more and more complex, then organisations need as many individuals as possible in possession of a more flexible and sophisticated mind to keep up with it. However, organisations have traditionally ignored the challenge of transforming people and raising consciousness. A second-tier organisation should intentionally support human transformation through all domains of growth and development. This support for transformation should be extended to all stakeholders (especially, collaborators and customers).

Something that organisations and its members partake in, is that they are all on an evolutionary journey. Becoming a Teal organisation is a developmental decision with significant implications for everyone involved. Human beings span very different levels of development. The way to raise organisational consciousness is to move a critical mass of people to a higher stage. Being a Teal organisation does not imply that every single member should own the stage (in most cases that would entail 95% layoffs!), but the more the merrier, so attracting the highest value meme individuals and helping people develop is crucial. As Barrett (2014: xxiii) rightly states, if the organizational culture is less advanced in its development than the person is, he/she will find obstacles to explore their full potential. If the culture of the organisation is more sophisticated, it will support the individual's development over time, up to the effective value meme the organisation has attained. Laloux (2014: 41) puts the following example:

> *"Suppose I am a middle manager looking at the world mostly from a Conformist-Amber perspective. My natural style with my subordinates would be to interact in very hierarchical ways, telling them exactly what they need to do and how they need to do it. Now let's say I work in a Green Organization, where my leaders urge me to empower employees that work for me. All around me, I see other managers giving their subordinates lots of leeway. Twice a year, I receive 360-degree feedback, including from my direct reports, telling me how well I'm doing on empowerment (which can affect my bonus); every six months, I'm asked to sit down with my team and discuss how well we are doing in living company values (which include empowerment). Within such a strong context of Pluralistic-Green culture and practices, I'm likely to espouse some Green management skills and behaviors. The context has pulled me*

> *up, leading me to operate in more complex ways than I would if left to my own devices. And just perhaps, over time, when I'm ready for it, the context will help me grow and genuinely integrate into that paradigm."*

Organisations could be a springboard to boosting human potential. Wilber (2006, 2012) introduced the interesting metaphor of the conveyor belt. He says that the influence of certain institutions and leaders can act as "conveyor belts" for vertical development, helping people move up the ladder of transformation. In his canonical book, *Integral Spirituality* (2006), Wilber argues that religion can serve as the great conveyor belt for human transformation. As I have argued elsewhere (Robledo, 2018a), business, as the most important institution of our time, can be at least as critical in supporting our development.

Kegan and Lahey coined the term *Deliberately Developmental Organisation (DDO)* to explain the phenomena of organisations and business ventures that consider, as necessary, the development of each employee as the maximisation of the bottom line[87]:

> *"What if a company did everything within its power to create the conditions for individuals to overcome their own internal barriers to change, to take stock of and transcend their own blind spots, and to see errors and weaknesses as prime opportunities for personal growth? What would it look like to "do work" in a way that enabled organizations and their employees to be partners in each other's flourishing?" (Kegan and Lahey, 2016: 86-87).*

They conducted research that proves that organisations that included people's development as a central objective outperformed those that ignored it, not only with an overall more satisfying work experience but with higher profits. They offer a simple test to ascertain to what extent an organisation is a DDO:

[87] And rightly so. My main issue with the DDO philosophy is that it doesn't take into account all dimensions of management reality. Making money is the primary objective of the scientific dimension, and people's development is partially the objective of the artistic dimension, but ethics are not included in this model. Moreover, none of these fulfills a higher purpose in itself, and all of then should be subordinated to the higher spiritual dimension. Development could only be a principal purpose for some very particular organisations, such as coaching firms, schools, or universities.

- Does your organisation help you identify a personal challenge that you can work on in order to grow?
- Are there others who are aware of this "growing edge" and who care that you transcend it?
- Are you given supports to overcome your limitations?
- Do you experience yourself actively working on transcending this growing edge on a daily or at least weekly basis?
- More specifically, is there any process in place by which you are helped to see how you could have done your work better?

Based on Kegan's DDOs, Wilber and DiPerna (2016) subsequently examined the notion of a Deliberately Developmental Civilisation. Their integral approach offers a more comprehensive understanding of the various types of development than Kegan's original research. In his survey of the vast array of orientations toward the further reaches of human potential, Wilber (2006) sustains that there are three core elements of transformation and development. He refers to these three elements as *states*, *structures*, and *shadows*. According to him, any integral understanding must take them all into account. According to his view, human development is a three-dimensional journey of growing up (through structures of consciousness from beige to turquoise or even beyond), waking up (through mastering the different states of consciousness, in particular, the nondualistic ones) and cleaning up (through the integration of our own shadow[88]).

[88] The topic of shadow integration falls outside the scope of this book. Still, I would like to make a few remarks about it. As defined by Jung, the shadow is our "dark side" or personal unconscious, a kind of dissident sub-personality made up of the repressed part of us. It is a "litter bin" filled with denied aspects of ourselves, including all the feelings and abilities rejected and banished by our egos. Usually, it appears in childhood when we identify with certain ideal characteristics and dismiss others. Shadow integration is of fundamental importance because even if a person succeeds at mastering states and gets to higher structures of consciousness (of greater complexity, care, and perspective-taking), he or she can still be a victim to unconscious motivations, desires, and attachment patterns that create deep suffering for themselves and others. As Jung pointed out, when we suppress shadow aspects of ourselves or other people push them out of conscious awareness, they become more powerful drivers of behaviour. Only by re-owning and re-integrating them through therapy or techniques such as Integral Life Practice's 3-2-1 process, can its corresponding expression be reduced or eliminated. The shadow can appear (I should better say hide) both at individual and

Any map of human growth and development that fails to include all three dimensions is falling short of a comprehensive analysis. Partial models will, by their very nature, create conditions for the development of partial/stunted human beings. The bottom line for Wilber and Diperna (2016) is that our world needs human beings who are both evolved through the various structures of consciousness, as well as awake to the full spectrum of states of consciousness:

> *"The higher the structures of growth in spiritual intelligence, and/or the higher the states in waking up, and/or the fewer shadow elements present, then the more loving, more truly spiritual, more conscious and more caring an individual is."*

An integral approach to development also means not restricting it to punctuated moments separate from the day-to-day running of the company (like a course, external coaching or sending employees to an MBA program) but having it ingrained in the fabric of the organisation.

The artistic dimension, as it applies to human beings, aims to promote the integral development of the members of the organisation (including states, structures, and shadow) so that they can unleash their full potential. That means leveraging human capacity and building people to greatness, offering them the means to discover, develop, and use their innate talents. Those efforts should not be restricted to associates, but include all stakeholders: suppliers, customers, and society in general. Paradoxically, that objective was already stated by Frederick Winslow Taylor in the foundational book of Orange-level management, *Principles of Scientific Management* (1911: 2): *"On the contrary, the first object of any good system must be that of developing first-class men."*

Many people think that developing is just getting better at what we do (i.e., acquiring skills and knowledge), but it is not only about learning new things, it also includes transformation (i.e., changing the way we know and understand the world). For this reason, we need to distinguish between horizontal and vertical development:

---

collective levels. Individually, the shadow is what can't be thought about consciously; collectively, the shadow is simply what is not talked about, but it is manifested through social mechanisms such as prejudice, scapegoating and marginalisation (Murray 2017: 210).

- Horizontal Development focuses on technical learning. It is about acquiring more knowledge, skills, and competencies. Horizontally focused education would aim to pour new content into the person, such as how to use some software or how to communicate effectively.
- Vertical Development is about how one thinks. It is the advancement of a person's thinking capability. It refers to the stages that people progress through to make sense of the world. The outcome of vertical development is the ability to think in more complex, systemic, strategic, and interdependent ways.

In short, horizontal development is about transferring information to the person, whereas vertical development has to do with the transformation of the person. In metaphorical terms, horizontal development is like pouring water into an empty glass. The vessel fills up with new content (e.g., a foreign language). But what if the glass is already full or is not adequate to hold what we want to pour in? In this case, the limiting factor is no longer the content (our knowledge); it is the cup (our mind). Thereby, vertical development places less emphasis on the content and more on the container itself (the mindset, identity, and mental models of the person). The aim of vertical development is not to add more content to the cup but to change it. Using a technological analogy, it is the difference between getting new software (horizontal development) or upgrading to a new operating system (vertical development). There comes a time when you have to buy a new mobile phone because all of the latest apps are not compatible with your outdated operating system. I don't remember who said this, but it is very well said indeed: to be truly free, don't change your cage, change yourself.

The methods being used to develop people in organisations are mostly focused on horizontal development. The learning that takes place is basically what Chris Argyris would call "single loop" learning (improvements and adjustments of the current mindset). Vertical development is about "double-loop" learning (changes to the assumptions and thinking upon which the incumbent worldview is built, which will finally lead to a shift in mindset). As the challenges of the future require more complex thinking, more emphasis on vertical development is needed. As Kegan observes (2016: 238): *"People will need to change their mindset, not just their skill sets."* The good news is that according to Clayton Alderfer's Existence, Relations, Growth (ERG) model of human needs, the need for growth is never met (unlike physical wellbeing and relational needs that can be satiated). So, if people get started on the path of vertical development, the more they grow, the more they want.

However, keep in mind that growing into a new stage of consciousness can't be forced onto someone. As the creator of the STAGES model of development, Terri O'Fallon, once said at a conference: *"We have developmental rights. We should be allowed to stay at whatever developmental level we are at."* The only thing we can do is to create the frameworks that are conducive to propelling growth into higher stages of psychological and cultural development. 3D-management organisations understand in what stage of evolution every person is and try to design the conditions for a healthy emergence to the next level. There are four possible ways this can be done[89]:

1. Create opportunities for people to have transformational experiences.
2. Provide support to understand and integrate the insights from those experiences.
3. Give people practices, training, and tools to adopt a new way of being in their everyday lives and work activities.
4. Connect people with relationships and communities that support the new way of being.

I am very fond of Barrett's model of evolutionary coaching (2014: xxxi). Evolutionary coaching is about helping people find out who they really are and assisting them in becoming all that they can be (in more technical words, helping them to individuate and fully self-actualise) so that they can be truly independent. The purpose of evolutionary coaching is to facilitate the full emergence of people's potential. Evolutionary coaching is not about merely helping people become more proficient at what they do (horizontal development), *"but helping them participate in their own evolution, the evolution of their organisations, the evolution of our global society and the evolution of our species"* (vertical development). The model of Evolutionary Coaching takes into account, among other things:

- A person's stage of development, i.e., level of consciousness, and worldview.
- The stage of organisational development, and if the culture corresponds with the desired stage of development.

[89] Adapted from Vieten and Estrada (2017: 291)

- The degree of fit between the organisation and its members.

Nick Petrie (2014), from the Center for Creative Leadership, defines vertical development as thc process of how to grow "bigger" minds. He has developed an interesting process based on three conditions that can trigger vertical development (2014b: 3):

1. Heat Experiences *(The What—Initiates)*. These are complex situations that disrupt and disorient the individual's usual way of thinking. They come with the realisation that the current form of making sense of the world is inadequate. The mind starts to open and search for alternatives.
2. Colliding Perspectives *(The Who—Enables)*. The person is then exposed to people with different mindsets, ideas, backgrounds, and experiences. This both challenges the existing mindset and increases the number of perspectives.
3. Elevated Sensemaking *(The How—Integrates)*. Finally, through a process or a coach, the person integrates and makes sense of these perspectives, and experiences a more elevated level of consciousness that is gradually embodied and stabilised.

According to Petrie, any one of these conditions has value, but it is not until you combine all three that development takes off. The absence of one or more of the elements often leads to anaemic development and insufficient results. For example, a program that includes *Heat Experiences* and *Colliding Perspectives* but not *Elevated Sensemaking* can motivate participants to grow and be exposed to new perspectives, but they won't have the time and support necessary to integrate them into a broader worldview. When no *Colliding Perspectives* are offered, the program will fail to expose participants to fresh perspectives, and they will fall back into their old way of thinking. Finally, a program lacking *Heat Experiences* will result in participants not finding a reason to grow. They will treat the development process as an intellectual exercise and not much will be transferred back to their lives.

Petrie's process demonstrates how growth is maximised through challenge and support. A self-management environment is a perfect setting for vertical development because people are constantly challenged with making decisions, seeking advice, working on new tasks, and picking up skills and knowledge that elsewhere would be reserved for managers. Research has shown that 70% of organisational learning comes from challenging work assignments. As job scope increases, it is a requirement to acquire skills that are broader and different from the ones we already have. With that idea in mind, Semler (1993: 157) introduced job rotation at Semco. The employees decide if they rotate and where to rotate, but they can stay in one job a minimum of two years and a maximum of five. If they want to stay longer, they are required to set new goals. They plan the rotations a year in advance, so they have time to learn the new job.

An integral approach to development is vital. AQAL is an excellent tool to do that. The individual first assesses him or herself from the inside (UL quadrant), then from the outside with the help, for example, of a questionnaire (UR). Later, colleagues provide feedback to each other making assessments with a coaching approach (rather than blaming or pointing out mistakes), first subjectively (LL), and then based on a questionnaire (LR). Once this integral 360º assessment is done, each person identifies a development plan and colleagues provide peer coaching in many different ways. If this process is followed, the organisation becomes a mentoring society. Tools such as the Leadership Circle Process or Kegan's Immunity to Change (2009) are recommended here.

I particularly like some practices used by Quantum Monkeys, a small consultancy firm in Montreal, specialised in agile methodologies and cultural improvement. As one of his employees, Maurice Lefebvre (2017) explains, they were inspired by the baseball cards devised by investment company Bridgewater (see Kegan and Lahey, 2014). The card groups information about your personality type, the ways in which you truly shine, and the areas you can improve upon, as voted by your peers. Quantum Monkeys baseball cards feature three aspects in which the employee can be a role model for others and three that he or she wants to improve upon. Each individual first proposes them after a self-assessment, and then they evolve during weekly group consultations with their team. In some instances, they are simply determined through discussion, with the "looking to improve" list set as a personal continuous improvement goal along with the team's goals. In other instances, teams have developed satisfaction surveys for every member to send to anyone (other employees, other workgroups, managers, even clients after offering a service), and the answers are used to fuel their team and their personal continuous improvement efforts. As a whole, Lefebvre reports that the baseball-card approach fosters a very positive, rapid learning environment, with less resistance and has resulted in a rapid deepening of skillsets, not only of the listed subjects but of coaching and mentoring skills also.

Another excellent example is Buurtzorg, where all nurses are trained in "Intervision," a peer-coaching technique where they call on colleagues to think about issues they encounter in their work, share the existing knowledge and experience, and make better use of it. It is about learning from and with each other, to gain expertise and improve the quality of work.

I don't want to forget Next Jump, the company I am going to talk about below. Every Next Jumper has a coach assigned who is responsible for their growth, which includes setting up their environment with training, feedback loops, and coaching.

5.4. Case in Point: Integral Development at Next Jump[90]

Next Jump is a $2-billion e-commerce platform founded in 1994, headquartered in New York, and with offices in Boston, San Francisco, and London. Its core product is PerksAtWork, an employee discount platform used by over 70% of the Fortune 1000 to help their employees save money. It also has a new product line of various apps and tools to measure and manage employee performance and company culture.

In 2016, Next Jump was recognised as one of the nine healthiest workplaces in the US, but it has become more popular after Kegan and Lahey included it in the book *An Everyone Culture* (2016), as a Deliberately Developmental Organisation (i.e., an organisation with a culture explicitly designed to advance the mutual development of the organisation and its people).

Their developmental culture is condensed in the mantra *"We want to do little things so that others can do the great things they're meant to do"* and further summarised in the equation: Better Me + Better You = Better Us. "Better me" describes the importance of self-improvement, "better you" uses that knowledge to help others, and "better us" is the result that contributes to creating a better company and a better world. Supporting others is an essential element of Next Jump's culture, so, they have a policy whereby the biggest bonuses and highest form of recognition (the "Avengers Award" which recognises the Next Jumper who most

---

[90] This case was primarily prepared with information from Kegan and Lahey (2016) and Next Jump's wonderful main site www.nextjump.com, which includes tons of information about the company's distinctive culture.

exemplifies steward leadership) goes to those people who have helped others the most.

Next Jump has devised a series of programs to help employees grow as people and leaders. These programs allow employees to experiment in areas where they are required to develop without having to fear the consequences of failure.

Super Saturday is Next Jump's hiring process. They run three events a year, inviting top applicants to spend a day with them. They review thousands of resumes and perform hundreds of screenings to narrow down the list of candidates to 40. These potential Next Jumpers are flown to the host office for a full day of skills tests, practical exercises, and interviews. They also have the chance to connect with Next Jumpers on a more casual level, for example, having lunch in small groups. Additionally, they meet senior leaders and get a presentation and Q&A with the Co-CEOs, Charlie Kim and Meghan Messengers. Next Jump doesn't want to be a company of, as they call them, "brilliant jerks." Their main hiring criterion is humility, as they believe that this is the most critical predictor of personal growth. Coachability, responsibility, and absence of victim mentality are other key features.

The onboarding process at Next Jump starts the same for everyone (whether they are straight out of college or senior executives), in Personal Leadership Bootcamps (PLBC) for three weeks as a way to assimilate to Next Jump culture and work on areas of development. The program starts with participants learning to identify their "backhands," a very descriptive tennis metaphor they use to refer to weaknesses. To be a great tennis player, you need to be very well-rounded. Even if you have a devastating, dominating stroke (a forehand or a service, in most cases), you have to work hard to bring all of your game to a reasonable level (including the backhand, which is the weakest point for most of us), or else your opponents will beat you by hitting to your vulnerable areas. At Next Jump, everyone is required to work on their backhands, the areas where they feel less comfortable or less skilful, or those that hold them back from fulfilling their potential. While generally, we all try to cover up our backhands, hiding our flaws and portraying an image of perfection (especially the case at work), at Next Jump they want you to keep working on your flaws and getting support to improve. Next Jump excels at creating trust and safety for employees to experiment without fear. For example, they have a no firing/lifetime employment policy as a statement of intent for employees so that they can show their vulnerabilities, weaknesses, and faults without the fear of losing their job. They have reduced people's more profound limitations to being too confident or being too humble, and everyone there knows if you lean towards arrogant or insecure. They suggest to hesitant people that in meetings they should speak up in the first fifteen minutes. On the other hand, overconfident individuals are advised to wait 45 minutes before talking. At the end of the boot camp, a committee evaluates your performance and decides whether you graduate or not. Those who do leave the boot camp, do so with a practice plan for working on their backhands. Those who don't graduate will have to stay in the boot camp and engage more fully and authentically, or else they can leave the company with compensation of $5,000.

Once on board, Next Jump provides daily, weekly, and monthly frameworks of development. Every day, there is the *Talking Partners* (TPs) programme, a co-mentoring activity designed to help employees increase their awareness and improve judgment when making a decision. From among individuals who were hired at the same time, every employee is assigned a Talking Partner who complements their weaknesses. Talking Partners starts every workday, first thing in the morning, usually while eating a company-sponsored breakfast. The idea is to talk about each other's strengths, frustrations, and problems, and to use the partner as a second screen when making important decisions. Each TP meeting is organised around a framework: meet, vent, work.

- Meet: Signals the need for consistently meeting every morning, and getting into a daily ritual of practice.
- Venting: Involves "getting the toxins out" – anything from home life or work life is fair game for discussion. TP is a place that honours frustrations and anxiety as part of who we are. It also gives a structure for reducing the hold of negative thinking.
- Work: TPs are expected to push each other for greatness, set high expectations, and help each other talk out both small and large decisions.

Weekly, two sets of Talking Partners and a more experienced colleague, acting as a mentor-coach, meet for a two-hour *Situational Workshop* (SW) in which the participants use a real challenge they faced that week to learn about themselves and their problem-solving skills. Charlie Kim, co-CEO of Next Jump, describes what he thinks makes this kind of weekly workshop structure powerful:

> *"At this weekly workshop, each of the four of you describes some challenge you've met at work in the week and what you've done to meet it, or not. You might not be sure if how you handled the situation was optimal or not. The mentor-coach is there to encourage you to reach a higher level of self-awareness so that you might identify new options for responding to similar future challenges and so avoid reacting in the same old way.... Over time, you see people growing immensely from these weekly sessions."*

As Charlie explains, the focus is *"on the training of judgment, rather than on technical training."* As a result, the discourse and pace of a situational workshop can be a bit surprising to a first-time observer. A typical workshop question might be, "what are you learning about yourself in having this problem?" People are identifying "problems of practice," snags they run into, but the coach's response is rarely direct problem-solving. Next Jump's practices are geared to help people change from the inside out. Solving problems too quickly, without the benefit of uncovering underlying assumptions, means no change. If you don't uncover the underlying assumption, you are most likely going to be reproducing new versions of the same problem you think you have already solved.

Finally, every month, in an event called the *10X Factor*, ten employees give five-minute presentations to the entire company about the progress they have made in culture or revenue building[91]. 10X is a unique opportunity for Next Jumpers to reflect on their personal and professional development and share it with the entire company twice a year. It started as a way to show that "something extra" engineers and business people brought to their daily work. Over time, the program has evolved from a showcasing of raw talent and tangible results to a reflection on an employee's personal and professional development that can be shared with the rest of the company twice a year. Each employee gets the unique opportunity to share their journey with the company and receive honest feedback from a panel of judges, and on-the-spot coaching to understand if they are moving in the right direction to improve their backhands. This

[91] Revenues and culture are equally important at Next Jump. Everyone works half their time on HR and culture, from the software engineer to the CEO. Compensation takes evenly into account what you do for the business and the culture. Lastly, performance reviews are 50 per cent based on revenue contributions and 50 per cent on cultural contributions. No matter how good your performance is, if you don't work on your development, you will be penalized.

feedback is useful, both professionally and personally, because mistakes and challenges in work are closely aligned to the problems and weaknesses in personal life.

Next Jump's development follows a 3D Management approach, as it contemplates physical, emotional, mental, and spiritual training, addressing the Fantastic Four dimensions of body, mind, heart, and spirit.

- Physical Training: A robust physical base that takes into account fitness, nutrition, and sleep, is the foundation to start growing. The company provides healthy meal choices and Next Jumpers are encouraged to visit the company gym twice a week, where they offer a wide range of activities, from spinning to yoga nidra. To make working out regularly easier, they have created a weekly company-wide fitness competition. Every week, teams compete to see how many employees are able to exercise at least twice a week. The winner is the team with the highest percentage of employees hitting the target. FitNut (Fitness & Nutrition) is Next Jump's in-house health & wellness program created to help employees understand their own health. It offers free biometric tests and bi-annual onsite blood screenings and flu vaccinations for employees, family, and friends.
- Emotional Training: Next Jumpers participate in psychological training and receive feedback in programs such as the already mentioned talking partners, 10x, situational workshops, etc.
- Mental Training: While they believe 90% of the training should be on the job, they also offer weekly, monthly, and annual training sessions in real-life scenarios. Technical Situational Workshops provide mentoring to tech teams and leaders on a bi-weekly basis. They focus on skills and overall technical knowledge and are run by the most senior technical leaders. First Fridays is a monthly platform for Next Jumpers and guests to learn from thought leaders and experts on a monographic topic. Initially set up as a spin-off of Next Jump University, CEOTalks[92] offer the rare opportunity to gain valuable insights and learnings from CEOs, thought leaders, and industry experts aligned with Next Jump's corporate culture. The list of guests is

[92] https://www.youtube.com/playlist?list=PLeX0W94H3mZQmJzOuHSiMI_mV1SEcncsC

impressive, including Tony Hsieh, Simon Sinek, Arianna Huffington, and Bob Chapman.

- Spiritual training: The activities they organise under this heading are about changing the world for the better and changing the work culture. The revenue that Next Jump generates from its employee savings platform is used to help public schools, entrepreneurs, non-profits, the US Military, and many others. Their "Better You" giving-back platform includes successfully established programs such as the following:
    - Next Jump Leadership Academy is a three-day, full-immersion, pro bono workshop, taught by Next Jump's master coaches, designed to share Next Jump's developmental culture.
    - Through the Adopt-A-Public-School program, Next Jump partners with public schools to build long-lasting relationships that serve and support students, teachers, and parents. For example, on July 27th, 2015, they adopted PS 119 in the Bronx, a school where 75% of students live below the poverty line.
    - Code for a Cause pairs teams of Next Jump engineers with non-profits for two weeks free of charge to help scale and build charitable products.
    - Vendor Appreciation Day is a Christmas tradition through which Next Jump employees say thank you to everyone who keeps their offices running by buying presents for their children.

5.5. Humanising the workplace

The business of business is people. (Herb Kelleher, Co-founder of Southwest Airlines)

Today I bumped into a friend of mine. He is a regional executive of a well-known multinational company, and he told me about the bitter situation in his company. Ever since they were taken over by investment funds, everything focused on short-term results, and the pressure increased to unbearable limits. Maybe a new company has been bought out, and you are no longer deemed necessary after the merger, or perhaps the company has been acquired by another, whereby your job is equally threatened. The employees feel the sword of Damocles constantly hanging above their heads. Some people resign because they can't endure the pressure; others take medical leave because of stress or depression. It is heartbreaking to witness.

Workers feel increasingly alienated and powerless with the progressive deterioration of working conditions disguised under euphemisms such as right-sizing, labour-market flexibility, and outsourcing. Nowadays, only a privileged few have stable contracts, while most must conform to low wages and insecure, precarious employment terms. Treating people like this is not only wrong in moral terms, it is terrible for business. When people are down and exhausted, they tend to act more short-term, performance and creativity drops, and self-control is lost more easily.

Unfortunately, this happens even in some of the most admired companies, where employees have fun playing table tennis and take naps on the couch in front of their bosses. Take Netflix, an organisation whose best practices I have highlighted several times throughout this book. One of Netflix's fundamental principles reads: *"Build and maintain a culture that rewards high-performers, and weeds out continuous, unimproved low performers."* An expression of that is a policy known as the "keeper's test" designed to detect and get rid of the low performers. The way it works is simple: supervisors ask workers if they would fight to keep a particular colleague or not; if the answer is no, the person is dismissed. As the Wall Street Journal reported in a 2018 article, people in those positions have recognised that they feel pressured to lay off workers because they don't want to be considered softies, which entails the risk of losing their jobs. Regardless of its vanguard practices, Netflix's culture is mainly Orange. Netflix's CEO, Reed Hastings, compares the company to an Olympic Team, and natural selection is a prerequisite to maintain its culture of excellence. The intense competition to be among the high performers turns workers into rivals. I'm sure that working there often feels like being on a high-performance sports team, but I also imagine that it can feel like being in "The Hunger Games." That's not right, not only from a Teal perspective but from a human perspective.

What kind of world have we created? For far too many, work is a curse and suffering a requirement to make a living. We spend around half of our waking time at work. It should be something that gives us happiness and fulfilment, not something that takes from us. Enough! There must be a better way.

A Teal culture is incompatible with the insecurity associated with cutthroat environments, exploitative employment practices, and rock bottom wages.

3D Management is a humanistic philosophy that considers people never as a means but as an end in themselves. It aspires to humanise the workplace, respect individuals, and improve their satisfaction and fulfilment by creating spaces where they feel more secure, authentic, and happy. 3D Management conceives having more satisfied workers, not as a utilitarian goal ("the happier the cow, the better the milk"), but as an end in itself because it is the right thing to do.

Southwest Airlines, the only consistently profitable major airline since 1973, has built an exemplary humanistic culture. They have an unconventional hierarchy of stakeholders that ranks employees first, customers second, and shareholders third: *"We believe that if we treat our employees right, they will treat our customers right, and in turn that results in increased business and profits that make everyone happy,"* the airline explains in a blog post about company culture. Southwest evidences its people-first philosophy in many different ways. In the notoriously cyclical airline business, they have never had a layoff. It has employee turnover rates of 4 to 5%, more than half the industry average. Finally, it was the first major airline to introduce profit-sharing to its employees. In 2016, the company gave its 54,000 employees a record $620 million in profit sharing. In 2017, it shared $586 million, which equated to about a 13.2% average bonus for each employee, or roughly the equivalent of six weeks' pay.

The Greek word Eudaimonia (εὐδαιμονία) etymologically derives from the words "eu" ("well") and "daimōn" ("spirit") which refers to a minor deity or a guardian spirit. Eudaimonia literally means achieving a condition similar to that of a benevolent deity, or being protected and looked after by a benevolent god. As it is regarded as the most favourable state to be in, it is commonly translated as happiness. However, some experts suggest "human flourishing" as a more accurate translation, since it includes an experience of meaning and development, to become the person one is meant to be. A Gallup study of human happiness in 155 countries supports that point of view, as its number one determinant was having a meaningful job in the company of people we care about.

Freinacht (2017c: 266) is a strong proponent of making people happy as a societal goal, including both *hedonic* happiness (pleasure, enjoyment, fun) and *eudaimonic* happiness (meaning, purpose in life, and peace of mind). It is one of the tenets of his inspiring metamodern political agenda. I couldn't agree more with him, and I think that it should not only be a goal for society but also for organisations. 3D Management addresses both kinds of happiness to build workplaces for human flourishing and wellbeing. That entails generating the conditions for psychological thriving and growth to occur. Work has to be enriching, and rewarding or it is not worth doing.

Let's start with hedonic happiness. When employees switch on their computers at the beginning of a workday at Cyberclick, a Spanish online marketing business based in Barcelona, the first thing they see is a traffic light of emotions, a dashboard where they have to express how they feel that day. A green light means they are happy and ready to go, a yellow light indicates that they are so-so, and a red light means something is upsetting them. Managers review the results and check if there is something they can do to help the ones with problems. Semco came up with a more analogue device. A panel at the entry of the factory has the name of each worker written on a hanger. When workers arrive in the morning, they select one of the three pins on every hook. Again, green means happy, yellow means beware, and red means not today, please. Other companies such as Artiem Hotels have developed apps to check on the emotional state of the workforce after the working day.

Now, imagine a scale of happiness that goes, let's say, from 1 to 7, describing a whole range of states from horrific, to very uneasy, to so so, to satisfied, to good, to joyous, and ending in blissful. What would be the median of the happiness in your organisation? Just imagine how differently an organisation would function if many more of us were in higher states a more substantial portion of our time. If my median state is 6, I would feel much more secure and effective compared to a medium state of 5. As Freinacht asserts (2017c), *"Each state-level you shift up or down is a world of difference."*

Allow me to introduce at this point a concept I call the art of the states. Think of an organisation where people see work as an end in itself, where they work according to their intrinsic motivations or even transcendental ones. A space that allows them to return to the basis of their professions, to what brought them to choose it in the first place, or simply, to practice a passion that they love. Work would be meaningful, making the boundaries between work and leisure increasingly porous. Such kind of organisation would surely be creating the conditions to maximise flow states at work and generate satisfaction, fulfilment, and personal growth. Among the objectives of the artistic dimension of 3D Management is to optimise the likelihood for higher subjective states, flow states, and intrinsic and transcendent motivation. That is the Art of the States.

InfoJobs is the first privately owned career network in Europe, so prevalent in Spain that "InfoJobs" has more searches on the internet than "job" or "work." They are aware that physical spaces produce effects on people. If you have entered a Gothic church, you will have sensed how the atmosphere invites you to contemplation and spirituality. Likewise, InfoJobs has spaces to induce certain states. The headquarters have meeting rooms with names that correspond to the company's values, and they are decorated accordingly. For example, the happiness room is the room where people can relax and experience peace of mind. It offers yoga, meditation, and relaxation sessions during working hours. It has no chairs or tables, just pillows, blankets, and yoga mats. You have to go barefoot, and mobile phones and computers are not allowed.

Many organisations have created the role of the Chief Joy Officer. That is the case of the London-based coding bootcamp Makers Academy, where the position is filled by Dana Svoboda[93]. She defines her mission as "to help people connect with themselves." Among other things, she acts as a holistic coach for students and staff, as well as a yoga teacher, running Vinyasa sessions twice per week, and a meditation teacher leading classes daily. She has also introduced an emotional intelligence curriculum. At Makers, they believe that software developers must cultivate emotional skills. Gone are the times when coding was a solitary activity. Coding has become a team sport, and it is necessary to learn how to get the best out of oneself and other people. Likewise, at Ben & Jerry's, happiness is considered so important that they have created the joy gang, a volunteer team of employees that try to make work a bit more fun.

Mainstream organisations have marginalised not only happiness but all emotions in general. Since Descartes, emotionality has been opposed to rationality and has been repressed. The scientific dimension won the battle over the artistic one, and organisations became rational institutions. The way most organisations deal with emotions seems to be taken from one of those science fiction movies in which alien invaders with human form blast anyone showing human emotions with their laser guns. In the same way, people in organisations have to hide their humanness behind a facade of cold, abstract, and dispassionate technical knowledge and business jargon. They are paid to think, not to feel, so they leave their hearts at the doorway. Factors such as enthusiasm, passion, intuition, sensitivity, and

---

[93] Meet her at http://www.chiefjoyofficer.com

love are not part of the official history, nor are selfishness, hatred, fear, envy, or anger.

The idea that business is about numbers is ridiculous. We are emotional creatures. Our brain gives priority to emotions before reason. We need to recognise that the exchanges generated in an organisation are mainly emotional. Emotion makes people ignore facts, forget about logic, and justify any argument. Science has proven that we make our decisions emotionally and then explain them rationally because information gets first to the limbic system and later to the neocortex. So much for the *homo economicus*. Thus, the rational language of management is often merely rhetorical to preserve the appearance of rationality, and numbers are used to justify previous decisions. People are persuaded through emotions, not reason or numbers. It is emotions that move and motivate us (notice that all three words have the same etymology). If you want to accomplish anything, they are essential to make it happen. Emotions need to be honoured in the workplace. If being professional means being cold, inhuman, and emotionless, let's be unprofessional. Look at InfoJobs, a Spanish job searching site that exchanged handshakes for hugs as the standard salutation.

In any case, choosing between reason and emotion, putting mind over heart, is as stupid as walking on a single leg or covering an eye with a patch to see better. Pascal once said, *"The heart has its reasons, of which reason knows nothing."* The emotional and the rational are so intertwined that they are hard to separate. An Orange culture is wary of emotions. They want people not to show any feelings and only act logically and predictably. Green goes to the other extreme, rejecting analytical "left-brain" thinking and favouring "right-brain" feeling and intuition as a basis for decision-making. Teal is happy to tap into all the domains of knowing and being. The portrait of the people working in Teal organisations includes complex and holistic thinkers that are emotionally, socially, and spiritually intelligent.

Art is the emotional dimension, science the logical dimension, and ethics the moral dimension. We have to balance all of them. Employees who work with their hearts, minds, and souls are more productive than those who simply "do a job." Without emotion, there is no motivation, engagement, or creativity. The time has come for people not to leave their hearts on the coat rack when they get to work.

5.5.1. A New Language

Language does not describe the world. To a large extent, it creates it, and creation is power. The Gospel of Saint John itself reveals the cosmogonic power of language: *"In the beginning was the Word, and the Word was with God, and the Word was God."* (John 1:1). God created the world through the verb (the logos), and through the verb, man destroys it. Children know that words are magic. Utter the words "Open Sesame," and the cave of the treasure will unlock, shout "Shazam!" and you will turn into Captain Marvel. Language plays a determinant role in our way of seeing the world. As Wittgenstein argues, the limits of my language are the limits of my world. Consequently, in Kofman's words (2001a: 44): "*We don't talk about what we see, we only see what we can talk about.*" When an Inuit looks at the snow, he sees a different reality than the one I see. The Inuit has about forty terms to qualify the snow. I have only one, which is more than enough in Majorca.

Our language is an arbitrary system of signs that create meaning by difference ("face" is not the same as "race") and opposition (reason-emotion, man-woman, superior-subordinate). Inevitably, differentiation and contrast generate dominance and repression. Language is a double-edged sword that shows as much as it hides, and creates as much as it destroys. In any system of opposites, one is usually better or preferable (it is better to be the boss than an employee, reason has been considered traditionally superior to emotion…). In practice, as Derrida maintains, it engenders a hierarchy that marginalises all those values and beliefs that lost the war of opposites. As a result, language is often used to cover up and manipulate (as it is the case with some sadly current euphemisms such as collateral damage, pre-emptive warfare, downsizing, or rightsizing). As Kofman (2001a) notes:

> *"In the midst of games of words such as those described by George Orwell in his 1984 novel, the War Office is renamed the Ministry of Peace, abdication, and lack of leadership becomes "empowerment", resentment becomes "courtesy", aggressions become "honest communication" and wild criticism is considered "feedback."*

Let us think about the everyday language of business. Although Orange is the effective value meme, and it shows ("*achieving competitive advantage", "striving for excellence", "profit is the measure of our success*"), business language has profound Red undertones of aggressiveness and power ("*market dominance", "crush the competition,"* etc.) and warfare terminology ("*we need to rally the troops", "capture market share*").

What if we change the metaphor and we think of business less like an army or a competition where victory is the only option, and more like harmonious coexistence, co-creation, and collaboration?

Consider the word employee. It is loaded with Red implications of subservience. It comes from the verb employ, which has synonyms like use, utilise, or spend. The same goes for the term human resources. People are reduced to resources to use and throw away like toilet paper. Go and ask for their engagement. What about an operator? It would be a contradiction in terms if an operator thinks autonomously or takes initiative. All those words are the product of a very determined ideology that makes us think instrumentally about human beings. One more word that conjures up an undesired reality is patient. How is a caregiver going to take a complaint from a patient if a patient is, by definition, someone who suffers all evils and adversities resignedly? Just calm down and wait! Speaking of hospitals, the movie *"The Doctor"* (Randa Haines, 1991), offers another good example. William Hurt plays a doctor who treats his patients rather unemotionally since he believes that *"surgery is a matter of judgment, and you should not attach yourself."* However, when he gets laryngeal cancer, he begins to see things differently. One day, one of his residents talks about *"the terminal of the 1217"* and he replies angrily: *"Terminal of what? Of buses? (...) Call another patient terminal, and you will be describing the end of your career."*

For this reason, Jurgen Appelo (2011: 115) prefers to talk about team growing instead of team building. Let's follow his full explanation:

> *"People are careless in their use of language, and they often make a mess of terminology. They tend to talk about building living things, which is impossible. We don't build cities, we grow them. What we build are our individual houses, roads and trash cans. What we grow are families, businesses, trees and a large population of ugly pigeons. The sum of all that is a city and it grows. It is not just a construction. Likewise, we don't build companies. We grow them. And we can't build relationships. We grow them."*

We need to humanise the language of management if we want more human workplaces. The most progressive companies have replaced HR with People Departments. Artiem, a chain of hotels consistently on the list of Best Workplaces of Spain, calls it People and Welfare Department. Many others have also dropped the words employee and subordinate. Instead, they use terms like associates, members, partners, or colleagues. W.L. Gore was a pioneer in introducing this new language. They have no employees; they have associates. An associate is an independent person who works with you, not for you. Finally, at Gore, there are no jobs. There are commitments. A commitment is defined in the Cambridge dictionary as *"a willingness to give your time and energy to something that you believe in, or a promise or firm decision to do something,"* so is not an imposition, but something you freely decide to commit to and that you are responsible for. A job is static, whereas commitments are dynamic and fluid, so associates choose the commitments that are more appealing to them and most suitable to their capabilities.

Language can also be used to support transformation, as the words people use can determine the way they think. Every altitude has a jargon of its own. Beliefs, attitudes, motivation, or values are difficult to change, but language is different because it is directly observable (UR). Intervening in a certain way to change the language people use can help to move the centre of gravity of every member of the organisation. As that happens to one person and then another, the entire culture can change to a new stage. However, it is not wise to use a language too far removed from the centre of gravity of the people you are talking to. Integral Theory always recommends speaking in the language of the listener and introducing the Teal jargon very gradually.

5.6. Case in Point: Decurion[94]

Headquartered in Los Angeles, California, Decurion, is a corporation with several subsidiaries operating in the businesses of movie exhibition, real state, and senior living. They include Pacific Theatres, ArcLight Cinemas, Robertson Properties Group (RPG), and Hollybrook Senior Living. Decurion employs about 1,100 people they call "members."

The Decurion Corporation, one of the three DDOs of Kegan and Lahey (2016), is defined more by why it exists and how it operates than by what businesses compose its portfolio. Its identity comes not from running movie theatres or developing real estate but from the pursuit of its purpose and adherence to its values. Decurion's mission, the fundamental reason it exists, is to provide places for people to flourish. By "flourish," they mean to become fully oneself, which includes living a whole life and growing

[94] Decurion is one of the companies identified by Kegan and Lahey (2016) as a DDO. The information to prepare this case study comes from their book and Decurion's web page http://www.decurion.com/dec/

into what one is meant to be. Flourishing is the process of living into one's unique contribution and expressing oneself fully. While building each of its businesses, Decurion seeks to create the conditions in which that expression will emerge. By demonstrating the efficacy of their practices in generating financial and developmental returns, they hope to inspire and guide other companies in making work more profitable and more humane. In this way, they seek to change society for the better.

Decurion has developed the following set of axioms derived from some fundamental beliefs about people and work:

> *We believe that work is meaningful, that work gives meaning to people's lives. For us, meaning comes from three things: developing oneself, creating something excellent and enduring, and contributing to other people.*
>
> *We believe that people are not only means but also ends in themselves. Most businesses view people (employees, customers, suppliers, and others) as a means to some end, such as completing a transaction or meeting a goal. We feel that reducing people to a role in a process dehumanizes them. While honoring the roles they play, we approach people as fellow human beings, as ends in themselves.*
>
> *We believe that individuals and communities naturally develop. Much of the literature on development ends with the teenage years. But we know that adults continue to develop. Our structures and practices create conditions that pull people into greater levels of complexity and wholeness.*
>
> *And while we didn't begin with this belief, our experience has shown us that pursuing profitability and human growth emerges as one thing. They are part of a single whole, not two things to be traded off or two elements of a "double bottom line." We capture this axiom by saying that nothing extra is required.*

Those axioms are the foundations of the values that guide the company, namely:

- *Excellence: If we can't be proud of it, we don't want to do it.*
- *Respect: We feel a responsibility to treat people with fairness and decency.*
- *Clock Building: We believe in managing and building this company to last at least through the next century.*
- *Servant Leadership: We feel an obligation to contribute to the communities in which we operate.*

- *Learning: We believe in providing an opportunity for individuals to develop, grow, and contribute.*
- *Compassion: We care about people.*

Employees are not required to share Decurion's values or beliefs. They encourage questioning and recognise that wisdom begins in not knowing. They do, however, require that people adhere to their purpose and values when they act in or on behalf of the company. Building meaning into work, treating others as ends, and creating conditions for development (their axioms) as well as excellence, clock building, servant leadership, respect, learning, and compassion (their values) are not ideals to which they aspire. They are standards for action and requirements of behaviour.

Developmental growth lies at the heart of Decurion's approach to business. Their purpose, to provide places for people to flourish, includes creating conditions for people to develop more fully into themselves. They have established a consistent set of practices to achieve that.

They have, for a start, what they call *"developmental pulls."* Managers at Decurion intentionally identify and create situations and challenges for its members that will promote development because they exceed the person's current level of capability. For example, Decurion's ArcLight Cinemas has a sophisticated set of practices to promote appropriate developmental opportunities. The general manager at each location uses data about individual growth to identify ideal job assignments for every employee, every week. They are meant to serve both the crew member's development and the company's business needs. The management team at each location meets weekly to review the goals and performance of each worker and to determine whether someone is ready for more responsibility.

"Touchpoints" are an excellent way to connect work with personal growth. They are daily one-on-one meetings of employees with their managers, devised to discuss how to realise their own goals through opportunities tied to Decurion's business needs. The dream of one employee, for instance, was to become a film set decorator, so her manager made her responsible for the decor of events to align her interests with an organisational goal.

Lastly, *"competency boards"* are poster boards prominently set up in a central back-of-house location in each theatre that displays growth as public information. Coloured pins on these boards indicate the capability level of each employee in 15 identified job competencies. As they achieve one, they get a blue pin. This information is used to schedule shift rotations, facilitate peer mentoring, and set expectations for learning as part of a development pipeline. Everyone can see how crucial personal development is to the company and how everyone else is progressing. At weekly theatre managers' meetings, they review not only traditional business metrics on attendance and sales but also the number of crew members ready for a promotion.

5.7. Creativity

Mainstream Orange thinking considers creativity a highly desirable value from the recognition that those organisations that can leverage innovation are the ones with more possibilities to stay ahead of a changing marketplace. Almost every job advertisement is looking for creative, entrepreneurial, proactive candidates able to solve increasingly complex, non-routine problems. Then, the reality is that Orange organisations tend to undermine those very qualities. They are reluctant to give people the freedom to experience play and curiosity, and this is probably one of the most important reasons for the lack of creativity they suffer from. On the contrary, they have created rigid structures of hierarchical command and control and bureaucratic policies that sabotage creativity. Innovation is also bottled-necked from the top levels, where it is assumed that they can be the only ones that can devise original ideas. Teal organisations are much better equipped for creativity, thanks to decentralisation, flexibility, self-management, open communication, open innovation, and participatory decision-making.

Here are some tips for implementing a creative culture:

- Reward mistakes: Orange organisations, enslaved by a results-oriented culture, fear failure, but mistakes are an integral part of the creative process. As James Joyce said, the mistakes of a man are his portals of discovery. So, it is necessary to redefine the concept, as Bob Ross, the art instructor and host of the popular PBS TV show The Joy of Painting, did: "*We don't make mistakes, just happy little accidents.*" Edison made more than 1,000 unsuccessful attempts at inventing the light bulb. When a reporter asked him how he felt after failing 1,000 times, Edison replied, *"I didn't fail 1,000 times. I've just found 1,000 ways that won't work. You never know when you are going to need a light bulb that explodes."* An organisation that wants to promote creativity needs to reward positive mistakes because they teach you why you failed. The only recommendation is to make them early on when the cost and impact are smaller. This is the rationale behind methodologies such as QFD (Quality Function Deployment) and Sprint.

- Foster curiosity and experimentation: Young companies are more creative because they are more curious and open to experimentation, they take more risks, and make more mistakes. Thriving organisations and successful products and services owe much more to experimentation and accident than to rational planning. The most significant advances in surgery happen in times of war when there are more experiments. Google was famous for a policy that allowed employees to spend 20% of their time working on their personal projects. Gmail, Google Maps, and Google News were all created during this so-called “20% time”. Dabble time is how they labelled the same concept at W.L. Gore. One of its most representative products, the Elixir guitar strings, sprang from the mind of an associate in the company’s medical products division during that time. At Cisco Labs in Norway, they went even further, and they allow people to spend any amount of time on projects not directly related to their job. According to Appelo (2016: 96), the problem with these policies is that many employees argue they have no time. To get rid of those excuses, Australian software company Atlassian organises a ShipIt day once every three months, in which everyone in the company works on an idea of their choosing, and where awards are given to the best ones. They call it this because they must deliver a result within 24 hours. Facebook and Spotify organise similar events respectively called hackathons (every six weeks) and hack days. Some companies take the hackathons a step further and turn it into innovation markets by leaving the selection of ideas to employees. They are like an internal version of crowdfunding where all employees have a personal budget that they can use for investing in the ideas that, in their opinion, have the best chance of succeeding.
- Forget about the customer: Customers won’t innovate for you. They are beta testers, not soothsayers. The invention of genuinely new products never comes from big data consumer analysis. If Henry Ford had surveyed his customers, they would have asked for a faster horse. Many successful products initially failed but finally invented or reinvented a market. The list included Post-It notes, bubble wraps, pacemakers, VCRs, faxes, and mobile phones.
- Avoid paradigm paralysis: Countless companies have missed tremendous opportunities as a result of remaining fixated on a particular paradigm. It is what Joel Barker (1992) calls paradigm paralysis. When you work in a fish market, you stop perceiving the

persistent bad smell; if you live next to a highway, you don't hear the traffic noise. Things become invisible when we don't look at them attentively. The author reviews the case of the Swiss watch industry, the absolute leader of the sector about 50 years ago with an 80% market share. At a World Congress, they presented a battery-operated mechanism developed at their research institute in Neuchtel. For them, it was nothing more than a curiosity; watches were supposed to be made according to the traditional method. But Seiko noticed that the quartz mechanism was more accurate and convenient. It was the beginning of the end of the domination of the Swiss watch industry, and the rise of the Japanese makers. Quartz glass watches dominate the international market today, and spring-wound watches have become a thing of the past. Another example is the case of Chester Carlson, who in 1938 invented a new photography procedure he defined as electrostatic photography, which eventually would be known as a photocopy. He went from company to company, looking for funding to manufacture his invention. More than twenty potential investors rejected it, including Eastman Kodak, leader of the sector and inventor of the standard method based on the combination of photosensitive paper and emulsion. Kodak only saw Carlson's invention as an alternative way to take pictures and, from that point of view, it was clearly inferior. Only a company outside the photographic sector, Xerox, saw the potential of the invention.

- Action-orientation: In our increasingly uncertain and changeable work, whoever experiments the most wins. Do you think Amazon was created through a careful market study and a meticulous business plan? Nothing is further from reality. Jeff Bezos read in 1994 statistics that the growth of the internet would be 2300% and decided to get on that train as soon as possible. He left his job on Wall Street, took his family in a caravan, and set out on a journey to the West, just like the old settlers, without even knowing what he would do when he got there. He chose to stay in Seattle because it was a city with many computers. After making a list of products that could be offered online, he decided to market books and launched his company without a second thought.
- Hire unconventional people. When Edison selected a person, he invited him to eat soup. If the candidate threw salt on the soup without even trying it, he didn't hire him, because he had acted automatically. Steve Jobs used to hire people with "intriguing profiles" and "extraordinary taste" (poets, artists, historians). Most importantly, the new hires had to be people with the capacity to think outside the box

and challenge the system: When a student asked Einstein for advice to become a good researcher, he replied: *"Anyone who aspires to be a true scientist must devote at least half an hour a day to think differently than his colleagues."* As Cary Grant put it in "*I Feel to Rejuvenate*" (Howard Hawks, 1952) *"The history of discoveries is the story of men who didn't follow the rules."*

- Create diverse teams: Teams are more creative than individuals. Hall (2001) cites four experiments by Gene Burton, in which groups created 44%, 50%, 65%, and 93% more ideas than individually. But to achieve the most out of group creativity, it is essential to encourage diversity. How can organisations be creative with a workforce made up of men between 40 and 60 years old, of equal race, religion, culture, and nationality? A cluster of clones can hardly generate creative synergies. Captain Kirk of the classic Star Trek series has a psychologically diverse and specialised team: Mr Spock is exceptionally rational, Dr McCoy is empathetic and emotional, and Scotty is the one who pays attention to detail. Traditional organisations divide people into two categories: the few who have creative roles and then most of the others who have nothing to do with creativity. Vanguard organisations draw ideas from every corner. In fact, research shows that a diverse group of ordinary people works better than a homogeneous group of experts. Scott Page, a professor of complex systems at the University of Michigan, demonstrated mathematically that cognitively diverse groups of regular people outperformed groups of like-minded experts (Dennis 2010: 94). The first explanatory variable he found was diversity: diverse groups of problem solvers outperform groups of like-minded individuals. When we collaborate with people who are not like us we see a wider range of perspectives, we develop a fuller understanding of the causal connections between variables and a richer comprehension of the architecture of the problem, we are aided in identifying our false assumptions, we start to look beyond dichotomies, and we are able to make contradictions compatible. The results went even further: on complex problems, groups of ordinary people who were cognitively diverse routinely outperformed groups of like-minded experts. Page's work showed that they were stumped less often than the experts, who tended to think in similar ways.
- Introduce outsiders: A Buddhist story tells how a Zen student visits his master for the first time. The teacher serves him tea, the cup fills up, and although the tea overflows, he keeps pouring. The student asks him to stop. The master replies: *"Like the cup, you are full of*

ideas. How can you learn until you empty the cup?" Our cultural tradition considers ignorance a weakness or a sign of stupidity. Thus, we hide it from others. The Zen tradition calls this state the expert mind: we believe or pretend that we already know everything and close the door to learning. The beginner's mind is preferable, as ignorance frees us from the prison of knowledge. David Kelly from Ideo, says that some of their greatest breakthroughs were the result of adopting a beginner's mind. When Orson Welles started the production of his first film, *"Citizen Kane,"* Gregg Toland, the best cinematographer of his time, went to see him at RKO studios. He put on the table the Oscar he won for *"Wuthering Heights"* and told him that he wanted to work on his film. Welles asked him why someone of his prestige would want to work with a neophyte 24-year-old. Toland replied: *"Mr Welles, you just learn something new by working with someone who has no idea."* He was not mistaken: Orson Welles revolutionised the Seventh Art with his innovative use of flashback and documentary, and his style of violent low and wide angles for psychological purposes (which caused not a few technical problems to Toland). "*Citizen Kane*" is still one of the summits of the Seventh Art.

- Encourage travel and time away: Legs are as important to creativity as the eyes and the brain. When you leave your usual environment, you are much more attentive to any stimulus, and this often leads to innumerable new ideas. Sabbaticals are common in universities, Netflix, Intel, and Apple have an unlimited travel budget, Semco (1993:160) has what they call "hepatitis leaves" so employees can take time off for a few weeks or even a few months every 1 or 2 years to reflect upon work goals, plan for the future, and select priorities.
- Let people have fun: It is not proven that fun enhances creativity, but it certainly relaxes people and creates an environment conducive to collaboration. For companies like Southwest Airlines, PeopleSoft, and AES, fun is a fundamental corporate value. Dennis Bakke (2005: 174) clarifies that *"by fun, we don't mean party fun, we are talking about creating an environment where people can use their gifts and skills productively to help meet a need in society and thereby enjoy the time spent at AES."*
- No pressure: Creativity is an uncontrollable and unpredictable process. It is proven that people under pressure, stress, or threat resort to conventional thinking. Creativity is not efficient from a productivity point of view. It does not guarantee results, and it does not understand delivery dates, schedules, or Gantt diagrams. Creativity requires time. Retreats to quiet environments or meditation rooms can be helpful. On

the other hand, uncertainty at work, lack of security, the pressure to achieve targets, punishments, and even promises of incentives make individuals react defensively and with little imagination (they won't try anything new or assume risks). One experiment showed how patients who were going to be operated on gave more stereotyped answers in a Rorschach test than the average. In another one, subjects who received a cash prize had worse results than those who didn't.

- Design appropriate spaces: Winston Churchill said: *"First we shape our buildings, and then our buildings shape us."* If the office layout is divided into separated offices or cubicles, collaboration is close to none, and social interaction only happens when you schedule a meeting. Those physical spaces were built to separate and silo in a world of information scarcity. If you want collaboration and cross-fertilisation to happen, the workspace should enable social connections. It is advisable to create open spaces that allow casual encounters and foster a feeling of camaraderie and belonging. To take it to the next level, the radical design of leading-edge companies such as Zappos, Neosoft, SOL, IDEO, and Google is a reflection of their cultures. For a start, most of the Teal organisations I know have gotten rid of all material symbols of status (executive floors, fancy offices, reserved parking, or those executive washrooms portrayed in one of the classic episodes of the Simpsons) and they offer plenty of spaces for social interaction, relaxation, meditation, and fun.

5.8. Open Organisations: Unbounded Innovation

The innovation processes of the 20th century were designed for simple and stable environments. They were driven by a closed approach that worked under the assumption that successful innovation requires control (Chesbrough et al. 2006). Innovation was a top-secret kept within internal walls. Intellectual property rights, patents, and various other mechanisms were utilised to protect the investments when they were brought to light.

Innovation can no longer rise within organisational boundaries alone. The traditional and closed proprietary business model tends to be increasingly substituted with open source or open core options. Over the last decade, open-source solutions have proven themselves far superior. They enjoy the competitive advantage of hundreds or even thousands of minds developing, testing, and improving. Today's environment is one of relentless change and increasingly complex problems, often wicked ones, the more people thinking about them, the better. It is necessary to break the organisational limits to create a boundless and liquid organisation based on collaborative dynamics that involve multiple stakeholders –be it consumers, firms, public organisations, or communities. This eco-systemic view of organisations and innovation emphasises that value co-creation needs to be steered by a common motive, based on mutually connected opportunities and a collective value proposition.

Open organisations have a broader innovation supply because ideas coming from within cross-pollinate with ideas coming from without. An open innovation philosophy brings a shift in the locus of innovation from within the internal walls to communities and ecosystems for collaborative innovation. The active involvement of the multiple stakeholders through an open approach facilitates innovation, be it at the early stages of ideation and development, at the intermediate stages of validation and valuation, or for final implementation and diffusion. It is an open culture of radical transparency and inclusiveness that is continuously seeking links outside the company. Open organisations are based on trust, as they confidently share everything, in the hope of incorporating the insights of others.

Open innovation follows the underlying principle of "collective intelligence." It emerges from the collaboration of many individuals and groups, ideally structured in networks. Customers, in particular, can no longer be passive consumers fooled with false promises of participation and are called to play a much more significant role in the innovation process with advances in the open-source movement and technologies such as 3D printing. Co-creation incorporates them in the innovation process from the very beginning to make a product or service according to their needs, creating a unique user experience and strengthening their feelings of belonging.

There are different degrees of open innovation. The first type is the outside-in, also referred to as inbound OI or knowledge exploration. Outside-in open innovation is still close to traditional closed innovation, as all that changes is the access to additional knowledge. Thus, the focus is on establishing relationships with relevant stakeholders in the business ecosystem, such as other organisations, universities, research consortia, or incubators, in order to access external technical and scientific competence and resources through, for instance, collaborating, in-licensing, strategic alliances, university research programs, funding start-ups, living labs, and user integration. Here, firms access external knowledge through various contractual and collaborative agreements. The co-creation of products and services through harnessing ideas and collaborating with customers, also referred to as user innovation, is another example of the outside-in mode

(Kim 2013). These crowd-related activities are usually set up as contests such as tournaments, idea competitions, and innovation awards that are shared and hosted via an Internet platform and in which individuals or teams generally compete for a cash prize. In crowdsourcing, hackathons[95], or makerspaces[96], the sponsor organisation identifies a specific problem that needs to be addressed (sometimes even for societal causes, as it happens at Next Jump), and offers an award that is in alignment with the complexity of the challenge. People collaborate because they enjoy it and because they benefit from the solutions obtained. Thus, customers are involved in the organisation's objectives and become contributors adding value not only as promoters (which was the maximum level of involvement within the traditional model), but also with their ideas, reactions, services, products, assets, or personal networks. Other models of utilising external sources in the innovation process include feedback loops, reciprocal interactions with co-creation partners, and integration with external innovation networks and communities.

The second variety of open innovation is the inside-out mode, also called outbound OI or knowledge exploitation. The inside-out open innovation model gives unused or under-utilised ideas and assets to external organisations whose business models are better suited for their commercial exploitation (Chiaroni et al. 2011). Corporate spin-offs or spin-outs are examples of the inside-out model (Kim 2013). The parent company provides funding, technology, intellectual property, legal services, and so on. Out-licensing or donating intellectual property and technology, corporate venture capital, corporate incubators, joint ventures, and alliances

---

[95] Hackathons have their origins in 1995 in Berlin when C-Base, the world's first hackerspace, was launched. Hackerspaces started as places where a group of computer programmers could collectively meet, work, and share infrastructure to basically "hack" technology. They gained popularity in the 2000s when Facebook and Google started promoting them internally. Today they are competitive events in which computer programmers, developers, and designers work intensively in teams, at a specific venue, under tight timelines (typically hours or days), to solve complex software-related problems or produce innovative technologies. The process ends in a final pitch with judges.

[96] Hackerspaces and makerspaces are collaborative workspaces for making, learning, exploring, and sharing. As they don't have the short-term and competitive perspective of hackathons, they are better suited to maintain momentum in knowledge sharing, increase the level of engagement in the collective, support knowledge transformation, and facilitate the structuration of shared identities and joint enterprise in the long run.

through becoming a supplier to or a customer of a new initiative are other mechanisms of outbound open innovation (Chesbrough et al. 2014).

Finally, flash organisations (Valentine et al., 2017) mix outbound and inbound OI. Organisational structures are combined with computational crowdsourcing techniques, mobilising a potentially massive amount of people into collectives of unprecedented scale, drawing together experts and amateurs to create rapidly assembled and reconfigurable organisations composed of online crowd workers. Through flash organisations, anyone with an internet connection can construct a virtual organisation in pursuit of complex, open-ended goals. It is a jointly-built process between the organisation (if there was one beforehand) and the players invited to participate.

The actor-engagement level goes from the lowest of a crowd to the highest of a community. The crowd level is a group of individuals with different characteristics that don't necessarily know each other and who are loosely bound together by organic social practices (Wexler, 2011). The community level is a kind of community of practice where individuals become members of a collective that is structured around a specific purpose with shared practices and identities to create a sense of "joint enterprise" (Wenger, 1998) that increases the sense of belonging into the collective.

5.9. Case in Point: Barrabés.biz[97]

Barrabés.biz is a consultancy specialised in innovation and technology. What makes it different from others is its organisation as a cluster of companies in the field of innovation, entrepreneurship, customer experience, and emerging technologies. In spite of being independent companies, they operate as one big corporation with an extended team of more than 180 professionals and an activity of €10 million in innovative projects.

Barrabés.biz was born from Barrabés.com, an e-commerce platform for ski and mountain gear, founded by Carlos Barrabés, a pioneering and influential figure in introducing and popularising the Internet in Spain. The extraordinary success of Barrabés.com, made possible the creation of a

[97] This case is based on Martín et al. (2018)

consulting division, called Barrabés Internet, which was the seed of what today we know as Barrabés.biz.

Barrabés.biz is a startup ecosystem that represents one of the most advanced organisational responses to understand, develop, and provide value with leading technologies (Cloud, Big Data, IA, IoT, 5G or blockchain). It is modelled as a dynamic ecosystem that creates startups to respond to the opportunities that technology opens. The startups are the seeds of digital ecosystems and they are called extended organisations. An extended organisation does not limit itself to managing its value chain but also takes into account the rest of the links that make up an industry, from the end customer to the suppliers of raw materials.

There are two major activity areas in Barrabés' startup ecosystem: Barrabés.biz and the startups created or supported by StepOne, a venture capital fund established in 2008 in San Francisco for investing in the first stage of technological companies with high growth potential, mainly in Silicon Valley. StepOne can be considered the gear between the two sub-ecosystems. It operates, in this case, as a venture builder helping startups to consolidate their business, putting at their disposal capital and a wide variety of services, supported by the Barrabés Group.

5.10. Integral Leadership: Cracking the Leadership Code

> *"A leader is best when people barely know that he exists, not so good when people obey and acclaim him, worst when they despise him. Fail to honour people, they fail to honour you. But of a good leader, who talks little, when his work is done, his aims fulfilled, they will all say: We did this ourselves."* Lao Tzu

The story of leadership has been the story of the individual. It doesn't matter whether you admire Orange leaders like Steve Jobs, Green ones such as Anita Roddick, or Teal models like Jos de Block; the prevailing underlying narrative is one of heroic leadership.

The traditional concept of leadership makes us think of a heroic figure on a white horse. People like Alexander the Great, Joan of Arc, Braveheart, or Martin Luther King spring immediately to our minds. They are superhuman individuals that have all the answers to light our way to salvation. Creating poster boys or girls to represent movements or organisations can be useful. My main issue with the model of heroic leadership is how distant it is from reality. As Robertson (2015:188) asserts, no matter how caring, charismatic, and selfless the leader may be, the whole system is limited by his or her capabilities. Our postmodern times (and the metamodern times to come) need a new leadership metaphor. Teal leadership should be more like a multiplayer online role-playing game.

In the traditional leadership model, leaders are appointed and called managers. It is a domination hierarchy where only those at the top are recognised as leaders. This model has become less effective with time, as the fit between environmental challenges and the ability of the heroic individuals to solve them has begun to diverge. Imposing leadership is going against the very nature of the function. Traditional management is mistaken when the boss makes decisions because of his or her position in the organisational chart, not because he or she has a particular insight into what will produce the desired outcome (Bernstein et al. 2016). Teal organisations have substituted individual leaders by distributed leadership so that anyone can be a leader. Thus, the company is not run by managers but managed by leaders. Leadership is a natural process that happens spontaneously and organically. Anyone committed to sustaining or developing the organisation's purpose can exercise leadership, if only temporarily. It is not derived from a position; it comes from responsibility, expertise, willingness, and contribution. A leader is anyone whom the others follow naturally and for a particular purpose. Some of the most famous leaders of all time never held a formal position (Gandhi or Martin Luther King are the first ones to come to mind). This is the standard model for younger generations. They are accustomed to seeing in social networks that influence is based on contribution and reputation, not on position, and that leadership is distributed throughout a network. The more this kind of leadership is allowed, the better for the health of the system.

Leadership is a function of the relationship between leader and follower. My dear friend, Robert Perry, used to define leadership as inspired followership. A leader is someone who has followers. In a self-managed organisation, no one is anointed a leader by a higher power. Leaders emerge organically from those whose authority is recognised by their colleagues. Leadership is earned, not granted. As Robertson asserts (2015: 190), self-management does not remove the value of leadership; it just distributes it across more people. The new leadership is not a position or a label for an individual anymore; it is a role. It is a social process happening throughout the system. Margaret Wheatley's definition of a leader as *"anyone willing to help at this time"* is especially suitable for Teal organisations. It takes a lot of weight off our shoulders since we don't depend on one person being a great leader all the time; but that everyone can be a good leader on certain occasions. Sometimes you lead, sometimes you follow. Authority shifts depending on who has the most knowledge and experience in a specific context. Francesca Pick, from Ouishare, refers to this concept as a dynamic hierarchy.

Leadership is essential for second-tier organisations. Natural hierarchies require natural leaders—that is, individuals who can influence and inspire others despite a lack of formal authority. I believe the most critical feature of leadership in the future will be to inspire people and unify them around a sense of common purpose. According to Manz and Sims (2001:4) *"this perspective demands that we come up with a new measure of leadership strength –the ability to maximize the contributions of others by helping them to effectively guide their own destinies, rather than the ability to bend the will of others."*

Until recently, nobody had applied Integral Theory to leadership but, in a relatively short while, it has become the area of management that has received more attention by integral researchers (to the point that one of the most important journals devoted to Integral Theory goes by the name of *Integral Leadership Review*) and the one where more significant inroads have been made.

I will never tire of repeating that to be an integral leader you have to be an integral person, and that is a lifelong endeavour. Research has proven that leadership effectiveness is linked to adult development (Kegan, 2014; Spence and MacDonald, 2010). Integral leadership requires unique qualities such as wisdom, maturity, and a more sophisticated and complex way of thinking that those operating at lower levels of consciousness. Together with high levels of cognitive intelligence and technical competence, integral leaders excel in emotional intelligence and spiritual intelligence. In other words, they have a balanced integral psychograph with relatively high development in all different areas. Their internalisation of the AQAL model allows them to take into account simultaneously three distinct areas: the external world (the left quadrants), the internal world (UL), and the world of others (LL). The internal focus helps them connect with their intuition and the values that guide them, the external focus helps them navigate the world around them, and the focus on others improves the quality of their relationships. In a number of studies, leaders at higher altitudes were found to continuously adapt to changing market demands and consistently generate long-term positive and sustainable organisational transformation related to profit, market share, and organisational reputation measures, when compared to those located at lower levels

(Cook-Greuter, 2004; Rooke & Torbert, 1998). Models that can be useful to improve integral leadership skills include integral life practice (Wilber et al. 2008), Spiral Dynamics (Beck and Cowan, 1996), or the Leadership Development Framework (Cook-Greuter, 2004; Rooke & Torbert, 1998; Spense and MacDonald, 2010).

Three key factors of integral leadership correspond to the 3D-Management dimensions:

- Technical Factor: The leader needs knowledge and technical skills to manage and make decisions effectively and efficiently.
- Emotional Factor: Leadership only happens when there are followers. A leader needs to persuade, inspire, and influence others.
- Ethical Factor: The integral leader is a moral agent who follows strong moral principles and is a behavioural role model.
- Spiritual factor: Integral leaders transcend self-interest for the good of the group, and convey powerful and meaningful visions.

5.10.1. The Leadership Rosetta Stone: An Integral Model of Leadership

Leadership is one of the most studied phenomena of management. Researchers and practitioners alike are mainly concerned with one overarching question: How can people motivate and influence others to achieve significant positive results? In Brett Thomas' opinion (2014), no theory has given an entirely satisfactory answer. On the contrary, he maintains that leadership, as it is conventionally understood and taught, is fundamentally flawed. All the different leadership schools enthusiastically advocate the superiority of their singular approach. But, according to Thomas, one-size-fits-all approaches rarely work with any consistency: *"The result? A deeply confused, fragmented, vague, and contradictory body of knowledge around what should be one of the most important fields of human study."*

His premise is the following: *Most conventional leadership models work with some people some of the time. Few, if any, work with all people in every situation.* Thomas' integral approach to leadership seeks to incorporate the enduring truths of all the existing theories while drawing on a broader and more sophisticated model of human interaction to provide overarching guidelines for which approaches will work consistently, with which people, and in which situations. It is a comprehensive, integrally-informed, and practical leadership framework that transcends and includes all the other styles (and schools) of leadership.

Following Jago (1982), we can classify the different leadership theories in two main axes: universality versus contingency and traits versus behaviour. Approaches that focus on universal leadership traits are among the most traditional ones we can find, and they are a consequence of an Amber worldview. They believe some general principles should be followed in every situation. It all started with the Great Man Theory that postulated that leaders are born, not made. Its central idea is that some people inherently have better leadership capacities than others. Accordingly, they study leadership as a combination of personality traits that all great leaders share, including individual characteristics (e.g., extraversion, openness, discipline, etc.), or skills (technical skills, people skills, conceptual skills). Nowadays, the Trait Theory has lost most of its credence, although it keeps returning with new attempts to identify the universal characteristics of a leader, such as The Big 5 personality factors model (Vandenbros, 2007).

The relative failures of that school changed the research focus. The effect that the style of leadership (be it autocratic, democratic, or permissive) had over the behavioural patterns of the followers, became the central issue. The Schools of Michigan and Ohio are the leading proponents of that approach, and McGregor's Theories X and Y together with Blake & Mouton's managerial grid are the most well-known models. Some of the theories that emerged under its umbrella are still quite popular (visionary leadership, transactional leadership, transformational leadership, servant leadership).

The inconsistency of the "*one best way*" resulted in the substitution of the universal models with contingency models. Contingency models are relativistic and situational, and they come from a Green mindset. They contend that there is not a better way to be a leader; rather, the style depends on the circumstances. Fiedler's contingency theory suggests that task or people-oriented leadership styles effectiveness depends on the situation (e.g., the structure of work, position, or relationship). Blanchard's Situational Leadership theory encourages matching the management style with the preferred working method of subordinates based on the two poles of "direction" and "support." Contingency models based on leadership traits acknowledge that different styles can be useful depending on the situation, so they relate the personal characteristics of the leader with contingency situations (Fiedler and Mahar, 1979). Thomas (2014: 27) considers them an early intuition of the need for Integral Leadership. What he finds lacking in these approaches is a comprehensive, accurate, and reliable method for analysing different situations and the inclusion of the psychology and worldviews of the people and groups involved.

This quick overview of leadership theories shows how every level of development has elaborated its own theories according to its narrow worldview. A Red worldview develops autocratic leaders; Amber creates bureaucratic ones; Orange advocates for expert and meritocratic leadership; Green's group consciousness prefers participatory styles and servant leadership. The problem with all of them is that they define an ideal leadership style. Even the more relativistic or situational theories treat followers more or less as a constant, and place variability only at the leadership level. No wonder all of those one-size-fits-all approaches rarely work with any consistency: *"(they) fail to adequately take into account the fact that people with different worldviews interpret the same facts very differently and will —or won't— tolerate different leadership styles and approaches that can be closely correlated with those same worldviews."* (Thomas 2014: 40).

Thomas' Integral leadership model is a giant step forward in leadership theory. It is characterised by an evolutionary approach to human development based on the understanding of individuals and their social context. The fact that it takes into consideration the hierarchical nature of human development makes it different from any other previous leadership theory. If Laloux was the first to apply Spiral Dynamics to organisations, Thomas did it first with leadership. If only for that, he deserves some credit, but what is more important in both cases is not the application of evolutionary theory to leadership or organisations (any integrally-informed management researcher could have done that, sooner or later), but the quality of their analysis and the models they present.

Thomas' model promises to know when, where, and with whom a given leadership approach will reliably work (and when it will reliably fail). The key to understanding, motivating, and influencing people is to use the leadership style that is most resonant with the person's (or group's) dominant worldview. If we don't understand a person's meaning-making framework, it will be challenging to motivate and/or influence them.

Don't lead the way you would prefer to be led. It won't work with people that don't operate from your level. Integral Leadership is most fundamentally about "perspective-taking." Leadership is a function of the psychology both of the leader and the follower. A person's worldview defines what they care about, what motivates them, what they believe is worthwhile, and what they believe lacks value or is "wrong." It also dictates which leadership style they would be likely to follow, as well as which approaches would be likely to backfire. A leader needs to harmonise, balance, and integrate the different interests, voices, values, and cultures of the various stakeholders.

Thomas' (2014) tool for Integral Leadership is called the Leadership Rosetta Stone[98]. It correlates four universal leadership styles[99] with the four most common worldviews (Red, Amber, Orange, and Green[100]) so leaders can choose the leadership style that is most resonant with the person's (or group's) dominant meaning-making framework:

- Leading Red: People with a Red centre of gravity generally require very specific and unambiguous direction along with constant and close supervision. They need autocratic leaders[101] who are perceived to be strong, tough, and dominant. You have to define in advance the limits within which any kind of behaviour is accepted, lay down the rules, say what is going to happen, and have control mechanisms for them. It is very dangerous to give autonomy to this type of worker. Empowerment is not an option, whether you like it or not, you need command and control. So, assign tasks giving enough detail on the desired result you expect from them, establish limits to discretion, and set a completion date. Then, get out of the way, unless needed. The Red individual will show pride in doing a good job. Graves (2005:240) recommends managing these people through Skinnerian conditioning principles. As he or she seeks

[98] The Rosetta Stone, carved in 196 BC, was found by French soldiers in 1799 in a small village called Rosetta (Rashid). As it was written in two languages (Egyptian and Greek) using three scripts (hieroglyphic, demotic, and Greek), it allowed Jean-François Champollion to decipher hieroglyphs in 1822 for the first time in history.

[99] For the sake of clarity, Thomas only includes in his Rosetta Stone the most current levels of development (i.e., Red, Amber, Orange, and Green). He omits the levels above or below because they are rare.

[100] Thomas uses SD as a frame of reference (Red, Blue, Orange, and Green), but I will translate it to SDI colours for consistency.

[101] Autocratic Leadership is defined as the person with the most power leads using command and control.

immediate gratification, you should reward positive behaviour. Spend time pointing out things they do well and direct them with a specific action. If an individual centralised in Red makes an error, he recommends to confront the undesired behaviour by stopping it on the spot, but without giving any punishment or getting into a discussion, until given a positive response, and then reward, preferably with something extrinsic and immediate. According to Graves (2005:240), when you have to discipline, you never get into a discussion. Why? The Red individual has a high tendency to act aggressively. If you start discussing, it might end up in a fistfight.

- Leading Amber: Status is essential for Amber. People with a traditional mindset prefer to follow leaders who are perceived as having positional and/or moral authority. Their respect for leaders makes a paternalistic or bureaucratic style of management suitable for them. They need a predictable work setting with clear routines, structures, and regulations. As they respect authority, they can be influenced and changed by the leader. The leader has to lay down the rules of the game and be the impetus for change. However, if you try to change their fundamental beliefs, they will close down completely, so don't expect them to respond very enthusiastically to autonomy.
- Leading Orange: People with an achiever mindset prefer to follow leaders who are perceived to have the most expertise and ability to achieve goals. They find *Strategic Leadership* most motivating (Thomas defines Strategic Leadership as the most experienced person leads via strategic planning and tangible incentives).
- Leading Green: Naturally, they prefer to follow leaders who are perceived as being aware, valuing consensus, and always treating others as equals. They find *Collaborative Leadership* most motivating (i.e. democratically-based, self-managed teams lead themselves.)

When it comes to motivation, we find a similar situation. The failure of traditional motivational techniques is the root cause of the failure of conventional leadership approaches. According to a study carried out by the Gallup Institute, only two out of ten employees strongly agree that their performance is managed in a way that motivates them. We need a new and integral perspective on motivation:

> *"An integral view of motivation is based on the assumption that all previous motivation theories are accurate for certain people in certain circumstances, but in order to apply them effectively, they must be properly contextualized into a given person's (or group's) specific value system, life conditions, and abilities." Thomas (2014: 113):*

So, if you want to motivate people, you must understand what they value accurately, which is a result of value memes and worldviews. Every level of development has its specific drives and motivations, as Maslow and Barrett well understood. At the Infra-Red level, the focus is survival by satisfying physiological needs. Magenta seeks protection and a safe environment. Red is looking for power. Amber wants order and belonging. Orange is interested in achievement. Affection and connection guide Green. Self-actualisation and wholeness are Teal's main drives.

The distinction between extrinsic, intrinsic, and transcendent motivation improves our understanding of the matter. Extrinsic motivation is driven by external rewards such as money, reputation, status, and praise. A person's intrinsic motivation is their natural, inherent drive to act because of the satisfaction they anticipate in the process (UL/arts). A person's transcendent motivation is their willingness to work because of the benefit they expect others to experience as a consequence of what they do (LL/ethics/spirit). To understand what motivates people, you must first know their meaning-making frameworks. Traditional extrinsic motivators, like financial rewards and promotions, work well for Red, Amber, and Orange, but they lose importance at Green and beyond. But don't get carried away by authors like Daniel Pink (2011) that dismiss the importance of extrinsic motivation. While for many people and types of work, external motivators have limited value and can even backfire, for others, they remain incredibly useful. Try to eliminate financial incentives in a group of Orange-centred salespeople and see what happens. The problem with extrinsically motivated people is that they are not necessarily intrinsically engaged. One needs intrinsic and transcendent motivation to be really engaged, and those kinds of motivations are values-dependent. For example, many models (e.g., Pink, 2011; Manz and Sims, 2001) include purpose as one of the underlying factors explaining intrinsic or transcendent motivation. While that is true for people holding Traditional Amber and Green Postmodern beliefs, people with Red and Orange values don't care much about purpose.

CHAPTER 6

ETHICS:
CULTURE AND COMMON GOOD

"It has become clear that our technology has surpassed our humanity" (Einstein)

6.1. Whatever happened to Jiminy Cricket?

While the other animals are determined by their instincts, humans are, at least in appearance, free[102]. The human race is moral because it is free, and that makes ethics a fundamental dimension to guide individual action. In spite of its importance as the yardstick for decision making, ethics is the more marginalised dimension of management. Scientifically-dominated practices, like mechanistic rules and procedures, strict performance indicators, and top-down control, everything subordinated to the final objective of profit maximisation (or, in the case of non-for profits, cost reduction) has ruined the ethos of organisations all over the world.

The motto of the B Corps movement is *"use business as a force for good."* If we find this slogan so revolutionary, there must be something fundamentally wrong with business as we know it. If we read between the lines, the tagline implies that this form of social organisation, in its current form, is either a force for evil or. at least, is just not doing enough good.

The ethical debacle of many corporations in recent times is a compelling reason for questioning the conventional management model and claiming a moral regeneration. The crisis that began in the United States in 2007 and expanded with rising levels of unemployment and poverty all over the world was not just financial, but ethical. It was the result, not only of the

---

[102] The amount of freedom we have is highly debatable. To what extent are we determined by our needs, worldviews, family tree, groupthink, mass media, and many other conditionings? Much more than we think. And yet we are the freer species on the planet.

deregulation of the financial system, but of the violation of basic ethical standards, and ended with a widespread perception of impunity as some of the perpetrators were considered too big to fail (and jail).

Take Enron. A flagship of Corporate America, apparently hugely successful, lauded by Fortune Magazine as one of the most innovative companies in the world, and recognised as one of the best places to work in the US (reaching number 22 as all-time high). Orange people loved to work there. Teals wouldn't last a minute. Why? Because its 3-D Management triangle was out of balance. The company had very well developed scientific and artistic dimensions, but ethics were totally neglected.

Don't think of the case of Enron as an aberration of the system. During the difficult years of the crisis, there were plenty of examples of bad corporate behaviour, particularly among large financial institutions, and the news is still fraught with corporate scandals. It is the Orange value meme in berserk mode. To be more precise, the corporate world is Orange in the conceptual line, but Red in the moral line. The pre-conventional Red attitude of "anything goes, as long as they don't get you" is still sadly ever-present.

The heart of the problem here is the ontology of the current paradigm that subordinates ethics to profits. Don't be surprised if companies don't take ethics into account. Ethics is nowhere to be found in the right-hand-quadrant perspective that dominates mainstream management. Asking companies focused on profit maximisation to voluntarily embrace an ethical perspective is simply wishful thinking, especially when it brings uncertain returns, and sometimes even at its own expense. It will only be considered when there is a business advantage, but to expect the "right thing" to be done, against the company's core interests, is very naïve; especially when the more profitable option is not illegal. Why should a decent salary be paid when paying the minimum wage is legal? Why use recyclable materials when non-recyclable ones are cheaper? Why not tweak financial reports a bit to make them look more attractive to investors? Why not bribe government officials when it is a standard business practice in some areas of the world? The bottom line is that, in most cases, companies will prioritise profit maximisation at the expense of externalities[103] such as environmental depletion and social harm. Some companies will go even further, as Volkswagen did in 2015, and still not having enough, did it again in 2019, with the emissions scandal. The German car manufacturer understood that outstanding ecological performance could give them a competitive advantage. They didn't care much about the environment, but they did care about money, and the cheapest way to achieve that edge was by cheating.

Even corporate social responsibility (CSR), a positive development coming from the Green mindset, is only a minimal fix that does nothing to address the structural problems that lay at the foundation of how our business and society operate. The whole idea of CSR comes from a one-dimensional view of management subordinated to the tyranny of profits. Companies add it as an extra activity or department to compensate or redeem themselves from the evil that they do, or as a marketing tool or defensive PR measure to ward off criticism. No wonder CSR is too often just window dressing and green and social washing and is usually the first thing to be discarded in times of crisis.

Ethics can no longer be considered as second class to profit. Public consciousness has become much more sensitive to the social responsibility of organisations. Customers no longer only care about getting a quality product at a reasonable price. They are increasingly concerned about where those products come from and if the companies that supply them are good citizens. B-Corp expert Ryan Honeyman says that the new race is not about being the best in the world but being the best for the world (2014:1).

Many organisations are truly committed to contributing actively to society at large. That's the case of Sweetgreen. Founded in 2007, Sweetgreen is in the business of feeding people and changing what that means. Originally from Washington, it now operates in the District of Columbia and seven other states. The company defines itself as a destination for simple, seasonal, healthy food. Let me quote its mission statement:

> *"Our mission is to inspire healthier communities by connecting people to real food. We know that Sweetgreen is a critical link between growers and consumers, and we feel a responsibility to protect the future of real food. To that end, we're committed to supporting small and mid-size growers*

---

[103] Even language is skillfully crafted to reduce the feeling of moral responsibility. Externality sounds like "it has nothing to do with me."

> *who are farming sustainably, to creating transparency around what's in your food and where it came from, and to creating more accessibility to healthy, real food for more people. Because here at Sweetgreen, impact is not an arm of our business, it is our business, and it permeates everything we do, from what we source to who we hire and how we support local communities. We want to make an impact and leave people better than we found them, and we tailor our approach in each market to reflect the needs of the community."*

Sweetgreen's mission is set up in a way that attempts to align with our values. I love the inclusive language they use when they say that their main objective is to connect a growing network of farmers, who produce local and healthy ingredients, with us (the customers) since we are the ones who want to have more options for healthy foods of local origin. The point of connecting people is what makes this mission statement so powerful. That promise has gone beyond their website and the posters on their premises. They offer information to young children about healthy eating, physical activity, sustainability, and the origin of food. Its Sweetlife's music festival that attracted, at its peak, 20,000 like-minded people who gathered to listen to music, eat healthy foods, and contribute to a good cause: Sweetgreen's FoodCorps charity.

Business needs to elevate its centre of gravity. Only a second-tier integral consciousness can provide a balanced and virtuous paradigm that takes into account all fundamental dimensions of reality in a balanced and non-marginalising way. One that can fully contribute to the achievement of the highest aspirations of people and organisations; one where ethics is no longer subject to financial results. Only by granting ethics its legitimate status as a fundamental dimension of management will we achieve the objective that business goes from being an instrument for individual greed to a vehicle for the collective good. Only then, will ethics reach its highest potential. Freed from the individualistic standards of Red and Orange, in which you do good only when it leads to doing well, this new level of ethics does good just because it is the right thing.

3D Management is the first theory in the history of management that puts ethics in its rightful place. Ethics and social responsibility are part of the DNA of a 3D-Management organisation. In this model, the ethical dimension is not subordinated to the scientific one (i.e., to financial results). Both are equally indispensable aspects of management, and each pursues its specific ends (the scientific dimension looks for value maximisation, and the ethical aspires to the contribution to the common good). It is possible to do well in business while doing good. Companies need to integrate and balance both dimensions, becoming agents of humanistic and social welfare. What the company does has to be, one way or the other, socially significant. End of the story.

Ethics is located at the base of the 3D-Management equilateral triangle to signal it as the axis of the model, the compass for decision making. Ethics sets the limits, defines what action is considered to be acceptable and preferred, and determines the criteria to judge what is right and what is wrong, what can be done and what cannot. Unlike the other two dimensions, the ethical dimension has universal directives and denying this is one of the fundamental mistakes of extreme postmodernism. The other dimensions are relative: a company can have zero mistakes as one of its fundamental values, whereas another one may celebrate errors to encourage risk-taking. You may like your t-shirt more than mine, and that is just a matter of taste. But nobody dares to say, "I'm against honesty." If science tells us *what* and arts tell us *how*, ethics tells us *why*. The 3D-Management model always points to the North Star of ethics.

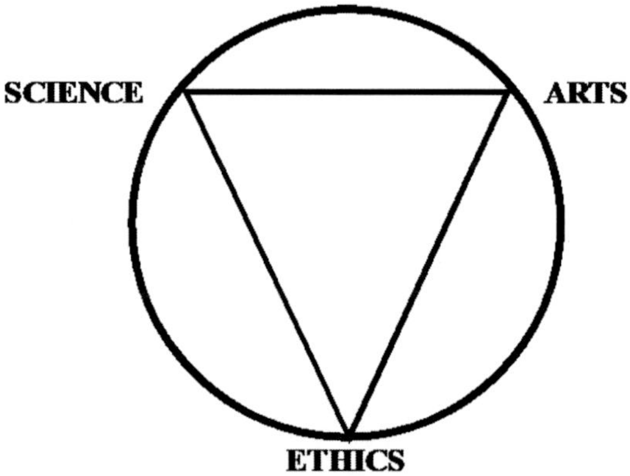

Figure 12: The 3D-Management Triangle.

6.2. A genealogy of amoral business

For centuries, economics and ethics went hand in hand. The merchants of the sixteenth century could do wrong, but they knew when they did it. It was a world in which ethics was fully seated. Even for Adam Smith, the father of liberalism, economics was a part of moral philosophy. He was a professor of moral philosophy at the University of Glasgow and published his *Theory of Moral Sentiments* well before conceiving *The Wealth of*

Nations, the work for which he is universally known. After the publication of *The Wealth of the Nations*, the study of economics got rid of ethics, supposedly because it was deemed unnecessary. Smith believed humans ultimately promote public interest through their everyday economic choices. That is, although individuals pursue selfish ends, a natural process (a miraculous and benevolent invisible hand) would establish a social order that would promote greater prosperity for everyone. This theory led to the differentiation between economics as a positive science and ethics as a normative doctrine. The rules of conduct formulated by ethics were believed not to be applicable to economics because they were simply the result of value judgments, reflecting ideological or sociological attitudes of no scientific value. In short, economics was placed outside the bounds of ethics, whose recommendations, however well-intended, were irrelevant. At that precise moment, economics became amoral.

Neoliberalism, which is still the hegemonic economic doctrine of our times, pushed the assumptions of classical economics to the limit. Neoclassical or neoliberal economists, such as Milton Friedman or Friedrich Hayek, only recognised one social responsibility for business: increasing profits. In any case, the Invisible Hand of the market would turn the pursuit of self-interest into a benefit for the entire community as easily as Jesus changed the water into wine. They argued that in a free-market economy, the social responsibility of business is limited to maximising profits without breaking the law. Business is thus reduced to its scientific dimension. Managers have no right to do anything other than increase the economic value for the shareholders, and they must forget about any ethical considerations if that diverts them from that goal. Anything else would violate their legal, moral, and fiduciary responsibilities.

Consequently, morality must be relegated to the private sphere. You are free to go to Mass on Sundays, give alms to the poor, or sponsor a child from a developing country if you want to, but in your own time and with your own money. Friedman[104] expressed it this way:

> *"What does it mean that an executive has a "social responsibility" in his capacity as a businessman? If this statement is not purely rhetorical, it must mean that he must act in a way that is not in the interest of those who have hired him. For example, it should refrain from raising the price of the product to contribute to the social objective of avoiding inflation,*

---

[104] At the end of his career, he moderated his position and admitted social responsibility, but only with a utilitarian view.

even if the increase were positive for the company. Or you must incur costs to reduce pollution beyond the amount that suits the company or that is required by law to contribute to the social goal of improving the environment. Or, at the expense of company profits, hire recalcitrant unemployed rather than better-qualified workers to contribute to the social goal of reducing poverty. In each of these, the executive would be spending the money of others in the general social interest "(cited by Kaptein and Wempe 2002: 113).

The kind of capitalism that emerged from this doctrine is, in contrast to the most controlled and regulated capitalism of the 1950s and 1960s, a much harder, more mobile, and more implacable version. Its fundamental objective is to serve the interests of investors, who only want to hear about EBITDA metrics, EPS, and the like. All obstacles to its ability to do so (regulations, controls, trade unions, taxes, state ownership, etc.) are unjustified and must be eliminated at all costs. It advocates for "flexible" labour markets and freedom of movement of capital to invest and disinvest in industries and countries.

The shareholder value movement, starting in the 80s, is a branch of this school. The prominent CEO of General Electric, Jack Welch, was its principal spokesman. Under Friedman's spell, and the influence of a scientific paper by Jensen and Meckling titled "*The Theory of the Firm*" (1976), the Shareholder Value Theory assumed that shareholders owned corporations and that directors and executives should focus on maximising their wealth. Jensen and Meckling's proposal was to turn executives into owners through stock compensation, to align their objectives with those of the corporation and its shareholders. The explosion in CEO compensation since the 1990s was the result of setting their remuneration not only relatively higher to that of other managers, as it used to be done, but in relation to the returns generated for the stakeholders. With the advent of stock options as the standard tool of executive pay, next-quarter thinking became the norm. Short-term focus made stocks boost, making executives and shareholders filthy rich at the expense of company performance and employee wellbeing. Corporations became obsessed with shareholder value maximisation, as manifested in meeting quarterly profits, and executive pay skyrocketed. Over the years, corporate raiders, leveraged buyouts, and activist hedge funds came into play and put even more pressure over short-term results. At the peak of this lunacy, corporations merged like crazy, companies downsized, whole industries were outsourced, and underperforming executives were fired just to keep stocks up. It is a system so perverse and absurd that it gave preference to fire people than to create employment. As Denning summarised in his brilliant chronicle of the development of the Shareholder Value Theory and its repercussions (2018:170), the pursuit of a single clear goal, if it was the wrong goal, became a financial, social, and moral disaster. Douglas Rushkoff (2016: 4) eloquently argues that unceasing growth has become the underlying objective of an economic model that goes against our wellbeing and prosperity:

> *"We are caught in a growth trap. This is the problem with no name or face, the frustration so many feel. It is the logic driving the jobless recovery, the low-wage gig economy, the ruthlessness of Uber, and the privacy invasions of Facebook. It is the mechanism that undermines both businesses and investors, forcing them to compete against players with digitally inflated poker chips. It is the pressure rendering CEOs powerless to prioritize the sustainability of their enterprises over the interests of impatient stakeholders. It is the unidentified culprit behind the news headlines of economic crisis from the Greek default to skyrocketing student debt. It is the force exacerbating wealth disparity, increasing the pay gap between employees and executives, and generating the power-law dynamics separating winners from losers. It is the black box extracting value from the stock market before human traders know what has happened, and the mindless momentum expanding the tech bubble to proportions dangerously too big to burst."*

The gloomy landscape Rushkoff paints is a product of scientific materialism and the Orange worldview; of organisations dominated by the scientific dimension, which only consider the material as real, reducing their complex nature to objective realities from a techno-economic perspective. Everything immaterial (vague and not measurable) is relegated to ostracism. The result of that mindset is a corporate world plagued by continuing scandals: Enron, WorldCom, Monsanto, Volkswagen, BP, Valeant, the entire 2008 financial crisis, etc. Ethics is not part of the equation for them.

Neoliberalism has received many criticisms. For example, in 2005, the internationally renowned academic, Henry Mintzberg, heavily condemned the doctrine of shareholder value:

> *"Shareholder value is an antisocial dogma that has no place in a democratic society. Period. It brings a society of exploitation of people as well as of institutions. It is bad for business because it undermines its respect and credibility. Look at the Enrons, the Andersons, and all that followed."*

Almost at the same time, another acclaimed business guru, Sumantra Goshal (2005), denounced in a brilliant posthumous article, the determinant effect that theory has had over unethical management practices by legitimising certain behaviours from a strictly economic point of view without regard to other variables. As Goshal points out, if our theories are amoral, we are implicitly freeing practitioners of any sense of moral responsibility. A CEO can justify the biggest atrocities just by saying "our job is creating shareholder value."

Ask (at jail visiting hours) supposedly evil CEOs such as Enron's Kenneth Lay, Tyco's Dennis Kozlowski, or Worldcom's Bernie Ebbers, and they will consistently answer that they didn't do anything wrong, they were just doing their jobs. In a way, they are right. Maximising shareholder value was their job. That is what they learned at college, and that is what everybody told them to do. They were not immoral. Their moral system just didn't include ethics. I am not saying they should not be in jail, but the prevailing order largely backed their crimes.

Mackey (2013: xii), CEO of Whole Foods and one of the foremost advocates of Conscious Capitalism, replied to Friedman and his late theory of shareholder value creation in this way:

> *"While Friedman believes that taking care of customers, employees, and business philanthropy are a means to the end of increasing investors profits I take the exact opposite view: making high profits is the means to the end of fulfilling Whole Foods Core Business. We want to improve the health and well-being of everyone on the planet through higher-quality food and better nutrition, and we can't fulfil this mission unless we are highly profitable"*

In the final analysis, the amoral argument is ontologically incorrect. Almost any business decision has some ethical content, and organisations need, for their smooth operation, a moral background. Companies expect their employees not to steal, the contracting parties in a commercial operation trust that agreements are going to be respected, consumers assume that what they paid for will correspond to what they will get, etc. In short, without ethics, business is not possible. In truth, the neoliberal principle that managers have only one responsibility, and it is with shareholders, is a moral statement. Therefore, the argument that business is amoral is merely absurd.

The neoliberal postulate that only science (and its quantitative expression) matters is unsustainable. Science is a value-free structure that needs ethics since the former only tells us what it is. It can't be applied to decide what should be, to specify the direction that things should take, to describe the future we should construct as a consequence of our actions. Such acts of valuation necessarily constitute moral decisions. We can use the information generated with scientific methods to guide those decisions, but not to tell us if they are correct. As Peterson (1999:10) points out, action presupposes moral valuation. To act is to manifest preference about one set of possibilities, contrasted to an infinite set of alternatives. The question of "what should be?" therefore includes three subqueries (Peterson 1999: 13):

1) *What is? – What is the nature (meaning, the significance) of the current state of experience?*
2) *What should be? – To what (desirable, valuable) end should that state be moving?*
3) *How should we therefore act? – What is the nature of the specific processes by which the present state might be transformed into that which is desired?*

The "what is" is a description of the present. We answer the question "what should be?" by formulating an image of the desired future. To decide a course of action is to think about the future. Every decision necessarily has a strong moral component. In the final analysis, we answer the question "how then should we act?" by determining the most efficient and self-consistent strategy for bringing the preferred future into being.

6.3. The Morality of Development

- *Just answer the question Georgia, can you name one time in the past year where you checked the tape and you didn't give the banks the AAA-percentage they wanted?*
- *If we don´t give them the ratings, they'll go to Moody's right down the block. If we don't work with them they will go to our competitors. Not our fault, simply the way the world works.*
- *Holy shit!*
- *Ah yes, now you see it! And I never said that!*
- *You're selling ratings for fees. A rating's shop. You could afford to make less.*
- *Make less… Nobody said that! And it is not my decision. I have a boss.*
- *Are you kidding me?*
- *No, I am not kidding you!*

- *Is that the angle you're taking? So now anybody who has a boss can't be held responsible for doing shitty and illegal things! What are you? Four?*

The Big Short (Adam McKay, 2016)

The moral line is one of the lines of development that Integral Theory takes into account. The American psychologist Lawrence Kohlberg (1973) developed a model of moral development of six stages. He grouped those different stages into three tiers, as compared to the dominant worldview in a particular society. His typology ranges from preconventional, to conventional, and finally to postconventional.

A. Preconventional: It is an egocentric, prenormative, and amoral stage where right or wrong is judged from the perspective of one's own interest. What is good is anything that satisfies my desires as long as I don't get punished. It is the kind of moral reasoning that prevails up to the Red altitude.
B. Conventional: It is a sociocentric tier that nowadays would include the Amber and, to a significant degree, the Orange level of development[105]. At childhood, we learn that the best way to experience pleasure and avoid pain is to conform to the desires of our parents and the rules of our culture. What we think and how we act is strongly influenced by what we assume others want us to believe and do. Our group-fostered identity is shaped by the norms, expectations, and interests of the group to which we belong, and that determines our moral stance. It is the level at which most individuals and organisations are. Many will never go beyond this stage.
C. Postconventional: At this tier, which currently includes all levels of development that come after Orange (Green, Teal, and Turquoise, plus the still negligible third-tier), the moral agent follows non-heteronomical norms or principles. Morals become, for the first time, autonomous from the pull of heteronomy, or "other-directedness." Heteronomic factors, such as natural inclinations and desires, mythic religion, or ethnocentric culture, no longer determine the rules to be followed. It is the moral agent (the individual or organisation), the one that decides the appropriate rules of behaviour autonomously, according to its

[105] The Orange stage is, by definition, worldcentric, but when it comes to business ethics, I would describe it as sociocentric at best.

own ethical criteria. Those are independent of external incentives, such as rewards or punishments, or sociocentric standards, as what the group of reference dictates. Once we move away from heteronomy, role identity is overcome, and we can move, using Peterson's terminology, from a morality of restriction based upon prohibition ("Thou shalt not") to a morality of possibility based upon what should be done. It is a morality that comes from within, from its own reasons, not from any external source whatsoever, and it includes the capacity of questioning and choosing the norms that one follows. Ethical decisions rest with the individual, who must assume responsibility for his or her own relatively autonomous choices. Ethics becomes a positive and affirmative knowledge, a categorical imperative that impels one to act in a certain way independently of any external judgment.

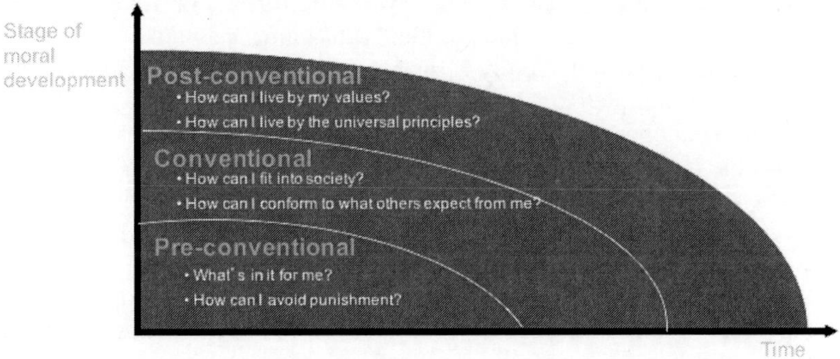

Figure 13: Kohlberg's categories of moral development.

This classification is dynamic and relative, as every stage can be preconventional, conventional, or postconventional, depending on the vantage point. Thus, Red consciousness was postconventional 50,000 years ago, but it was the conventional stage in the Middle Ages, and nowadays is preconventional in the Western world, which has its centre of gravity somewhere between Orange and Green. However, it remains postconventional for the Sentinelese of the Andaman Islands in India, one of the remaining foraging cultures today.

Increasing psychological and moral development is directly related to the number of perspectives one can take into account. The more views (i.e., the more of reality) that are acknowledged, the more ethical a decision will be. When I am acting egocentrically, I am a slave to my desires, and I am only able to consider my own perspective. An ethnocentric moral stance takes into account the point of view and needs of one's family, group, or nation. This second-person perspective is certainly broader but is still a slave to the herd mentality. As Kant advocated, I am truly free only when I act from a worldcentric stance following my own moral will. The birth of true morals or ethics occurs when I can take simultaneously, at least, a third-person perspective[106]. It is a worldcentric kind of ethics that takes into account all people on the planet but is still too anthropocentric. An integral approach to ethics goes even further, to a kosmocentric position. At this level, one identifies with all manifest and unmanifest reality.

As many ethical decisions involve making trade-offs, Ken Wilber has developed the Basic Moral Intuition, an integral rule of thumb based on holonic theory. All holons, as we have seen, are both wholes and parts (Wilber 1995: 544-5). As a part, all holons have instrumental value (also called extrinsic value). That is, they have value for others. Likewise, as a wholeness, any holon has "whole-value." It has intrinsic value. It is an end in and of itself, and not merely a means for something else. One of the fundamental principles of Integral Theory's holonomic theory is, the greater the wholeness, the greater the intrinsic value. Wholeness-value, in other words, is the same as depth-value. The greater the depth, the greater the value. There are also levels of significance: the greater the depth, or the greater the wholeness, then the more significant that wholeness is because more can be embraced in that wholeness and depth. Thus, cells are more significant than molecules because cells contain molecules, an ape is more significant than a cell, and so on. Depth also refers to complexity: a human has more depth of consciousness and is, therefore, more significant than a dog, which has more depth than a worm. Finally, the greater the potential depth, the greater the potential value: A new-born girl is more significant than a grown-up dog because she has more

[106] In this usage, "3rd person" means not the person spoken about, but the capacity to take the viewpoint of one person's viewpoint of another person's viewpoint. With a third-person perspective, three different viewpoints can be simultaneously held in mind. It can objectively be aware of a 1st and 2nd-person perspective. A fourth-person perspective would take four. Red altitude can only take the individual's own personal perspective; Amber can take a 2nd-person perspective, putting oneself in somebody else's shoes; Orange adds a 3rd-person perspective, from which an individual can take up a more reflective, objective, critical, and even sceptical view of his or her experiences and beliefs; Green can take a 4th-person perspective; Teal can take a 5th-person perspective; Turquoise can take a 6th-person perspective, and so on.

potential depth than the dog (despite the fact that she currently has less depth than the dog). The Golden Rule of integral ethics, or "Basic Moral Intuition" (BMI), pushes us toward the need to *"protect and promote the greatest depth for the greatest span"* (Wilber, 2000, p. 640). Span refers to complexity of size: the world has more span than one organisation, which has more span than one department or circle. This rule helps us navigate through some moral dilemmas. For example, because of his depth, it would be better to save the Dalai Lama than a worm, and because of its span, we should protect the Rainforest before our backyard. However, when we have to weigh depth and span simultaneously, things become more complicated: Is it better to choose the life of the Dalai Lama or all of the worms in the world? Probably the latter, because losing them would affect the entire biosphere, but as you see, it does get complicated.

Many organisations are still in their moral childhood. They behave like egocentric, impulsive, and capricious children, with their bullying behaviours. Most organisations have grown up to be like peer-pressured adolescents. They are satisfied with just following the rules by meeting the legal obligations and moral standards of the mainstream culture. Very few have reached moral maturity.

The business world averages a conventional centre of moral gravity that is hijacked much too often by preconventional impulses. Greed and self-interest are manifestations of the long Red shadow of the corporate world. That's why it is still necessary to develop more effective Amber legal frameworks for regulating corporate responsibility, both at the international and national levels, even though moral conduct is far more than merely complying with external norms to avoid the punishment which would result when they transgress.

The pre-conventional and conventional stances have resulted in environmental crisis, inequality, and injustice in the world. The biggest challenge we face is that our global digital society becomes postconventional in its ethical perspective. Until we collectively evolve, we remain incapable of seeing, much less changing, its many damaging ways. From this point of view, the moral evolution of business as a social institution is urgent. We need mature, morally autonomous organisations acting from worldcentric and kosmocentric perspectives more than anything else. As my friend, Daniel Wahl (2016: 23), puts it:

> *"Mature community membership means a shift towards a form of enlightened self-interest that goes as far as questioning the notion of a separate and isolated self at its very core. In the fundamentally*

interconnected and interdependent planetary system we participate in, the best way to care for oneself and those closest to oneself is to start caring more for the benefit of the collective (all life). (...) The "them-against-us" thinking that for too long has defined politics between nations, companies, and people is profoundly anachronistic"

6.4. Total Stakeholder Integration

Conventional organisations have a hierarchy of stakeholders: shareholders come first, customers second, then employees (I remember a Dilbert comic strip in which the boss rectified this and said that carbon paper came first), and eventually all the rest. They work under the assumption that one stakeholder group can only prosper at the expense of other stakeholder groups, for example, exerting pressure on suppliers to cut their prices (Sisodia et al. 2007: 258). This kind of mindset is no longer valid, as Hamel (2009) asserts:

"In tomorrow's interdependent world, highly collaborative systems will outperform organizations characterized by adversarial win-lose relationships. Yet today, corporate governance structures often exacerbate conflict by promoting the interests of some groups—like senior executives and the providers of capital—at the expense of others—usually employees and local communities. In the future, management systems must reflect the ethos of community and citizenship, thereby recognizing the interdependence of all stakeholder groups."

Putting shareholders first has jeopardised the True, the Good, and the Beautiful in our world. On the contrary, 3D Management organisations consider all of their stakeholders as equally important, interconnected, and interdependent. They aspire to optimise value-creation for all of them, so the objectives of each one can be met simultaneously. It is a significant paradigm change that moves from a zero-sum culture (win-lose) to a non-zero sum culture (win-win).

Total stakeholder integration is not about balancing the interests of one stakeholder group versus the other (for example, higher wages for employees versus higher profits for shareholders, or lower prices for consumers versus higher prices for suppliers). It is about actively aligning them and optimising value creation, as Sisodia et al. (2007:8) affirm:

"Instead of trading off the interests of one group versus those of another (for example, higher wages for employees versus higher profits for investors or lower prices for customers), they have carefully devised business models in which the objectives of each stakeholder can be met

simultaneously and are, in fact, strengthened by other stakeholders. (...) That's why these companies can do seemingly contradictory things such as pay high wages, charge low prices and get higher profitability."

Thus, they are freer from trade-off constraints, as evidenced by Southwest Airlines or JetBlue, which offer very low prices but a very high quality of service. Hence, value is multi-dimensionally redefined so that it contributes to the welfare and satisfaction of all stakeholders through products or services that make customers happy, through profits that make shareholders happy, through work that makes employees happy, and through the contribution to a better world that makes society happy. The purpose of business is still creating value but from an integral perspective. A 3D-Management company puts the wellbeing of the stakeholders at the forefront by adding value 3-dimensionally: economic value (science), human value (arts), and social value (ethics). In this new scenario, it is no longer necessary to choose between, say, social responsibility and profits, but to integrate and balance both.

All the stakeholders of a 3D-Management Organisation are, in one way or another, involved with and have a vested interest in the enterprise. For example, suppliers become real partners that establish long-standing relationships of mutual benefit. Ultimately the bonds between the organisation and its stakeholders can become so intimate that it even blurs the limits between them to the extreme of becoming a liquid entity in unity with its stakeholder community. Customers or suppliers, for example, become members of a boundless organisation, participating in the circles charged with designing or promoting new products or services.

The organisation should then be active in engaging stakeholders in its purpose, creating moments of contact to lay fertile ground for engagement.

6.5. Case in point: Drinks that refresh the world

There is a growing market of indie soft drinks that have appeared as an alternative against global giants like Coca-Cola and PepsiCo. Some of them are also local, organic, and fairtrade. Karma Cola, from New Zealand, sources organic kola nuts from farmers in the village of Boma in Sierra Leone. As its name implies, the community directly benefits from the proceeds (so much so that Fairtrade International crowned the brand World's Fairest Trader in 2014). Likewise, Ubuntu Cola takes its name from a Zulu word that describes the universal bond of sharing that connects all humanity. It was the first drink in the UK to get a Fairtrade Mark in 2007 and is made with Fairtrade sugar cane from Malawi.

Very special to me is Pep Lemon, a founding member of the 3D-Management Club of Conscious Organisations. Pep Lemon is a Majorcan company that produced organic soft drinks until 2018. Carme Verdaguer and Christoph Hafner had a lemon tree in their backyard that produced about 100 kg of fruit each year. Too many for one family! Wondering what could be done with so many lemons, they found out that, every year, tons of citrus are wasted in Majorca. They also discovered that in the north of Europe, indie local soda brands were beginning to be a trend. Joining these two ideas, in 2012, Carme, Christoph, and Tomeu Riutord created Pep Lemon, a 100% natural brand of local soft drinks, with a hipster attitude, based on circular-economy principles of upcycling. Pep Lemon was a collaborative project, inviting other companies on the island to provide their knowledge and resources. They took those lemons, carob, and oranges that due to their shape or size didn't reach the market. Then they produced lemon, cola, and orange soft drinks through Amadip Esment, an organisation whose mission is to integrate people with disabilities. All the pulp obtained from squeezing the lemons and oranges was also used to produce lemon and orange jam, so no waste was generated. The last independent bottler in Mallorca was rescued from extinction by being commissioned to make their eco-designed bottles of returnable glass. Unfortunately, they decided to rethink the whole project after PepsiCo sued them on the grounds that the name of its Cola drink, Pep Cola, was too similar to Pepsi. It didn't matter to them that the design was totally different and that the name Pep has nothing to do with Pepsi. Pep comes from the most widely used nickname in Catalan (meaning Joe), and they used it first for the original lemon drink to emphasise their local roots when they were not even thinking about making a cola. Being forced to change a very well-positioned brand name was quite a blow.

Finally, Premium-Cola is a soft drink brand founded in Hamburg, Germany, by a collective of fans of Afri-Cola, a traditional German brand. After a change of ownership, Afri-Cola secretly reduced the amount of caffeine in its recipe to reach a wider audience, and then it introduced plastic bottles without any announcement. Uwe Lübbermann, future initiator and "central coordinator" of Premium-Cola, was unhappy about this top-down decision that disregarded the customer. After running a protest website unsuccessfully, he decided to use the original recipe and began to produce Premium-Cola.

Premium-Cola is a postconventional firm. It has no offices, no salaries, and no bosses. They limit their growth, and its members choose the amount of time they will spend working. For some, Premium-Cola is a hobby they combine with their actual work or studies; for others, it is a full-time job. There is hardly any advertising; instead, art pictures are printed on the inside of the bottles' labels. The collective puts much thought into acting ethically in the economy instead of expanding or selling more. Premium-Cola is being sold only in selected outlets (mainly clubs and bars, but not exclusively) whose philosophy is similar to that of the brand.

They treat every stakeholder in their ecosystem – employees, truck drivers, beverage grocers, producers of ingredients etc.– as partners and equals. From their perspective, there is nobody who is "external" to the company. Anyone who has a connection to the company, no matter how remote, is considered "internal" and has the right to participate in the discussion. They share all information with all stakeholders, including strategy, sales figures, and obviously, costs and revenue, which are, in any case, public. All issues are decided collectively in a very Green consensual way.

6.6. Case in point: Whole Foods' Declaration of Interdependence

The motto of Whole Foods - *"Whole Foods, Whole People, Whole Planet"*- embodies its total stakeholder orientation. Their conscious model of business is governed by Whole Foods' "Declaration of Interdependence," which identifies the various stakeholders of the company, acknowledges their importance, and makes a commitment to ensure that their interests, desires, and needs are kept in balance. Here is the full text of the declaration[107]:

Our Purpose is to Nourish People and the Planet

Whole Foods Market is a dynamic leader in the quality food business. We are a purpose-driven company that aims to set the standards of excellence for food retailers. We are building a business in which high standards permeate all aspects of our company. Quality is a state of mind at Whole Foods Market.

[107] The Declaration was created originally in 1985 by 60 team members who volunteered their time. It has been updated in 1988, 1992, 1997, and 2018.

We recognize the interdependence among our stakeholders - those who benefit from or are impacted by our company. Our success is optimized by a win-win strategy, and all of our stakeholders are simultaneously benefitting.

Our Values:

- We Sell the Highest Quality Natural and Organic Foods

We appreciate and celebrate great food. Breaking bread with others, eating healthy and eating well - these are some of the great joys of our lives.

Our product quality standards lead the marketplace. We focus on growing methods, safety, ingredients, taste, freshness, nutrition and appearance.

We tirelessly develop and introduce delicious and healthy foods that our customers love.

- We Satisfy and Delight Our Customers

Our customers are the lifeblood of our business and our most important stakeholder. We strive to meet or exceed their expectations on every shopping experience.

We deliver outstanding customer service through our knowledge, skill, enthusiasm and operational excellence.

We continually experiment and innovate to offer a better customer experience. We create store environments that are inviting, fun, unique, comfortable, attractive, nurturing and educational. Our stores are community meeting places where people can join their friends and make new ones.

- *We Promote Team Member Growth and Happiness*[108]

Our success is dependent upon the collective energy, intelligence and contributions of all our Team Members. We design and provide safe and empowering environments where highly-motivated people can flourish and reach their highest potential.

We strive to build positive and healthy relationships. "Us versus them" thinking has no place in our company. We earn trust through transparent communication, open door policies, and inclusive people practices. We appreciate and recognize the good work that our fellow Team Members do every day.

We value the importance of fun, family, and community involvement to encourage a rich, meaningful, and balanced life.

- *We Practice Win-Win Partnerships with Our Suppliers*

We are part of an interdependent business ecosystem. There are tens of thousands of suppliers that we depend on to create an outstanding retail shopping experience for our customers.

We view our trade partners as allies in serving our stakeholders. We treat them with respect, fairness, and integrity - expecting the same in return.

We listen compassionately, we think carefully, and we always seek win-win relationships with everyone engaged in our business.

- *We Create Profits and Prosperity*

We earn profits every day through voluntary exchange with our customers.

---

[108] In 2017 Amazon bought Whole Foods. Many analysts wondered if Whole Foods would be able to keep to its business philosophy. Same as happened with Zappos (also acquired in 2009 by Amazon) the answer seemed yes, but with the recent coronavirus outbreak, the supermarket company is facing escalating tensions with employees demanding improved workplace safety and sick pay for employees affected by the pandemic. The company has suggested that employees donate their accumulated paid time off to their coworkers. As a subsidiary of Amazon, the world's biggest company, and a supporter of the Conscious Capitalism Movement, I think they should do a lot more to honour their philosophy and protect their own employees.

We know that profits are essential to create capital for growth, job security, and overall financial success. Profits are the "savings" every business needs in order to change and evolve to meet the future goals. They are the "seed corn" for next year's crop and the creator of sustained prosperity.

We are stewards for our parent company Amazon, and we have a responsibility to use their capital wisely and frugally with the goal to increase its value over the long-term. We will grow at such a pace that our customer satisfaction, Team Member happiness, and financial health continue to flourish together.

- We Care About Our Communities and the Environment

We serve and support a local experience. The unique character of each store is a direct reflection of a community's people, culture, and cuisine. We celebrate and strengthen each community through employment, investment in local non-profits, and a conscious commitment to our local producers.

We leverage our foundations to broaden our community impact. We champion nutritional education for children, food access in underserved areas, and microcredit for the poorest of the poor.

We practice and advance environmental stewardship. We balance our needs with the needs of the rest of the planet so that the Earth will continue to flourish for generations to come. Our industry-leading quality standards support sustainable agriculture, animal welfare, and ocean preservation. We are committed to reduced packaging, composting, and water and energy conservation.

6.7. Transparency and trust

> *Intelligent control appears as uncontrol or freedom, and for that reason, it is genuinely intelligent control. Unintelligent control appears as external domination. And for that reason, it is really unintelligent control. Intelligent control exerts influence without appearing to do so. Unintelligent control tries to influence by making a show of force. (Tao te king.* Laozi).

Trust is one of the more critical assets an organisation can have. Command-and-control systems create environments lacking in trust that fosters defensive, suspicious, and fearful behaviour, with all the negative consequences that ensue.

A lack of trust results in constant and expensive control and monitoring, whereas trust results in the freedom to act.

Trust is foundational to fostering an environment that brings out the best in people. The best performing and most fulfilled teams exhibit a high degree of mutual trust. When trust is established, great things can happen.

Trust works internally and externally between the company and its customers, suppliers, other business partners, communities, investors, government, and all the rest of the stakeholders.

Building trust requires constant, authentic communication. Communication is not just about words; it is also based on actions. Every action communicates something to employees. Too many companies say one thing and do another, breeding deep cynicism among stakeholders over time.

One of the things that creates trust is transparency. As the responsive.org manifesto states[109], in the past, information was power. In the industrial era, organisations secured information carefully and leveraged it as a competitive advantage. The result was a lot of information asymmetries as top management was keeping secret pieces of information from the bottom and vice versa. Today, we live in times of information abundance, and it is impossible to predict what information might be useful, or who might use it. Information hoarding doesn't make good business sense. Information is there to share and to be shared. In a world of information surplus and connectedness, the potential benefits of trusting people with information usually outweigh the risks of it being used in counter-productive ways.

Transparency requires that all information relevant to decision-making must be available to everyone involved or affected by it. As a result, progressive organisations make information open for self-regulation, innovation, learning, and control. Everybody has access to all information, including financial data, salaries, and team performance. Smarkets is an online betting exchange[110] headquartered in London, run on a self-

---

[109] https://www.responsive.org/manifesto/

[110] A betting exchange allows users to bet against each other, head-to-head, rather than the house.

management structure, and driven by trust and radical transparency. Information of all kinds is openly shared in real-time, from financials to salaries, to failures and successes. They make it happen through tools such as Slack, regular town hall meetings, and weekly stand-ups of 30-45 minutes[111].

In a self-managed environment, information transparency is a prerequisite for decision making and peer-based control. Employees must be able to know as much as possible to exercise freedom wisely and calculate the impact of their decisions. For example, employees settle on their own salaries at Semco, but they must take into account four criteria before giving any figure:

- How much could they earn at another company?
- What are other colleagues with the same responsibilities and skills making?
- What do other people with similar training earn in the marketplace?
- How much they need to make a living?

The company provides them with internal and external information about the first three points to help them decide on an accurate figure. What happens if you choose an unrealistic salary? Well, you are expected to perform accordingly. Your colleagues will let you know if you don't measure up since they know exactly how much you earn compared to their own salaries, and they will expect you to renegotiate the salary the following year. This is the power of peer pressure, as I have already explained. With the same intention in mind, Next Jump has designed a feedback app to allow everyone to provide anonymous, public feedback to everyone else.

It is the end of information privacy and secrets. The problem with secrets is that people tend to imagine the worse. They assume that the company is making tons of money and that the owner is a multimillionaire. Thanks to transparency, people don't waste time trying to guess, for example, what colleagues earn. Whole Foods' Wage Disclosure Report lists anyone's salary or bonus from the previous year, including executives and the CEO. John Mackey introduced the policy in 1986, only six years after he co-

[111] You can learn more about Smarkets and many other progressive workplaces in the "bucket list" of the indispensable blog Corporate-rebels.com.

founded the company. According to him, open salary information makes the compensation system fairer because there will have to be justification why some people are paid more than others (actually, he is not one of them. His yearly salary is just 1$). Whole Foods' managers post their store's sales every day and regional sales each week. Monthly, Whole Foods sends each store a comprehensive analysis of profitability and sales. Mackey says, *"If you're trying to create a high-trust organisation, an organisation where people are all-for-one and one-for-all, you can't have secrets."*

Transparency is an extremely efficient system of control. It is certainly more flexible and less expensive than a rigidly applied system because it is self-regulating. For example, most companies have detailed policies for business trips. Employees must have permission for travelling, abide by strict spending limits, and submit travel expenses for approval. Bogsnes (2016:13) reports on a revealing experiment on transparency the Swiss pharmaceutical company Roche carried out. In a pilot study, they disposed of the travel budget and almost all the travel rules and regulations. Instead, they introduced full transparency by publishing every employee's expense report ensuring that everyone could examine all the information about who, where, how, and how much was spent, thereby relying on peer pressure to rein in profligate spenders. Travel costs fell dramatically. Finext follows a similar policy for expenses: Employees submit their expense statement declarations, and without additional control, the declared amount is paid. The only condition is that the statement is visible for everyone on the company intranet.

CineCiutat has faced many difficult times. It is the bitter reality of an alternative kind of cinema, exhibiting undubbed independent movies (a small Iranian film is unlikely to be a blockbuster). The company has made all the financial information open to members and workers. Anyone can see the financial statements and salary information. Employees and members may feel anxious about finances when faced with difficulties, but at least everyone knows where the company stands. They don't want to give a false sense of security. At an operational level, daily stand-up meetings are held to review the status of work in progress. In these meetings, members share what work has been done, what will be done next, what problems they are facing, and where they need help. Periodic reports are also a regular occurrence in this company.

Transparency is not only restricted to sharing information, but to sharing knowledge, both internally and externally. I have already explained how

Buurtzorg has revolutionised home-care services in the Netherlands. One of the reasons is that the company not only welcomes competition to imitate its model, but they explain it to them free of charge. As a result, other healthcare providers such as ZorgAccent and Amstelring Wijkzorg have implemented self-managed neighbourhood teams, the Buurtzorg way. Disclosing competitive information would be anathema for an Orange company, but for Buurtzorg's Teal philosophy it is the right thing to do: the more companies share its philosophy the better the contribution to its core purpose: to maintain and improve people's capacity to live at home, as well as possible, for as long as possible.

6.8. Dealing with Workplace Conflicts

Freedom is a highly respected ethical ideal that must be linked with responsibility. You cannot have one without the other. Conflict is inevitable, because people have different needs and because at times freedom is not exercised responsibly enough. However, conflict is healthy. Diversity of opinions, disagreement, and divergence are at least as necessary as conformance, consensus, and cohesion.

In traditional companies, when one person does not deliver, the boss generally takes care of the matter. The rest of the people may complain or criticize, but they usually stand on the sidelines. The same happens with disputes and disagreements. When they arise, it is up to the boss to find a solution. Kids fight and daddy steps in to set things right.

In self-managing organisations, there are no managers to call people to order or settle disputes, and no one has the authority to force a decision. It is everybody's business to step up and confront colleagues who don't fulfil their obligations or address tensions, whether organisational, interpersonal, contextual or personal, and take immediate steps to solve the problems.

Conflict resolution is the process that allows for an objective examination of facts so that colleagues hold each other accountable for their mutual commitments. The mechanism should be clear and known to everyone, ideally publicised in a policy for handling conflicts. In most Teal organisations, the conflict resolution process is structured according to an escalation procedure. As there are no managers to judge and decide, the fundamental principle is that peers must resolve their disagreement between themselves involving as few people as possible.

Morning Star's Conflict Resolution and Accountability Process has always been a benchmark for other organisations. It starts with a call to responsibility: *"If anyone perceives any action on the part of a colleague that is not supportive of the mission or is counterproductive to the work of other colleagues, he or she will be obligated to directly speak with that person about the issue"* (Kirkpatrick 2010: 56). The process is divided into three parts:

1. Direct conversation between the parties, generally in the form of a request of one person to the other.
2. If the discussion between the parties involved didn't resolve the issue, they resort to a third-party mediator, trusted by both colleagues, who examines the facts and circumstances independently. The mediator can only give an opinion but doesn't have any power to resolve the issue. That power belongs to the parties involved.
3. If the differences are still not resolved by direct discussion or mediation, then it will be necessary to convene a panel of no more than 6 colleagues to sit down with both parties until a solution is reached. If they don't resolve the issue then the CEO, as the guardian of the mission, will participate in the deliberations and render a final decision.

Let's imagine you and I work together, and you complain that I didn't fulfil, in several instances, my responsibilities to you reflected in our CLOU (Colleague Letter of Understanding, see 4.3). As a first step, we would meet, and you would present your case. I might offer an excuse, agree to do better, or tell you directly to go to hell. If the two of us couldn't resolve the matter, we would pick an internal mediator whom we both trust and present our views. Let's say the mediator agreed with you, but I still objected to the reduction of my salary. At this juncture, a panel of six peers who are not involved in the situation and can be fair and unbiased would assemble to help us settle our dispute. This group might endorse the mediator's recommendation to reduce my salary, resume my responsibilities, or propose another solution. If I objected again, the CEO would bring the parties together, hear the arguments, and make a binding decision. It is highly unusual for a dispute to land on the CEO's desk, but in serious matters, the conflict resolution process can end with termination.

6.9. Ethical audits and certificates

An ethical audit is an independent and systematic evaluation of the ethical conduct of an organisation and its impact. It is often linked to a certification or label. For the organisation, receiving a certificate is a way to transmit a positive image of commitment and integrity. Labels tend to be associated with specific products or services, and they offer information on how products have been made, guaranteeing that they follow specific standards (related to the environment, societies, human and workers' rights, etc.). Some labels specify the origin of the product, others prohibit the use of a particular substance, others explain the product manufacturing process, etc. The number of certificates and labels is rapidly growing, especially the environmental ones. Among the most prominent, we can mention the following:

- European norm AA-1000 (created in 1999 by the Institute of Social Responsibility and aimed at improving the process of social and environmental accountability).
- SA 8000 Certification (which certifies the social responsibility of any industrial sector in any country).
- The labels of the Fair-Trade Labelling Organisation, mainly for food products.
- All the different environmental certifications, ISO 14000 and EMAS being the most notable ones.

Worthy of special attention are the B Corps system and the Common Good Balance Sheet, the models of choice of many postconventional organisations. Their underlying philosophy, high standards of social and environmental performance, public transparency, and legal accountability set them apart from the rest. The former has its stronghold in America while the latter is more important in Europe, but both of them are movements (more than just commercial certificates) that want to change the world for the better.

Benefit Corporations, B Corporations or, in short, B Corps, are companies that undergo a rigorous certification process to improve their social and environmental performance. They have their practices independently vetted by a non-profit established in 2007 called B Lab, the organisation behind the B Corp movement. It was founded by Jay Coen Gilbert and

Bart Houlahan after they sold their former company, AND 1[112], along with Andrew Kassoy, a former Wall Street investor.

B Lab's certification process is easy. First, they offer a free online self-assessment tool, called the B Impact Assessment, which measures the social and environmental performance of a company on a scale of 0 to 200 points. Eighty points are required for B Corp certification, and the median score for all certified B Corps is around 95 points. The platform gives access to best-practice guides, comparative data, and an individualised improvement report; everything free of charge. The B Impact Report shows how each certified B Corporation performs on five sections of its assessment: governance, workers, community, environment, and customers (table 12); then it's time for the audit. Lastly, B Lab makes its results transparent to anyone on the B-Corp directory. There are currently over 2,900 Certified B Corporations in more than 64 countries.

Governance	Mission and Engagement Ethics and Transparency
Workers	Financial Security Health, Wellness, and Safety Career Development Engagement and Satisfaction
Community	Diversity, Equity, and Inclusion Economic Impact Civic Engagement and Giving Supply Chain Management
Environment	Environmental Management Air and Climate Water Land and Life
Customers	Customer Stewardship

Table 12: Areas included in the five different sections of the B Impact Report.

[112] AND 1 is a popular basketball shoe and apparel company. Honeyman (2014) reports that under Gilbert and Houlahan's leadership AND 1 became the No. 2 basketball shoe brand in the United States (behind Nike) while enjoying a well-deserved reputation as a socially-responsible business (something quite uncommon in that industry). AND 1 was a pioneer in making organic shoes, using recyclable material (tires for the soles), and bought materials from local manufacturers. The company had a basketball court at the office, on-site yoga classes, exceptional parental leave benefits, shared ownership of the company, and it gave 5 per cent of its profits to local charities. AND 1 also had codes of conduct and strict control of the working conditions of its overseas suppliers.

It is necessary to distinguish between "B Corp" and "Benefit Corporation." B Corp is any for-profit entity that is certified by the B Lab. By contrast, a Benefit Corporation, Public Benefit Corporation, or PBC is a type of corporate entity, like "Inc." or "LLC." It is a legal status of incorporation already recognised in some places with legally protected requirements, and it means that the organisation exists not only to make a profit but also to serve a higher societal purpose. It arose because the B Corp movement felt that the B Corp certification could not provide the kind of legal protection that a government-recognised legal form could provide. It is a mechanism to protect the company's core values during succession, as baby-food manufacturer Plum Organics did in 2013 when the Campbell Soup Company acquired it. Plum's stated public benefit is to deliver nourishing, organic food to babies and to raise awareness and advance solutions for childhood hunger and malnutrition in the United States. Other famous PBCs are Patagonia and Ben & Jerry's. As a PBC, Plum is legally required to prioritise that purpose regardless of what its shareholders think about it.

The Economy for the Common Good (ECG) is a very influential social movement, launched by Christian Felber in 2010, which advocates a more ethical economic model in which the wellbeing of people and the environment become the ultimate goal. It calls for organisations working towards the common good and cooperating, rather than merely generating money and competing. The movement has gained the support of nearly 3,000 companies in 50 countries. They have developed a model that leads to a certification called the Common Good Balance Sheet. The Common Good Balance Sheet measures, from a 360° perspective, how firms fulfil the following constitutional values: human dignity, solidarity, justice, environmental sustainability and transparency, and co-determination.

Organisations that want to be recognised need to follow a three-step process very similar to B Corp's (Blachfellner et al. 2017). First, they self-assess their activities and produce a Common Good Report according to a list of indicators organised in 20 Common Good themes. Those are specified in the Common Good Matrix (refer to table 13), which is the framework for the evaluation of business activities that gives guidance on how to evaluate based on Common Good principles. The report should include a description of how the company's activities relate to each of the 20 Common Good themes and how developed each value is within the company. Second, the results are examined by external auditors that evaluate the individual themes and assign an overall score. Points (or seedlings, as they are also called) are awarded for all the activities. In all cases, they go beyond the fulfilment of the legal minimum standard. In an evaluation, levels are allocated following an assessment scale (getting started, advanced, experienced, and exemplary). Each level builds on the previous one, so for example, to be awarded the experienced level, all criteria under advanced need to be met. Each evaluation level is given a score depending on how ECG-driven the theme is within the company and the extent to which the criteria for each level have been met. In addition to evaluating each theme, an overall evaluation is made by allocating Common Good Points. The maximum total score is 1000 points, and the minimum is a negative score of -3,600. Up until now, the average rating of all the companies certificated is around 300. Finally, the Common Good Balance Sheet, which comprises the Common Good Report and the Certificate awarded by the auditors, is published upon the condition of valid membership of a recognised ECG association.

VALUE / STAKEHOLDER	HUMAN DIGNITY	SOLIDARITY AND SOCIAL JUSTICE	ENVIRONMENTAL SUSTAINABILITY	TRANSPARENCY AND CO-DETERMINATION
A: SUPPLIERS	**A1** Human dignity in the supply chain	**A2** Solidarity and social justice in the supply chain	**A3** Environmental sustainability in the supply chain	**A4** Transparency and co-determination in the supply chain
B: OWNERS, EQUITY- AND FINANCIAL SERVICE PROVIDERS	**B1** Ethical position in relation to financial resources	**B2** Social position in relation to financial resources	**B3** Use of funds in relation to the environment	**B4** Ownership and co-determination
C: EMPLOYEES	**C1** Human dignity in the workplace and working environment	**C2** Self-determined working arrangements	**C3** Environmentally friendly behaviour of staff	**C4** Co-determination and transparency within the organisation
D: CUSTOMERS AND BUSINESS PARTNERS	**D1** Ethical customer relations	**D2** Cooperation and solidarity with other companies	**D3** Impact on the environment of the use and disposal of products and services	**D4** Customer participation and product transparency
E: SOCIAL ENVIRONMENT	**E1** Purpose of products and services and their effects on society	**E2** Contribution to the community	**E3** Reduction of environmental impact	**E4** Social co-determination and transparency

Table 13: The Common Good Matrix version 5.0 (Blachfellner et al. 2017).

The ECG is a comprehensive alternative economic model, and the Balance Sheet is just one of its constitutive elements that is interrelated with the others. For example, one of ECG's proposals is to convince governments to develop a system of economic benefits for sustainable and socially responsible organisations. Companies with a high score in the balance sheet would qualify for tax breaks, low-interest loans, and would be given preference in public purchasing and government contracts.

CHAPTER 7

SPIRIT:
PURPOSE AND COMMUNITY

"When the complete comes, the partial will come to an end." Corinthians 13.10

7.1. The Fantastic Fourth

To be human is to be spiritual. In the final analysis, that is what sets us apart from other species. No other creature that we know of is capable of posing questions related to meaning and transcendence, such as: Who am I, why am I here, what do I stand for, or where am I going? Human beings have thus been defined as the questing animal, because the search for meaning in life, the spiritual quest, is essential for them. The term "spirituality" derives from the Greek *pneumatikos* (spiritual). St. Paul originally coined it to describe any reality that is related to the transcendent. Spirituality thus concerns an individual's search for meaning in life.

It is increasingly common, especially among people in midlife and beyond, to find a craving for transcendence that makes them look for higher meaning in their lives and work. More often than not, they can't find it in their jobs and they become "dispirited." But when an organisation covers their spiritual needs, they feel deeply fulfilled and discover their true potential through work. From this perspective, workplace spirituality would be *"a framework of organizational values evidenced in a culture that promotes employee's experience of transcendence through the work process"* (Giacalone and Jurkiewica, 2003:13). For those who are literally "spirited", work is not something they do for a living, it is a calling, a vocation, something they feel passionate about, and that gives them value and satisfaction beyond the paycheck.

But spirituality is a concept that also applies to the organisation as a whole. When I talk about spirituality, I mean much more than building a chapel or mosque in the workplace or allowing time for mindfulness or tai chi at work. Indeed, that would address the spiritual needs of the members of the organisation and have some positive effects, but it is not the holistic approach to spirituality that 3D Management suggests. The dominating Orange altitude has instrumentally abducted many of these spiritual practices (like mindfulness or yoga) to have workers at their desks, stress-free and more productive, doing business as usual.

So, what am I talking about? Similar to human beings, every organisation needs to ask some fundamental questions of meaning and transcendence: What is our purpose? What is the business we are in? Who are our customers? Which and where are our markets? What is our vision? Every time we think about that, we are asking questions of spiritual content for the organisation.

Mitroff and Denton (1999) authored what is regarded as the seminal study on spirituality in the workplace. It concluded that employees perceived companies with a greater sense of spirituality as better and more profitable and that they could bring more of themselves to work without having to renounce their principles. To sum up, organisations that are more spiritual get more from their members and vice versa. Following the footsteps of this trailblazing study, a growing body of research is showing the link between meaningful work and factors such as work motivation, absenteeism, engagement, job satisfaction, stress, and performance (Lips-Wierma and Morris 2011; Rosso et al., 2010).

The language of spirit should become a part of organisational jargon: words like community, soul, contribution, transcendence, authenticity, and vocation have long inspired humanity to extraordinary accomplishments. They deserve to be as much a part of the management vocabulary as the usual ones of profit, productivity, competition, and value. Do you want to stir people? Then use the right vocabulary. Are you using words like meaning, vision, community, and creativity or is profits, productivity, and competition everything you talk about?

The spiritual dimension is the dimension of unity. Making the organisation useful to society, satisfactory to its stakeholders, as well as profitable and competitive is challenging, and at times, these are conflicting tasks. The spiritual is the fourth dimension of 3D Management, the Fantastic Fourth, which, in the event of a conflict, harmonises the objectives of the three constituent aspects of management. The spiritual dimension unifies the organisation and elevates it in unison to higher degrees of performance, development, and ethical commitment. This corporate spirit is articulated through two sub-dimensions, namely communion and purpose.

From this spiritual dimension, 3D Management defines an organisation as a community of purpose, and business as a community of purpose that provides goods and services for the betterment of humanity. This definition is quite close to Tami Simon's (CEO of Sounds True) spiritual vision of business: *"My view of business is that we are coming together as a community to fill a human need and actualize our lives."*

7.2. A Purpose Beyond Profit

> *And God said, "Let Us make living creatures out of mud, so the mud can see what We have done." And God created every living creature that now moveth, and one was man. Mud as man alone could speak. God leaned close as mud as man sat up, looked around, and spoke. Man blinked. "What is the purpose of all this?" he asked politely.*
>
> *"Everything must have a purpose?" asked God.*
>
> *"Certainly," said man.*
>
> *"Then I leave it to you to think of one for all this," said God. And He went away."*
>
> (*Cat's Cradle.* Kurt Vonnegut)

> *"Simple, clear purpose and principles give rise to complex intelligent behavior. Complex rules and regulations give rise to simple stupid behavior."* Dee Hock.

The first facet of organisational spirituality is the search for deep purpose.

Purpose is teleology. It defines the way the organisation fits into the world, the reason it exists. It is the compass that provides direction, the GPS that matches the disparate objectives of the three dimensions and aligns each member with a common cause.

In the old-time classic *"It's a Wonderful Life"* (Frank Capra, 1946), when George Bailey is about to commit suicide, his guardian angel, Clarence, shows him how his town, family, and friends would have turned out if he had never been born. A variation of this idea is an excellent exercise to determine an organisation's *raison d'être*. Ask yourself: What would happen if the company closes? If there is some personal or social reason that dissuades you from doing so, then that's the purpose of your company.

Every organisation needs a purpose of spiritual nature, what I call an integral purpose. It is a lofty calling that transcends and includes the objectives of all the 3D-Management dimensions. A higher purpose can't be only scientific, artistic, or ethical. It has to be as inclusive as possible. It could be building a better world, making dreams come true (for a tourism company, for example), or ending poverty in the world (Oxfam's purpose).

Profit maximisation is the purpose of business within the traditional paradigm. You have a healthcare company, and you want to discover its purpose? Easy, it's profit. Education? Profit. Consultancy? Profit. *"Companies of the world unite!"* claims the traditional paradigm, and they do so around money.

Making a profit is fine, but by no means is it a higher purpose. On its own, it is a one-dimensional objective, not lofty enough to be spiritual. The final organisational end must inspire and engage people aiming at a higher cause that solves problems of people and the world, not just be about financial goals.

As early as 1954, Peter Drucker, the most influential management thinker of the 20th Century, refused to accept profit maximisation as the purpose of business and argued that the concept is not only meaningless but also dangerous, antisocial, and immoral. However crucial it may be, for Drucker (1973: 59) *"profitability is not the purpose of, but a limiting factor on business enterprise and business activity. Profit is not the explanation, cause, or rationale of business behavior and business decisions, but rather the test of their validity*".

Profit is not so much a goal in itself as a means to a higher end. It is only the objective of the scientific dimension. If the economic value is the only concern of a business, the other dimensions will be disregarded or marginalised, and they have their own particular objectives, independent and by no means subordinated to that one. In particular, the ethical dimension aspires to make a better world, and the artistic dimension pursues the development of the organisation and its members.

Stating that maximising economic value is not the higher purpose of an organisation does not, by any means, minimise its importance. As Collins and Porras (1994: 8) argue: *"Profitability is a necessary condition for existence, but it is not the end in itself for many visionary companies. Profit is like oxygen, food, water, and blood for the body; they are not the point of life, but without them, there is no life."*

Brad Bird, Oscar-winning director of Pixar movies such as The Incredibles and The Iron Giant, resorts to a different metaphor to defend the same notion: *"Speaking personally, I want my films to make money, but money is just fuel for the rocket. What I really want to do is to go somewhere. I don't want to just collect more fuel."* Profitability lacks the power to mobilise people (especially when the pie is so unevenly distributed). As Unilever's CEO, Paul Polman, provocatively puts it: *"Why should the citizens of this world keep companies around whose sole purpose is the enrichment of a few people?"*

Sisodia et al. (2007:132) maintain that *"achieving business success is less a matter of obsessing over the financials than about focusing on how a business adds value to society by contributing to solving its problems and enabling its members to better achieve their potential and otherwise improve their quality of life"*

They conclude (Ibid. p.152): *"what it takes to be an enduring great company can't be as precisely measured as financial activities and results can. The stuff of corporate greatness can only be approximated. It is more a product of the unseen than of the seen. It can't be fathomed through accounting paradigms."*

Leading-edge companies are fuelled by purpose, not cash. Profit is not an end in itself, but a means for a higher purpose. *"Choose a mission that is bigger than the company"* and *"create a cause, not a business"* are the respective bits of advice of Amazon CEO Jeff Bezos and management guru Gary Hamel. Mackey and Sisodia (2013: 33) highlight the benefits of having a higher purpose:

> *"Business has a much broader positive impact on the world when it is based on a higher purpose that goes beyond only generating profits and creating shareholder value. Purpose is the reason a company exists. A compelling sense of higher purpose creates an extraordinary degree of engagement among all stakeholders and catalyzes creativity, innovation, and organizational commitment."*

Aware of that, Tom Morris (1997: 155) provides an excellent definition of business based on the Aristotelian dimensions of truth, goodness, beauty, and unity: *"The essence of business must never be viewed as the attempt to move money from other people's pockets into our own. It should be viewed as a performance art, the creation and care of structures within which people can join together in partnerships of living well."*

According to 3D Management, the organisational purpose must be spiritual, and therefore, it should transcend all three dimensions and integrate them into an essential unit. The litmus test for a spiritual purpose is that it must answer the following questions while going beyond them:

- Does it create economic value, or, in the case of non-profits, does it make efficient use of limited resources? (scientific purpose)
- Does it promote the development of the organisation or its agents?
- Does it contribute to the common good?

The purpose of the Spanish chain of hotels Artiem is *"Inspiring people to be happy,"* a spiritual purpose that exquisitely combines the ethical, scientific, and artistic dimensions. If so many philosophers from Aristotle to Wittgenstein, have identified eudaimonia (i.e., the attainment of happiness) as the human race's life purpose, why should that not be the purpose of a business? Creating happiness is a higher purpose. You do that through products or services that make customers happy, through profits that make shareholders happy, through work that makes associates happy, and through a contribution to society that makes all of us happy.

There are many examples of integral purposes. Following the trail of Southwest Airlines, the New York-based low-cost carrier JetBlue, began service in 2000 with the mission of *"bringing humanity back to skies"* to restore that missing human touch in the air travel experience. This purpose is then three-dimensionally deployed in their commitment to bettering the lives of their customers, crewmembers, and communities, by providing exceptional customer service, caring for their employees, recognising their responsibility to the world, and inspiring others to do the same.

There are many t-shirt manufacturers, but the purpose of the company Life is Good sets them apart from the rest. Their mission statement goes beyond the creation of fun garments, and it focuses on *"Spreading the power of optimism."* They do that primarily with the neat designs and positive slogans on their shirts, such as *"Today is a good day to have a good day"* or *"Forecast: mostly sunny."* It all started in 1994 when, after five years of less-than-stellar sales, brothers Bert and John Jacobs designed their first Life is Good t-shirt and discovered how those three simple words could help people focus on the good. That is not the only thing they do to achieve their purpose. They have implemented programs in support of their mission, such as the #GrowTheGood initiative, and the Life is Good Kid's Foundation that positively impacts over 1 million kids each year by providing childcare professionals with the resources they need to inspire optimism in our most vulnerable children.

Another good example is outdoor gear and apparel maker Timberland, a company that has based every aspect of its business upon a sustainable outdoor lifestyle. As a consequence, they work hard to be Earth keepers in everything they do. This involves making their products responsibly, protecting the outdoors, and serving the communities where they live and work. They put together all those concepts beautifully in their mission statement:

> *"Our mission is to equip people to make a difference in their world. We do this by creating outstanding products and by trying to make a difference in the communities where we live and work".*

Making a difference brings together science, arts, and ethics (I, we, and its) in a spiritual purpose that aims to support people to be change agents who bridge the gap between what Jeff Swartz (Timberland's CEO) calls "commerce" and "justice."

Also, I would like to talk about Emprogage, a recently established group of Swedish consultants who share the desire to make a better world. Its name stands for empathy, pro-activity, and engagement, the values that form the basis of their philosophy. As a result of those values, and the model developed by one of the founders, Stellan Nordahl, they help their clients become creators of opportunities rather than victims of circumstances.

Finally, SAP AG is the third-largest independent software supplier worldwide and the largest producer of standard enterprise-wide business applications for the client-server software market. The company's principal business activities are the development and marketing of an integrated line of computer software for over 1,000 predefined business processes, from financial accounting, supply chain management, and business workflow to human resources, sales and distribution, and customer relationship management. SAP came out of the 2008 financial crisis with good financial results, but at the expense of disappointing customers for the price increase of its products, and employees for the cost reductions and the restructuring programme that the company introduced. In 2010, a new management team decided to launch a holistic management model focused on achieving a better connection with all stakeholders. The slogan *"The Best-Run Companies Run SAP"* had been a successful one, but they decided to revisit it to make it more inspiring and relevant to all stakeholders. The new storyline they presented in a commercial starring

Clive Owen[113] is that we have big problems, and solving big problems is what business does best, so, the best-run businesses make the world run at its best, and you know what those companies run, don't you? Voila! SAP AG had a brand-new purpose: *"Help the world run better and improve people's lives."* When their customers have the next big idea to save a species, transform an industry, feed the hungry, or support equality, SAP delivers the right technology to help them run at their best and achieve their vision.

Integral purpose has to be deployed and operationalised in the objectives of the other dimensions, so the organisation brings more goodness, truth, and beauty into the world. As you surely remember, the aim of the scientific dimension is the maximisation of economic value; the artistic dimension aspires to the growth and development of the organisation, its products and services, and its members; and the ethical dimension's goal is the common good. However, all such concrete objectives can and should subordinate to a metaobjective, which is purpose.

Whole Foods' motto – *"Whole Foods, Whole People* and *Whole Planet*" is an excellent integral purpose, reminiscent of the triple bottom line. The concept of "the triple bottom line" was coined in 1994 by John Elkington, the founder of a British consultancy called SustainAbility. The triple bottom line (TBL) consists of three Ps: profit, people, and planet. The first bottom line is the traditional measure of the profit and loss account. The second is the bottom line of the "people account"—a measure of how socially responsible an organisation is internally. The third is the bottom line of the company's "planet" account—a measure of how environmentally responsible it has been. In sum, the TBL aims to measure the financial, social, and environmental performance in an integrated business report over a period of time. The ultimate aim of the TBL movement is to make the three components equally important for the business.

According to the 3D-Management philosophy, and with the inclusion of spirit, an organisation extends the triple bottom line of profit, people, and planet, to a quadruple bottom line of 4 Ps: profit (science), people (art), planet (ethics), and purpose (spirit)[114], purpose being the one that

---

[113] Available at www.sap.com/corporate/en/purpose.html

[114] It is worth mentioning that one of the heavyweights of Integral Theory, Sean Esbjorn-Hargens, has designed the MetaImpact Framework based on AQAL and integral theory, and dedicated to the design of wisdom economies through the integration of multiple types of impact, multiple forms of capital, multiple types of

integrates the other three in an essential unit. Thus, purpose is the ultimate objective, which is then deployed in the objectives of the three other dimensions, subsequently expressed through subdimensions, and finally delivered in concrete KPIs for performance management to develop holistic metrics that can make up an integral scorecard, such as the ones depicted in table 11.

DIMENSION	SUBDIMENSION	OBJECTIVE	KPI
SCIENCE	Productivity Quality Financial performance	Maximisation of economic value	Profitability ROI ROE Sales Inventory Turnover Budget compliance Market share Productivity Customer satisfaction Customer complaints Customer loyalty Number of defects
ARTS	Organisational growth Organisational Learning Integral human psychographic development Innovation and product development Beauty/aesthetics/ design	Development	Market growth Innovation/NPD Time to market Ideas generated R&D Expenditure Motivation Turnover rate Associates' satisfaction Training indicators Skills development Vertical development

perspectives, and the four bottom lines. You can find all about this model at https://www.metaintegral.com

ETHICS	Integrity Justice Transparency Respect Legality Social responsibility Community involvement	Common Good	Reputation Contributions to the community Women and minorities integration Reduction of emissions/ consumption Environmental protection measures Transparency Charitable giving
SPIRIT	Communion Purpose	Happiness	Stakeholders' Happiness Stakeholder engagement Alignment Meaning

Table 11: Dimensions and objectives of 3D Management.

A pioneer in the introduction of the TBL concept is Costa-Rica based Florida Ice & Farm Co. (FIFCO). Initially focused on just maximizing profit, they started a transformation process to become a source of value to all of its stakeholders using the UN Global Reporting Initiative (GRI) standard as a framework. In 2016, FIFCO was the first company in the world to present an integrated GRI report. A bit earlier than that, in 2014, FIFCO started a company-wide process to define its purpose: *"We share with the world a better way of living,"* consistent with its TBL philosophy[115]. Every decision made at FIFCO has to fulfil the criteria of making the world a better place, and they have specific goals in each of the TBL areas:

- Planet: Go beyond neutrality and achieve a positive balance in water, emissions, and waste.
- People (internal): Be champions with their employees.
- People (external): Be champions in the community and promote the conscious consumption of alcoholic beverages.
- Profit: Double the company's sales and profits.

[115] Hansmeyer, Mendiola, and Snabe (2018) have written an excellent case study about them.

For 2020, they have deployed that in 7 ambitious commitments[116]:

1. Eradicate poverty within FIFCO: The programme "FIFCO Oportunidades" aims to eradicate poverty internally in three years. So far, this has been implemented only in Costa Rica, but they intend to extend it to Guatemala and the United States.
2. Be recognised as one of the best companies to work for in the world: In 2017, FIFCO hit the first position in the Great Places to Work ranking among large companies in Central America and the Caribbean. For 2020, the objective is to reach a score of 90 points.
3. Promote the smart consumption of all its food and beverages in the world.
4. Complete one million hours of volunteering work: At the end of 2017, FIFCO reported 468,292 hours of volunteering.
5. Become water, carbon, and solid waste positive.
6. Achieve 100 per cent recycling of its bottles and packaging: At the end of 2017, FIFCO reported a 65% recovery of post-consumer packaging, that is, for every 100 containers placed on the market, 65 were recovered for proper recycling.
7. Lead through brands that make the world a better place, an initiative they call "FIFCO Air Brands." They want their brands to be "as light as air" so that their life cycle does not imply negative environmental or social footprints, but rather that they generate positive value for the world.

KPIs are wonderful to let you know how well you do things, but one can't measure success according to KPI compliance, as many Orange organisations do. As Simon Sinek conveniently states, you have to start with why, not with what or how. Success is based on how well you fulfil your why, your purpose. If we forget about purpose, we will follow the wrong path no matter how many performance measures we use. As usual, Nietzsche found the perfect words to articulate the same concept: *"He who has a why to live for can bear almost any how."* FAVI's former CEO, Jean François Zobrist, differentiates between what he calls a "why" company and a "how" company:

> *"How" companies spend their time telling workers how to do their jobs—where to place the machinery, when to come to work and when to leave,*

[116] http://www.fifcosostenible.com/compromisos-2020

and so on. This has two consequences. The first is that you end up judging employees by everything except what counts, which is whether the job gets done and the customer is happy. The second is that it becomes difficult, if not impossible, to change any of the myriad rules about how to get things done. You want to move that cart to a different spot on the shop floor? You need clearance from your manager, who may have to ask his manager, and so on, creating a never-ending "chain of comment[117]".

In a "how" company, it is complicated to get the work done without disobeying somebody in the chain of command. A "why" company is different. It replaces all the "hows" with a single question: Why are you doing what you are doing? The answer for FAVI is to keep the customers happy. As long as what you do satisfies that commandment, it doesn't matter how you do it.

The purpose of a business needs to be intimately related to the customer. All stakeholders are equally important, but the customer is the stakeholder that defines what we do. It is all about the customer, not about the things we do, as Denning (2010: 65) describes in this beautiful way:

"The meaning of work isn't in the bread that we're baking: it is in the enjoyment the customers get from eating the bread.

The meaning of work isn't in the words the actor is reciting; it is in the response of the audience to those words.

The meaning of work isn't in the toy that we're putting together; it is in the smile on the face of the child.

The meaning of work isn't in the bricks and mortar of the house we're building; it is in the happiness we generate in a family with a house that precisely meets their needs.

The meaning of work isn't in the words or the musical notes of the song that we're writing; it is in the feeling of yearning we generate in the heart of the listener.

The meaning of work isn't in the paper and print of the insurance policy we've issued; it is in the security that we're providing to the spouse and the children.

---

117 Zobrist introduces here a play of words between "command" and the French word "comment",which means "how."

The meaning of the boutique hotel that we're running isn't in the rooms and the physical facilities; it is in the feeling of being at home away from home that we generate in people who stay there.

The meaning of the software we're coding doesn't lie in bits and bytes; it is in the cool things that users can do with the software.

The meaning that we see in work resides in the responses of the people for whom we are doing the work.

Patagonia grew out of a small company that made tools for climbers. Its purpose reflects the values of its founders, who were climbers and surfers in love with nature and the minimalist style they promote. They are committed to building the best products while doing the least harm to the environment and use business to inspire and implement solutions to the environmental crisis. Patagonia reduces ecological impacts by making goods that are organic, recycled, durable, and with no toxic dyes. However, they are perfectly aware that our consumerist society, enslaved by the cycle of buying-throwing-away-buying, is not good for the planet. To lighten our environmental footprint, everyone needs to consume less. Patagonia took its responsibility to the next level with its famous 2011 thoughtful-consumption campaign, *"Don't buy this jacket."* It is not that they don't want you to buy a North Face jacket; they don't want you to buy any jacket, even if it is one from Patagonia. Instead, what they propose is that you repair your old clothes. The campaign was part of its "Common Threads Initiative", which tries to reduce (making clothes that last longer and not pushing consumers into buying more), repair (fixing Patagonia gear for its customers), reuse (the company resells your used clothes on eBay or in their stores' Worn Wear sections), and recycle (you can return your worn-out garments, and they will recycle them). What, at first glance, might look bad for sales, is just the opposite because they stay true to their purpose and they get a level of customer loyalty that allows them to charge an average premium of about 20% over competitors' prices. In fact, Patagonia's sales revenues tripled between 2008 and 2015, rising to USD 750 million. Their current marketing strategy continues very much along the same lines. In the 2016 campaign, Patagonia declared that it would donate its total sales revenue obtained on Black Friday to environmental groups. Instead of the forecasted two million dollars, the company made ten million.

For the co-founder of HolacracyOne, Tom Thomison, purpose is much more than a simple redux or repackaging of the old mission. Traditional missions were sacred and untouchable statements carved in stone that came from the top. Such static documents soon become irrelevant to the people that actually do the work, (if they ever even had relevance.). By contrast, purpose is evolutionary, as one of Laloux's Teal tenets states. It is much like our own. My personal purpose has shifted over time, and I am sure yours will have too.

So has OuiShare's changed. In the image of one of its core values, "permanent beta," OuiShare's purpose has been modified several times since it was created. It all started in 2011 in Paris when a small group of like-minded individuals, seduced by the possibilities of the sharing economy, started meeting every month for potluck dinners. It soon evolved into a Facebook group to share ideas and knowledge about the collaborative economy. Less than two years into its existence, OuiShare was mobilizing dozens of self-organised groups that enabled them to run almost 200 events in 75 cities. This collective energy gathered around one core idea: they wanted to better understand the change underway and accelerate the transition to a more meaningful society by empowering the pioneers of the collaborative economy from across the globe. Their initial purpose was to build and nurture a collaborative society by connecting people, organisations, and ideas around fairness, openness, and trust. But soon enough, the collaborative economy label became too restrictive, and they set out to focus on the impact of technology in the way we work and live to change society. And again, this purpose evolved into how to bring about collective change, especially in the world of work. At the moment, OuiShare is officially defined as a distributed network of local communities that connects people and accelerates projects for systemic change based on collaboration, openness, and social justice.

Companies with a distinguished purpose outperform not-for-purpose companies in the long run. Research from the EY Beacon Institute and Harvard Business School shows that 85% of purposeful companies showed positive growth. In comparison, 42% of non-purpose led companies showed a drop in revenue (Purpose at Work 2016 Global Report). A year and a half after it introduced its new purpose, FIFCO conducted a study based on the "Strong Sense of Purpose Key Driver of Business Investment" study published by Deloitte (Hansmeyer, Mendiola, and Snabe, 2018). The findings revealed that 94% of the employees believed that FIFCO was really committed to attaining its purpose and saw an immediate correlation between purpose and the TBL approach. It also stated that managers were more attuned to the company's TBL goals and paid more attention to nurturing talent and innovating with purpose. Eighty-nine per cent of the employees were optimistic regarding the company's future, and 80 per cent enjoyed work more, had a better sense of balancing life and work, and had found more growth opportunities at work. Ninety per cent agreed that engagement had grown with the new purpose and stated that it was the main reason they were happy at the company and desired to stay there. Employee satisfaction increased at the highest rate ever. They said the company's purpose "helped them transcend," "set an example for their families," and "give back to the community."

Mackay and Sisodia (2013: 55) find a clear correlation between corporate purpose, business performance, and personal satisfaction. When there is a strong purpose, clearly and consistently communicated, the organisation naturally attracts people who align with it, and they are most fulfilled and happiest when their work is aligned with their own inner passions and values[118]. In this case, it is critical to hire individuals who align strongly with the purpose of the organisation. Hence, Patagonia tries to hire people who are passionate about mountain climbing and the environment.

Having said that, a brilliant purpose does not automatically create meaningful work. Schools and hospitals have noble objectives, and yet they have many unhappy, disengaged, and burned-out employees. Meaningful work for employees does not only depend on whether individuals can contribute to transcendent goals, it also depends on being able to bring all of themselves to work, being able to grow and flourish, being encouraged to act autonomously and responsively, being creative, being part of a community, etc. It needs to be aligned with what makes their hearts beat and what makes work worthwhile to them. All those elements are deeply instilled in people and can't be prescribed in a mission statement, as Lips-Wierma and Morris found in their research on meaningful work (2011:133):

> *"People don't want someone else's meaning. Our research shows that they have and want their own. They don't want to be motivated. They want to be given conditions that allow them to remain connected to or enable them to reconnect with what they consider makes their work meaningful."*

There is an important relationship between motivation and meaning. Without meaning, intrinsic or transcendental motivation is impossible,

---

[118] The opposite is also true: differing values generate repulsion.

only external motivation is possible, and at the end of the day, what this kind of drive aims for is to get people to do things they don't want to do.

Lips-Wierma and Morris identified four elements that make work meaningful (ibid. 2011: 17):

- Developing the inner self: An inward and reflected pathway that includes three main sub-themes: moral development, personal growth, and being true to self.
- Expressing full potential. An outward and active pathway with three sub-themes: creating, achieving, and influencing.
- Unity with others: Three sub-themes were found within this pathway: working together, shared values, and belonging.
- Serving others: It includes two sub-themes: making a difference and meeting the needs of humanity and the planet.

They also discovered that meaningfulness didn't only come from a combination of those four pathways but also from the right balance of them over time. This balance should be integral since each pathway belongs to a different quadrant. If we analyse the four aspects with AQAL, we realise that each one fits in one quadrant of the matrix, as table 14 portrays. That means that a balanced approach to meaning at work should be all-quadrant, all-level. In other words, it should encompass the dimensions of science, arts, and ethics.

	INTERIOR	EXTERIOR
INDIVIDUAL	Developing the Inner self	Expressing full potential
COLLECTIVE	Unity with others	Service to others

Table 14: Quadrants of development and pathways to meaningful work.

7.3. The For-Purpose Enterprise

One of the fundamental tenets of Holacracy is that purpose is the ultimate authority figure, the only boss an organisation should have. It is the Greater Other that everyone should serve. In Holacracy's governance meetings, the boss is purpose, and everyone is sensing around and into how we can best structure and align our work in its service.

If purpose is the only boss, what happens to the CEO? Can we talk about self-management if we still have a sovereign on top with the highest paycheck and the ultimate decision-making power? Most SMOs still have a CEO, and that is a contradiction in terms. Granted, that person is not the omnipotent ruler that calls all the shots. Actually, three prominent CEOs of Teal organisations such as FAVI's Jean-François Zobrist, Patagonia's Yvon Chouinard, and Semco's Ricardo Semler try to get out of the way as much as possible. They have declared that the goal of a CEO is *"to do as little as possible,"* or as Chouinard puts it *"managing by absence (MBA)."* That is very liberating for everyone, especially the CEO, who can do other things with his life. For example, Olivier Gesbert told me that he devotes one hour a month to Pressto Peru. The rest of the time, he does consultancy and other dissemination activities to spread the Gospel of liberated companies. As for Ricardo Semler, you can find him playing electric guitar or launching projects like Lumiar, an alternative school system based on democratic principles where children follow their interests and curiosity, overseeing Hotel Botanique, a luxury hotel, of course, managed democratically, and Mellos, his village of the future. In the same way, Bob Davids, who in 2006, after selling his successful video game business, Radica Games, to Mattel, founded the prestigious California winery Sea Smoke (featured in the Academy Award-winning movie "Sideways"), has refused, since the very beginning, to give solutions to his employees:

> *"I'm gone for eight months...If you feel that it is critical to contact me, that I get involved in your problem, what I want you to do is to lie down. When that feeling goes away, I want you to get up, solve the problem, and then send me an e-mail with the solution." (Carney & Getz, 2016)*

Even so, the CEO is critical when transitioning to Teal. All Teal organisations I know started with an individual who eventually became the CEO, shared a vision and made every single person own it. Jos de Block, Tony Hsieh, Koldo Saratxaga, Jean François Zobrist, Olivier Gesbert, all of them enlightened individuals at the Teal level of development whose driving force stemmed from an inner imperative to act by their values.

According to Laloux (2014: 240), "*The general rule seems to be that the level of consciousness of an organization can't exceed the level of consciousness of its leader*." His reasoning is as follows :

> *"What determines which stage an organization operates from? It is the stage through which its leadership tends to look at the world. Consciously or unconsciously, leaders put in place organizational structures,*

practices, and cultures that make sense to them that correspond to their way of dealing with the world." (Ibid., 41)

Therefore, for an organisation to go Teal, at least one leader (usually the founder or CEO) needs to be able to operate from that altitude. Laloux's assumptions have been recently confirmed by Reynolds (2019). In a qualitative study, he compared the STAGES assessment (O'Fallon, 2011) of 3 Founders/CEOs from Laloux's book (2014) with a STAGES assessment of their respective organisations. The companies showed similar distributions of scores to the 3 participants, implying a direct relationship between the Founder's/CEO's level of development and those of the organisation. In particular, the findings placed 2 participants and their associated organisations at 4.0 (equivalent to Green, in spiral dynamics) on the STAGES model and one at 5.5 (Turquoise), with the other organisation at 4.5 (Teal).

Once the organisation has made a move to Teal, the functions of the CEO turn out to be very different from the traditional ones (to the extent that CEO becomes a misleading term). According to Laloux (2014: 240), only one role remains the same: the CEO is the visible face and representative of the company to the outside world. He also identified two new and critical roles: creating and maintaining a space for Teal ways of operating, and role-modelling of Teal behaviours.

Ganescu (2107:30) compares the function of a CEO with that of a gardener: You can't make a flower grow by pulling on it. Olivier Gesbert resorts to the same analogy to describe his role at Pressto. The only thing a gardener can do is to create the necessary conditions for the plants to thrive. Accordingly, it is his job to create the best conditions for people to grow and perform or, as Ganescu puts it, hold space for people to do their work. They create an environment of trust, transparency, development, care, and support so that employees are working because they want to, not because they are forced to.

Tom Kelley, founder, and chairman of IDEO, and Terri Kelly, CEO at W.L. Gore, agree that their role is to be the stewards of the culture, to maintain it, and to make it evolve healthily. Bob Davids elaborates: *"My job now is the keeper of the culture. That's my job. I do it by talking to everybody every day, reaching everybody every day: "Hello, how are you, how's it going, what do you need?"*

However, that's not good enough for Tom Thomison. If we want to build a genuinely democratic organisation, no one should have unilateral authority over others. You have to put everyone on an equal footing and move beyond bosses, CEOs, and employees. You can't have sacred cows and privileged classes if you want to be true to your principles. And that certainly includes the boss of all bosses. He compares the change to self-management to a shift from alternating current to direct current. It is either-or. You can't have them both ways. The institution of a new power system requires an act of surrender as the very first move. The power holder (i.e., the CEO, the board, the founder…) needs to surrender his or her power to the new system. Every single Holacracy deployment process starts with a power holder saying yes to the power shift in a signed document. Thus, the power holder surrenders to the system and holds himself accountable to the same rules that apply to everyone else.

In 2016, Tom, teaming up with Christiane Seuhs-Schoeller and Peter Kessels, set out on a mission to push the boundaries of self-organisation and distributed authority even further. They founded Encode.org to bring to the world the beautiful model of the *For-Purpose Enterprise.* According to their proposal, purpose is the one and true boss, and independent *purpose agents* organically flock around the projects that attract them, supported by the necessary structures, rules, and agreements to make it possible. The shift to purpose allows all contributors to serve something greater than themselves. It is a genuinely spiritual and transcendental act of servant leadership because individuals fulfil their role to the best of their ability, as it is defined, and because they are part of an organisational holarchy connected to a broader purpose that they care about. In doing so, they surrender part of their autonomy and agency, and they tap themselves in as role fillers to serve the purpose.

The For-Purpose Enterprise model put forward by Encode.org is a massive contribution to making the power shift that is so incredibly needed to liberate purposeful work. It manages to create companies with self-organisation encoded in the DNA and no single trace of personal ownership or power. The model works without a board of directors, CEOs, C-Suite executives, bosses, managers, silent partners, or outside investors. It takes the self-organizing principles that we find in Holacracy and embeds them in legal structures so that all individuals who want to contribute to a purpose can do so as legal partners, not as employees.

Everyone is a purpose agent, a freely associated member/partner that cares about the purpose of the organisation and shows up to participate in its running instruction and to sense and respond to whatever's needed. As such, they become "investors in the purpose" and receive a slice of capital.

Unlike traditional equity-distribution models, this slice is not fixed, and is continuously re-evaluated as Mike Moyers' ground-breaking model of dynamic equity establishes (2012). Whether you invest money, time, talent, or energy, you are an investor in purpose all the same. The shift from employee to investor creates an entirely new game that renders impossible the existence of hierarchies of dominion. Getting rid of hierarchies of power and making everyone an investor, as they propose, is the most coherent answer for any organisation wanting to be called Teal.

The model is extremely flexible. Someone might want to commit only money; somebody else just work. It is up to you how much you invest, as long as that is clear for everyone else. When you invest your money, everybody knows how much you contribute, when you give your time and work, you also have to make a firm commitment to fulfil the responsibilities of the roles you assume. That can change over time, but you will have to be unequivocal about it upfront, so everyone else knows what to expect from you. You can commit yourself to work full-time, or you can only work part-time, and devote the rest of your time to your family or to anything else that you fall in love with. Tom jokingly says the model is compatible with a whole range of relationship arrangements, from monogamy to polyamory. Also, you can engage with a company for a long time or only for a temporary project. The model is also compatible with the ecosystemic nature an open organisation needs. In a world where technology makes it increasingly easier and cheaper to contract for the performance of specific tasks, a model such as this is especially timely. We can find Orange expressions of that trend in sites such as Upwork, CrowdFlower, Clickworker, or Toluna, and crowd-sourcing marketplaces such as Amazon Mechanical Turk[119]. Customers and other stakeholders can easily turn into investors in purpose if they desire to do so and have something to contribute. An individual can thus perform different roles for the organisation and be, for example, a customer and an investor, at the same time.

Another significant contribution of the For-Purpose Enterprise is to fill some of the gaps that the new paradigm of work still has. Holacracy, for example, is a brilliant model, but there are things that it does not address by design. In particular, by focusing on the organisational system, it

---

[119] Obviously, what I am suggesting here is a Teal version of this idea, not the shameful sub-minimum-wage, unregulated, digital sweatshops most of these platforms are currently promoting.

intentionally leaves behind two sub-systems; the financial and capital system, and the people system. Encode.org felt that tension as an indicator of an evolutionary purpose that needed to be created, so they designed an end to end system to fill all of the legal, financial, and social gaps that Holacracy, or other explicit rulesets of self-organisation, such as Sociocracy, are not covering. It provides financial models that facilitate the operational execution of dynamically and equitably accounting for shared risks and rewards; legal agreements that encode distributed-authority management and dynamic-equity profit sharing at the legal corporate level; and social and cultural models of cohesion to integrate individual differences in the new world of inter-personal and operational complexity. Encode's model radically upgrades the organisational, legal, and people structures by conceiving an enterprise as an entity made up of 3 different containers (see figure 14). Failure to distinguish and conveniently address the following three aspects can result in important legal, financial, and social gaps, and in misalignments with other foundational areas of the organisation:

- Organisation: The organisational space in the lower-right quadrant where the work gets done. That's the space of Holacracy's systems and processes to get work done and help the enterprise find its own unique identity and structure to make it independent from human agendas, egos, politics, etc. It encodes tactical operations and governance processes, as well as all the different structures within the organisation in order to get the job done. As for today, the ruleset for this container is the holacracy constitution.

- Association: Holacracy is fundamentally focused on the organisation and its purpose. It was never designed to take care of the people. Not in vain, it was designed to separate people from the roles they energise and focus on the latter. A corresponding home for the interior space is needed in order to not marginalise the left-hand quadrants as the traditional management model does. We need a rule set on how to encode culture, that defines what the behavioural social norms at play are between all contributors. Encode.org does that through the creation of the association space. The association space is the people container, a separate but connected depository for them to come together and interact with one another through a set of behavioural norms, cultural norms, and a tension processing system. Wittrock (2017) explains it as follows:

"It encompasses all the human aspects, our belonging needs, our culture, our values, our ethics, etc. Here we can show up as we are, outside of roles, taking care of ourselves and each other in various ways, giving and receiving personal feedback, mentoring each other, forming special interest guilds and -most importantly- friendships. Here we can relate to each other as free and equal Purpose Agents that flock together to express a shared purpose that overlaps with our individual purpose. Finally, there is a defined space for processing of personal and interpersonal tensions that fall through the cracks of the Holacracy processes."

Wittrock (ibid.) does not want us to consider organisation and association as separate boxes, but as interpenetrating realities that can be present simultaneously, yet are distinct in nature:

"We don't want to fuse them (pre-Holacracy), we don't want to leave the human side to its own devices without stewardship (Holacracy), rather we want to hold and inhabit both dimensions consciously as differentiated, yet integrated wholes. The For-Purpose Enterprise gives us the language and the tools to do so."

- Company: The focus of this container is the property, the assets, and the legal issues, including the operating agreement and bylaws. Its mission is to address all the problems an enterprise might encounter at this level (e.g., How do you make sure that purpose remains the boss? How do you prevent individual power from having excessive influence over the business?). It is a container nobody had taken care of before, and a crucial one for Encode.org, as in their model everybody is an investor and a legal partner. They have encoded rules that tie everything together so that the legal operating agreements include purpose. Thus, those documents are alive, lived, relevant, and encoded with the philosophy of the organisation. They have considered every possible scenario, including the creation of a new enterprise. Entrepreneurs can come together and take the first step of surrender from the personal imagining of what is possible in the world, to surrendering that into an organisation that is separate from themselves. That first act of resignation has been encapsulated in a document to launch a for-purpose enterprise not as founders but as founding members of something bigger. The operating agreement encodes all the rules they agree to play by in a legal way, including new capital structures, dynamic equity, etc.

These three containers conveniently address the different dimensions of an enterprise. The organisation and the company focus on the external realities (the governance and the legal issues), while the association pays particular attention to the people and cultural issues. Everybody is a member of the organisation, an investor in the company, and an associate in the association, and there is a clear set of rules for each of those areas.

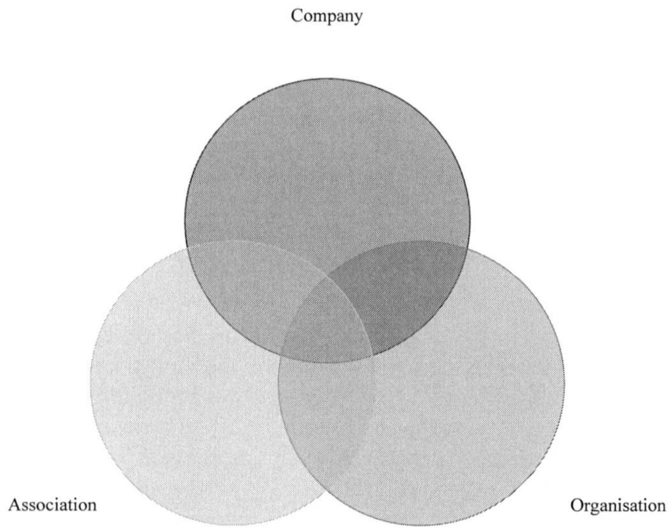

Figure 14: The Three containers of a For-Purpose Enterprise (image courtesy of Energized.org)

As a metatheory, 3D Management can potentially shelter under its umbrella many different options, be it self-management systems like Holacracy or Sociocracy, or even hierarchical ones. Even so, some go better with its philosophy than others, and the For-Purpose Enterprise model which, in my opinion, represents the vanguard of organisational thinking, is a particularly good fit for 3D Management.

7.4. Communion[120]

"Where two or three are gathered in my name I am amongst them." (Matthew 18:20)

The spiritual experience is one of both inner and outer connections. Social and environmental connectedness is a fundamental facet when we talk about organisational spirituality. From this perspective, *"spirituality is about the connections between the whole person and the whole community"* (Edwards, 2004). It refers to the connectedness that exists between individuals, groups, organisations, and communities in terms of their mutual responsibilities, ethical behaviours, and care. It aims to relate all the constituent holons of the organisation, internally and externally, with all its different stakeholders and its environment.

Edwards (ibid.) acknowledges that many individuals make their most significant contribution to society through work, so the workplace has become our primary source of community:

> *"As social capital and community involvement diminish across much of the western world, the importance of the workplace as a source for personal meaning and community values is growing. It is often through their work that people today find ultimate purpose or at least the focus of their goals and values in life."*

In an interesting Ted Talk[121], Margaret Heffernan reviews research that shows that what makes some groups more successful than others is the social connection. She contends that it is crucial for organisational success to give time for people to get to know each other, even if that implies to stop working for a while. A simple initiative she recommends is banning coffee cups at desks, so people hang out around the coffee machine and talk to each other. With the same idea in mind, Idexx Laboratories has created vegetable gardens on its premises, so that people from different parts of the business work together and get to know each other.

---

[120] I am aware that communion also fits in the lower-left quadrant, the one expressed in "we" language. However, that quadrant is expressed in the 3D-Management model with the dimension of ethics. Thus, I have preferred to elevate that "we space" to the spiritual dimension. In this manner, it gets a higher meaning while still being in accordance to the literature on spirituality at work.

[121] https://www.ted.com/talks/margaret_heffernan_why_it_s_time_to_forget_the_pecking_order_at_work

In organisational theory, the distinction between a group and a team is common. A group is a bunch of people who share physical space but remain as a sum of individualities. A team achieves coordination between people so that they can work together efficiently. The group moves in the physical order. The team also does but includes the intellectual, emotional, and moral. Beyond groups and teams, there are communities. A community is a group of people with shared interests and values. In a community, people feel part of something bigger. Their interests, objectives, and principles are in perfect harmony with one another. The best motto for a spiritual community is *"all for one and one for all."* Members feel that way because the community fosters strong and healthy relationships among them. That is the case of the cloud computing giant Salesforce (2018 winner of the Fortune 100 Best Companies to work for), which has entire floors celebrating the company "Ohana" (Hawaiian for family), or AES where all teams call themselves families.

The level of collective consciousness plays a significant role in that evolution. As Gunnlaugson and Brabant (2016: 21) contend, the We line of development follows a more similar pattern of growth than the rest of the lines. Under a Red altitude, the individual remains disconnected from the group field, caught in his or her web of narcissism. It is all about me, and there is no understanding of we. Amber altitude is characterised by social conformity. The I is backgrounded and deprioritised in favour of the group. Orange is based on social agency, so the individual can stay connected and in resonance with the group field while simultaneously offering his or her unique perspective. Green consciousness is more aware of context showing a more profound sensitivity to issues such as race, gender, sexual orientation, and religious affiliation. The Teal stage is holistic, so the individual develops heightened metacognition that can sense into the collective experience as a whole. This level can see, sense, and feel the intersubjective field almost as if it is a single entity and in such a way that is not so caught up in the self or others.

3D-Management organisations nurture strong forms of community, so the individual does not feel alienated or disconnected from the objectives of the organisation. They strive for the spiritual unity of all members of the organisation who feel engaged in the organisation in mind, body, and soul. Having that in mind, they spend more time in the education of employees and the building of strong cultures.

The challenge is finding the balance between agency and communion, two of the four main drives of a holon[122]. Agency is the drive to be a whole and not a part. It is a horizontal drive for functional autonomy and wholeness. People have a strong need to protect their independence, and whenever they feel that they are not free to choose, they are likely to resist. Agency's pathological expression is alienation, isolation, separation, repression, inability to commit, and even inability to communicate. Its complementary opposite is communion. It is the relationship drive of every holon to join or be part of a larger whole, with an emphasis on care, relational concerns, responsibility, and loving-kindness. Its pathological expression is fusion, herd mentality, and hypercommunion. If we create the conditions for people to be able to express all of who they are in service to something larger, we will have overcome the challenge.

An easy way to discover the degree of community in any organisation is to listen for the "we's" and the "they's" used. The larger the sense of community, the larger the sense of we. The "they syndrome" is a pathology whose symptoms are the constant complaints of its members against abstract theys: "it is their fault," "they don't care," "they never do that," "they wouldn't let us do that." "They" is somebody out there that is responsible for their problems. As a preventive measure, years ago the company AES organised a major "anti-they" campaign to get people to say we rather than they.

At the beginning of CineCiutat's operational meetings, there is a slot of time for positive recognition. After checking in, anyone can express appreciation and gratitude to other members of the organisation for something they did recently together, some favour, or even just qualities of somebody they like. To make it less formal and more context-specific, we use the formula: *"and the Oscar goes to…"* I found the idea from Kegan and Lahey's Seven Languages for Transformation. The rationale is that a meeting is an occasion, not only to deal with the pressing issues of the business, but also to experience being part of a whole, and building community by directing the collective attention to a person we care about and want to acknowledge. Many companies have similar systems to enable people to give each other tokens of appreciation for doing a good job. Whole Foods finishes all meetings with time for voluntary acknowledgements, Appelo (2016: 31) calls them kudos; Zappos has Hero

[122] The other two are Eros and Agape, which I will introduce later on.

awards; Ikea gives *tacks* (Swedish for thanks), and they are written on boards in the hall.

Celebrations are other strong community glue. Some companies have installed celebration bells in their offices. At Sun Microsystems Argentina, every time a team meets a target or goal, a bell rings and everyone stops to celebrate. Makers Academy, a coding bootcamp that aims to turn people into software developers, has gone one step further and introduced a giant gong that rings whenever one of its students gets a job. They pay much attention to create a strong sense of community, both internally and externally. Their motto: "*Once a maker, always a maker*."

Storytelling is a powerful tool with immense engaging power. Is there anything more compelling than a great story? Most of us can hardly wait to gather around the fire and listen to it. It is what we have done since the beginning of time. Sharing stories, especially personal experiences, brings people closer together. It helps to build relationships, turning the individual "I" that tells the story into "we." Telling our stories as a community makes us part of something bigger, part of something that matters to us. If you are not convinced yet, there is nobody better than Tyrion Lannister to make the point: *"What unites people? Armies? Gold? Flags? (denies with the head). Stories. There is nothing in the world more powerful than a good story" (A Game of Thrones,* S8E6). Some companies emphasise finding and sharing stories. Smucker's is a US-based manufacturer of fruit spreads, ice cream toppings, beverages, shortening, peanut butter, oils, and other products, founded in 1897. They encourage employees to share "tribal stories" about the company to pass along the lessons learned. That is precisely the idea behind Loomio's 6-monthly retreat. Richard Bartlett (2016), one of the co-developers and co-founders of Loomio, explains what it is: *"We go away for three days, crack open our chests and weave our heart stories together. This creates the affective bonds and trust that makes our bossless organisation extremely productive, aligned, and mutually accountable."*

Finding a common language is essential. In CineCiutat, we pay special attention to that. Drawing from our film industry roots, we have developed our own jargon to foster a sense of community and help to get organisational concepts across more clearly. We give *Oscars* when we express appreciation or recognition for someone, we have *auditions*, to provide the opportunity for any member to come and talk to the board, there are *castings* to hire new members, etc.

The hiring process is also crucial because each new member either strengthens or disrupts the community spirit. It is essential to prioritise in the recruitment process the degree of fit of the candidate with the organisational culture. In the case of the software development firm Menlo Innovations, cultural fit is paramount, as his CEO Richard Sheridan makes clear:

> *"Unless our people fit the culture, we won't have a chance of maintaining our culture over time. When we need new staff, we bring people in and get them to 'speed date' with our own staff. The question is always: would you like to work with this person? If the answer is yes, then we bring them in to work with us for a day, then a week, and then a month. If the answer is still 'Yes, I would like to work with this person' then they are hired"* (Denning 2018:40)

Leading-edge organisations devote a considerable amount of time to inform candidates about values and practices and to make sure that they fit the culture. At Artiem hotels, the last stage of the hiring process is an interview with the CEO, José Guillermo Díaz Montañés, focused on the culture of the company. Extensive training, selection by colleagues, and trial periods are other familiar feats of the onboarding process of those organisations. Whole Foods' new candidates undergo a 60-day process that involves a variety of interviews, including phone interviews, interviews with store leaders, and panel interviews with teams built from recruiters, managers, and select employees. Once selected, associates are assigned to a team for a trial period of four weeks. Once the period is over, the team votes and the recruit can only stay if he receives at least two-thirds positive votes. New associates who don't get voted in must either find a new team — repeating the trial period — or leave the company. This team selection process happens for every new member. FAVI's process involves two months of training. In the end, newbies write an open letter to the group they have joined, as a way to express gratitude and joy for being accepted in the community.

State-of-the-art group practices have to do with the concept of "we-space." Interesting we-space applications are presencing, circling, systemic constellations, and Theory U. These methodologies intend to develop an ongoing presence, connection, and surrender to what is revealed in the relationship. They operate across all the different states of consciousness ranging from concrete[123] (the realm of the senses), subtle (mind), causal (awareness or witness state), and non-dual (selfless). There are also really exciting technological developments that can be very useful for community building. For example, Mickey Siegel has designed a system called HeartSync, which links a maximum of 24 people via EEG headsets to a computer hub. Using audio cues over speakers, it lets the group sync its collective heartbeat and breathing. Just before a meeting, you can hook everyone up to a headband and a heart-rate sensor to get people out of their ego states and into a group state of coherence, thinking as one.

The enterprise community should embrace all stakeholders. I'm not referring to social media here (or at least, not exclusively). Social media is the Orange way to create community dynamics, and it is bluntly superficial. It turns real human relationships into likes, followers, and retweets, thus reducing people to measurable metrics organisations can control. Real community dynamics run much deeper than that. Community is a deeply embedded value that has a central position in CineCiutat's mission statement: *"CineCiutat is more than a cinema. It is a space to dream and share."* This space is for all stakeholders to share, that's why the cinema selects its partners carefully not only in financial terms but in terms of whether the association with this particular partner would be consistent with the shared values of the company.

7.5. Case in point: Community building at OuiShare[124]

What happens when your community is a distributed network of more than 1,500 people living in more than 20 countries? OuiShare has grown to be one of the more interesting open communities and social laboratories I have come across.

OuiShare is, first and foremost, an association whose activities are for the general interest - intellectual production and awareness-raising events

[123] Murray (2017: 201-202) points out that much of the experience of we-spaced practice is about embodiment and is pre-language. Often the non-ordinary or peak experiences achieved through we-space draws on a lower animal nature as opposed to a higher or spiritual quality. They manage to disengage the discursive or symbolic mind allowing more embodied pre-linguistic and preconscious aspects of the mind-body to be present.

[124] This section was prepared with the help of Ana Manzanedo, connector at OuiShare.

open to all. Its flagship event is the OuiShare Fest. The first one was launched in 2013 and brought together over 1,000 people from across the world. One OuiShare Fest soon led to five in Paris, each gathering 1,500 entrepreneurs, free thinkers, and activists striving to create a fairer, more open, and resilient society through alternative models. Now, OuiShare Fest has become a hub for all those looking to escape their comfort zones and create unique collaborations that connect its attendees on a deep and authentic level. To allow for the long-term sustainability of the associative project, they have developed a commercial arm that does studies, consultancy, training, etc. A non-negligible part of the results of the business activities they carry out is reinvested in the associative projects of general interest.

The OuiShare community is built and maintained around a strong culture nicknamed the OuiShare Style. Three of its five fundamental values - collaboration, openness, and care- are designed for communion[125]

- Collaboration: OuiShare has always wanted to make decisions collectively. That was the case from the very beginning, but being a distributed network of 1,500 active members, that goes up to 8,000 if we include supporting members, they have been forced to balance the combination of virtual and physical interaction spaces. OuiShare excels at relating and working through digital tools such as Loomio (an online tool created by Enspiral to make collaborative decisions). Still, they believe that real connections happen face to face, so *Meet people in real life* is one of their mantras. The summits are the most important physical encounters they have. Since its origins in 2012, summits have been a fundamental part of OuiShare's development and a chance to bring expertise to the communities that host them. Global Summits are where the international community meets to develop the organisation and its vision together, set strategic goals, kick-start new projects, and build relationships between the distributed team of connectors and members. All of that happens equally at a country level on Local Summits. They hold an international meeting each year (until 2017 there were two) and at least one local one. Participating in a Summit is also a great way for new

[125] The remaining two are permanent beta and do-ocracy. They will be explained later in this chapter.

people who would like to get involved in OuiShare to meet the most active members and get a glimpse at how OuiShare works.

- Openness: Transparency and openness are part of OuiShare's DNA. They are core values deeply encoded in the organisation, starting from its name: Yes, we share. OuiShare operates in a distributed network. Each member has potential access to all the accumulated knowledge. The challenge is to know how to navigate the network and activate the mechanisms so that knowledge is shared. That's something they learned from *stigmergy*, a form of self-organisation, initially inspired by the behaviour of termites, which produce complex structures, without need for any planning, control, or even direct communication between the agents. They have copied from ants how to leave traces of knowledge so that other members can find them and use them to improve a project or create a new one. Thus, everything is documented and shared: community meetings, minutes, experiences with clients, etc. Their biggest stigmergy experiment ended in 2017 with the consolidation of OuiShare Open Source, a gateway to connect the world to the knowledge they generate and which also serves to organise and exponentially improve the exchange in an agile and efficient way. Everybody can easily access online their knowledge maps, handbooks, and toolkits from how they are structured and make decisions, to how they operate on a daily basis.
- Care: Hosting and caring are so relevant and necessary to the community that is part of OuiShare's current values. The area of care, like everything else in OuiShare, arose out of necessity. At the 2014 London Summit, some people shared ideas about the potential of an organisation whose priority is to take care of each other. They started experimenting with this idea, since until that moment, these events were very focused on work and not so much on the people, and were quite exhausting. OuiCare was born from this opportunity: eight people were dedicated to exploring how to soften the effects of *chaordicity*[126] and make it more effective without harming people. The first implementation

[126] The term "chaordic" was initially formulated by Dee Hock (1995) when he was VISA's CEO. It is formed from the words "chaos" and "order". He intended to design an organisation that allowed for the harmonious coexistence of chaos and order and the simultaneous cooperation and competition of the member banks of the VISA issuing network.

was the facilitation and organisation of the next summit. They sought to cultivate deeper conversations, and methodologies were prepared accordingly. Nowadays, it is difficult to imagine a summit without careful design. The OuiCare group also played a key role in introducing personal development formats in the community's flagship event: The OuiShare Fest. Techniques were also introduced on how to give and receive feedback using Non-Violent Communication. Currently, the OuiCare group is not active, but its spirit has become embedded in the culture. Meetings in a circle and sharing emotions and concerns are examples that are part of their day-to-day practices. At the same time, it is necessary to balance the care of the organisation and the local communities to ensure their survival. The OuiShare Commons are all the backbone activities that are shared by the entire OuiShare community. They need to happen in order to keep operating smoothly on an international level and ensure maximum connectivity between communities. The global operations team generally manages them. The official contribution to the OuiShare Commons is 10% of each project. The contribution to the local communities varies. In France, for example, most projects are starting to leave at least 20% of the budget. In Spain, to the official 10% per project, they add another 10% for the remuneration that each member receives for their participation, and they channel it through Cobudget in the form of a donation. In parallel to those experiments, OuiShare is currently benchmarking other friend organisations, such as Las Indias in Spain or Enspiral in Australia, that have applications in which members have a common income, but they allocate a percentage of this total for monthly "salaries" (allowances). This communal fund allows a monthly payment to members that can't be active at some periods (due to holidays, maternity or paternity leaves, etc.)

7.6. The power of love

If I speak in the tongues of mortals and of angels, but don't have love, I am a noisy gong or a clanging cymbal. And if I have prophetic powers, and understand all mysteries and all knowledge, and if I have all faith, so as to remove mountains, but don't have love, I am nothing. If I give away all my possessions, and if I hand over my body so that I may boast, but don't have love, I gain nothing. (Corinthians 13.1-3)

Some of you might be shocked to read about love in a management book. You shouldn't be surprised if you got this far into the book. Even if it sounds touchy-feely, you have to agree with me that love is the fundamental force of the Universe, then why don't we use such energy? The most powerful organisation is the one that arises from love. Patagonia is in love with the environment, CineCiutat loves the 7th Art, and Buurtzorg adores its patients. Most organisations begin with an act of love, and they continue to be acts of love.

If we analyse the two main aspects of the spiritual dimension, purpose and communion, we will find that love is one of their main building blocks. Purpose is a reflection and a consequence of what you love. Ask yourself what is it that you love most deeply, and you will be on the path of identifying your true purpose. And what about communion? A community is as strong as the relationships among its members, and the love they feel for the project. Those are the ties that bind, because love is the ultimate and most potent force of the Universe. Everything comes out of love, and love is all there is. Without it, all moral, emotional, and intellectual capabilities are valueless.

Some enlightened leaders have adopted love as the driving force of their organisations. That was the case of Herb Kelleher, the legendary co-founder of Southwest Airlines, who said: *"A company is much stronger if it is bound by love rather than by fear."* Kelleher nicknamed Southwest as the "Luv Airline" not only because their headquarters are in the Love Field in Dallas. LUV is the company's three-letter symbol on the New York Stock Exchange, and they try to share that love with their employees, customers, society, and the planet. Also, there is Bob Chapman, CEO of Barry-Wehmiller, who declares: *"Our approach is extraordinarily successful because we have tapped into something far more fundamental to our true nature which is the opposite of fear: love"* (Chapman and Sisodia, 2015:83). Barry-Wehmiller - a global provider of manufacturing technologies - adopted a guiding principle, to which they attribute much of their success, including over 75 acquisitions globally and a combined $2 billion in assets: *"We measure success by the way we touch the lives of people"* (Chapman, 2015: xi). The company rejects the idea that employees are simply functions to be moved around, "managed" with carrots and sticks, or discarded at will. Instead, Barry-Wehmiller believes that every single person matters, just like in a family. That's the bedrock of the company's philosophy.

> *"You know, we measure success the wrong way in this country. We measure it by the financial performance and growth of a company, and yet we've got people whose lives are being destroyed every day by the way in which many companies operate. We are going to measure success by the way we touch the lives of people. All the people: our team members, our customers, our vendors, our bankers. For every action we take, we need to understand the impact it has on all the people whose lives we touch. If every business did that, the world would be a much better place than it is today." (Chapman and Sisodia, 2015: 54)*

Barry-Wehmiller's guiding principle does not only refer to employees or customers but all of their stakeholders. They challenge themselves to make a positive impact on all the lives they touch through the course of their business, including team members' families, suppliers, shareholders, and the communities in which they work and live.

Notwithstanding what I just said, love is like an X-file in the workplace. What is even worse, managing by fear has become acceptable and even desirable. If organisations don't give love, how can they expect to receive love? How are they supposed to have loyal customers or associates? When you fill others' buckets with love, it pours back into your bucket in limitless amounts. The Argentinian consulting company Quinto Impacto launched a very successful virtual campaign called "The Most Beloved Company." Since 2018, the people of the province of Mendoza have to vote for the company they love most, an assessment that goes beyond the recognition of quality, to highlight the ten most cherished companies because they have made an important contribution to the community.

It is about time for love to play a central part in management, especially in two of its forms: Eros and Agape. The four main drives of a holon are agency, communion, Eros and Agape. I already talked about the first two, which are the two major types of action, according to Ken Wilber. Let's consider now Eros and Agape, the two major types of love. Evolution is driven by love. If you notice, spelt backwards, love is in the four first letters of the word evolution. Eros and Agape are two fundamental evolutionary impulses of every organisation. Eros is ascending love. It is the vertical drive of a lower holon to "reach up" towards the higher. It is a call for evolution and self-transcendence, an urge to find higher, deeper, and wider wholeness. In its turn, Agape is the love of the higher reaching down to the lower. It is the vertical drive of the higher to embrace, protect, enfold, or, at the end of the day, "love" the lower. It refers to the involutionary force that pulls evolution from above. In a nutshell, Agape is a holon embracing its subholons and Eros a holon looking to become a subholon of a new and greater holon (Wilber 2017:479).

These two dynamics are present not only in individuals but also in organisations. Edwards (2004) points out that this evolutionary dynamic is seen in the need to expand and grow, in the push to exponentially increase profits and sales, and in the effort to reach new goals. The integrative dynamics are seen in the need for stability and sustainability, in attempts to form connections and to resolve past problems, in respecting the traditions of the organisation, and in the efforts to create community. Integral Theory considers both of them essential:

> *"It is a basic principle of Integral Theory that real health is only found in the balancing of growth and integration and that development is only sustainable when our striving for bigger and better is matched by our desire to retain, include and respect what we already have (...) (Ibid.)*

In development, one ascends via Eros (or expanding to a higher and broader identity) and then integrates via Agape (or reaching down to embrace with care all lower holons). Balanced development transcends but includes—it is negation and preservation, ascent and descent. Purpose, again, will be the primary yardstick for choosing between Eros and Agape. The organisation will often be pushed to reach its higher purpose, but at the same time, it will have to be careful to stay true to it and not lose its way or sense of community. Eros and Agape working together make a great circle of love through the organisation. A dance of refluxing Eros (the Many returning to the One) and effluxing Agape (the One becoming Many).

7.7. The End of Strategic Management (as we know it)

We need a vision of the future if we want to achieve our purpose. It is one thing to think about the desired future to focus our mind and efforts, and quite another to believe that we can forecast it.

Strategic management is a discipline and a business process that is supposed to prepare an organisation for the future. The mainstream approach to strategy and planning is based on causal determinism: The future can be predicted because it is an extension of the past. The prediction relies on a scientific approach in which qualitative data and intuition are usually discarded as unreliable. As quantitative data is required, and there is no data about the future, historical information is used instead. As Bogsnes (2016:24) says, quantitative data is instrumental in dealing with the present and the past. Data about results, costs, profitability, and the like, help us understand how we are doing and how we got there. The problem starts when we want to carry the same or almost the same level of detail into the future. An accurate prediction of the future would require knowing all of the unknown factors of the equation, and no methodology can do this. Prediction technologies such as Big Data can be useful for operations management, but they are very unreliable for strategic management since the future will never be a linear extrapolation of the past.

The big difference between the past and the future is that one is certain, and the other is uncertain. The flux of the present invalidates the static presumptions of history. The future is slippery, and it could not care less about our plans. You think you've got it and it sneaks out of your reach. You have figured out its next move, and it turns in the opposite direction.

If we scratch the surface of traditional strategic management, we discover it leans on a Newtonian paradigm and an Orange worldview that worked well in more stable times. But you can't apply old thinking to new problems. How can that be done if many of yesterday's solutions have become today's problems? In other fields, such as meteorology, the future can be predicted with an acceptable degree of accuracy by applying Newtonian physics. Though a myriad of factors influence the weather, it is a moderately isolated system that can be reasonably forecasted with computer models. In stable environments like the ones we used to have, we could apply that logic and predict the future by extrapolating what happened before. Unfortunately, that is no longer the case of our VUCA world. The scientific methods of strategic management, no matter how sophisticated or the amount of big data compiled, have as many chances to reliably predict what lies ahead as a person with Diogenes' Syndrome winning an interior design contest. So much so that Dartmouth professor, Brian Quinn, compares the traditional strategic planning process to a rain dance:

> *"A good deal of corporate planning is like a ritual rain dance. It has no effect on the weather that follows, but those who engage in it think it does. ... Moreover, much of the advice related to corporate planning is directed at improving the dancing, not the weather."*

Both of them are full of inaccuracies derived from the limited assumptions on which they are built. Ultimately, they are just futile attempts to invest the anticipatory act of an impossible certainty.

All this paraphernalia creates an illusion of control over the process. The illusion that we have done all the analysis, that we followed a plan, that those at the top have all the answers. But complexity and certainty are uneasy bedfellows. Robertson (2015:128-130), the developer of Holacracy, warns us of the consequences of all that:

> *"When we attempt to predict the future in an unpredictable world, not only are we deluding ourselves, but worse, we are actually inhibiting our ability to sense and respond to reality in the present moment. When you impose a "should" -as in "I should be X in 5 years' time"- you create an attachment to that outcome; the attachment limits your ability to sense when reality is not going in that direction or when other possible opportunities arise that might conflict with what you first set out to achieve (...)*
>
> *When we become attached to a specific predicted outcome there is a risk we will get stuck fighting reality when it doesn't conform to our prediction. If we find that we are not on the path we set out for ourselves, we may conclude, sometimes subconsciously, that something must be wrong. That judgment of reality then inhibits our ability to respond and encourages us to push against the unwelcome truth -to try to force reality to conform to our predicted vision. That's not a very effective strategy for navigating the ever-changing complexity of business today. When reality conflicts with our best-laid plans, reality usually wins."*

No matter how hard we try to make order out of chaos, we can't force the real world into our planning methodologies. Leading-edge theories such as Lean, Agile, or Holacracy, do the opposite and instead of trying to predict and control as mainstream planning methodologies do, they change to a steering modality based on trying to sense and respond.[127] Robertson resorts to a metaphor from the world of Agile Software Development to contrast the traditional process with dynamic steering:

---

[127] The Manifesto for Agile Software Development you can read below incorporates this change of philosophy:
"We are uncovering better ways of developing software by doing it and helping others do it.

- *Through this work, we have come to value:*
- *Individuals and interactions over processes and tools.*
- *Working software over comprehensive documentation.*
- *Customer collaboration over contract negotiation.*
- ***Responding to change over following a plan.***

That is, while there is value in the items on the right, we value the items on the left more."

"Imagine riding a bicycle the way we manage most modern organizations. You would hold a big meeting to decide the angle at which you should hold the handlebars; you'd map your journey in as much detail as possible, factoring in all known obstacles and the exact timing and degree to which you would need to adjust your course to avoid these. Then you would get on the bicycle, hold the handlebars rigidly at the angle calculated, close your eyes, and steer according to plan. Odds are you would not reach your target, even if you did manage to keep the bicycle upright for the entire trip. When the bicycle falls over, you might ask: "Why didn't we get this right the first time?" And maybe: "Who screwed up?"

That ridiculous approach isn't so far from the approach many organizations take to strategic planning. By contrast, Holacracy helps an organization operate more like the way we actually ride a bicycle, using a dynamic steering paradigm. Dynamic steering means constant adjustment in light of real feedback, which makes for a more organic and emergent path." (Robertson 2015: 129)

When you ride a bicycle, steering can't be planned. You have a direction, but to get there, you have to put your five senses on the present moment, and based on the information you get from them, respond and re-adjust by steering and countersteering in a continuous flow. He further clarifies and defends his dynamic steering process:

"I should note that embracing a more Dynamic approach for gaining control is not at all the same as just not predicting any more than riding a bicycle is a process of not steering. It is about changing how we relate to our predictions and plans, seeing them as sometimes useful fallacies but not the primary tools used to control the organization. And it is about being fully present in the here and now so we can steer continuously in response to actual reality. When dynamic steering is done well, it enables the organization and those within it to stay present and act decisively on whatever arises day to day, like a skilled martial artist or the stereotypical Zen master." (Ibid., 130)

Strategy guru Gary Hamel (2009) makes a similar proposal:

"Management processes that seek to arrive at the "one best strategy" through top-down, analytical methods must give way to models based on the biological principles of variety (generate lots of options), selection (use low-cost experiments to rapidly test critical assumptions), and retention (pour resources into the strategies that are gaining the most traction in the marketplace). In the future, top management won't make strategy but will work to create the conditions in which new strategies can emerge and evolve."

As Laloux (2016) reports, FAVI relies on an agricultural metaphor to describe the same paradigm shift. Traditional organisations look five years ahead and make plans for the next year. In contrast, FAVI believes we should think like farmers: look 20 years forward, and plan for the next day. We can plan which fruit trees to plant or which crops to grow, but it makes no sense to schedule the exact harvest date. The new paradigm of strategic management has to forget about forecasting the future and making plans around it. We should trust the unfolding of the present moment without being weighed down by the past or attempting to control the future. As we can't predict the future, the process should focus on detecting signals of change and responding quickly and effectively to them through a process of adaptive evolution that learns to work with reality as it unfolds by encouraging experimentation and rapid learning. The process would be as follows:

1. Scanning: Observing and detecting change through sensing and exploring the directionalities of the VUCA reality. That is what Sociocracy 3.0 calls "navigating via tensions." In Sociocracy 3.0, people act as sensors (nerve endings) that sometimes come across tensions. Tensions are the fuel of the organisation. They express the dissonance between what is and what could be, challenges or opportunities that become drivers of change.
2. Planning: Making sense of the changes and their implications, acquiring knowledge not about the future, but about how to respond to the current changes.
3. Acting: Developing adaptive responses by identifying and coordinating the relevant resources and taking the necessary actions.

So, we start with a long-term vision, but make progress through experimentation and iteration based on an approach of probe, sense, and respond:

> *"Teal Organizations make peace with a complex world in which perfection eludes us. They shoot explicitly not for the best possible decision, but for a workable solution that can be implemented quickly. Based on new information, the decision can be revisited and improved at any point." (Laloux 2016: 211)*

These are fundamental principles of Holacracy and Sociocracy. The focus is always on quickly reaching a workable decision and then letting reality tell us what to do next. "Good Enough for Now" and "Safe Enough to Try" are the guiding principles, meaning as soon as it doesn't make things worse, let's try it again, and let's do it as quickly as possible. The decision can be reviewed at any time if new information comes up or someone has a better idea. You know the saying: "too much analysis is paralysis." For example, in Holacracy, a strategy meeting typically takes place in each circle once every six months. If the conventional strategic planning process looks for a specific plan, these meetings are about equipping the team with the right compass to navigate the tensions being sensed and guide them along the journey (Robertson 2014: 135). There is nobody designing. Everybody is sensing, responding, and dynamically steering. The new strategic process is more like ready, aim, shoot, as Laloux implies (2016: 211):

> *"Companies that work this way, that make many fast iterations instead of a few mighty leaps, progress much faster and much more smoothly toward their purpose. No energy is wasted figuring out the supposedly best decision; no time is wasted waiting for more data and more certainty before making decisions. Just as important, when decisions are small and we are used to revising them often, it also becomes much easier to correct a decision that proves mistaken."*

Two of the core values of OuiShare, Permanent Beta and Do-ocracy, are designed to make the organisation as responsive and adaptive as possible:

- Permanent Beta: OuiShare is a work in progress. Its governance structure has been designed to reflect the vision of an emergent organisation that is in Permanent Beta and adapts to rapidly changing environments. Influenced by concepts of self-organisation, stigmergy, and distributed leadership, they aim to keep contributions and governance structure as organic and agile as possible. In each complex or conflictual situation, new operating rules are devised, and only sometimes documented. Although loosely based on classic sociocratic principles, OuiShare chose not to follow a standardised organisational model. They want to be a highly organic entity that is not constrained by unnecessary structures. In 2013, some members designed the first version of the OuiShare handbook, which was rejected because it was introduced in a top-down fashion and it didn't match the lived reality of the organisation. After that experience, they decided to trust each other and to design together operating rules based on their shared culture only when they face a problem, leaving room for chaos. They have since documented these minimum viable common rules in an open-source handbook as well as a map to communicate internally and generate an external community of reflection.

- Do-ocracry: OuiShare's common culture is built around the concept of Do-ocracy, a neologism that means power to the one who does, or in other words, decision-making based on actions. At OuiShare, the projects and the teams that form around them emerge spontaneously. OuiShare sticks to creating interactive spaces, physical and online, so that ideas, conflicts, needs, etc. can arise. Rather than collectively deciding who does what in the organisation, the one who takes on a role becomes responsible. Over time, competence has become an indispensable argument for taking over a given role. Thus, forms of distributed leadership emerge temporarily in the collective as project leaders that act as crystallisers will, following the notion of sense and respond, observe behaviours, and then create the minimal necessary structures to support them.

If the epistemology of the traditional strategic management process was primarily scientific, a new integral paradigm needs to be much more balanced in accordance with the 3D-Management philosophy. It will still need a scientific method, but at the same time, it will have to rely heavily on arts to conveniently sense and respond to the challenges and opportunities that arise, on ethics, to make responsible decisions, and on spirit, to stay true to the organisational purpose.

Let me highlight the spiritual aspect: As Sociocracy 3.0 suggests, people act as sensors for the organisation that needs to adopt a meditative stance of present moment awareness to detect and process tensions. Tension is an energy that arises between the perception of what is now and a desired future state. The process of governance is a sacred space, where role fillers come together for a group meditation to sense in the present moment. Being in the here and now, open to intuition, is of paramount importance.

The traditional strategy was based on left-brained rational thinking. Now it is whole-brained integral thinking what is required. New tools are accordingly needed: Theory U, Co-creation, Open Space, Appreciative Inquiry, Gamification, Three Horizons, Systemic Constellations, Lego Serious Play, and Design Thinking are increasingly popular techniques whose principles significantly differs from traditional quantitative and rational approaches.

In addition, an integral strategic management process is much more open and democratic. Under the traditional paradigm, management was divided into two categories: strategy and operations. Strategy was the activity of the managing elite and operations were for the masses. Strategizing was like playing chess, a highly intellectual mind game where the brains above controlled the subordinate hands of the organisation. Under the new paradigm, strategy is no longer reserved for the management elites. Open and crowd-sourced practices open up the strategic process to a larger number of more diverse contributors incorporating other stakeholders outside the organisation. The collective ability to meet challenges, take advantage of an opportunity, and respond to threats is far more significant when the responsibility for doing so is distributed as widely as possible. The benefits of these practices lie in the integration of multiple views, greater transparency, and improved insights generated from a wider variety of perspectives.

In 2018, Artiem hosted its first participatory Strategic Planning Workshop. It was a two-day event bringing together 87 people across the company (almost half of the total workforce, which is 187 employees) using Appreciative Inquiry as the root methodology. As a result, they came up with a map of opportunity areas which has resulted in the creation of 8 project teams that will work on their development supported by a sponsor from the top management team. The eight resulting areas are:

1. Lean philosophy.
2. Development of FreshPeople (that's what they call the members of the company), Ambaworkers (a combination of the words ambassador and worker), and Artiemise (spreading Artiem values internally and externally).
3. Experience culture.
4. Sustainable business growth.
5. Distribution 5.0.
6. Circular economy.
7. Zero emissions.
8. Social value.

There is one team responsible for the development of the projects of each area, with the support of a sponsor from the management team.

7.8. From Big Data to Great Wisdom

Where is the wisdom we have lost in knowledge?
Where is the knowledge we have lost in information? (T.S. Eliot)

Organisations operate thanks to their ability to process information. They can be considered, from this point of view, as information, communication, and decision-making systems.

There is a big fuss about big data. As the Orange mindset views information as a scarce resource and a source of power, big data analytics is considered a sort of philosopher's stone for competitive advantage.

But data, information, and knowledge are just scientific variables. If we have all the information in the palm of our hand, why are we none the wiser? The paradox of our days is we know more and more about less and less. Most organisations have limited themselves to creating sophisticated business intelligence systems, pushing aside the arts and the ethics of all of that. An integral approach would take the three dimensions in, as equally important. Data would be just the junior holon in a hierarchy that goes from data to information, then to knowledge, and finally to wisdom.

Data is raw. It has no significance beyond its existence, and no meaning in itself (think of a spreadsheet and you will get the idea). When data is processed to be useful (i.e., when it has been given meaning), it becomes information. In turn, when information is eventually processed and assimilated by a human being, it becomes knowledge. In short, formatted data becomes information, and formatted information turns into knowledge. The Internet is full of data that does not become information until the user finds what she is looking for and decodes it. The moment information is assimilated and interpreted (by a person, or also by a machine), it becomes knowledge.

But we need a final level to complete the holarchy. The next stage is wisdom, which is integrated knowledge. Data, information, and knowledge are monological; wisdom is integral. It is the know-what (science), the know-how (arts), and the know-why (ethics) all together. Information tells us what there is, knowledge what we can do with it, and wisdom what we should do. Unlike the previous three levels, wisdom asks why. It requires judgment. Wisdom is, therefore, the process by which we discern, or judge, between right and wrong, good and bad, ethical and unethical. It is responsible knowledge because it incorporates a moral filter. The first three categories relate to the past; they deal with what has been or what is known. Only the fourth category, wisdom, deals with the future because it incorporates decision-making. Wisdom involves using knowledge for the greater good. And so far, only humans can attain this level. Artificial intelligence and algorithms are not able to match wisdom yet. It is a uniquely human faculty that requires having a soul since it involves as much of our heart as our mind.

As Wahl (2016:29) wisely asserts:

> *"As the radius of the circle of what is known expands, we become aware of the expanding circumference of our own ignorance. We have to come to grips with the fact that knowledge and information, no matter how detailed, will remain an insufficient and uncertain basis for guiding our path into the future. We will increase our chances of success if we have the wisdom and humility to embrace our own ignorance, celebrate ambiguity, and befriend uncertainty. More often than not, certainty is not an option. We are invited to 'live the questions more deeply', to pay attention to the wisdom of many minds and diverse points of view, and to continue the conversation about whether we are still on the appropriate path. "*

Big data won't transform the world. Only great wisdom will. And by its very nature, wisdom is integral.

AFTERWORD

> *"Amid all the doom-laden exhortations to change our ways, let us remember that we are striving to create a more beautiful world, and not sustain, with growing sacrifice, the current one. We are not just seeking to survive. We are not just facing doom; we are facing glorious possibility. We are offering people not a world of less, not a world of sacrifice, not a world where you are just going to have to enjoy less and suffer more—no, we are offering a world of more beauty, more joy, more connection, more love, more fulfilment, more exuberance, more leisure, more music, more dancing and more celebration." – (Charles Eisenstein 2013:159)*

Evolutionary purpose is a defining element, not only of teal organisations but of any organisation. Every organisation is on an evolutionary journey. Red, amber, orange, green, teal, turquoise, and so on, are the inescapable stops in that journey. At this moment, the direction of organisational evolution is pushing towards teal. We can be witnessing the dusk of traditional management and the rising of a golden dawn. Amber, orange, and even the incipient green organisations are no longer a good fit for market conditions. If we look far enough on the horizon, we will see that the future is teal. The world is asking organisations to evolve to that. Put differently, the future is integral. Integral is more than just a theory, even more than just a metatheory. It is an inescapable stage in our evolutionary journey if we manage to get there. We know this because every developmental model has found in its research that stage at that particular point.

The number of individuals and organisations operating from the integral tier is still small but is growing day after day. Some pioneers have paved the way, and many are following the trail towards a more conscious, holistic, meaningful, and caring way of doing business. Soon there will be a legion. Experts say that only 10% is needed to reach the critical mass of social transformation. It is a process similar to the metamorphosis of the caterpillar into a butterfly. One day, some tiny cells, known as imaginal cells, begin to appear within the chrysalis and they are the catalysts for the transformation. At first, the imaginal cells are identified by the organism as alien enemies and are attacked, but soon enough, they become the genetic directors of the future butterfly. They start connecting and clustering for the transformation to take place. We are those imaginal cells, emerging with a new consciousness and vision of the future, which will transform our caterpillar organisations into beautiful butterflies.

Remember the movie Pleasantville? It is a variation of Plato's allegory of the cave that I drew upon at the beginning of chapter 3. David and Jennifer, two 1990s teenage siblings, are magically transported to a 1950s TV sitcom. They find a world in black and white, apparently safe and stable, but inflexible and oppressive if you scratch below the surface. Under their influence, the predictable and complacent world of Pleasantville begins to crumble. As the certainties of yesterday blow away with the wind, there is a time of turmoil, but gradually the grey town begins to show full and vibrant colours. The more rules that are broken, the more colourful life gets in Pleasantville.

It is time to break some rules. The traditional management's table of commandments that is carved in stone is no longer valid. In this book, I have shown many organisations and theories (3D Management being one of them), that are changing the rules of the game. We have to understand these examples, not as exceptions or rarities, but as the true promises of the teal consciousness that will define the forthcoming metamodern era.

Initially published in 2004, 3D Management is a pioneer teal theory, and the first integrally-built management theory ever to appear. That is no small feat. The enormous influence of Wilber's work has resulted in many integrally-informed theories and models, but there is only one integrally-built management theory to date, and that is 3D Management. Being integrally-built, using AQAL, makes 3D Management more than just another theory. It is a metatheory. It does something that no other management theory has done before. Rather than competing against other approaches, a metatheory like 3D Management tries to include as many legitimate theories as possible. 3D Management is the result of an AQAL analysis of organisational theories with the explicit aim of including all of their truths weaved together in a single metatheoretical framework. In practical terms, it is a non-prescriptive model that holds as many perspectives as possible within its frame and is able to host many different theories, even conflicting ones. It is totally up to you to use, say, Holacracy, Sociocracy, Sociocracy 3.0, or your own homegrown self-organisational system. If the evolutionary circumstances require it, you could even resort to a formal hierarchy. It is a radical evolution of conventional management, doing away with its pathologies, deformations, and limitations while preserving its achievement and benefits.

More important than this epistemological contribution, is the ontological one. 3D Management reprograms organisations from the inside out and reboots management with a fundamentally different ontology that overcomes the flatland one-dimensionality of the traditional paradigm where only profits matter. Instead, it proposes a balanced triad of science, arts, and ethics, three equally important, independent, and interrelated dimensions that finally converge into a fourth spiritual dimension. This updated ontology entails a profound transformation of organisations whose focus moves away from the domain of the material to the realm of the spiritual. From matter to what really matters.

Thus, 3D Management is a *summum bonum* of science, arts, ethics, and spirit, four key dimensions to achieve sustainable excellence, bring prosperity to everyone they touch, unfold organisational and individual potential, rediscover personal satisfaction at work, raise consciousness, and reinvent corporate spirit. As a model, 3D Management not only gives its rightful place to each of its constituent dimensions, it also reinvents them. The scientific dimension is redefined by replacing the old authoritarian regime with a holarchical governance system based on responsible autonomy. The artistic dimension breaks the organisation's boundaries to merge it with an ecosystem of stakeholders, all equally important and valued, and creates the appropriate mechanisms to spur the horizontal and vertical development of them all. Finally, the ethical dimension gets promoted for the first time to its rightful place, no longer subordinated to economic results, and geared by kosmocentric values.

As I write these sentences, the world has been swept by a global health crisis and it remains at the edge of ecological disaster. Do we still need more reasons to urgently change our ways? I believe that business can be a primary vehicle for transforming society and building a better world. As Charles Eisenstein so wonderfully expressed it, it is all about creating the more beautiful world our hearts know is possible. The teal future is within our grasp. If you have come this far in reading this book, you probably agree it is a splendid and highly desirable future. But it is not an assured future, not by a long shot. Powerful attractors guide us in that direction, but there are so many variables at work, and their interactions are so complex, that any event, however insignificant it may be, can delay its advent temporarily or even forever. If you want a new world, as you'd always dream it could be, you will have to earn it. Be an imaginal cell and start the transformational process that will give our organisations wings to fly high, wide, deep, and away. It is the right thing to do, the sensible thing to do, the beautiful thing to do, and more importantly, it is one of the most meaningful things to do that I can think of.

Appendix 1

YOU SAY YOU WANT A REVOLUTION?

ORGANISATIONAL PARADIGMS FOR A NEW ECONOMY

(Originally published for the New Economy and Social Innovation Forum 2016).

Our current business model is more than a century old and is built on premodern traditional and modern industrial rational structures based on a linear and Newtonian world view. It is founded on some questionable premises, and it has clear limitations that are becoming more and more apparent.

Going beyond merely denouncing the conventional business model, some theories and models are laying the foundation for a new management paradigm. As a result, a revolutionary way of managing organisations is emerging, and my prediction is that it is going to be the norm in the future. Important companies such as Whole Foods, Zappos, Ben and Jerry's, L.L. Gore, Semco and Buurtzorg are already being managed that way, and they are only the visible side of an iceberg that could sink business as usual.

The purpose of this article is to be a modest guide on some of the theories that are defining this new management paradigm. Obviously, the list is not all-inclusive, so I apologise in advance if I have not included your theory or your theory of choice.

If, as the Beatles sang, you say you want a revolution, and you believe another business is possible, here you have some real solutions to make business and organisations more humane, socially responsible and sustainable.

CULTURAL THEORIES

These sets of theories focus on the evolution of culture and values in business. The underlying assumption they all share is that the system of beliefs and values that shaped our organisations during the twentieth century is just not good enough today and they try to describe the cultural traits of the organisations of the future.

Cultural transformation and Value assessment: Richard Barrett is one of the true pioneers and should be considered as one of the gurus of the new management paradigm. He is responsible for developing the theory of the Universal Stages of Evolution, the concepts of personal and cultural entropy, and creating assessment instruments to map the values of individuals and collectives to his Seven Levels of Consciousness Model. He put it all together in the Cultural Transformation Tools (CTT).

Managing by values: Dolan, García, and Richley draw upon Plato's philosophy to propose a triaxial theory to understand organisational culture as a combination of three groups of values: 1) economic-pragmatic values; 2) ethical-social values; 3) emotional-developmental values. They advocate an evolution of conceptual management approaches from Management by Instructions and Management by Objectives towards Management by Values, a model based on a shared system of values between the owners and employees of companies.

Deliberately developmental organisations: Harvard Professor Robert Kegan coined the term Deliberately Developmental Organisation (DDO) in his book *An Everyone Culture* to explain the phenomena of organisations and businesses that develop cultures with a specific approach to growth that consider the development of each employee of the organisation at least as important as the bottom line. Kegan argues that those organisations outperform the average organisation in profits and employee satisfaction.

ECONOMIC THEORIES:

This block is about theories and movements whose main interest is economics in general, but that also includes management and organisations as subtopics.

Economy for the Common Good: A very influential social movement initiated by Christian Felber advocating for an alternative economic model. It calls for organisations working towards the common good and cooperating rather than only making money and competing. Its more important tool is the "common good balance sheet", which evaluates organisations on how cooperative they are with other companies, whether their products and services satisfy human needs, and how humane their working conditions are. A score is awarded accordingly.

Memenomics: A theoretical framework developed by Said Dawlabani which applies the Spiral Dynamics model to economics. By integrating economic development with human development, Memenomics provides a whole system's understanding of the historical trajectories of the past economic theories and potential solutions for a healthier "next generation economic system" and business model.

Conscious capitalism: A movement initiated by John Mackey, Whole Foods CEO, and professor Raj Sisodia. Conscious capitalism is more about management than economics, but I have included it within this section because of its defence of capitalism as a valuable system. Conscious Capitalism builds on the foundations of Capitalism but intends to elevate it to a more complex form of consciousness for its purpose, its impacts on the world, and the relationships it has with its stakeholders. It is based on four principles: higher purpose, stakeholder integration, conscious leadership, and conscious culture and management. Fred Kofman should not be forgotten here, as he has a book (2006) devoted to conscious business, and his brilliant Metamanagement (2001 a,b,c) trilogy follows similar principles.

SOCIAL RESPONSIBILITY THEORIES

These theories are concerned with increasing the responsibility of business towards society and the planet, and accordingly, they develop a set of tools and practices for that purpose.

B Corps: A global movement of for-profit companies holding a private certification issued by B Lab. To be granted and to preserve certification, companies must receive a minimum score on an online assessment for "social and environmental performance", satisfy the requirement that the company integrate B Lab commitments to stakeholders into company governing documents, and pay an annual fee.

The Economy of Communion: The Economy of Communion (EoC) was founded by Chiara Lubich in 1991 as an initiative of the Focolare Movement. It promotes an economic culture imprinted on the Christian values of communion, gratuity, and reciprocity. They propose an alternative lifestyle to the dominant one within our capitalist system and it is a concrete attempt to address acute social problems with businesses that are integral parts of their communities. Member businesses are required to commit a part of their profits to direct aid for those in need and another part toward nurturing a "culture of giving".

INTEGRAL THEORIES

Since the American philosopher Ken Wilber first used the word "integral" to refer to his approach in 1995, Integral Theory has become one of the most influential theories of our times. Integral Theory is the comprehensive study of reality from a holistic, all-embracing, and non-marginalising point of view. It has been applied to all fields of human knowledge including management and organisation theory.

Many authors have applied integral theory to specific areas such as strategy, coaching, organisational development, and some of the integral tools (AQAL, spiral dynamics) to business and management. The three theories that stand out in terms of comprehensiveness and relevance are:

Teal Organisations: The teal organisation movement was started by Frederic Laloux with his book "Reinventing Organisations". The book resulted from two years of research about how organisations have evolved over time, using the Spiral Dynamics Integral (SDI) model as a frame of reference, and it identifies the emergence of a new management paradigm. The Teal paradigm refers to the next stage in the evolution of human consciousness according to the colour scheme used by SDI. Organisations of this type consciously operate as complex adaptive systems based on evolutionary purpose, with distributed authority, structured as decentralised, self-managing teams or networks that encourage wholeness so that people have the opportunity to present themselves fully at work.

3D Management: An integrally built metatheory of management developed by Marco Robledo. It stands for Three-Dimensional Management, in reference to three fundamental and irreducible dimensions: science, arts, and ethics, which refer respectively to the techno-economical, the developmental- emotional, and the moral aspects of organisational reality. Those three are integrated in an essential unit by a fourth one, the spiritual dimension, which strives for unity and meaning. 3D Management denies the absolutist imperialism of the economic in business and replaces it by a harmonic triumvirate that takes equally into account other objectives such as the vertical development of people, social responsibility, and total stakeholder orientation, all of them integrated towards a higher purpose.

Integral Leadership: Leadership is the area of management that has received more attention due to integral theory (there is even a journal devoted to it, the Integral Leadership Review). One of the more important contributions to recent leadership theory comes from Brett Thomas. His integral leadership theory attempts to integrate all major styles of leadership as a result of the recognition that all of them will work with some of the people some of the time, but no single approach works with all types of people all of the time. Accordingly, Thomas has developed a breakthrough model called the Leadership Rosetta Stone. The tool correlates four universal leadership styles with the four most common worldviews according to Spiral Dynamics.

ORGANISATIONAL THEORIES

The organisations of the future will surely be more person-centric. Democracy, transparency, no hierarchies, and self-management are common characteristics of this kind of organisations. This is not as new as it sounds, self-management has been used by traditional companies such as General Electric, Monsanto, and Xerox in their quest for productivity and profits since the seventies, and lean manufacturing (as developed by Toyota and Honda) has self-organisation as one of its fundamental principles (and has influenced general management theories like radical management). Software developers were also self-organising pioneers, with their agile and scrum methodologies, and there are agile management models for all kinds of organisations. Still sounds like anarchy? So what? Anarchy means "without bosses", not "without order." There are models devoted to defining the structure and operating system of these kinds of organisations:

Sociocracy is a collaborative governance method based on effective organisation, distributed authority, and inclusive decision-making based on cybernetic principles. Modern Sociocracy was initially developed by Gerard Endenburg in the 1960s, and it is currently in its 3.0 version.

Holacracy is a comprehensive practice for structuring, governing, and running an organisation. Clearly inspired by Sociocracy, it was developed by Brian Robertson in his firm Ternary Software, and later marketed by his consulting company HolacracyOne LLC. It replaces the traditional management hierarchy with a peer-to-peer "operating system" of self-organising teams. Encode.org is another important contributor to the development of Holacracy.

REFERENCES

Anderson D. (2013) An Integrated System for Organizational Transformation *Journal of Integral Theory and Practice*, Volume 8, Issue 1&2. Pages 1-18.

Arnsperger, C (2010) *Full-Spectrum Economics: Toward an inclusive and emancipatory social science.* Routledge.

Appelo, J. (2011): *Management 3.0: Leading Agile Developers, Developing Agile Leaders.* New Jersey. Addison-Wesley.

Appelo, J. (2016): *Managing for Happiness: Games, Tools, and Practices to Motivate Any Team.* N.Y. John Wiley & Sons.

Appiah, K. A. (2011). *The honor code: How moral revolutions happen.* WW Norton & Company.

Bakan, J. (2004). *The Corporation: The Pathological Pursuit of Profit and Power.* The Free Press.

Bakke, Dennis W. (2005): Joy at Work. A revolutionary Approach to Fun on the Job. PVG: Seattle.

Barrett, R. (1998), *Liberating the corporate soul.* Butterworth-Heinemann.

Barrett, R. (2011). *The new leadership paradigm.* Lulu Press, Inc., Morrisville, North Carolina.

Barrett, R. (2014). *Evolutionary Coaching: A values-based approach to unleashing human potential.* Lulu Press, Inc., Morrisville, North Carolina.

Bartlett, R. (2016). *Bootstrapping a bossless organisation in 3 easy steps.* Retrieved from https://medium.com/the-tuning-fork/bootstrapping-a-bossless-organisation-in-3-easy-steps-afc653e8f5e6. May 19.

Batle, J. & Robledo, M. A. (2018). "Systemic crisis, weltschmerz and tourism: meaning without incense during vacations". *Current Issues in tourism*. Volume 21, Issue 16 pp. 1386-1405.

Beck, D. E., & Cowan, C. C. (1996). *Spiral dynamics: Mastering Values, Leadership, and Change.* Malden, MA: Blackwell Business.

Bernstein, E., Bunch, J., Canner, N., & Lee, M. (2016). Beyond the holacracy hype. *Harvard business review*, vol. *94*, number 7, July-August. pp. 38-49.

Biddle, G. (2018), "How Netflix's Customer Obsession Created a Customer Obsession". *Nir & Far.* Retrieved from https://www.nirandfar.com/2018/04/customer-obsession.html?utm_source=ActiveCampaign&utm_medium=email&u

tm_content=How+Netflix+s+Customer+Obsession+Created+a+Customer+Obsession&utm_campaign=New+Article%3A+How+Netflix+s+Customer+Obsession+Created+a+Customer+Obsession. 30th April 2016.

Blachfellner et al. (2017). *Compact Balance Sheet 5.0 Workbook.* The Matrix Development Team.

Bogsnes, B. (2009). *Implementing Beyond Budgeting – Unlocking the Performance Potential*, Hoboken, NJ: John Wiley.

Bozesan, M. (2013). "Demystifying the future of investing". *Journal of Integral Theory and Practice*, *8*(1&2), 19-40.

Burke, L., Forman, J., Thomas, B., & Putz, M. (2006). Integral Business and Leadership: An Introduction *AQAL: Journal of Integral Theory and Practice, 1*(1), 71-87.

Burkus, D. (2016). "Why Whole Foods Builds Its Entire Business On Teams". *Forbes.* Retrieved from https://www.forbes.com/sites/davidburkus/2016/06/08/why-whole-foods-build-their-entire-business-on-teams/#6003b3583fa1. June 8.

Cacioppe, R. (2000), "Creating spirit at work: re-visioning organization development and leadership – Part I", *Leadership & Organization Development Journal*, Vol. 21 Issue 2 pp. 48 – 54.

Campbell, J. (1949). *The Hero with a Thousand Faces*. Princeton: Princeton University Press.

Carney, B.M., and Getz, I. (2016). *Freedom Inc.: Free Your Employees and Let Them Lead Your Business to Higher Productivity, Profits, and Growth.* Crown Publishing Group.

Chapman, B., and Sisodia, R. (2015) *Everybody Matters: The Extraordinary Power of Caring for Your People Like Family.* New York: Penguin.

Collins, J. C., and Porras, J. (1994). *Built to Last: Successful Habits of Visionary Companies.* New York: HarperCollins.

Collins, J.C. (2001). *Good to great: Why some companies take the leap and others don't.* New York: HarperCollins.

Commons, M. (2008). Introduction to the model of hierarchical complexity and its relationship to post formal action. *World Futures, 64*, 305-320.

Compagne, O. (2014). "The Organization is Not the Tribe: Why Holacracy® Is Not About the People." *Medium*. Retrieved from https://blog.holacracy.org/the-organization-is-not-the-tribe-244d6dedc5f2. September 16, 2017.

Cook-Greuter, S. (1999). *Post-autonomous ego development: a study of its nature and measurement.* Harvard, UMI.

Cook-Greuter, S.R. (2004). Making the case for a developmental perspective. *Industrial and Commercial Training*, 36(7), 275-281.

Csikszentmihalyi, M. (1990). *Flow: The Psychology of Optimal Experience*. New York: Harper and Row.

Dawlabani, S.E. (2013). *Memenomic: The Next-Generation Economic System.* New York. Select Books.

De Angelo, M. (2016). "The Holacracy Experiment in Washington (State) Government." *Enlivening Edge.* Retrieved from http://www.enliveningedge.org/organizations/Holacracy-experiment-washington-state-government/ August 12, 2016.

de Bree, E., & Stokman, B. (2013). "Getting from Top-Down To All-On-Top". In Moravec, J. (Ed.) *Knowmad Society*. Minneapolis: Education Futures.

De Ciantis, C. and Hyatt, K. (2014) *What's Important: Understanding and Working with Values Perspectives.* Tucson. Integral Publishers.

Denning, S. (2010). *The Leader's Guide to Radical Management: Re-inventing the Workplace for the 21st Century*. San Francisco. Jossey-Bass.

Denning, S. (2018). *The Age of Agile*. New York: AMACOM.

Drucker, P. (1954). *The practice of management*. New York: Harper & Brothers.

—. (1973). *Management: Tasks, Responsibilities, Practices.* New York: Harper & Row.

Dubin, R. (1978). *Theory building.* New York: The Free Press,

Edwards, M. (2002a). "Through AQAL eyes Part 1: A Critique of the Wilber-Kofman Model of Holonic Categories." Retrieved from http://www.integralworld.net/edwards5.html.

Edwards, M. (2002b). "Through AQAL eyes Part 2: Integrating Holon Theory and the AQAL Framework." Retrieved from http://www.integralworld.net/edwards6.html.

Edwards, M. (2003). "Through AQAL eyes Part 7: "I" and "me" and "we" and "us" and "you" and "yous." Retrieved from http://www.integralworld.net/edwards11.html.

Edwards, M. (2004). Good for business: An Integral theory perspective on spirituality in organizations. *Journal of Spirituality Leadership and Management*, vol. 3 pp. 2-11.

Edwards, M. (2010a), *Of elephants and Butterflies: An Integral Metatheory for Organizational Transformation.* In Esbjörn-Hargens (ed.) *Integral Theory in Action: Applied, Theoretical, and Constructive Perspectives on the AQAL Model*: 385-412. Albany. Suny Press.

Edwards, M. (2010b), *Organizational Transformation for Sustainability: An Integral Metatheory*. Routledge.

Eisenstein, Charles. (2013). *The More Beautiful World our Hearts Know is Possible.* North Atlantic Books.

Fairtlough, G. (2005). *The Three Ways of Getting Things Done: Hierarchy, Heterarchy, and Responsible Autonomy in Organisations*, Bridport: Triarchy Press.

Forcadell, F. J. (2005). Democracy, cooperation and business success: the case of Mondragón Corporación Cooperativa. *Journal of Business Ethics*, *vol. 56, no 3, p. 255-274.*

Frank, R., and Pettit, P. (2018). "Corporations in the Economy of the Esteem". In Rangan, S. (Ed.) *Capitalism Beyond Mutuality?: Perspectives Integrating Philosophy and Social Science*, 229-255. Oxford, UK. Oxford University Press.

Freeman. J. (2015) "Reinventing Organisations" and the Teal impulse, Integral Leadership Review. *Integral Leadership Review.* August-November.

Freinacht, H. (2017a). "From Premodern to Metamodern Mind: a Brief History of Human Evolution." *Metamoderna*. Retrieved from http://metamoderna.org/from-premodern-to-metamodern-mind-a-brief-history-of-human-evolution?lang=en.

Freinacht, H. (2017b). "The Reign of Hackers, Hipsters & Hippies" *Metamoderna*. Retrieved from http://metamoderna.org/the-reign-of-hackers-hipsters-hippies?lang=en.

Freinacht, H. (2017c). *The Listening Society: A Metamodern Guide to Politics Book One.* UK: Metamoderna.

Gallup (2017), State of the Global Workplace: Executive Summary. Washington. Gallup.

Ganescu, N. (2017): The CEO's Playbook. New York. Morgan James Publishing.

Garcia, S., and Dolan, S. (1997). *La Dirección por Valores: El cambio más allá de la dirección por objetivos*. McGraw Hill.

Gebser, J. (1985). *The ever-present origin*. Athens, Ohio: UP.

Giacalone, R A & Jurkiewica, CL (2003) "Toward a Science of Workplace Spirituality" in *Handbook of Workplace Spirituality and Organizational Performance,* eds. R. A. Giacalone & C.L. Jurkiewica. M.E. Sharp, Armonk, NY, pp 3-28.

Gidley, J. (2007) "The Evolution of Consciousness as a Planetary Imperative: An Integration of Integral Views", *Integral Review: A Transdisciplinary and Transcultural Journal for New Thought, Research, and Praxis,* 2007, Nº 5, p. 4-226.

Gilligan, C. (1993). *In a different voice: psychological theory and women's development*. Cambridge Mass.: Harvard University Press.

Gómez, C., and Serrano, S. (2018). "La organización evolutiva como marco de referencia para la transformación de las administraciones públicas". *Economía industrial* 408, pp. 63-75. Available at: http://www.minetad.gob.es/Publicaciones/Publicacionesperiodicas/EconomiaIndustrial/RevistaEconomiaIndustrial/408/GOMEZ%20MU%C3%91OZ%20Y%20SERRANO%20CALLE.pd

Goshal, S. (2005), "Bad Management Theories are destroying good management practices". *Academy of Management Learning and Education,* vol. 4, nº 1, 75-91.

GrantTree's Journey Towards Self-Management (2018, January 29). Retrieved from https://www.organizationbuilders.com/blogoudoudoud/2018/1/29/granttrees-journey-towards-self-management.

Graves, C.W., Edited by C. Cowan & N. Todorovic (2005). *The Never-Ending Quest: Dr. Clare W. Graves Explores Human Nature.* Santa Barbara, CA: ECLET Publishing.

Gunnlaugson, O., Brabant, M. (2016). *Cohering the Integral We-Space: Engaging Collective Emergence, Wisdom, and Healing in Groups.* Integral Publishing House: San Francisco.

Hackman, J. R. (2011): *Collaborative Intelligence.* San Francisco, CA: Berrett-Koehler.

Hamel G. (2009) "Moon shots for management". *Harvard Business Review,* February, Vol. 87 No. 2, pp. 91-99.

Hamel G. (2011) "First, Let's Fire All the Managers". *Harvard Business Review,* December, Vol. 89, No. 12, pp. 48-60.

Hansmeyer, E., Mendiola, R., and Snabe, J. (2018). "Purpose–driven business for sustainable performance and progress." In Rangan, S. (Ed.) *Capitalism Beyond Mutuality?: Perspectives Integrating Philosophy and Social Science*, 161-190. Oxford, UK. Oxford University Press.

Heydebrand, W. V: (1989) "New organizational forms", *Work and Occupations,* 16(3): 323-57.

Hock, D. W. (1995). The chaordic organization: Out of control and into order. *World Business Academy Perspectives*, 9(1), 5-18.

Honeyman, R. (2014). *The B Corp Handbook: How to Use Business as a Force for Good*. Berrett-Koehler Publishers.

Jago, A.G. (1982). Leadership: Perspectives in theory and research. *Journal of management science* 28(3) 315-332.

Kaltenecker, S., and Peter Hundermark (2014). "What are self-organizing teams?" *InfoQueue*. Retrieved from https://www.infoq.com/articles/what-are-self-organising-teams.

Kegan, R. (1994): *In Over Our Heads: The Mental Demands of Modern Life.* Cambridge, MA: Harvard University Press.

Kegan, R. and Lahey, L. (2009) *Immunity to Change: How to Overcome It and Unlock the Potential in Yourself and Your Organization.* Cambridge, MA: Harvard Business School Publishing.

Kegan, R. and Lahey, L. (2016) *An Everyone Culture: Becoming a Deliberately Developmental Organization. Cambridge,* MA: Harvard Business Review Press.

Kirkpatrick, D. (2011), *Beyond Empowerment.* Morning Star Self-Management Institute.

Koestler, Arthur (1967). *The Ghost in the Machine* (1990 reprint ed.). London: Hutchinson (Penguin Group).

Kofman, F. (2001a) *Metamanagement. Principios.* Barcelona: Granica.

Kofman, F. (2001b) *Metamanagement. Aplicaciones.* Barcelona: Granica.

Kofman, F. (2001c) *Metamanagement. Filosofía.* Barcelona: Granica.

Kofman, F. (2002). "Holons, heaps and artifacts (And their corresponding hierarchies)". Retrieved from http://www.integralworld.net/kofman.html. May 24, 2018.

Kofman, Fred. (2006) *Conscious Business: How to Build Value through Values*. Boulder, CO: Sounds True.

Kupers, W. and Russ Volckmann. (2009). "A Dialogue on Integral Leadership". *Integral Leadership Review*, Volume IX, No. 4 - August.

Laloux, F. (2014). *Reinventing Organizations: A guide to creating organizations inspired by the next stage of human consciousness.* Brussels, Belgium: Nelson Parker.

Larkin, H. (2006). Integral Management and the Effective Human Service Organization. *AQAL: Journal of Integral Theory and Practice, 1*(3), 184-203.

Lee, M. Y., & Edmondson, A. C. (2017). Self-managing organizations: Exploring the limits of less-hierarchical organizing. *Research in organizational behavior*, 37, 35-58.

Lefebrvre, M. (2017). My experience with a Deliberately Developmental Organization. Retrieved from https://www.happymelly.com/deliberately-developmental-organization/April 24th 2017.

Lewis, M.W. y Grimes A.J. (1999). "Metatriangulation: Building theory from multiple paradigms". *Academy of Management Review,* vol. 24, nº 4, 672-690.

Lips-Wiersma, M. and Morris, L. (2017) *The Map of Meaningful Work: A Practical Guide to Sustaining our Humanity* (2nd edition). Milton Park, Abingdon, Oxon, UK: Routledge.

Loevinger, J. (Ed.). (1998). *Technical foundations for measuring ego development: the Washington university sentence completion test.* Mahwah New Jersey: Laurence Erlbaum Associated, Publishers.

Mackey, J., & Sisodia, R. (2013). *Conscious Capitalism: Liberating the Heroic Spirit of Business*. Harvard Business Review Press.

Manz, C. and H. P. Sims Jr. (1995*), Business Without Bosses: How Self-Managing Teams Are Building High- Performing Companies*. NY: John Wiley & Sons.

Manz, C. and H. P. Sims Jr. (2001*), The New SuperLeadership: Leading Others to Lead Themselves*. San Francisco: Berrett-Koehler.

Martín, L, Moreno, A., Alías, S., y García, A. (2018). La organización extendida, una nueva forma de crear ecosistemas digitales. Caso Barrabés, Biz. *Economía industrial* 408, pp. 41-53. Available at: http://www.minetad.gob.es/Publicaciones/Publicacionesperiodicas/EconomiaIndustrial/RevistaEconomiaIndustrial/408/MARTIN,%20MORENO%20AL%C3%8DAS%20Y%20GARC%C3%8DA%20ESTEVE.pdf.

Merry, P. (2009). *Evolutionary Leadership: Integral Leadership for an increasingly complex world.* Pacific Grove: Integral Publishers.

Mezirow, J. (1995). "Transformation theory of adult learning." In M. R. Welton (Ed.), *In defense of the lifeworld* (pp. 39-70). New York, NY: SUNY Press.

Mitroff, I.I. y Denton, E. (1999), "A Study of Spirituality in the Workplace". *Sloan Management Review,* Summer; 83-92.

Moreno, A., Martínez, M., and Maroto, A. (2018). "La transición hacia organizaciones evolutivas teal". *Economía industrial* 407, pp. 61-72. Available at http://www.minetad.gob.es/Publicaciones/Publicacionesperiodicas/EconomiaIndustrial/RevistaEconomiaIndustrial/407/MORENO,%20MART%C3%8DNEZ%20Y%20MAROTO.pd.

Morris, T. (1997) *If Aristotle Ran General Motors.* Henry Holt and Co.

Moyer, M. (2012). *Slicing Pie: Fund Your Company Without Funds.* Lake Shark Ventures.

Murray, T. (2016), "We space practices: Emerging themes in embodied contemplative dialogue". In Gunnlaugson, O., Brabant, M. (eds).

Cohering the Integral We-Space: Engaging Collective Emergence, Wisdom, and Healing in Groups. Pp 200-212. Integral Publishing House: San Francisco.

Neilsen, T. (1984), *"Becoming an Organization Development Practitioner"*, Englewood Cliffs, CA: Prentice-Hall.

O'Fallon, T. (2011). StAGES: Growing up is Waking up—Interpenetrating Quadrants, States, and Structures. Retrieved from https://www.stagesinternational.com/wp-content/uploads/2016/04/StAGES_OFallon.pdf.

Paulson, D. S. (2002), *Competitive Business, Caring Business: An Integral Business Perspective for the 21st Century*. Paraview Press.

Petrie, N. (2014), *Future Trends in Leadership Development.* Center for Creative Leadership. Colorado. Retrieved from http://www.ccl.org/wp-content/uploads/2015/04/futureTrends.pdf.

Pinchbeck, Daniel (2006). *2012: The Return of Quetzalcoatl.* New York: Jeremy P. Tarcher/Penguin.

Pink, D. H. (2011). *Drive: The surprising truth about what motivates us*. New York: Penguin.

Pór, G. (2015). "Reinventing Yourself". *Enlivening Edge.* Retrieved from http://www.enliveningedge.org/columns/our-individual-journey-to-teal/.

Putz, M. (2006). Integral Business and Leadership: An Intermediate Overview. *AQAL: Journal of Integral Theory and Practice, 1*(1), 88-108.

Reynolds, E. (2019). Next-stage organizations: A transdisciplinary case study. Unpublished PhD thesis. Saybrook University. Retrievable at https://www.academia.edu/40219785/NEXT-STAGE_ORGANIZATIONS_A_TRANSDISCIPLINARY_CASE_STUDY.

Ridderstrale and Nordstrom (2000) *Funky Business*. Prentice-Hall.

Robertson, B. (2015). *Holacracy: The New Management System for a rapidly changing world;* Henry Holt and Company: New York, NY, USA.

Robledo, M. A. (2004) *D3D: Un Enfoque Integral de la Dirección de Empresas*. Ediciones Díaz de Santos. Madrid, Spain.

Robledo, M. A. (2011) "D3D: Hacia un nuevo paradigma empresarial" *Harvard Deusto Business Review*. Núm 202 (junio) pág. 26-35.

Robledo, M. A. (2013) "Integrating Management Theory: Using the AQAL Model for Multiparadigm Management Research". *Journal of Integral Theory and Practice*, Volume 8, Issue 1&2. Pages 57-70.

Robledo, M. A. (2014). Building an integral metatheory of management. *European Management Journal, 32*(4), 535-546.

Robledo M. A. (2016) 3D Management: An integral Business Theory. Integral Leadership Review. Pp. 72-85. Available online: http://integralleadershipreview.com/14840-3d-management-an-integral-business-theory/.

Robledo, M.A. (2018a). "Conveyor Belts for Societal Transformation". Global Journal of Archaeology & Anthropology. 2018; Vol. 4 Issue 5. DOI:10.19080/GJAA.2018.04.555648.

Robledo M. A. (2018b) Hierarchy of Anarchy: Holarchical Structures and 3D Management. *Integral Leadership Review*. Available online: http://integralleadershipreview.com/16562-the-hierarchy-of-anarchy-holarchical-structures-and-3d-management/.

Robledo, M. A., & Batle, J. (2017). Transformational tourism as a hero's journey. *Current Issues in Tourism,* Volume 20, 2017 - Issue 16 pp. 1736-1748.

Rooke, D., & Torbert, W.R. (1998). Organizational transformation as a function of CEO's developmental stage. *Organization Development Journal*, 16(1), 11-28.

Rosso, B.D., Dekas, K., Wrzesniewski, A. (2010) *On the meaning of work: A theoretical integration and review*. Research in Organizational Behavior 30, 91–127.

Rushkoff, D. (2016). *Throwing rocks at the Google bus: How growth became the enemy of prosperity*. NY: Penguin.

Scharmer, C. Otto (2009), *Theory U: Leading from the Emerging Future as It Emerges: The Social Technology of Presencing.* San Francisco, CA: Berrett-Koehler.

Semler, R. (1993) *Maverick!* London: Random House.

Simpson, S.; Fischer, B.; Rohde, M. (2013). The Conscious Capitalism Philosophy Pay Off: A Qualitative and Financial Analysis of Conscious Capitalism Corporations". *Journal of Leadership, Accountability & Ethics*. Vol 10(4) 19-29.

Singer, A.E. (2010) "Strategy as Metatheory." *Integral Review,* Vol. 6, no. 3, pages 57-72.

Sisodia, R. S., Sheth, J. N., and Wolfe, D. B. (2007). *Firms of endearment: How world-class companies profit from passion and purpose*. Pearson Prentice Hall.

Spinder, P. (2013). "Knowmads Business School: Empowering and enabling knowmads". In Moravec, J. (Ed.) *Knowmad Society*. Pp. 164-173. Minneapolis: Education Futures.

Tasset, T. (2010). An Integral Exploration of Leadership. *Journal of Integral Theory and Practice*, *5*(2), 96-116.

Thomas, B. (2015). *Integral Leadership Manifesto.* Retrieved from http://integralleadershipmanifesto.com/.

Valentine, M. A., Retelny, D., To, A., Rahmati, N., Doshi, T., & Bernstein, M. S. (2017, May). "Flash organizations: Crowdsourcing complex work by structuring crowds as organizations." In *Proceedings of the 2017 CHI conference on human factors in computing systems* (pp. 3523-3537). ACM.

Volckmann, R. (2014) Generativity, Transdisciplinarity, and Integral Leadership, *World Futures*, 70:3-4, 248-265.

van den Akker, R., Gibbons, A., and Vermeulen, T. (2017) 'Periodising the 2000s, or, the emergence of metamodernism', in R. van den Akker, A. Gibbons and T. Vermeulen (eds.), *Metamodernism: Historicity, Affect and Depth after Postmodernism.* London and New York: Rowman and Littlefield, 2017, pp. 1-20.

Vermeulen, T. and van den Akker, R. (2010). "Notes on metamodernism". *Journal of Aesthetics & Culture* Vol. 2, DOI: 10.3402/jac.v2i0.5677.

Vieten, C., and Estrada, M. (2017). "Making Change". In Kuntzelman, E. and DiPerna, D. (eds.) *Purpose Rising: A Global Movement of Transformation and Meaning* (pp. 291-28). Bright Alliance.

Wahl, D. (2016) *Designing Regenerative Cultures*. Axminster. Triarchy Press.

Whetten, B. (2013). "Integrating Money and Meaning: The Role of Purpose and Profit in Integral Business". *Journal of Integral Theory and Practice*, Volume 8, Issue 1&2. Pages 149-161.

Wilber, K. (1995). *Sex, Ecology, Spirituality: The Spirit of Evolution.* Boston. Shambhala.

Wilber, K. (1996). *A brief history of everything.* Boston: Shambhala.

Wilber, K. (1998). *The Marriage of Sense and Soul*. Boston: Shambhala

Wilber, K. (2000a) *A Theory of Everything: An Integral Vision of Politics, Science and Spirituality.* Boston: Shambhala Publications.

Wilber, K. (2000b). *Integral psychology*. Boston, MA: Shambhala.

Wilber, K. (2002) *The Many Ways We Touch -Three Principles Helpful for Any Integrative Approach.* Retrieved from https://integrallife.com/many-ways-touch/.

Wilber, K. (2003) *Foreword.* In Visser, F.: *Ken Wilber: Thought as Passion*, pp. xii-xiii. Albany. SUNY Press.

Wilber, K. (2006). *Integral spirituality: A startling new role for religion in the modern and postmodern world.* Boston, MA: Shambhala.

Wilber, K. (2017). *The religion of tomorrow: A vision for the future of the great traditions*. Boulder, CO: Shambhala.

Wilber, K., and DiPerna, D. (2017) "Toward a Deliberately Developmental Civilization: Illuminating the Three Key Elements of Spiritual Transformation and Purpose." In Kuntzelman, E., and DiPerna, D. (eds.) *Purpose Rising: A Global Movement of Transformation and Meaning* (pp. 13-28). Bright Alliance.

Wilber, K.; Patten, T.; Leonard, A.; Morelli, M. (2008). *Integral Life Practice: A 21st-Century Blueprint for Physical Health, Emotional Balance, Mental Clarity, and Spiritual Awakening*. Boston: Shambhala publications.

Wittrock, D. (2017), "Does Holacracy Have Blind Spots? From Holes to Wholeness." *Medium.* Retrieved from https://medium.com/encode-org/does-Holacracy-have-blind-spots-b0b8b052b661.

Zohar, D. (1997). *Rewiring the Corporate Brain.* Berrett-Koehler Publishers. San Francisco.

Zohar, D. and Marshall, I. (2004), *Spiritual Capital. Wealth we can live by.* London. Bloomsbury.